LIBERAL CHRISTIANITY AND WOMEN'S GLOBAL ACTIVISM

LIBERAL CHRISTIANITY AND WOMEN'S GLOBAL ACTIVISM

The YWCA of the USA and the Maryknoll Sisters

AMANDA L. IZZO

RUTGERS UNIVERSITY PRESS

New Brunswick, Camden, and Newark, New Jersey, and London

Library of Congress Cataloging-in-Publication Data

Names: Izzo, Amanda L., 1977– author.
Title: Liberal christianity and women's global activism : the YWCA of the USA and
the Maryknoll Sisters / Amanda L. Izzo.
Description: New Brunswick : Rutgers University Press, [2018] | Includes
bibliographical references and index.
Identifiers: LCCN 2017012784| ISBN 9780813588483 (hardcover : alk. paper) |
ISBN 9780813588476 (pbk. : alk. paper) | ISBN 9780813588490 (ebook (epub)) |
ISBN 9780813588506 (ebook (web pdf))
Subjects: LCSH: Church and social problems—History—20th century. | Maryknoll
Sisters—History—20th century. | YWCA of the U.S.A.—History—20th century.
Classification: LCC HN37.C3 .I99 2018 | DDC 261.8082—dc23 LC record available at
https://lccn.loc.gov/2017012784

A British Cataloging-in-Publication record for this book is available from the British
Library.

∞ The paper used in this publication meets the requirements of the American
National Standard for Information Sciences—Permanence of Paper for Printed
Library Materials, ANSI Z39.48–1992.

www.rutgersuniversitypress.org

Manufactured in the United States of America

CONTENTS

LIBERAL CHRISTIANITY AND WOMEN'S GLOBAL ACTIVISM

INTRODUCTION

Turn-of-the-century Smith College seems an unlikely place for the genesis of an American Catholic women's foreign mission movement. Its student body was drawn largely from wealthy families of the Northeast, who counted few Catholics among them. Moreover, the Catholic clergy exerted considerable pressure on the faithful to keep their children in the parochial educational system.[1] Nevertheless, Mary Josephine Rogers frequently identified her student days at Smith as the inspiration for founding the Maryknoll Sisters of St. Dominic, a Roman Catholic religious order established in 1920. Though at Smith she was an anomaly as a Catholic, she fit the profile as a well-to-do Bostonian, and like many other students there, she felt a call to religious service after becoming involved in campus Christian life. The transformative experience of witnessing a student missionary ceremony at the end of her junior year set her on this path. That evening in 1904, a biographer later wrote, Rogers watched from afar as her Protestant classmates sang hymns and "filled the night with exultation," pledging to enter the foreign mission field after graduation. She was overcome. The evangelistic commitment of these "fine types of young American womanhood" inspired a vision. The US Catholic Church had not yet participated in the foreign mission movement, and as Rogers reflected on the student volunteers, she "reached something that was part realization, part decision, part prayer: she would do something for the missionary work of the church."[2]

It might also seem incongruous that an elite women's college was caught up in the evangelical fervor more commonly associated with denominational and Bible schools of the Midwest. Yet the wealthy, mainline Protestant women of Smith had become captivated by the campus revival spirit. Many of them would carry this spirit of socially engaged Christianity into the growing realm of female professional employment. Rogers might have crossed paths with one such student, Mary van Kleeck, a senior and an Episcopalian, at the missionary ceremony. Van Kleeck was then president of the college's Association of Christian

Work. She had recently come into contact with the Young Women's Christian Association (YWCA) as Smith's delegate to a Christian women's student conference in New York. The YWCA was in the process of assembling over six hundred local groups that were scattered across American cities and colleges into a national organization. The interdenominational Protestant voluntary organization, already widely celebrated for its outreach to working-class women, introduced van Kleeck to the Social Gospel. This brush with a religious movement that historian Sidney Ahlstrom tagged the "praying wing of Progressivism" inspired her to take up settlement work and industrial sociology after college.[3] Connecting theories of scientific management to Social Gospel principles of cooperative Christian justice, van Kleeck went on to become one of the most influential researchers of women's labor in the 1910s and 1920s. Although she spent her professional career at the Russell Sage Foundation, she maintained a long affiliation with the YWCA as a consultant, speaker, and author. The YWCA provided an accommodating forum for van Kleeck's vision of a "new conception of religion": a conviction that "the standard of life for all people must be an adequate standard of life." Such standards could be achieved, she told a 1920 YWCA convention, when this diverse Christian women's organization set "free in our national life [a] spiritual force that is needed to work out a new conception of collective action."[4]

Twenty years after Smith College's missionary celebration, the Maryknoll Sisters and YWCA were thriving organizations in a supposedly secular age, one characterized by a post-World War I disillusionment with Christian crusades. Inspired by their participation in a religious community, Rogers and van Kleeck followed separate denominational routes into careers built on shared ethical and institutional foundations. Rogers infused the sanctified community life of women religious with an evangelical spirit, carrying the foreign mission movement to the US Catholic Church. Van Kleeck conducted her professional and voluntary activities under Christian imperatives devised by Protestant women dedicated to progressive reform.

The intersection between Catholic and Protestant religious life at the ceremony points to a liberal Christianity of twentieth-century women that went beyond Smith and the sectarian life of churches. The celebration was part of an environment that gave rise to an active religion that, for many, became the springboard for lifelong activism. It demonstrated how women's realms, those of single-sex religious organizations, prompted the pursuit of social change on a global scale. It proclaimed the belief that Christian ethics provided the road map for the improvement, even perfection, of the world. And it was a performance of solidarity among white American women, an assertion of confidence in their unique contribution to public life.

This book traces the evolving means by which these two profoundly influential US religious women's groups put a gendered, activist Christianity into motion by creating bridges between the grassroots realm of small-scale interpersonal encounters and social movements that were both local and global in scope. Amid a historiography that continues to privilege men as instrumental actors in religious life, the narratives presented here call attention to an often-overlooked religious politics crafted by and for women. Offering a counterpoint to histories of gender and religion that emphasize conservative evangelical women's mobilizations as imagined protectors of the domestic sphere, this account demonstrates that liberal Christian women produced an equally gendered blueprint for activism. Maryknoll and the YWCA thrived by taking an expansive view of gender; while men's and women's roles in the church might differ, women's work was no less vital, and women's souls no less valuable, than men's. And in contrast to scholarship that reinforces denominational divides by treating Christian sects as isolated entities, these stories reveal convergences in the ethical frameworks and methods of social action that emerged from liberal branches of the churches.

Ultimately, this account of religious activism makes three major interventions into the history of faith traditions and women's social movements in the twentieth-century United States. First, it underlines the central place of women in Christian political life, both Catholic and Protestant. Whether viewed through the lens of the turn-of-the-century foreign mission movement or from the perspective of 1970s feminist theology, organizations like Maryknoll and the YWCA created an institutional setting for religious practices and principles crafted by women who were often shunted to the margins of mainstream churches. The extent to which women collectively disseminated and put into action a body of theological, ethical, and missiological thought is rarely emphasized in US history. By taking seriously the intellectual, pastoral, and professional efforts of Maryknoll and the YWCA, this book places women at the forefront of American religion.[5]

Inquiries into US women's separatist organizing strategies point to the years before the ratification of suffrage as the time in which a reform culture of single-sex organizations yielded a "public female world" that had political leverage distinct from the formal polity.[6] The histories of Maryknoll and the YWCA defy the assumption that separatist organizing strategies disappeared after the suffrage victory. The separatist tradition in the churches had deep roots, and women continued to find spiritual sustenance in these settings. The clerical domain remained (and, for Catholics, remains) largely inaccessible to them, but marginalization alone does not account for the endurance of women's communities. Rather, the rewards of single-sex organizing and a sense that women had a particular gift of service to offer humanity fueled this dedication. The commitment not only revealed the strength of separatist traditions in American women's reform, but it also shored up an organizing method that helped foster international connections. The all-female configuration of the groups contributed in multiple ways to their success in sustaining transnational projects. As diverse religious and cultural traditions reinforced ideals of gender separatism, and as women continued to have uneven access to civic forums, international single-sex coalitions offered groups such as Maryknoll and the YWCA opportunities to seek solidarity and exert political influence.[7]

The second major intervention of this book centers on the evolution and enduring importance of liberal religion in twentieth-century activist mobilizations. This history has been overshadowed by the attention given to conservative groups in both historiography and contemporary political movements.[8] As representatives of liberal wings of mainline Protestantism and Catholicism, Maryknoll and the YWCA confirm what scholars have described in respect to conservative Christianity: religion fueled a variety of social movements well beyond the nineteenth century. The evolution of the organizations' political influence over the course of the century also highlights the shifting fortunes of liberalism, in terms of both goals and impact. The celebrated Cold War-era, American Century-style internationalism of the Maryknoll Sisters provides an instructive point of comparison to the maligned visions of world governance promoted by the YWCA in the same period, and also instructive is the censure experienced by both organizations amid reactionary attacks on subsequent initiatives to eradicate poverty, racial prejudice, and war.

The third intervention of this book is its account of US Christian women's persistent determination to forge a global community. Crusades to spread Christianity have been a long-standing component of the imperialist thrust of globalization, but it has been less recognized that such crusades provided foundations for present-day transnational feminist organizing. The missionary impulse that first inspired the organizations was built on biblical injunctions to evangelize, a New Testament insistence that the Christian faith be spread to nonbelievers. Mary Josephine Rogers explained the special purpose of her congregation as "obedience to the Saviour's command: 'Go, teach all nations,'" a biblical verse often cited by missionaries as the inspiration for their ministry. The YWCA of the USA similarly expanded overseas under the reasoning offered by its first staff member stationed in a foreign country, Agnes Gale Hill: "foreign mission . . . is the natural outcome of life which follows God fully." After all, she asserted, the Bible revealed that "God makes *world* plans."[9]

In an era of imperial expansion, such women imagined they had the spiritual power to evangelize the entire world. But hopes for a globally influential Christianity outlasted the scramble for empire. The foreign mission movement was the seedbed for an American women's Christian internationalism, a religious wing of the "worlds of women" that downplayed divides of race and nation in a quest for gender solidarity.[10] First preoccupied with winning the world to Christianity, the YWCA and Maryknoll, like other liberal elements in the churches, ended up celebrating pluralism, criticizing nationalism, and scrutinizing the aims of foreign mission. Domineering approaches to evangelization and tacit national and racial prejudices existed in tension with hopes for global harmony. An examination of the interplay between these US organizations and the overseas settings in which they operated complicates simplistic accounts of cultural imperialism, demonstrating that mission could never be a simple act of Western domination. As historians have emphasized more generally, American women's mission efforts were not "a unidirectional exercise of power." Rather, an evolving understanding of the meaning of religious outreach came out of "encounter and exchange" in the field; the viability of Maryknoll and the YWCA's international work depended on relinquishing expectations of dominance.[11]

As the model of mission changed from evangelization to world fellowship, Christian women's advocacy networks became oriented toward what would come to be called the human rights movement. Scholars of human rights discourses frequently highlight the intellectual underpinnings of the Enlightenment and the legal machinery of the United Nations, but the conceptions of human rights that are examined in this book were oriented toward the interrelationships between the public and private spheres rather than formal political operations.[12] The groups' activities situated women's everyday responsibilities as practicing Christians, family members, and workers within an imagined global community. The organizations produced a vocabulary of justice and rights that addressed matters of citizenship, but more often they used such terms as "family," "fellowship," and "friendship" to describe human unity. They allied their efforts with those of other organizations and offered their service to such intergovernmental forums as the United Nations and the International Labor Organization at the same time that they supported on-the-ground projects. In so doing, they aimed to create emotional connections among individuals as well as change laws and political structures.[13]

Because the organizational histories of the YWCA and Maryknoll are so distinct, the rationale underlying the book's juxtaposition of the two groups may not be obvious. Yet while stand-alone accounts of each could yield much of value to historians, a larger picture emerges when they are examined together. This study is not designed to demonstrate that the organizations were fundamentally alike, or that creedal differences, institutional structures, and distinct chronologies are somehow immaterial. Nor is its emphasis comparative, a narration of similarities and differences. Rather, it follows the two organizations through separate but overlapping journeys across a broad terrain of women's

Christian ethics and politics. The faith in action examined here was staged from the setting of single-sex institutions, immersed in an evolving milieu of liberal social movements, and directed at a global vision of community.

The connections and divergences between the journeys of the two groups beg a reexamination of the standard periodizations of twentieth-century social movements. This book traces how the inheritors of the women's movement navigated the Age of Empire, the American Century, the revolts of the 1960s, and the reactionary insurgencies of the 1970s, all the while retaining historical moorings in single-sex organizing and a New Testament ethics of love. The groups provide evidence of the lively organizing strategies that link the so-called first wave of feminism to the second, showcasing the spiritual resources that consistently infused efforts to improve women's lives. This is an influence usually overlooked in accounts of feminism in the 1960s and 1970s.[14] Relevant to the arc of American religious history, the work calls into question conclusions about the enervation of liberal Christianity, whether that enervation is attributed to the inexorable appeal of an ascendant religious right or to the impact of secularism on left-leaning religious bodies.[15] Directing attention to a string of antiradical campaigns that could be called a long Red Scare, which stretched from 1920s anticommunist crackdowns to the 1930s Dies Committee and on through four Cold War decades, the histories of these groups suggest that the moral authority once conferred on liberal Christian institutions in American life was not simply ceded in face of shifting allegiances on both the right and the left; in instrumental ways, that authority was seized. This seizure of power can be apprehended through the accusations of subversion that were persistently and powerfully hurled against liberal Christian women's groups. Ultimately, the vehemence of such attacks—and the high levels from which they were made—helped render liberal Christianity illegible and illegitimate as a form of religious politics. Several generations of reactionary coalitions drew on the power of the state to shift the discursive framing of expressions of religious ethics in the public sphere. Over time, attempts of groups like the YWCA and Maryknoll to enact New Testament principles became less visible as articulations of Christian mandates and more likely to be portrayed as veneers for nefarious political allegiances. Meanwhile, the domain of Christian activism came to be represented primarily by proponents of women's submission, bellicose isolationism, and the supposed protection of family values.[16]

The histories of the YWCA and Maryknoll deserve to be considered in concert not simply because of the scope of their impact but also because they show the contours of a larger set of social movements shaped by women's religious institutions. The organizations represent a fraction of the many groups whose members labored to enact a socially conscious spirituality by carving out autonomous spaces within religious bodies dominated by men.[17] A number of other women's organizations—and mixed-sex ones that relied on women's contributions—navigated this terrain. Their members circulated in the same activist and theological networks. Groups that bear comparison to the YWCA and Maryknoll include the women's reform communities that blossomed in settlement houses. There are connections to the organizations that participated in the long civil rights movement: Methodist women's and youth groups; inter-denominational mainline organizations such as the Commission on Interracial Cooperation; and Catholic religious congregations, including the Sisters of Saint Joseph and Sisters of Loretto, who were noted for their ministry across racial divides. Dimensions of women's religious politics can be seen in general interest, mixed-sex groups, including the Catholic Interracial Council, Young Christian Workers, and Dorothy Day's Catholic Workers; and in ecumeni-cal Protestant efforts like the World Student Christian Federation and Student Volunteer Movement.[18] Relationships could be drawn to US Jewish women's groups: Hadassah, in which women's Zionism was expressed in the "educational and spiritual nurturance" of single-sex religious solidarity as well as in support of medical missions in Palestine (and later Israel), and the National Council of Jew-ish Women, with its long history of social reform.[19] While all such groups differ in terms of their range of interests and spiritual traditions, in the aggregate they point to a dynamic, politicized landscape of women's religious service.

As much as they were part of this larger landscape, the YWCA and Maryknoll Sisters stand out for their innovation, influence, visibility, and scope of politici-zation. Though, as historian Anne Firor Scott regretfully notes, there "is as yet no comprehensive scholarly history of the organization," the YWCA has received significant inquiry from women's historians.[20] Investigating the pioneering pro-gramming and racial diversity of the association's membership, many of these scholars have documented the YWCA's interracialist ambitions and its contri-butions to the African American civil rights movement. Others have looked to the YWCA as a venue for addressing labor issues, a node of international exchange, and an exemplar of the gendered built environment.[21] Statistics from peak moments in the early 1920s give some sense of the group's importance: its membership was over 600,000 in 1922, making it the third largest US women's membership organization, following the General Federation of Women's Clubs (with a million members) and the Woman's Christian Temperance Union (800,000 members); it had an institutional presence in over 1,100 US com-munities and campuses, from heartland farm towns to industrial metropolises; and it employed nearly 4,000 women, with 250 of them stationed overseas.[22] But even when its numerical strength was not so vast, the YWCA set the pace in fields that ranged from physical education to social work, from sociology to biblical scholarship, and from public affairs to public health. Opportunities for professional and volunteer leadership enabled YWCA women to be visible participants in social and intellectual movements—labor, antiracist, ecumenical, and feminist—that stretched across the twentieth century.

Unsurprisingly for a religious order, the membership and institutional life of the Maryknoll Sisters does not match the scale of those of the YWCA. At its peak in 1966, 1,675 women belonged to the congregation; over time the numbers ranged from the roughly 100 who were associated with the group at its official formation in 1920 to about 420 sisters in 2016. However, the congregation has had an influence that belies its size. The name Maryknoll, in reference to both the sisters and their companion group, the Catholic Foreign Mission Society of America (Maryknoll Fathers and Brothers, founded in 1911), frequently arises in discussions of foreign mission and the Catholic left. While the number of sisters who belonged to Maryknoll was comparable to the membership of such other major US congregations as the School Sisters of Notre Dame, Sisters of Charity (Cincinnati), and Sisters of Saint Joseph, Maryknoll secured a unique visibility as the face of American Catholic mission.[23] Popular media accounts of missionary heroics and scandals placed Maryknoll priests and sisters in the spotlight, and many Catholics encountered the group by subscribing to Maryknoll's magazine, a *National Geographic*-style publication that proffered an education on distant lands and peoples as it called on "American Catholics to share their gift of the Faith" by supporting missions.[24] But it was a tragedy in 1980 that brought unprecedented attention: two Maryknoll sisters, along with two other missionaries, were tortured and killed by security forces in El Salvador, triggering an international incident whose repercussions continue to be felt into the twenty-first century.

Though this study is not strictly comparative, some comparison may be useful for understanding the groups' places among women's religious organizations. Both the YWCA of the USA and Maryknoll were founded in the first decades of the twentieth century, and both have survived into the twenty-first. Considerable differences distinguish the Roman Catholic religious congregation, which was administered through a chain of ecclesiastical hierarchy, from the loosely structured interdenominational Protestant voluntary group, which was led by a professional staff. Despite their distinct histories, many connections can be drawn between the two organizations' religious principles and strategies for social change. They remained women's groups even as single-sex networks lost ground to more integrated institutional life, and though they held to an older style of gendered religious practice, they welcomed new roles and responsibilities for women. The theology and political interests of both organizations grew steadily more liberal over time. Each group found inspiration in interpreting the New Testament as a Christian mandate to remake the world as a loving, cooperative community. From the beginning, both groups were committed to modern, rather than reactionary, solutions for social problems, and Christianity was the basis of these solutions. With interventions that ranged from small-scale educational and medical institutions to ambitious plans for eradicating poverty and racism, the organizations searched for contemporary meanings of Jesus's ministry and new responsibilities for those faithful to God's directives.

The unique impact of each organization in its own right can be apprehended from even a brief overview of their organizational histories, for they were both pioneers in their faith traditions. Springing from a transatlantic evangelical Protestant revival, the YWCA had its origins in the 1850s when, inspired by the Young Men's Christian Association, a group of London women founded interdenominational prayer circles and boardinghouses intended to serve the spiritual and material needs of urban working-class women. By the end of that decade, US women had organized similar groups—some under the YWCA name, others using a variation of it—that offered intercessory prayer for the well-being of young women and introduced social services for the uplift and evangelization of workers, including boarding facilities, recreational activities, and vocational assistance. The story told in this book centers on a specific manifestation of the multilayered, international YWCA operation: the YWCA of the USA, which was established in 1906. This organization was formed as a national federation to consolidate the associations that had proliferated on college campuses and industrial cities during the late nineteenth century. Administered by an entity called the National Board, which was composed of an sizable professional staff as well as volunteer committees, the YWCA of the USA was responsible for establishing programming put into motion by hundreds of community YWCAs throughout the United States.[25] At the same time that it coordinated US association programming, the YWCA of the USA took an active role in the World's YWCA (later renamed the World YWCA), an international umbrella organization that oversaw global expansion.

This book's investigation of the programming and professional leadership of the YWCA of the USA does not do justice to the stories of local associations. Nor can it convey the diversity of other associations in the World YWCA network. Yet as the interface designed to coordinate community efforts into a global movement, the YWCA of the USA has a history that provides considerable insight into other arenas of association work. Its impact reverberated through all levels of the wider organization.

Connecting women across social divides—those of age, class, nation, and denomination—underwrote the idea of association from the start. Interpreting Jesus's ministry as a call to unite humanity in bonds of loving cooperation, YWCA leaders sought to create a spirit of fellowship and mutual assistance among women of dissimilar circumstances. After the establishment of the national group, YWCA women spoke of their burgeoning membership, committed leadership, and ambitious horizons as a movement, "a great movement [that] is going to live for centuries." A "sense of kinship" among women and a "sense of power and strength to do large things" fueled their movement, and they directed their energies toward solving "the problems that confront the women of today" through Christian service.[26]

The founders of the national organization designed the group to be "an effective agency in the bringing in of the Kingdom of God among young women," and they drew from two major theological currents in Protestantism in their earthly pursuit of the heavenly kingdom: evangelicalism in the aim to bring personal salvation to young women and the Social Gospel in the desire to bring social structures into conformity with the "ideals and principles of Jesus Christ."[27] A Gospel ideal of fellowship, a "spiritual democracy" that united the community of believers, proved a wellspring for efforts to bring women together in mutual concern. Directing the membership toward the "great social problems of the day"—a swirl of changes in family, labor, technology, education, and politics—YWCA leaders promoted the application of ideals of fellowship to social issues.[28] Shifting in emphasis from the devotional priorities of evangelicalism to the reform interests of the Social Gospel, the YWCA became deeply involved in political, labor, and social work activities in the 1920s.

The YWCA in turn exerted its influence on the Social Gospel. Addressing the perceived needs of all types of women, its social services, publications, and programs had a breadth matched by those of few other organizations, including the Young Men's Christian Association and the Woman's Christian Temperance Union. The YWCA's commitment to women indeed outpaced that of many labor organizations. It was commodious enough to attract the participation of factory and clerical workers, affluent reformers, volunteer housewives, immigrants, university students, African American clubwomen, and teenagers. With ties to the missionary movement, its Foreign Division sent scores of people overseas. The association's structure was adaptable to many circumstances. It nourished women's education and social morality activism in post-Meiji Japan, engaged the interest of women workers in revolutionary-era China, and provided a welcoming space for women of diverse creeds and ethnicities in the new Turkish Republic.[29] At the same time that US women supervised overseas YWCAs, on-the-ground experience and global anti-imperialist movements reshaped the US organization's visions of national identity and international outreach.

Despite fragmentation in the women's movement after World War I, the YWCA invoked its authority as a diverse body of Christian women to advocate for humanitarian social change. As a member of political coalitions such as the Women's Joint Congressional Committee, the publisher of works by thinkers such as Walter Rauschenbusch, and a forum for reformers such as van Kleeck, it served as a hub of liberal religious activism. Because of this advocacy, reactionary anticommunists regularly took aim at the "revolutionary flavor" of the organization's religious principles, and they identified the association's support of labor, desegregation, and world governance as markers of dangerous radicalism.[30]

Such attacks may have buffeted the YWCA, but its religiously influenced activist consciousness endured. This was in evidence most prominently during the interracial, church-based period of civil rights organizing. The group's long-standing concern with race relations primed YWCA women to take leadership roles in local and national struggles alike.[31] Yet while finding a renewed sense of purpose with the rise of black power and feminist movements, the YWCA of the USA faced organizational difficulties in the latter decades of the twentieth century, becoming a victim of financial troubles and an unwieldy administrative structure. It has continued to operate as a nominal umbrella for the many community YWCAs still in existence. Until 2009, the YWCA acknowledged "its roots in the Christian faith," but most associations no longer make reference to Christianity. Instead, they highlight the group's identity as "the oldest and largest multicultural women's organization in the world."[32] Though only faint traces of its religious origins remain, the YWCA's heritage of politicized outreach is evident in its current interests, many of which have connections to the association's historical roots: women's health, child care, transitional housing, violence prevention, and emergency services for victims of domestic and sexual assault.

Just as the YWCA of the USA came into being in the first decade of the twentieth century, Mary Josephine Rogers was sowing the seeds for the creation of the Maryknoll Sisters. Shortly after her graduation from Smith in 1904, she joined forces with James A. Walsh, a Boston priest who had been similarly inspired by Protestant missionary fervor, and embarked on the formation of religious orders dedicated to overseas proselytization. By 1911, Rogers and Walsh, along with a growing cadre of supporters, had made considerable progress in realizing this vision. They launched a foreign mission magazine called *The Field Afar*; established a center of operations in New York's Hudson River Valley, which supplied the name Maryknoll; and received papal approval for a clerical society of missionary religious, the Maryknoll Fathers and Brothers. Rogers's interest in expanding opportunities for women—who, in the early days, prepared mailings and meals—came up against considerable obstacles. However, after a decade of organizing without Vatican recognition, she gained formal authorization in 1920 for the establishment of an apostolic congregation of women religious, the Maryknoll Sisters of St. Dominic.

As the US YWCA shed its evangelical emphasis in a turn to the Social Gospel, Maryknoll missions were in their earliest stages. The congregation described its "particular and special end" as "the conversion of pagans in heathen lands and of Asiatics in Christian countries." Although sisters endeavored to maintain cultural respect while adapting Catholicism to local conditions, the overriding emphasis on winning conversions and sacramental devotions often undermined Maryknoll's constitutional directive not to "impose on native people our customs."[33] With this charge, the Maryknoll Sisters became the US Catholic Church's first group of women religious singularly dedicated to foreign mission. The sisters' labors were propelled by the legacy of the cloister as well as the charismatic vision of their founder. Rogers incorporated the evangelical influences that had captured her attention at Smith College into the religious community, and she pursued new avenues for women's active service. However, she remained fundamentally committed to Catholic traditions of women's spirituality that centered on piety, self-sacrifice, and acts of charity and mercy. Though institutionally and financially the congregation functioned independently, sisters continued to perform the behind-the-scenes support to Maryknoll priests.

The ecclesiastical hierarchy proved receptive to Rogers's vision of a distinctly American missionary force, and it commissioned the sisters' labor as health care workers, teachers, and support staff. Before World War II, Maryknoll established a presence in China, Japan, Korea, and the Philippines, as well as in Asian communities in California, Washington, and Hawaii. In the frontier conditions of foreign missions and the imagined frontiers of American immigrant enclaves, sisters embraced expanded opportunities for religious service. They engaged in direct religious ministry, and as they established successful institutions such as schools and clinics, they garnered recognition for their professional skills as well as for their sacred vows.

After the war, Maryknoll grew in territory and ambitions. The congregation came to articulate a deeply politicized sense of mission as the US church turned to liberal, anticommunist internationalism as the future of the faith and the nation. Bolstered by the financial support of devout churchgoers and the dedication of a growing number of women joining the order, Maryknoll's charitable interventions aligned with the US government's Cold War battle for spheres of influence. With a view of developing nations as potential pawns in the atheistic Soviet quest for world domination, Maryknoll women labored to awaken foreign populations to the salubrious influence of US values, institutions, and policy goals. Armed with a sense of triumphal Catholic righteousness and American know-how, the sisters turned away from the legacy of submissiveness.

Maryknoll embraced the changes in theology and community structures ushered in by the Second Vatican Council (1962–65) just as enthusiastically as it had endorsed anticommunist internationalism. Sisters responded to Rome's call for renewal from a position of direct witness to global unrest. A longtime affinity for ministry to the poor and an emphasis on community-level empowerment placed Maryknoll at the forefront of the postconciliar liberation theology movement, and this search for a grassroots Catholicism supplanted the authoritarian approach to mission.

As liberation theology transformed Catholicism in Latin America, where Maryknoll had concentrated its postwar missions, sisters incorporated public advocacy into their ministry. Critiquing US foreign and economic policy, Maryknoll became known, perhaps unjustifiably, as an activist and even radical congregation. The execution of its sisters in El Salvador, one of the most galvanizing events of twentieth-century US Catholic life, put this identity into high relief. The very public martyrdom became an emblem of the global struggle for human rights. The resulting opprobrium unleashed by Catholic conservatives and the presidential administration of Ronald Reagan marked the profound distance the congregation had traveled from the cautiously liberal internationalist commitments of its early years.

The principle that most united these two organizations throughout their histories is the pillar of liberal Christian ethics: the commandment of love. In Maryknoll and the YWCA, strategies for evangelization radiated out from an evolving doctrine of agape. This doctrine defines Christianity as a religion that springs from God's love for his people, and it focuses on the ethical implications of the Gospel tales of Jesus. The New Testament-oriented practice emphasizes that Jesus called on his followers to love one another as God loved them, and that just as he dedicated his ministry to the loving care of marginalized members of society, they too had responsibilities for service in the worldly realm. In its simplicity, the directive proved adaptable, a rich inspiration for renewal.

Gender frameworks of liberal religion were not as constrictive as those in conservative religious bodies, many of which interpreted biblical portrayals of gender roles as an unchanging natural order or rendered women's submission so extensive as to efface their presence in the church. Maryknoll and YWCA women hardly viewed Christianity as a patriarchal religion. Their work was premised on the notion that women were an instrumental force in Christian ministry, a force that a YWCA speaker named "a great army of Christian women" and a "sisterhood in Christ."[34] Whether intent on winning converts or struggling to achieve secular reform, both groups' conception of evangelization produced an active religion; at times, this evangelization became religious activism. The organizations were not simply preaching a message of Jesus but were also establishing an institutional framework to reshape the temporal world around this message. Christian love provided the women of Maryknoll and the YWCA with a capacious mandate in assuming of the role of evangelizer, and it prompted them to direct their ministry toward humanitarian outreach. Because the commandment to love focused evangelization on interpersonal encounters—those of association and community-based mission—it affirmed women's emotional labor and traditional duties as fundamental modes of religious service.

Religion remained important to women's activism in the twentieth century because religion adapted to broader changes in women's lives. From their beginnings, Maryknoll and the YWCA relied on the imprimatur of religious service that had long legitimized women's claim to authority beyond the household. This imprimatur did not limit them to traditional roles. They spoke to women not simply as mothers and wives, but also as professionals, sanctified religious figures, humanitarians, and citizens. At the same time, religious service provided a safety valve from some of the pressures of changes in women's roles. These single-sex spaces fostered emotional ties among women and created a refuge from the expectations of heteronormativity. While women continued to have unequal access to power and material resources, they had control of most facets of organizational life in Maryknoll and the YWCA. They held positions of leadership, controlled funds, and devised programming. At times, their ambitions were unobtrusive and inoffensive, bringing rudimentary health care to remote settlements or providing boardinghouses for people who had few other places to go. At other moments, however, women of the YWCA and Maryknoll discerned that the teachings of Jesus called for rigorous confrontation of social injustice. They continued to claim the righteousness of their work as a religious calling even as their hopes for change took them in controversial directions.

In the following chapters, these agendas—and the impact they had on the world around them—will be described through an intersecting account of the organizations' institutional lives and political commitments. Roughly ordered by chronology and divided into three parts, the chapters center on, first, a postsuffrage nexus between women's professional outreach and gendered ambitions for cooperative social change; second, a split in midcentury liberal internationalism, which positioned the YWCA and the sisters on opposite sides of Cold War anticommunism; and finally, a reconvergence of the organizations' political and spiritual ambitions amid the leftist ferment of the 1960s and 1970s. Taken as a whole, the political and religious trajectories of the YWCA and Maryknoll Sisters over the twentieth century reveal the complexity and endurance of women's commitments to female-centered institution building and mobilizations for social change.

PART I

WOMEN AND CHRISTIAN FELLOWSHIP IN THE EARLY TWENTIETH CENTURY

The YWCA's experience of dramatic growth at the turn of the century underscores the importance of the activist energies of religious organizations in the "woman movement."[1] While struggles for the ballot have come to be the most visible manifestation of this upsurgence, the reform and community-building activities of the YWCA and other women's groups nurtured by evangelical revivalism left an indelible influence on what would come to be called feminism.

As described in the introduction, the YWCA of the USA was the product of mid-nineteenth-century women's transatlantic organizing, in which the success of the Young Men's Christian Association inspired the creation of a parallel women's organization.[2] The first YWCAs were convened by middle-class and elite Protestant women to look after the spiritual welfare of young women affected by urbanization and industrialization. Already in 1858, when the Ladies Christian Association was founded in New York City, US women in urban centers were organizing prayer circles and social services for workers on the model of the London groups. The US organization took root on college campuses, where student YWCAs attracted the participation of the growing population of women in higher education. Working in concert with student YMCAs, they established a strong influence on the missionary movement. While many Christian groups took on reform projects and foreign mission work in the second half of the nine-teenth century, both city and campus YWCAs stood out for their interdenomi-nationalism and single-sex ethos. This fostered an inclusiveness that brought mainline Protestants together outside of the atomized setting of churches. In a context where male representatives of church bodies often "expressed opposi-tion to women's activism," the YWCA created an outlet for women's energies "where there were no men to hamper them," in the estimation of Anne Firor Scott.[3]

The late-nineteenth-century groups established an institutional identity pre-mised on what the YWCA called the "association idea": "that all kinds, condi-tions, and classes of young women in the community shall be united in Christian fellowship, each to give according to her ability, each to receive according to her capacity," according to a 1907 pamphlet.[4] Founders envisioned the YWCA as a boundary-crossing space. The space was both literal and figurative, as the organization's mission to bring women together in the spirit of Christianity was interknit with the construction of facilities to provide the recreation and services a diverse population required. One association author underscored the excite-ment that accompanied the creation of these tangible spaces, noting that "wom-en's groups in the past had had little opportunity to feel the thrill of ownership."[5] This celebration of the power of women's unity included the conviction that the association had the unique ability to bring egalitarian social values to life. Though "the experience, advice and help of older women [were] always needed," the YWCA endeavored to be a group "for young women, and largely by young women." The YWCA's identity was perhaps most defined by its commitment to reaching across the divisions of social class: "inside the Association there can be no class distinction—from the board member, the wife of the wealthy manu-facturer, to the girl who works in the factory."[6] YWCA facilities offered work-ers spiritual and material services in an attempt to create wholesome outposts in noisome cities. Housing and employment training and referrals proved popular in an urban landscape that was particularly inhospitable to single women. But however much the association positioned itself to transcend the boundaries of class, racial divides were largely left undisturbed. African American groups that were affiliated with the YWCA, where the logic of Jim Crow prevailed in admin-istrative structures, brooked the inequalities of turn-of-the-century interracial-ism that were the cost of access to the institutional resources of majority-white organizations.[7]

In an effort to streamline administration and orchestrate growth, YWCA leaders brought the loosely affiliated campus and city groups together under a unified umbrella organization, the YWCA of the USA, in 1906.[8] With its inception as a national federation, the YWCA of the USA joined a number of nationally organized women's mass membership organizations that were simultaneously faith driven and dedicated to female-led social change. The Woman's Christian Temperance Union, formally organized in 1873, was the largest in scope and membership, parlaying the battle to eliminate alcohol abuse into a comprehensive international campaign of lobbying and direct action in service of the purification of the public sphere. Affiliates of the National Association of Colored Women's Clubs, founded in 1896, discerned a divine mandate for women to pursue uplift as an avenue for racial justice. Created after a gathering at the World Parliament of Religions in 1893, the National Council of Jewish Women launched programming that claimed a place for Jews in the American body politic, provided direct social services to a growing population of impoverished immigrants, and linked its policy ambitions to those of the broader women's movement. Nineteen years later, Henrietta Szold and her compatriots in a Zionist women's study group created the transnationally focused Hadassah and launched a women-led public health infrastructure for Jews in Palestine.[9]

During the years in which the YWCA of the USA came of age, the Maryknoll Sisters were born. While the YWCA rode the cresting wave of Protestant women's institution building and community work, Mary Josephine Rogers faced an ecclesiastical hierarchy that was suspicious of developments in the US Catholic Church and indifferent to women's service in the mission field.[10] The institutional differences between the YWCA and Maryknoll were particularly pronounced in the 1900s and 1910s. The Maryknoll Sisters, attempting to establish themselves within the rigorous framework of apostolic women religious, were in an embryonic state, while the YWCA, thanks to the support of wealthy funders and a well-established network of women's voluntary clubs, had tremendous momentum. However, the nascent Maryknoll effort was built in part on the foundations established by Protestant women's organizing. Though they were not in the same stage of growth as the YWCA, the Maryknoll Sisters were similarly impelled by the rise of women's educational and professional opportunities in religious institutions. The sisters were also inspired and goaded by the successes of Protestant women in the mission field.[11]

In addition to presenting the background for the Protestant religious outreach that spurred the creation of Maryknoll, the following chapters explain how, in these early years, the YWCA combined the energies of the women's movement with a liberal Christian quest to perfect society according to Gospel tenets. They show how the YWCA built the "association idea" into a national entity that was at once a vibrant membership group, a corporate provider of social services, and a hub of women's religious, intellectual, and political life. The reach of the organization was considerable. It began a presence in six hundred cities and colleges as well as a handful of foreign missions, and within twenty years, four hundred more associations were added in all sorts of communities across the United States. Additionally, it oversaw dozens of new associations in foreign cities and schools.[12] In tiers of organization that went from the community level to the national federation and ultimately to an international network, members and staff collectively advanced a faith in action that was a vital, if now under-recognized, presence in the Social Gospel and foreign mission movements. While scholars of the YWCA have documented the powerful impact of the organization on the early labor movement and the long civil rights movement, various dimensions of its story remain untold. This examination of the first decades of the organization highlights how an attempt to enact the ethics of Jesus inspired an innovative program of Christian advocacy that extended from small-group organizing to community-level programming and national electoral politics. At the same time that the challenges of international institution building steered the YWCA into an anti-imperialist revolt that reverberated throughout the foreign mission infrastructure, circumstances in the United States placed the organization in the reactionary crosshairs of a Red Scare that flared intermittently until the 1950s. In facing these challenges, YWCA women contributed to the vitality of mainline Protestantism as a launching point for local and global social engagement.

1 · "LIFE MORE ABUNDANT"
The YWCA and the Social Gospel

The first convention of the YWCA of the USA, held in New York City in December 1906, captures something of the alchemy responsible for the YWCA's rapid growth in its first two decades: an emotionally charged mixture of evangelicalism, the Social Gospel, and ambitions for female-centered social change. The atmosphere of this and later national membership conventions must have felt something like a combination of a revival, Chautauqua-style edification, and a political convention. Programs were scheduled from morning to night, with hymns and prayer services, sermons and lectures, and procedural matters such as committee reports and membership resolutions. Representatives of community and campus associations gathered to hear from some of the most prominent figures in mainline Protestantism, with Charles Stelzle encouraging ministry to laborers, Robert Speer describing the "supreme good" effected by the YWCA's work among college students, and John Mott waxing enthusiastic about the role the group could play in the "great advance" of "great Christian civilizations."[1] Passing motions to determine the direction of the organization, delegates enthusiastically participated in a simulacrum of the electoral machinery that then barred their access to it. The meeting was convened after several years of sometimes contentious negotiations over coordinating the efforts of autonomously operating associations. The tasks at hand were, first, the pragmatic work of articulating an institutional identity and determining the scope of association activities, and second, the inspirational work of issuing a charge for Protestant women to unite in the spirit of Christian service.

The women gathered in New York affirmed a YWCA plan of action with three points of emphasis: to serve as the "door through which young women are led into the Church of God," to break down the "lines of class and caste" through cooperative service, and to unleash the "mighty power" of "earnest consecrated women" in solving the "many perplexing problems" of modern life.² This plan fostered a synergy between the personalist passions of evangelicalism and the Progressive impulses shaping both women's organizing and the Social Gospel movement.

By the YWCA's sixth convention in 1920, which made the national press for its controversial calls for workers' rights, women's participation in electoral politics, and ecumenicalism, it became evident that this was an unstable alchemy. The dramatic increase in working-class women's participation in association life, as well as the shifting religious affiliations of the rising generation of YWCA leaders and members, tipped the balance away from the evangelical concerns of piety, social morality, and personal salvation. Instead, an emphasis on the "social principles of Jesus" and Progressive coalition politics prevailed.³ This transformation opened the way for the YWCA to become a pacesetter in liberal Christian activism.

The YWCA's institutional mission, the "ultimate purpose" adopted at the 1909 convention, can be credited with providing an expansive directive that inspired the search for a practical application of Gospel ideals. This purpose, the YWCA's constitution declared, was to bring women to "such a knowledge of Jesus Christ as Saviour and Lord as shall mean for the individual young woman fullness of life and development of character."⁴ The declaration, combining a Gospel paraphrase ("I have come that they might have life more abundantly" [John 10:10]) and the cadences of uplift, guided a pursuit of religious service that extended into the era of women's liberation and liberation theology.

The YWCA's persistent affirmation of the value of single-sex women's organizations in shaping the public sphere can be credited with establishing a powerful infrastructure that pushed the organization's members to connect the interpersonal to the political and the local to the global. The professional staff who steered the association's operations and the members who participated in its programs brought to life what YWCA of the USA founder Grace Hoadley Dodge called "a spirit of womanhood and girls, a spirit of working together and being in touch with each other, trusting one another, with the loving Christ."⁵ Religious mission dovetailed with dedication to gender separatism as the group blossomed into one of the largest and most diverse American women's membership organizations in the early twentieth century. Its success should not be measured solely in numbers, however. For one thing, it should be marked in the reach of its programming. The YWCA became so robust that by the 1920s, four major (and still operating) organizations had been spun off from the parent group to focus on more specialized interests: Travelers Aid, which stationed matrons in transportation centers to intercept women travelers before they could be swindled or led astray; the International Migration Service, which aided refugee resettlement; the International Institute, an immigrant service provider; and an organization for career women, the Federation of Business and Professional Women.[6] For another, the YWCA's importance can also be gauged in the degree to which it fostered an international network of women intellectuals and activists. Finally, its influence can be apprehended in the visibility it achieved as an advocacy organization. The latter proved a source of contention. As this chapter concludes, although the YWCA's roots as an evangelical women's club initially warded off criticism of its religious politics, the association became ensnared in the Red Scare of the 1920s. As troublesome as charges of radicalism may have been, attacks on the YWCA denote the organization's success. In ways that lone ministers, denominations, and single-issue interest groups could not, the YWCA brought an ethos of politically engaged Christianity to well over a thousand communities, campuses, and foreign missions. The ethos was rife with tensions: declarations of egalitarian fellowship were paired with considerable institutional segregation; democratic organizational procedures designed to empower minority constituencies were overseen by paternalistic administrators; and calls for social change favored moral suasion over confrontation. The tensions were ultimately productive, as the organization was persistently compelled to examine the disjuncture between its ideals and practices.

"THE KINGDOM OF GOD IN ITS FULLNESS"

The executive staff and volunteers who operated the national organization at its founding drew on an organizational legacy that addressed two registers of the abundant life of the New Testament. Most important for the founders was the abundant life of salvation in the hereafter. Their programming continued in the vein of YWCA predecessor organizations, as YWCAs evangelized participants through a number of exclusively religious activities—including proselytization of the unchurched as well as worship and study for the devout. Yet the association had long been known for the variety of its offerings, reflected in the sprawling goals stated in its founding documents that aimed "to advance physical, social, intellectual, moral, and spiritual interests of young women."[7] Its work was accordingly very much directed at addressing the temporal realm. For the middle-class and affluent white clubwomen and professionals who made up most of the members of the volunteer committees and hired staff, social morality concerns served as a natural bridge between the call to evangelize and the drive to shape the public sphere.

Publicity material described the organization as "a great preventative and constructive agency," "preventative because it offers to young women opportunities which lessen the power of temptations; constructive because in the all-round building up of character is being laid the foundations for the homes of the succeeding generations."[8] As a constructive agency, the YWCA offered all sorts of young women a salubrious path to self-development. Still, the group designated the evangelization of working women a favored category of work, which explains the emphasis on prevention—the prevention of moral ruin among women loosened from the controls of domesticity. YWCA leaders shared the preoccupations of rescue agencies that served "fallen" women like prostitutes, unwed mothers, and delinquents in the conviction that such women's susceptibility to bad health and morals threatened the state of womanhood in its entirety.[9] However, while rescue groups sought to mitigate the contagion of immorality by isolating and rehabilitating its carriers, preventative work had a prophylactic purpose. The YWCA's strong institutional presence, which had grown from 616 community and student associations in 1906 to slightly more than 1,000 in 1915, provided a variety of means to do so. Affordable accommodations steered self-supporting women away from immoral boardinghouses. Cafeterias replaced saloons, and calisthenics—or, ideally, vigorous prayer and hymns—substituted for the dance hall. The association offered factory workers both bread (employment bureaus and training) and roses (music, reading rooms, and vacation camps in country settings).[10] With a pledge to "develop a nobler womanhood in our country, more efficient women wage-earners and, above all . . . , win young women to . . . Jesus Christ," the YWCA promised funders that it was contributing to a stronger industrial workforce, one populated by workers with more rest, training, and obedience than women made inefficient and unruly by the enervating conditions of their employment.[11] The uplift of Christian womanhood would improve labor productivity. Reinforcing the perceived moral shortcomings of an indolent working class, one 1907 pamphlet advertised that the YWCA "wields a powerful influence among girls who are in the heart of and to an extent constitute the labor problem," an appeal aimed at attracting the financial support of outfits on the management side of "the labor problem."[12]

YWCA founders touted their selfless service in helping young women reach the abundant life, but such sentiments naturalized middle-class white women's assumption of leadership. The premise of uplift rested on an unequal relationship between privileged and disadvantaged women, and racial segregation and white paternalism prevailed as African American women claimed their place in the movement. Though the YWCA would come to stand out among women's organizations for its racial diversity and early interest in interracial activism, the historian Nancy Robertson underscores the fact that from the beginning, the association "established that white people—especially southerners—were to control the race question."[13] Its posture of deference to southern customs gave cover to widespread segregation throughout the network of YWCAs. Black women secured the national association's moral and, to an extent, material support of black YWCAs at the cost of publicly affirming the association's questionable claims of fellowship. Privately, they struggled for basic concessions as they established, by dint of their own efforts, strong community institutions designed by and for African Americans.[14]

The uplift politics of social morality that captivated the organization's earliest leaders may have prevented them from achieving their ultimate aim of unifying women in cooperative service. Still, the organization's quest to realize Gospel ideals provided tools for challenging the hierarchies written into its own rhetoric and practices. In describing the YWCA's "Beginnings among Colored Women," Addie Waites Hunton, a clubwoman and activist whose "intimate understanding of the special problems of her own race [gave] authority to the publication," invoked the kingdom of God and a language of Christian democracy to call for collective support of African American women's association efforts. Hunton underscored the fact that white women had a religious obligation to pursue egalitarian fellowship: "this leaflet hopes to awaken a larger co-operative sympathy to all those who believe in the democracy of Christianity and who have recognized that the supreme call of the hour is the extension of God's kingdom here on earth."[15] African American women waged a long struggle to convert such sympathy into policy change, but the struggle eventually bore fruit.

FIGURE 1.1. "The Favorite Pastime. YWCA Colored Recreation Center, New York City," circa 1919. Credit: Photo courtesy of the World YWCA

FIGURE 1.2. "Great Sport on a Warm Day. YWCA Student Conference, Blue Ridge, N.C.,"
1919. Credit: Photo courtesy of the World YWCA

Contingents in which white women were the majority faced fewer obstacles
in advancing their interests. To some degree, Dodge's instrumental position in
the organization during its early days may account for the national leadership's
receptiveness to new directions in programming. "No one ever hears of Grace
Dodge," asserted a 1910 article in the Christian general interest magazine *The
World Today*. "Her name rarely appears in a newspaper, her picture, never. . . . She
declines all interviews."[16] Within the world of the YWCA, however, she was a
revered figure. Though no particular individual could claim credit for launching
the association, Dodge had a singular role. She had been recruited to oversee the
unification of predecessor YWCA organizations, and after she had succeeded in
doing so, she served as president of the US YWCA until her death in 1914. An
heir to the Phelps-Dodge family fortune—accumulated from the import and
mining businesses of her father, William E. Dodge Jr.—she put her wealth
and experience in New York City's religious and philanthropic networks to
use in building the association's infrastructure. She helped craft a federation of
groups that resembled her family's corporate ventures in its emphasis on scale,
efficiency, and expansion.

Dodge's leadership ability went well beyond material resources and organizational acumen. Inspired by a very uncorporate sense of kinship with young
working women, she also cultivated an emotive ethos of democracy and care as

the premise of association. As these ideals came to shape the YWCA's operating structures, they undermined the hierarchical relationships engendered by the trope of uplift that saturated evangelical efforts at social outreach.[17]

Dodge identified herself with the wage-earning women she had longed to influence in earlier philanthropic ventures. Before her recruitment into the YWCA, she had sponsored the Working Girl's Society, a club that emphasized self-reliance and mutual support, and the 3 P's Circle, which was devoted to purity, perseverance, and pleasantness. Claiming to have "earned her wages in advance" by an inheritance that enabled her to dedicate her life to social improvement, Dodge counted herself a confidante of young women navigating the difficulties of coming of age. She named the "American girl . . . the one great interest of my life," and she proclaimed that the desire to serve young woman-hood inspired her outreach: "I came into this work because I love the girls so much. . . . They have meant to me my life for twenty years."[18]

Her experiences as a single woman philanthropist may have given her some sense of the isolation and disempowerment felt by the working women who sought out the YWCA for leisure and social services. When Dodge organized and funded the creation of Columbia University's Teachers College, her vision of a school of vocational pedagogy was usurped by male academics who instead created a scholastic program.[19] The YWCA of the USA, she imagined, would be a place governed by mutual decision making, where women of her privileged standing would bring young members into the association as beloved partners. Young members in turn would animate the YWCA's Christian purpose as they determined what the meaning of "fullness of life and development of charac-ter" meant in the context of their own lives. With her intention to enlist work-ing women in the leadership of the movement, Dodge signaled her interest in challenging the prevailing presumptions of philanthropic work. Her remarks at the 1909 national convention expressed both an optimism about the power of Christian sisterhood and a sense that the association was not living up to its ideals. She questioned whether the well-to-do delegates truly recognized the everyday implications of their avowed commitment to Christian fellowship: "have you ever thought what the girls have who have given your breakfast, the women who have made the things you wear?" Assuming that her listeners had not, she told them, "they are our sisters." The time would come, she predicted, when workers themselves would stand before the convention and assert their vision of "what a great woman should be—they perhaps know better than we do."[20] This sisterhood was to be secured by the bonds of Christian fellowship.

As blinkered as such yearnings may have been, Dodge and her associates were not disingenuous in professing devotion to young working women. Given the limits of uplift, evangelicalism may seem like an unlikely influence on the social justice impulse that would become manifest in the YWCA. Evangelicalism's doctrinal foundations muted denominational differences between Protestants through shared convictions of biblical revelation and "the proclamation of Christ's saving work through his death on the cross and the necessity of personally trusting him for eternal salvation," in the words of the historian George Marsden.[21] Accordingly, its social agenda is most often associated with proselytizing, devotionalism, and purity issues, which indeed were priorities for early association leaders. Still, evangelical commitments to overcoming the divides of class, age, and nationality through effusive expressions of faith and the interpersonal encounters of evangelization gave the organization impetus to push its outreach in new directions.

Initial programming priorities were set according to the premise that a cascade of social transformations could be put in motion when a large group of women embraced Gospel principles. While these beliefs emphasized personal devotion to Jesus and the authority of the Bible, they contained a universalizing vision of a shared humanity. As much as they focused on millennial hopes for the afterlife, YWCA leaders directed their attention to secular arenas when they set out to realize the "Association idea."[22] At the first YWCA convention, Mrs. C. R. Springer pointed to the importance of these principles in the tangible work of recruitment, explaining that she "never had the least success in reaching my hand down" to bring young women into the St. Louis YWCA. Instead, she referred to a partnership engendered by Christianity: "I reach my hand up and try to make that girl feel that she and I are just the same in the good Master's keeping, and that we are coworkers with Him."[23] Notably, she identified the YWCA collective with a labor term, not with a familial one: its members were coworkers on an equal plane, with a benevolent God as their mutual foreman.

Significantly, early YWCA leaders saw no disjuncture between biblical principles and the entrance of women into public life. While the rhetoric of uplift frequently referenced the aim of preventative work to be preparation for marriage and motherhood, the organization consistently expressed support for single women as paid laborers and asserted that it had a responsibility to shape the public sphere. Dodge mentioned her own unmarried status and independence as a point of pride, writing in a pamphlet styled as a "A Private Letter to Girls": "girls, I would rather that you should all die 'old maids' than that you should be in a hurry to take a man just because you want to get married." She assured her readers that "there is much that can come into a woman's life who is not married," for unmarried women could devote themselves to both extended family and social betterment.[24] The evangelical confidence that God had given all people the responsibility to spread the Gospel made it incumbent on women to provide moral leadership beyond the home. While they did not forge direct alliances with women's rights efforts at the turn of the century, evangelical YWCA members embraced the belief that women had a duty to rebuild society using Christian principles. They also insisted that they deserved resources and authority to carry out those duties.

Wealthy evangelicals may have occupied the most visible positions in the leadership of YWCA of the USA at its founding, but the professional staff who populated the central administrative apparatus—called the National Board—carried forward day-to-day operations. These professionals were instrumental in integrating Social Gospel principles into programming, principles instilled at the types of student conferences and campus organizations that had transformed the consciousness of Mary van Kleeck. In their desire to apply the ideals of Christian love, the second generation of administrators changed the formula that had made the early YWCA so powerful, transforming the religious rhetoric and, ultimately, the operating principles established by the founders. When the Social Gospel displaced evangelical priorities in the programming, the YWCA came into its own as an activist organization.

More so than many of the other women's membership organizations that proliferated in the late nineteenth century, the YWCA took the professionalization of religious outreach to new heights with its expansive, regimented administrative structure. From the beginning, the National Board sought an expert staff to be the labor force behind the YWCA movement, and it enlisted educated women to become secretaries—a term that designated a professional, not a clerical, post. The multiple departments of the National Board, regional offices, and local associations generated significant demand for staff members. Only women could be secretaries, whether assistant or executive. These roles provided opportunities for advancement, autonomy, and recognition. Despite the culture of racial paternalism, the organization recruited black women and immigrants to carry out programming for specialized constituencies.

Although a number of secretaries were employed by the association for decades, many women with shorter tenures at the YWCA moved on to exert considerable influence in the wider domains of women's professions. The Progressive reform impulse and premium placed on scientific management created a demand for social science training for women, which the YWCA provided in-house. One woman called the Women's Bureau of the US Department of Labor the YWCA's "graduate school" because of the many women who parlayed association experience into government employment.[25] For many years, the National Board consulted with van Kleeck, who—in the years after her Smith College encounter with the YWCA—had become a leading figure in industrial sociology and the first head of the Women's Bureau. Crystal Bird Fauset, the first African American woman elected to a state legislature (Pennsylvania's), developed programs for black women during her time on the national YWCA staff during the 1920s. Before her appointment to the faculty of Columbia University, the anthropologist Ella Cara Deloria had worked in the 1920s as a secretary of health education in the YWCA's Native American programs.[26] The roster of distinguished alumnae could continue for pages.

Women professionals may have been marginalized or ridiculed in the culture at large, but the YWCA pinned the salvation of society on their capabilities. In the *Association Monthly*, the YWCA's nationally circulated magazine (later renamed *Womans Press*, spelled without an apostrophe for unknown reasons), Helen Barnes called the work a "new profession for woman [that] asks the very finest type of womanhood for the gift of her life." Similar to the settlement house workers who embodied the new spirit of social service, the YWCA secretary was expected to devote herself passionately and altruistically to her work. However, departing from the settlement house model, the YWCA provided women with careers, financially compensating them for their specialized training. The spiritual wages of religious service were touted as an even more significant motivation to take on this work. Like Barnes, Emma Bailey Speer, president of the National Board from 1915 to 1932, described secretaries as women of noble character and monumental influence. The "unselfish, utterly self-sacrificing services of the secretaries" nurtured careers with "value as great as the recognized learned professions of the past, [a] profession on which human progress is dependent."[27]

The women most visible in creating YWCA programming in the late 1910s employed the rhetoric of the Social Gospel and democratic self-governance in a way that the association's founders had not.[28] Many of the younger women had been active in college YWCAs, which had helped steer them to association employment after graduation. They were exposed not only to the emotive worship practices and devotionalism of late-nineteenth-century evangelical revivals, but they were also captivated by the millennial ideals of what the Social Gospel theologian Walter Rauschenbusch called "the immense latent perfectibility in human nature."[29] Responding to an increasingly diverse membership that had lost interest in social morality and resisted paternalist proselytizing, they turned the organization's focus to the practical application of Gospel ethics as the path to abundant life. The founders had worked from the base of women's clubs that often established indirect connections to public advocacy. In contrast, the next generation of National Board secretaries witnessed women's Progressive political mobilizations that were propelled by a confidence that technological innovation and the social sciences provided the practical tools for such perfection.[30] Moreover, they saw the decades-long struggle for citizenship rights culminate in the women's suffrage amendment to the US Constitution.

Social Gospel and evangelical impulses in liberal Protestantism were hardly mutually exclusive. Anna Rice, director of religious programming, affirmed the association's dedication to the two dimensions of salvation: "If Christianity is to triumph and bring the Kingdom of God in its fullness it must save not only individuals, but society as well."[31] She articulated both the evangelical quest to bring individuals to Christian salvation in the afterlife and the Social Gospel crusade to remake life on earth following the model of Jesus's social teachings. In both types of doctrine, love was an animating force, the engine of fellowship and Christianization. Whether evangelicals and Social Gospel adherents viewed the Christian purpose as individual uplift or structural reform, they found common cause in the YWCA's identity as a service provider. They expressed confidence that the tools of modernity—economy of scale, secular education, social science—could be put to use in the service of religious directives.

These currents of Protestantism fundamentally differed in their ultimate aims. While Social Gospel and evangelical enthusiasts shared an interest in exerting Christian influence on reform efforts, the political thrust of many Social Gospel allegiances diverged from the evangelical principles of spiritual conversion, biblical authority, and redemption earned through the crucifixion of Jesus. Theological elaborations of the Social Gospel placed "the social principles of Jesus," a frequently used shorthand term for a New Testament-oriented activist ethics, at the center of religious practice.[32] Social Gospel supporters answered fears about the dislocations unleashed by modern life, particularly the struggles of urbanization and industrialization, with a confident faith that contemporary developments, such as social planning and international communication networks, provided solutions.

From the beginning, the YWCA recruited Social Gospel theologians to articulate the institution's religious mission to its members. Conventions showcased the high-profile personalities of the movement—particularly Rauschenbusch, often cited as Social Gospel's "most representative thinker."[33] Many of the male theologians who participated in various YWCA ventures had personal ties to the association's mission, affirming the YWCA's special contribution to their Social Gospel ambitions. Harry Emerson Fosdick (husband of Florence Whitney Fosdick, a volunteer member of the National Board) lectured and published extensively through the YWCA, which continued to support his work when he became a lightning rod for criticism amid the fundamentalist revolt. The YWCA counted on the contributions of the Labor Temple founder Charles Stelzle (father of secretary Hope Stelzle), missiologist Robert Speer (husband of Emma Bailey Speer, a secretary and later president of the YWCA), and ecumenicalist pioneer John Mott (husband of Leila Mott, a volunteer National Board member). Still, the organization was not a passive audience for men's religious thought. Building on these foundations, association thinkers advanced their own vision of applied Christianity.

"AN INFLUENTIAL UNIT IN THE BODY
OF CHRISTIAN PUBLIC OPINION"

At the 1911 national convention in Indianapolis, four years of growth elicited excitement about the successes of the expanding association movement. As had occurred at previous biennial conventions, delegates from throughout the United States came together to determine the contours of the leadership and programming that held together a geographically dispersed confederation of associations, which varied considerably in interests and constituency. Their reports, debates, and resolutions determined program priorities, authorized the scope and composition of the National Board, and provided a forum for a collective discussion about the state and future of the YWCA's work. An incursion into the realm of advocacy proved to be one of most significant outcomes of the convention. A resolution concerning living-wage legislation struck a balance between evangelical and Social Gospel impulses, demonstrating delegates' willingness to enter a battle in the public sphere as well as their attachment to the uplift model of social change. It marked the beginning of public affairs programming launched from the level of the National Board.

The proposal endorsing the living wage—a goal of the women's labor movement, which pursued a minimum wage for male and female workers alike—stirred a lively discussion. The resolution drafted by the National Board staff highlighted the association's "responsibility as an influential unit in the body of Christian public opinion" in calling for policy intervention.[34] It nudged the group not only toward a declaration of solidarity with the labor movement, a contentious field of cross-class alliance that the YWCA had not previously entered, but also toward participation in a women's political culture that was edging toward a national suffrage victory. The plight of women workers was front-page news, for the Triangle Shirtwaist factory fire had occurred a month before the meeting. Indirect references to that tragedy peppered the discussion. Citing her encounter with the 1909 garment workers strike, Mrs. Barnes of the New York City YWCA reported that not one striker could be persuaded that the association "cared if she lived or died in the streets." Rather, working women responded "with scorn" and accused the YWCA of "dealing with disembodied spirits" in its offers of spiritual help. It was time, she asserted, for the association to show it cared for those who were literally dying in the streets.[35]

The wording of the resolution, however, draped this potentially controversial endorsement with the blameless cover of social morality. The preamble noted that "the utterly inadequate wages paid to thousands of young women throughout the country often hamper and stultify the work of the Association as a great preventative agency" and attributed "the white slave traffic" to "the lack of the living wage." The YWCA proposed using its influence to support a woman's "inherent right . . . to a living wage which shall insure her the possibility of a virtuous livelihood." It also acknowledged that favorable public opinion alone would not secure this right; protective legislation would be necessary to regulate hours and wages. In contrast to the organizing efforts of the Women's Trade Union League (WTUL) or the wildcat activities of the shop floor, the resolution did not speak of struggle. Rather, it proposed a cooperative relationship between employers and labor. The living wage would bring a "higher standard of faithful service and achievement for the worker and of justice and consideration for the employer."[36] The resolution promised better service from women workers, referencing concerns about working women's tendencies toward poor health, poor morals, and poor work performance. The YWCA's disinterested Christian declaration would put moral weight behind regulatory legislation, making Christian employers aware that sufficient wages safeguarded young women's virtue.

The convention considered the matter only two years after the WTUL endorsed the living wage. It was expected for mainstream early-twentieth-century women's organizations to lobby for the regulation of vice. But it was a new step for the YWCA to support a movement associated with radicalism, not to mention Catholicism and Judaism. Linking the demands of the women's labor movement to ideals of purity had contributed to the success of a number of protective legislation campaigns, and YWCA convention delegates responded positively to this strategy, passing the resolution with a large majority.[37] Some supporters cited the exigencies of moral panic to urge ratification of resolution. A St. Louis delegate stated that the organization's stand against the white slave traffic would help YWCA work in the South, where women's chastity was the "one thing that is held sacred." For others, the stance reflected a measured evolution of the YWCA's interest in women workers. Without "rushing into hasty legislation," the YWCA's support of the living wage would offer "the hand of fellowship to girls whose minds and bodies are starved" by the conditions of their work.[38]

Delegates representing the association's members (who numbered 228,412 at the time) may have been open to this dimension of the increasingly politicized women's movement, but it was National Board staff members who pushed them in that direction. Florence Simms, a charismatic secretary who engineered the YWCA's program for industrial workers, elaborated the links between the association's Christian purpose and the demands of factory workers. In the *Association Monthly* she asked, "Since the matter of wages, hours and conditions of industry has direct bearing upon the life of the girl employed, and since the mission of the Association is to bring to that girl a more abundant life, is it not plain that the Association must be concerned for the practical matters which have such a large influence in molding and shaping that life?"[39]

One means of addressing these practical matters was the application of principles of scientific management—a tool of the wider women's movement—to association programming.[40] YWCA women were not praying the kingdom of God into being but systematically pursuing it, and Walter Rauschenbusch praised the association's membership for this vision of joining "the power of social science to the impulses of Christianity [for] social redemption." Secretaries promoted "investigation, study, experiment, adaptation, [and] constructive planning" as resources to carry out the group's Christian purpose.[41] The professional fields connected to YWCA programming grew organically from the intertwined Progressive and women's movements: academia, particularly sociology; health and hygiene, which encompassed physical education; and social work; among others. The YWCA's multifaceted institutional mission called for a wide range of expert guidance.

The YWCA expressed its commitment to the reform professions with one of its first projects after incorporation, creating an institute of higher education. In 1908, the National Board established the National Training School (NTS) at its Manhattan headquarters. Designed as a graduate school for the professional development of secretaries at a time when the first social work schools were getting underway, the NTS mixed religious, professional, and practical instruction in its curriculum. Mainstays like Bible study and hymnody supplemented courses in economics and sociology, while training in management, finance, parliamentary procedure, and public speaking supplied the pragmatic foundations for association employment.[42] Although a number of stalwart YWCA secretaries attended the NTS, it never drew a critical mass of students and closed in 1928. The NTS's existence nevertheless testifies to the degree to which the YWCA provided an intellectual space and activist network for Social Gospel Progressives. Renowned ministers, academics, and reformers participated in the NTS. In making faculty appointments, the school affirmed the expertise of women like the Barnard economist Emilie Hutchinson and the Adelphi (later University of Chicago) sociologist Annie Marion MacLean in ways that their home institutions, where "low status and limited opportunities" prevailed, did not.[43] Their presence conferred scholarly legitimacy to the YWCA's endeavor. Between 1908 and 1920, the NTS hosted guest lecturers including Mary van Kleeck; the educator Mary Wooley, a volunteer National Board member who was deeply involved in YWCA ventures; settlement house pioneer Mary Simkhovitch; prison reformer Katherine Bement Davis; and Margaret Drier Robins, president of the WTUL. Later, the YWCA became a home for female religious thinkers. In the 1920s, it provided speaking and publication opportunities to the British theologian and activist A. Maude Royden, and it enlisted the services of Mary Ely Lyman, a YWCA secretary who had become a biblical scholar.[44]

The first major study commissioned by the National Board showcased the distinctiveness of the early YWCA's vision of the Social Gospel. It sent Annie Marion MacLean into the field in 1908 to investigate women's labor conditions. Reporting her results in the *Washington Post*, MacLean highlighted the woman-centered organizational culture underwriting the study. The investigation, she explained, "was in various respects the first of its kind in the world: the first ever conducted entirely by college women . . . , the first systematic study of the conditions surrounding women in industry ever ordered by a religious body . . . , and the first instituted, conducted, and paid for entirely by women."[45] While MacLean touted the study's empirical nature, with six thousand interviews of workers at four hundred places of employment across the United States, she did not present it as an impersonal, statistical report. Rather, she analyzed the research in a spirit of cross-class solidarity, prompting Grace Hoadley Dodge to wax enthusiastic over the potential to realize Christian fellowship through educated outreach. In a convention speech, she effused that the study would enable the organization to better "take part in the divine plan to bring to our sisters, who in many respects are so much more worthy of our opportunities, some of the privileges we have." From factory cities of the Northeast and Midwest to the "Oregon hop fields" and the "fruit picking, packing and drying of San Jose and Fresno," MacLean investigated working conditions by taking employment alongside young women. She documented their social and personal longings as well as the conditions of their work. As she became aware of an informal working women's culture of mutual support, she concluded that "there's a lot of real nobility among the working girls," a tacit counter to association rhetoric that promoted its programming by warning of the hedonistic, improvident tendencies of workers.[46]

Another early study, a 1910 report on "Some Urgent Phases of Immigrant Life," similarly viewed qualitative data through the frame of yearnings for Christian fellowship. YWCA researchers examined Ellis Island statistics and elicited expert counsel to plan programming for immigrants settling in the United States. They enlisted multilingual women to conduct 550 interviews with immigrants. The method underscored the fact that though the YWCA made ample use of quantitative analysis, it sought to have dialogues with the objects of study. The National Board hoped surveys would enable it to address the needs of diverse groups of women. The immigrant report stated one "definite conclusion": the "fundamental need is not of more statistics but of more contact in life."[47]

MacLean's perspective indicated the ways in which the YWCA's quest for fellowship made a more welcoming atmosphere possible for women who did not share the class and ethnic background of the majority of the members. Using the tools of social work, female professionals of the YWCA cultivated contacts with the rank-and-file workers in factories and offices to gain a sense of their material and psychological needs. But bridges between classes were forged not simply through National Board studies or by sympathetic secretaries. Employed women—both "industrial" and "business and professional" in the YWCA's parlance—did not join the association because of evangelical attempts at uplift, such as the "weekly noon meetings in factories, with hymn singing to the accompaniment of portable organs," touted in early programming.[48] Rather, workers used the association's mechanisms of democratic self-governance to orient programming toward their well-being and personal empowerment. The historian Dorothea Browder provides a compelling account of how working women held the association accountable to its claims of cross-class solidarity in establishing their own programming priorities. "Neglected by labor unions," working-class members "used the YWCA's discursive and institutional resources—meeting spaces, staff, and organizational religious purpose—to make claims for a greater share of power and autonomy" within and beyond the YWCA.[49]

Working women's success at leveraging the rhetoric of cross-class, cross-generational fellowship shored up the Social Gospel influence in the association's religious life, which led to its immersion in political advocacy. While touting the heterogeneity of the membership, the National Board reported that "diversity of background, environment, nationality and race means, of course, diversity of opportunity"—an opportunity to improve society and spread fellowship. The sudden growth of the industrial program (from 375 local clubs in 1915 to 823 in 1918) marked the leading edge of the YWCA's pursuit of a pluralistic membership, one it increasingly defined as breaking barriers.[50] As YWCA leaders solicited the perspective of these workers, it became clear that they believed that material needs were inseparable from spiritual development.

The growth of industrial programming occurred at the same time as the decline in explicitly religious work. "For an organization that is frankly religious," a 1916–17 statistical yearbook warned, "it may be discouraging to note that the enrollment in Bible and mission study, which increased by nearly 50,000 from 1907 to 1915, has decreased by nearly 14,000 in the year between 1915 and 1916."[51] Few leaders in the National Board found cause for despair. The board discerned innovative spiritual impulses at the root of the organization's increasingly pluralistic culture, and it marshaled a variety of resources to allow this new spirituality to take expression.

If the 1911 national convention, with its resolution addressing white slavery and the living wage, marked a balance between evangelical and Social Gospel approaches to advocacy issues, the 1920 convention in Cleveland demonstrated the twilight of evangelical influence. The delegates approved two resolutions that set a new course for YWCA work, one that pushed the organization to engage more fully in direct political advocacy and another that relaxed the religious requirements for its student members. And though the advocacy resolution led one of the organization's most prominent volunteer board members to walk out, proponents of the Social Gospel took charge of a new sort of religious programming with the overwhelming support of the association as a whole.

The shift evident at the 1920 convention cannot be attributed to religious factors alone. World War I brought a new exigency to democratizing impulses at the same time that it supplied momentum to women's movements. The war sparked a period of unparalleled growth in budget, membership, programming, and facilities for the YWCA. Nancy Robertson attributes this growth to "the particular fit between perceived wartime needs and the YWCA's expertise in housing, cafeterias, and recreation—all infused with Christian values." Its patriotic service "brought it resources and new recognition."[52]

The period invigorated the YWCA's Christian purpose as well. The association's religious thinkers came away from the war convinced that the collective horror about the destruction made a Christian social order more, rather than less, likely. The age called for a new approach to geopolitics. YWCA women such as Lillian Chambers, an American secretary stationed in Japan, were stirred by the Wilsonian "spirit of world brotherhood." The League of Nations, Chambers and like-minded colleagues believed, promised to make this spirit a governing force. The YWCA had mobilized to facilitate women's war work; it now hoped to turn this collective power toward reshaping the postwar world with women's values. Endowed with what Harriot Stanton Blatch, in a YWCA publication, called the "protective duty towards not only [their] own offspring but towards the race itself," women now could use their unique capacity for care to further the public good.[53]

The YWCA had not formally weighed in on the issue of suffrage as an organization, though several of its efforts suggest its support of a women's rights agenda. Still, the final push of the suffrage struggle and President Woodrow Wilson's oratorical commitment to spreading democracy infused the YWCA's spiritual meditations with a language of Christian citizenship. For the architects of YWCA programming, suffrage was not solely a matter of securing political citizenship. They aimed to "Christianize the woman's movement" and transform civic life with Christian values. "The latent power of womanhood . . . released . . . through suffrage must be given the Christian emphasis," insisted the religious educator Katherine Gerwick in the YWCA's magazine.[54] Like international women's suffrage activists of that era, she described the women's movement as global, but she highlighted the universalizing gestures of Christian love instead of the sense of "common subordination" that Leila Rupp identified as the mobilizing force behind international women's groups. Gerwick described citizenship as an indispensable tool in creating world fellowship: "Women must see in

citizenship an opportunity to set into motion an ever-widening circle of friendship which shall reach from the woman in a small Ohio village to an isolated
group in an Indian purdah."[55] In her account, political involvement and citizenship education replaced evangelical proselytizing as a form of caring outreach.
Still, this care was couched in the terms of the imperialist, feminist discourses of
foreign mission and domestic uplift. For Gerwick, the ministrations of midwestern YWCA women were linked to the enlightenment of their benighted friends
overseas.

The 1920 convention was held in mid-April, four months before the suffrage
amendment was ratified. The outcome of a convention debate over whether
to endorse the Federal Council of Churches' statement on the "Social Ideals
of the Churches" demonstrated that women of the YWCA were committed
to active citizenship. The statement demanded, among other reforms, occupa-
tional health and safety measures, a six-day workweek, protective legislation for
women, and the right of workers to organize. The National Board's decision to
advance the resolution of endorsement was, to a significant extent, a product of
the agitation of the industrial contingent of the YWCA's membership. The 1911
call for a living wage had provoked an examination of the association's place in
the public sphere, and the 1920 resolution stated decisively that the organization
had the responsibility to help shape public opinion. It proposed that after "careful study of social and economic conditions," the National Board should "use its
resources and influence to help secure such legislation as shall promote the welfare of young women."[56]

In fighting for this resolution, working-class members drew on the organization's Christian purpose to frame "socioeconomic problems as moral and political issues," Browder notes.[57] Insisting that the abundant life meant economic
security, they issued a charge for fellow delegates to show their interest in young
women's development by supporting legislation beneficial to workers' welfare.
At the same time, they demanded autonomy within the organization to put forward their own vision of a cross-class women's movement. The social ideals resolution centered on contentious labor issues during an eruption of antiradicalism.
The YWCA nevertheless elected to support organizing rights.

The YWCA's endorsement of the social ideals generated considerable controversy within the assembly. The students' motion to relax religious requirements
in their membership criteria created even more. Participation in YWCA activities was open to all women, regardless of creed (at least in policy). However,
the YWCA administration upheld a religious requirement that restricted full
membership, which conferred association governance privileges, to women who
belonged to evangelical Protestant churches.

Representatives of the student division and industrial and immigrant groups
argued that an individual pledge of Christianity, instead of a formal church

affiliation, was sufficient ground for full membership. They maintained that this change was necessary to bring more of their peers into the association. Official membership in a church congregation had been a matter of course for the older women of the association, but this was not the case for many Protestant students. The industrial and immigrant groups were unique in having Catholic (and even some Jewish) participants.

To some of the old guard, the membership proposal repudiated the very purpose of the YWCA. Mrs. J. J. Fisher "grieved" on sectarian grounds, warning that the measure would "give access to Romanists, Unitarians, Jews, and Scientists." It was a "disloyal" action, a rejection of the church that had inspired the movement and offered the sole gateway to God's salvation. Helen Gould Shepard—a prominent volunteer member of the National Board who had inherited the railroad fortune of her father, Jay Gould—feared that the banner of Christianity had been appropriated for unsavory ends. Invoking the authority of social science in citing a personal study, she warned that the language of Christian fellowship concealed socialist forces at play: "I have been making a special study of the great currents leading away from Christianity, and . . . the fundamental step of departure in those movements and in the political movements for subversion of our government . . . is the emphasizing of brotherhood instead of the atonement of Christ and his divinity." She pointedly resigned her voluntary committee post in the midst of the convention. She did so out of "loyalty to my Lord and Saviour," issuing a denunciation of the "wedge that is separating [the association] from the highest purposes of its constitution."[58]

Still, delegates opted to emphasize fellowship on earth rather than salvation in the hereafter. The assembly passed the new, less restrictive membership pledge with reservations, making it subject to periodic review.[59] Meanwhile, the authorization given at the 1920 convention to pursue legislative interests gave National Board activists a new tool for perfecting society according to Gospel principles. The association's political diversity ensured that collective mobilization behind legislation would happen slowly, but politicized groups, including the national staff, yearned to deploy the association as a political force. Rhetoric far outpaced action. Nevertheless, as it thrust social consciousness to the center of its spirituality, the YWCA made itself a target for reactionaries.

"SUMMON THE RESOURCES OF THE SPIRIT"

The 1920 convention is when the YWCA of the USA, as reflected through the work of the National Board, fully incorporated advocacy into its institutional identity. Previous actions, such as the 1911 living wage resolution or the qualitative studies of specialized constituencies of young women, demonstrated that even when evangelicalism set the tenor of the organization, the YWCA endorsed women's action in the public sphere. But the 1920 convention ushered in a new forthrightness in the group's political goals. This development had an uneven influence on the wider membership, as local associations had wide latitude in adopting or rejecting programming. Still, the national organization devoted considerable energy to public affairs.

The consequences of this became clear as forces of antiradicalism took notice of convention actions. The YWCA of the USA's political endorsements in 1920 were accompanied by attacks on its programming and religious ideals. Earlier that year, Attorney General A. Mitchell Palmer had rounded up immigrants affiliated with leftist causes, which resulted in the deportation of hundreds of suspected subversives, and this climate encouraged business interests to redouble their mobilization against the labor movement. In publications and whisper campaigns, manufacturers' groups targeted the YWCA for its support of the "Social Ideals of the Churches" and workers' right to organize. The criticism did not debilitate the YWCA, as it did other groups involved in liberal social movements in the period after World War I, but it marked a starting point for cycles of accusations that would be repeated over the coming decades.

Critics' rhetorical strategies established patterns that would be evident in later Red Scares, particularly the conceit of infiltration and a gendered interpretation of subversion. The idea of infiltration posited that nefarious forces could surreptitiously ensnare innocent victims. According to this reasoning, individuals established radical allegiances not out of political commitments, but instead because of ignorance and passivity. A *Manufacturers Record Daily Bulletin* article reported on a student conference at which a radical minister was "Turning the YWCA into a Scheme for Teaching Socialism." A business group distributed warnings against the "radical and bolshevik elements" seeping into the churches and the YWCA, "interjecting impractical and restrictive ideas into the practical conduct of industry."[60] Groups encouraged donors to withhold funds from the YWCA to force it to retract its endorsement of the social ideals.

Antiradical attacks also took on a gendered dimension. Critics spoke with a voice of paternalistic authority, contending that the YWCA had been victimized by radicals who "would not hesitate to try to seduce an angel itself in the interest of their propaganda" and that the association's student groups "were a fertile soil in which to sow the seeds of socialism." The reforms of the social ideals, detractors argued, were not a progressive vision of Christian society but rather "weapons with which to destroy industry." Association women were "amateurs who . . . know nothing about the subject," and manufacturers' groups demanded that the YWCA follow the lead of "its big brother organization, the YMCA" in adopting an industrial program amenable to employers' interests.[61]

Blindsided by the criticism from well-funded business groups engaged in the postwar open-shop campaign, the National Board went on the defensive.

Long viewed as a genteel women's group, the YWCA was unaccustomed to such treatment. Association leaders contacted various business organizations to explain their program, request retractions of misleading statements, and foster the cooperative spirit that they had confidently assumed would fall into place between employers and employees. Predictably, they met with little success.[62]

In the wake of its endorsement of the social ideals, the YWCA gained as much esteem among the groups that rose to its defense as it lost from antilabor forces. Speaking at a 1921 rally, Frank Morrison, secretary of the American Federation of Labor, roused sentiment against a "great conspiracy" of employers' associations attacking the YWCA's call for "social and economic justice for the workers."[63] YWCA women likely felt more comfortable with the outrage expressed in the religious press. The *Churchman* pointed out that since "leaders of the YWCA have no other purpose than the welfare of young women in America," they might have "sensible ideas of what will benefit the country." Other publications applauded the fact that the YWCA had "taken the 'Social Ideals of the Churches' seriously enough" to make business groups "realize that they meant something." Journalists mocked the paternalist tone of the attacks with indictments of "unchivalrous" behavior.[64] To the progressive press and churches, the organization's achievements as a Christian women's movement made plain that a stand for labor was a stand for righteousness.

At the level of the National Board, the attacks sparked a new resolve. The turn to advocacy did not have an adverse effect on the YWCA's membership, which reached a height of 600,000 in 1922, when it was the third largest US women's organization.[65] The association did not retract its support of the social ideals, nor did it shy away from its prolabor industrial program to curry the support of well-funded anti-union activists. In this respect, it parted company from the Young Men's Christian Association, whose steadfast support of business interests and studiously apolitical programming helped it secure better finances. The National Board intensified the call for responsible citizenship. The YWCA's "sincerity and unselfishness of purpose [was] indispensable to the welfare of the community" and needed to "be given opportunity for expression."[66] This conception of citizenship was premised on a notion that democracy rose out of mutually supportive everyday actions, which included the collective participation in civic life. A more Christian society radiated outward from the level of individual encounters to national and international governmental structures.

The National Board acted on the 1920 convention's authorization to embark on political advocacy by establishing a Public Affairs Committee. The committee consisted of a staff of National Board professionals who gathered information on political issues and represented the YWCA in forums such as the National Committee on the Cause and Cure of War and the Foreign Policy Association. Initially, the board stipulated that it would confine public affairs activity "in so far as possible to the range of subjects mentioned in the Social Ideals . . . , particularly . . . those subjects of which we have knowledge based upon the experience of young women within the membership."[67] Its political interests soon extended beyond labor concerns, however.

Most public affairs work consisted of voter education, not unlike that provided by the League of Women Voters. The Public Affairs Committee tracked state and federal legislative issues and sent local associations informational mailings. Attempting to present a balanced account of pending questions, committee members urged association women to make their own assessments and become involved in the civic process. "Because we learn by doing," one pamphlet explained, "the greatest means of education for citizenship in the YWCA is the practical work for securing legislation and helping to build the policy of the government." The vote was one of several tools that could be used to create change. With petitions and telegrams; public meetings; letters to the editor; the educational "pantomime, charade or play"; and persistent, personal contact with elected officials, YWCA women could fulfill the duties of responsible citizens.[68]

The National Board's political endorsements were used judiciously, even infrequently, as the leadership labored to identify the issues that could create a coalition across the association. Still, a cohort of YWCA women, including many of the National Board professionals who were steeped in women's reform culture, waged a vigorous effort to mobilize behind liberal policy initiatives. Although these women publicized these initiatives in YWCA publications and the inspirational atmosphere of conferences, they faced difficulties in organizing community YWCAs to support the agenda of the National Board. Voter education efforts attempted to be "consistently representative of local needs and desires and to be helpful and stimulating without causing annoyance to Associations that do not wish suggestions or service."[69] The political spectrum of the membership, which ranged from conservative matrons to communist workers, complicated this effort.

Nevertheless, the association weighed in on most of the women's issues of the 1920s. The YWCA pursued its political ambitions through the postsuffrage nonpartisan women's bloc—which, at moments, included such strange bedfellows as the Daughters of the American Revolution and the Women's International League for Peace and Freedom.[70] The YWCA gained a central place in this bloc as the National Board backed a slate of legislation that included the Sheppard-Towner maternal health care act, the establishment of the Women's Bureau in the Department of Labor, decency in films, enforcement of Prohibition, a Constitutional amendment against child labor, and the Kellogg-Briand Pact, among other causes. Other issues came out of the organizing efforts of the association's specialized constituency groups. In an age when xenophobia prevailed, the YWCA hoped to intervene on behalf of the "foreign-born" women who formed a significant contingent of its membership. The National Board appealed to members to proclaim "faithfully the attitude of a Christian organization," which meant "faithfully declaring the equal worth of all nationalities in its international family."[71] Similarly, US secretaries stationed in Japan sent a telegram to the 1924 convention to protest the Japanese exclusion clause that had prevailed in recent immigration bills. American policy, they wrote, baldly contradicted the spirit of Christianity: "Can we your representatives teach Christian brotherhood in face of blow to world fellowship which present racial discrimination inflicts we depend upon you."[72] YWCA women registered their disapproval in a collective telegram to President Calvin Coolidge urging a veto of the measure. They turned the civic act of protest into a show of international Christian fellowship, a commitment obviously not shared by the supporters of the devastating restrictions that became policy.

In addition to voter education and policy endorsements, the National Board lent its secretaries' labor to outside groups that were more dedicated to direct lobbying. In the decade following the storm and stress of the endorsement of the social ideals, the YWCA furthered its labor politics through affiliations with the Women's Bureau, National Women's Trade Union League, and National Consumers' League. The Women's Joint Congressional Committee (WJCC), an umbrella women's legislative coalition, attracted the YWCA's interests with a structure in which "no group is ever compelled to work for any measure which it does not wish to promote."[73] The YWCA became an enthusiastic member that lent resources and support to a range of WJCC ventures.

The YWCA's alignment with the women's bloc plunged it into another wave of antiradical attacks in the mid-1920s. It is widely recognized that the pacifist cause, which largely gained traction as a women's issue, was the primary lightning rod for antiradicalism in the mid-1920s.[74] However, the extent to which women's religious organizations were accused of subversion marks a departure from predominating secular narratives of the Red Scare. Certainly, secular mobilizations of the left—organized labor, socialism, and anarchism—enflamed antiradicalism. But the liberal Christianity of a mainstream membership organization also drew rebuke.

The YWCA had been able to neutralize the 1920 criticisms from manufacturers' groups. Controversy sparked by a notorious 1924 attack on the women's bloc proved more difficult to evade. Mrs. Samuel MacClintock, a low-profile National Board member whose given name remains elusive, served as the YWCA's representative on the "spider web chart," the connect-the-dots demonstration of how "socialist-pacifist" women's organizations were an "absolutely fundamental and integral part of international socialism." Created by Lucia Maxwell, a librarian in the US War Department, the chart circulated widely among right-wing patriot groups in the year before it was published in a March 1924 article in Henry

Ford's *Dearborn Independent* titled "Are Women's Clubs 'Used' by Socialists?"[75] The chart singled out members of WJCC organizations in a visual depiction of a tangled syndicate of subversion. The "spider web" identified these women's con-current membership in peace groups as proof of their disloyalty.

Once viewed as an innocuous venture of the postwar women's movement, the WJCC withered under this smear campaign. Despite a retraction from the War Department, the spider web chart lingered, and a conservative women's movement, which labored to publicize these charges, established itself as a key force in the interwar network of "patriot" activists. The Daughters of the American Revolution figured prominently in this vocal cluster of women's groups, but women mobilized in other venues. The *Woman Patriot*, originally an antisuffrage magazine that remained "dedicated to the defense of the family and the state *against* feminism and socialism," predicted that acrimonious volleys between conservative women activists and feminists spelled the end of the women's reform movement. Such hostilities "have torn to shreds the disguise of sex soli-darity upon which Feminism depends for political power!"[76] The universalizing declarations of sex solidarity of Progressive women might have been more of a misapprehension than a disguise, but the *Woman Patriot*'s editor nevertheless correctly identified that centrifugal forces were unraveling what remained of the turn-of-the-century women's movement. Conservative women rejected the maternalist claim that political activism was a blameless extension of domestic-ity, casting it instead as a subterfuge that undermined nation and family. In their pursuit of social legislation, Progressive women reformers had taken for granted their claim to represent women's values in the public sphere. Their female critics made it obvious that all women did not speak with one voice.

Unlike the WJCC, the YWCA rebounded. Though caught off guard by the resources and influence of antifeminist groups, the National Board instructed local associations to stand unapologetically behind the political program. In official communications and YWCA publications, the board's activist contin-gent addressed the criticisms as part of their battle to shape the public sphere, and they exhorted association women to rely on Christian righteousness as their weapon in this battle. As Henrietta Roelofs, head of the Public Affairs Commit-tee, warned in 1927, "the worst thing" for local associations to do in the face of scrutiny "is to ignore or hush up questioning." Rather, they should "admit with pride and courage" the YWCA's positions on international peace and social leg-islation that benefited women and children. Likewise, the National Board execu-tive Rhoda McCulloch called on association women "to summon the resources of the spirit" necessary to face controversy. She pointed to the Gospel to explain the forces at play: "criticism of our course is an inevitable experience of the Jesus way of life," a way premised on confronting injustice. "There is both comfort and challenge for us in the undebatable fact that criticism and opposition are inevitable if we are true followers of Jesus," she wrote, drawing parallels to the opposition Jesus faced when he confronted the powerful.[77] As Social Gospel theologians pointed out, those who followed the teachings of Jesus could not be complacent about the status quo.

Though the YWCA persevered through the flurry of attacks, these controversies ushered in changes. The landscape for social reform had been transformed. The women's bloc had few legislative victories, losing the child labor amendment, renewal of the Sheppard-Towner Act, and the spirit of solidarity that had given it so much political influence. However, the difficulties that confronted the YWCA did not diminish its hopes for the Christianization of society. The religious rhetoric of the YWCA of the USA in the late 1920s would have been indecipherable to many of the evangelical women who had formed the organization in 1906. Reformers who replaced evangelical philanthropists in the leadership advanced a Christianity that attended to the material conditions of the lives of a diverse membership. Progressive Social Gospel activism, distilled into a discourse of Christian citizenship, continued to offer the promise of the perfection of society through an ethics of love and mutual support.

The changes in religious and political emphasis that unfolded during the early years YWCA of the USA were nested within an important set of shifts affecting women in the United States, particularly rising levels of wage labor, educational attainment, and participation in the formal political sphere. But these shifts also transformed the work undertaken by YWCA women who traveled overseas to spread the association movement. The next chapter examines that transformation.

2 · "BY LOVE, SERVE ONE ANOTHER"

Foreign Mission and the Changing Meanings of Evangelization

When the World's YWCA was organized in 1894, it took as its motto an Old Testament verse prophesying the reign of God: "not by might, nor by power, but by my spirit, saith the Lord."[1] The verse evoked the millennial impetus driving foreign mission, the coming of the kingdom of God on earth, and the optimistic visions of the international Christian women's movement that had produced the YWCA. In this vision, moral righteousness, rather than dominance, would bring global uplift.

By the 1930s and 1940s, a number of YWCAs in nations affiliated with the World's YWCA had adopted a different biblical verse for their mottoes, a New Testament directive of the apostle Paul: "By love, serve one another."[2] The change in tenor from the triumphalism of the World's YWCA's inaugural mission statement to the cooperative and emotive ethos of the New Testament verse is telling. This chapter describes how an evolution in the practical work of the YWCA of the USA's Foreign Division, the administrative department that oversaw overseas efforts, shadowed these shifting sentiments. It highlights resistance to the presumptions of "woman's work for woman," the European and US Protestant theory of mission driven, in the words of historian Dana Robert, by a "maternalistic, albeit idealistic, belief that non-Christian religions trapped and degraded women, yet all women in the world were sisters and should support each other."[3]

The extension of the YWCA movement beyond Protestant Western Europe and North America came out of a process of realizing more fully a founding vision of global Christianity. It resulted from interactions—sometimes collaborative, sometimes contentious—between YWCA participants in missionary-receiving lands and the architects of international association work, a group in which US staff members figured centrally. And as much as mission was a vector of domination, the case studies examined in this chapter show how such institutions came to be vehicles for the formation of coalitions and the exchange of ideas. Mission was a means by which women negotiated the power imbalances between races, religious creeds, and nations to forge cross-cultural connections.[4] Successful YWCA expansion proceeded from the imperial foundations of the foreign mission movement, but it did not reflect the exultant "evangelization of the world in this generation"—the goal proclaimed by turn-of-the-century student missionaries.[5] Rather, the disjuncture between democratic visions of Christian fellowship and unacknowledged orientalist inequalities of mission practice came to the surface quickly.

The European and US leaders who directed overseas institutions were compelled to contend with associations that were not the blank slates on which the dream of Western Christian stewardship could be written. By the 1920s, challenges to ethnocentric models of mission had produced new interpretations of the meaning of evangelization and international outreach, supporting Jane Hunter's contention that the YWCA was "at the forefront of efforts to reconceptualize and internationalize" Protestant mission work.[6] These changes came out of negotiations of power that were staged in interpersonal interactions as well as in larger political struggles. When confronted with the realities of sustaining transnational institutions, Europeans and Americans could not implement their domineering designs. In the end, the utility of the association in a variety of contexts, rather than the triumphal progress of Western Christianity, spurred growth.

After a flush of success of expansion into mission lands, three overlapping developments elicited eruptions that reoriented the international work of the YWCA of the USA between the 1910s and 1930s. First, the approach to the Christianization of the world shifted from the cultivation of souls to the transformation of social conditions. Second, as YWCAs in mission territories became self-sustaining, women from outside of Europe and the United States held the movement to its claims of world fellowship. They labored, often successfully, to exert influence on policy and to assume leadership posts in institutions founded in their countries. Finally, to maintain transnational relationships, the US YWCA adapted its institutional identity to meet local needs. These developments provide an instructive lesson in how women's institutions rooted in the foreign mission movement survived after orientalist fantasies of the conversion of the East had faded.

"IT IS AGAINST ALL OUR PRINCIPLES TO PROSELYTIZE": EARLY YEARS OF EXPANSION

The YWCA movement had been growing in scope and geography for forty years before the establishment of the World's YWCA in the 1890s. Economic shifts and evangelical ferment that had inspired the original London efforts affected Protestant Europe, North America, and Australia alike. British women initiated associations in the colonies, creating Christian outposts that subsumed denominational allegiances to forge connections among settlers as Protestants and Europeans. By the end of the nineteenth century, these scattered associations had been established on every continent.[7]

International expansion was launched under the same two sets of premises that shaped the creation of the YWCA of the USA. One was an evangelical drive to bring disadvantaged women—working-class and non-Protestant—under the sway of middle-class uplift, Christianity, and the process of civilization. The other emphasized the equalizing principles of Christian fellowship. The association advocated an international women's movement that, in the words of a late-nineteenth-century publication, "links us together, not in any great and showy enterprise, but in loving sympathy and service all the world over, uniting every class and well-nigh every race."[8]

The World's YWCA, administered primarily by women from the United States, Great Britain, and Northern Europe, established a distinct place for itself in the foreign mission movement that bloomed at the turn of the century. The world group was charged both with asserting a collective identity for the dozens of YWCAs that had been organized at the national level and with carrying out the practical work of extending its own geographic reach. To the latter end, national YWCAs designated funds from their operating budgets to support work in countries where associations were not financially self-sustaining. The single-sex structure imparted freedoms that women engaged in denominational mission activities, which were subject to the oversight of male religious leaders, usually did not find. Energized by a transatlantic swell of ambitions and material resources, the YWCA consortium was able to create an institutional infrastructure that made it a peer of the major denominational mission boards and an outlet for single women hoping to embark on an exotic professional career.[9]

YWCAs were designed to be distinct from, but complementary to, denominational mission groups. Insisting that "as YWCA workers it is against all our principles to proselytize," association leaders aimed to supplement religious evangelization, providing wholesome social services, recreation, and socialization to women of a variety of backgrounds.[10] YWCAs might serve as the setting for revival-style conversions, but they targeted other domains such as health and entertainment for Christianization and personal development. Impressed by the "truly trained and professional officers" who pioneered the multifunctional community centers of urban YWCAs, leaders of the World's YWCA encouraged US associations to export their workforce and institutional infrastructure. The YWCA of Toledo, Ohio, was the first to respond to such a call and sent Agnes Hill to Madras (Chennai), India, in 1895.[11]

The World's YWCA self-consciously modeled its expansion strategy on imperial spheres of power: representatives from European associations supervised development in territories they colonized while US women claimed a broad terrain for an informal empire, bolstered by the rise of their homeland as a global power. A representative to the World's YWCA asserted in 1906 that the US association "should control as fully . . . the work in those countries which [it] ought to claim," referring to the hemisphere that US politicians and business leaders labored to bring under their sway, as well as new territories they pursued in the Pacific: "China, Japan, the Philippines, the West Indies, and North and South America."[12] Because of this broad geographical purview and its resources, the YWCA of the USA had considerable responsibility for staffing, funding, and administering associations in missionary-receiving countries.

Plans for expansion were built on a Janus-faced perspective on global relationships among women. On the one hand, despite overt references to the designs of empire, European and American leaders conceived of their organization as part of a cooperative international women's movement, a Christian arm of the "worlds of women" who came together in a turn-of-the-century coalition to raise women's collective status.[13] As staff members fanned out to create new associations in the Balkans, Middle East, and East and Southeast Asia, they hoped to inspire a sense of connection among women that superseded national borders. They expected that associations would not be foreign outposts, set apart from their indigenous context. Supporters believed that under the tutelage of Western professionals, women in mission territories, whom they called their sisters, would embrace the association movement and make it their own. A World's YWCA president explained that the goal was "to develop leaders in each nation," not to install colonies of Western women.[14]

As was the case in most women's movements of that period, efforts of the YWCA were premised on universalizing declarations of women's concerns and capacities. The YWCA's view of the shared strengths and needs of the world's women contrasted with ethnological models of racial difference, which placed women on an evolutionary scale that reinforced biological and sociological hierarchies.[15] European and US YWCA leaders instead emphasized connections among women as children of God and global citizens. They made liberal reference to the apostle Paul's declaration of the radical equality of Christianity—"for in him, there is neither Jew nor Greek, bond nor free, but all are one in Christ Jesus"—as the source of their responsibility not only to make

Christianity global but also to seek emotional connections to women in distant lands. In such fashion, US secretary Mary Hill identified Christianity, rather than the sexed body or common conditions of oppression, as the root of the feminist trope of sisterhood when she told the 1911 US YWCA convention that "we, of America, think of the women in India as being our sisters because we are all one in Christ Jesus." Women were also connected, the association proposed, by social, political, and economic changes occurring around the globe: "the same dangers, the same sins, the same temptations, the same aspirations, the same human nature, with increased freedom from restraints."[16]

There was no shortage of negative changes in women's lives for which the YWCA could be put to use as a preventative agency. Young women faced the temptations of new liberties, the dislocations engendered by migration, and the intemperances of the political sphere, where they might be "in danger of turning to . . . Revolutionary Committees [because of the] need of an opportunity for expression" in nationalist struggles. Still, positive changes had come in the lives of women throughout the world, and the association could help them seize new opportunities. In 1913, Clarissa Spencer, a US woman then serving as general secretary of the world organization, encouraged the association to address the "widespread restlessness among women and the desire for the larger and the larger life" as a global matter: "it is not confined to Europe or America, but is world-wide."[17] Grace Hoadley Dodge encouraged Euro-American women to recognize their own yearnings for progress in the context of a world movement: "women in all parts of the Orient are rising and claiming a place in their country's development." Agnes Hill was stirred by the civic impulses animating anticolonial struggles, and she "praised God" that she could witness "the rise of the patriotic and national spirit tending to liberty such as seen in young Egypt, young Turkey, young India."[18]

On the other hand, even if—unlike some of their contemporaries—Europeans and Americans in the YWCA leadership yearned to transcend national and racial divisions in the creation of a global movement, they unsurprisingly crafted hierarchies that naturalized their control of association development and underwrote their sense of a global sisterhood. They justified this through imagined cultural differences between West and East, a construct that encompassed creed, racial character, temperament, and social structures but defied geography—Argentina was occasionally listed among the "oriental" associations.[19] European and American women reasoned that despite the inimical effects of so-called heathen culture, women in mission lands would join the movement as equals as they experienced the salubrious effects of Christianity and civilization.

Given their belief that the "foundations for the larger civilization of the West are founded deep-down on the bedrock of Christianity," YWCA leaders imagined that their call to evangelize would catalyze the uplift of the world's women.

This stewardship model of internationalism proceeded from the feminist missionary conviction that Christian civilization uniquely held the key to women's advancement. As one contributor to a World's YWCA magazine noted in 1914, it was axiomatic: "the spread of Western civilisation to mission lands undoubtedly raises the status of women, and our sympathy must go out to all those who are seeking to take advantage of the new possibilities."[20]

Discerning God's guiding hand in the social and intellectual progress of his followers, the leadership proclaimed a divine endorsement of the unique capacities of Europeans and white Americans. Effie Price Gladding, a member of the National Board of the YWCA of the USA, attributed Americans' "unique responsibility . . . to the world's work [to] God's providence." Lucy Tritton, an Englishwoman who served as president of the World's YWCA, vaunted the cultural inheritance of the "Anglo Saxon races," who "have had great privileges, an open Bible, with God-fearing teaching for generations." She underscored the duties this engendered: "*therefore* our responsibilities are great toward those who have surroundings of darkness, of atheism . . . , superstition, and . . . ignorance."[21]

This orientalism can be characterized by its wide scope. Although YWCA women employed generalizations about the "different countries of the Orient" that might sweep "Japan, China, India, Norway, Russia, Italy" into the same category, they also enumerated particular national and racial conditions crying out for feminist Christian solutions.[22] In India, with "that awful caste system" and "religions so vile [that] they believe in the sanctity of the cow and the depravity of women . . . , all of the western, civilizing influences . . . are going to have an effect in molding the lives of young women." In Japan, it was "the relationships and principles governing . . . homelife [that] doubtless hold the secret of the lack of initiative and of the sweet docile spirit and submissiveness of Japanese women," and the YWCA set out to bring them into their "rightful place in the work and service and life of the world." Convinced that "the needs of women are always pathetic in countries of Mohammedan prejudice," the association celebrated that "new liberty has come to the women of the Near East" in the wake of World War I.[23] Contrasting themselves with their countrymen who sought to gain influence through gunboats and treaties, YWCA internationalists viewed an "evangelism of intimacy" as the source of their influence, hoping to effect individual transformations through emotional connections and sentimental attachment.[24]

While the world leadership pursued the empowerment of women under fantasies that Western, middle-class Protestantism held the key to liberation, the growing influence of the Social Gospel laid the groundwork for conceptions of transnational linkages among women that went beyond the orientalist uplift mentality rife in foreign mission work. The process by which foreign YWCAs (the National Board's designation for overseas associations administered by the YWCA of the USA) came under local control paralleled the development of autonomous membership units for workers, immigrants, and students in the United States. Though domestic and foreign work logistically proceeded on separate tracks in the YWCA of the USA, the shift to a socially conscious Christian ethics occurred simultaneously in both divisions.

The evolution in doctrinal emphasis could be detected in the gatherings of World's YWCA delegates, which, as with conferences convened in the United States, became occasions for the dissemination of Social Gospel principles. The 1910 World's YWCA convention in Berlin explored the "social awakening" and turned its attention to the "social teaching of Jesus." In directing national associations to study the "industrial conditions of the day" and to investigate the "means of amelioration which legislation and private endeavor offer for conditions under which women live and work," the convention gave reform a place in an agenda otherwise centered on proselytization.[25] Florence Simms, the National Board secretary who nurtured the politicized industrial program of the US YWCA, urged the international assembly to pursue a more audacious agenda to meet the needs of wage earners. Simms's interpretation of social awakening put a premium on self-leadership and self-expression among workers, who were calling on US and overseas associations to intercede in the material conditions of their labor rather than in their spirituality. She encouraged YWCAs to become involved with labor advocacy and to "identify [themselves] more and more with organisations having an industrial and economic interest in women." "Industrial and social work," she argued, "could help to give a new interpretation of Christianity to a world which often seems not to understand much of the Christian message." Her theory of mission placed labor at the forefront of the Christian struggle: the association "must seek to unify society by applying the spirit and teaching of Jesus Christ, the only hope of the world . . . , where class divisions and hatreds are at their bitterest."[26]

The social awakening discussed at the Berlin convention encompassed citizenship claims increasingly made by women, an interest that worked in tandem with new perspectives on labor. Ferment over women's access to the political sphere affected many within the YWCA's orbit, though suffrage had by no means a preeminent place. Matters of citizenship arose in diverse contexts: the Chinese revolution, nationalism in the Ottoman Empire, and home-rule agitation in India. Even before World War I put women's rights into relief, many leaders of the YWCA expressed confidence in citizenship as a tool in the arsenal of evangelical reform. The World's YWCA convention held in 1914 further emphasized women's increasing influence on nation building. Noting the "great need of a Christian standard of National Righteousness in all parts of the world," convention materials encouraged associations "to place before their members the duty of good citizenship, to endeavor to fit them more adequately for loyal and efficient service to the State, and to urge . . . members, as a matter of Christian conviction, to avail themselves of opportunities of civic and national service."[27] Such rhetoric designated the state as a domain of religious practice. Though it highlighted civic involvement as a path to moral and religious growth, it opened the way for secular policy goals to take on an importance once reserved for piety.

Building on the foundations established by the social awakening, YWCAs at the national level forged alliances with other organizations and used these blocs to influence political processes otherwise inaccessible to women. While Esther Fahmi Wisa agitated for Egyptian independence through the Sa'dist Ladies' Committee, an auxiliary to the nationalist Wafd Party, she advanced women's social welfare interests through fifty years of service to the Alexandria YWCA. Likewise, women's social services and political activities came together in the career of Kim Hwallan (Helen Kim), who in the 1920s was a founding member of both the Korean YWCA and Kunwuhoe, a feminist, anti-imperialist consortium of women's organizations. Through her work in the YWCA, her long tenure in the administration of Ewha College, and her employment in the regime of the South Korean president, Rhee Syngman, Kim promoted women's education and civic service in overlapping forums.[28]

World War I hastened the developments identified as the social awakening and interrupted the plans of the association movement with emergency demands. It also challenged the conflation of Christianity and Western civilization that underwrote international association work. As the YWCA of the USA conceded in 1915, with the present "conflict of many Christian nations, questions have arisen in the minds of many as to the true value of Christianity." The chastening effect on evangelical millennialism prompted the World's YWCA to acknowledge that even Western nations required profound transformation to meet Gospel standards. It fastened its "great hope for the civilization of the future [on] the permeation of the democratic movements and political bodies in every country with Christian ideals," and it encouraged Christian women to dedicate themselves to promoting cooperative political and economic goodwill. Over time, the Foreign Division of the YWCA of the USA replaced millennial conceptions of the kingdom of God with ideals of world governance. A 1929 report encouraged the adoption of a pragmatic sense of the Social Gospel: "While heretofore we have had an ideal world concept in 'The Kingdom of God,' we now begin to have the more concrete possibility of political world organization . . ., and see accordingly that 'our task is to build a world order in our heads.'"[29]

The rhetorical gestures of conference reports and religious declarations were less of a test of the avowed Christian social commitments of the YWCA of the USA than were the day-to-day operations of overseas associations administered by its secretaries. While the organization identified itself with goals of fellowship and active citizenship nested within an international women's movement, its leadership faced tacit and explicit rejection of the imperialist thrust of foreign mission. US secretaries had financial power and set policy, but local women involved in association life had their own leverage.[30] Their participation was integral to realizing the ideals of a world movement and necessary for the survival of YWCAs in mission lands. They compelled the organization to advance world fellowship not only in its advocacy work but also in its own operating structures.

Michi Kawai's path to local control of the Japanese YWCA in the 1910s indicates how the emotionally charged interactions staged in missionary settings could be used to militate against Western women's assumption of authority. Kawai's response to the demands of her YWCA of the USA supervisors reveals pragmatic strategies that women in missionary-receiving countries used to resist the domineering practices of overseas administrators. Under her influence, the volunteer and professional leadership of the YWCA of Japan, founded in 1901, was quickly turned over to Japanese women.

A "FOREIGN EXECUTIVE IS ABSOLUTELY NECESSARY": NEGOTIATING ADMINISTRATIVE AUTHORITY

This transfer of control was set into motion when Caroline Macdonald, a Canadian assigned by the World's YWCA to oversee the emerging Japanese association, recruited Michi Kawai in 1905. Early YWCA histories described Kawai as literally the answer to their prayers. The story went this way: Macdonald wheedled Kawai, a recent college graduate employed as a teacher, to join the association as a full-time secretary. Initially, Kawai "stubbornly refused to give up her teaching in the college." Macdonald told her: "'Well, I shall pray you into the work.' And before Miss Kawai knew how it came to pass, the prayer was answered."[31] In 1916, Kawai became the first Japanese woman to serve as the general secretary—akin to executive director—of the YWCA of Japan.

Kawai answered YWCA prayers in a broader sense. A devout Protestant and a proponent of the Christianization and Westernization of Japan, she had extensive experience as both an educator of Japanese women and an informal cultural ambassador who embodied the promising future of Japan to mission supporters. Her leadership portended the indigenization of the association and the evangelization of the East—and, accordingly, the coming of the kingdom of God. She demonstrated, though perhaps only as a token, that the association was truly a world women's movement.

Kawai had found her life path through Christianity and the support of missionary enthusiasts around the globe. Born in 1877, she was the daughter of a Shinto priest who had been displaced from his post at the imperial shrine in Ise under Meiji-era reforms. Starting a new life in Hokkaido, the family weathered their profound social dislocation through their immersion in Christian faith and community. Kawai distinguished herself among the pupils of the North Star Girls' School, which was operated by the American Woman's Board for Foreign Mission of the Presbyterian Church. Nitobe Inazō, a renowned intellectual and educator, served as her mentor. Nitobe and his American wife, Mary (née Elkington), put Kawai in contact with not only a network of Quaker mission sponsors but also Tsuda Umeko, a women's education activist. Kawai, whose missionary education had made her fluent in English, was a natural candidate to participate in Tsuda's campaign to give more Japanese women the opportunity to study overseas. With the personal and financial assistance of the Quakers, Kawai graduated in 1904 from Tsuda's alma mater, Bryn Mawr College. Kawai received informal training in transnational projects in these years as she earned her education by giving speeches at Christian student conferences, visiting the homes and churches of mission supporters, and allowing herself to be regarded as an exotic symbol of the successes of an international Christian movement. She then settled in Tokyo and took a teaching post at the Joshi Eigaku Juku (Women's English School), the pioneering postsecondary institution for women founded by Tsuda.[32] Kawai divided her time between teaching and volunteering for the YWCA until she accepted the position of general secretary.

Kawai was able to give expression to her interests in education and evangelicalism in the YWCA. Japanese associations—which by the 1910s included groups in Tokyo, Kobe, Osaka, and Yokohama—focused their programming on support services for students, religious activities, and outreach among factory workers. One prominent area of programming had ties to the evangelical Protestant tradition of social morality but also was relevant to transformations in Japanese family life tied to the "good wife, wise mother" (ryōsai kembo) domestic ideal promoted under Meiji modernization. As part of a purity campaign that called for temperance and attacked prostitution, concubinage, and the profession of geisha, the discourse of "good wife, wise mother" assigned mothers critical responsibilities in imparting civic virtue. Conferring on women a crucial role in building the Japanese state without politically enfranchising them, it asserted the value of women's "hard work, their frugality, . . . and their responsible upbringing of children," and it inspired an outpouring of reform efforts.[33] To further such goals, the YWCA lent support to groups such as the Japan Woman's Christian Temperance Union, which led efforts to criminalize prostitution, and offered courses in health and housekeeping that emphasized piety, hygiene, and companionate marriage as foundational to good families and a strong nation.

Although the recruitment of Kawai was seen as a major coup, the administrators of the YWCA of the USA, which oversaw association work in Japan, fretted about her ascension to the executive post. She did not fit the fantasy of a docile student who eagerly deferred to her elder sisters in the movement. At times, US secretaries used the term "imitators" to describe Japanese people, projecting expectations of deference and dependency.[34] Coming into the position with considerable experience traversing missionary networks and Japanese Christian communities, Kawai defied these preconceptions. Friction between her and her supervisors in the US association never turned into open conflict, but American women struggled to impose their plans on this woman who had well-developed ideas about the direction of the work.

The installation of a Japanese board and staff was foremost among Kawai's priorities. As she explained to executives of the World's YWCA, "we Japanese members have come to see that our Association work should be represented by a Japanese, otherwise it will be understood as a foreign work." Accordingly, it would not be an effective force for evangelization for those who saw Christianity as a means of foreign domination. Obliquely criticizing the imperial thrust of Western interventions, Kawai noted that missionary efforts "were sincere and good [but] their means were criticized as unwise and . . . some of them cannot have the sympathy of the natives."[35]

While Kawai's receptiveness to the Western reform spirit appealed greatly to the international leadership, her management of the association often did not. The divergent expectations of Kawai and the US YWCA could be seen most plainly in conflicts over staff and money. Americans held the purse strings in Japan. To turn an overseas YWCA over to local control, the US group stipulated that the association needed to be professionally and financially self-supporting, compelling the Japanese staff to secure funding for their own salaries as part of training for financial independence. The US association provided programming and building funds, and it paid the salaries of its own secretaries working in Japan. Kawai pointed out to the US administrators the bind this created for Japanese leadership: it was the indirect means by which American women reserved power to themselves. She wrote: "Our difficulty is that while you furnish us with splendid workers from America we cannot keep pace with our Japanese workers. Neither workers or money can be had." When the US association proposed sending more American staff members in the late 1910s, Kawai rejected this strategy for growth, one that depended on giving nonnative secretaries new responsibilities. Prioritizing indigenization, she wrote that "unless we can secure more native workers I do not wish to ask for a great many foreign workers to Japan."[36] On a personal level, Kawai was a profound believer in the power of cross-cultural exchange to undo the prejudices that divided nations and races, and her appraisal of women involved in foreign mission and international YWCA endeavors was consistently effusive. But it seems likely that she was sensitive to the growing Japanese resentment of US threats to Japan's sovereignty and of the racism experienced by Japanese immigrants in the United States. Still, she couched her plan to indigenize in pragmatic rather than political terms. Like other Japanese Christian activists, she labored to evangelize by actively transforming Christianity "from a foreign religion into a Japanese creed."[37]

In private, American administrators revealed their difficulty in treating Kawai as a peer in building a world movement. They described her as "unquestionably one of the most superb and outstanding women of Japan today, the greatest asset that the association has" and judged that "the future of our work in Japan depends upon our being able to hold her in our organization."[38] But they were not as enthusiastic about Kawai's assertions of executive power. When personnel trouble in the Japanese association (triggered by a US secretary of "questionable mental balance") prompted Charlotte Adams, a high-ranking secretary in the US association, to travel to Tokyo to evaluate the situation in person, she concluded that a "foreign executive is absolutely necessary in Japan." Like others working in the liberal missionary tradition who, in the words of the historian William Hutchison "championed autonomy in principle [but] found it inapt in particular situations," she sought to remedy problems by taking charge herself.[39]

Adams came to this conclusion by identifying a host of personal shortcomings rooted in Kawai's racial and national background. A nonnative executive was necessary to supplement what Adams interpreted as the insufficient leadership capabilities of Asian women. Adams explained to the World's YWCA executive committee that over time, Kawai had become "constrained, aloof, and, worst of all . . . anti-foreign," a mind-set that Adams believed was the root of the Japanese YWCA's troubles. "To keep the [association] Japanese is a master passion" of Kawai's, she wrote. Adams charged that Kawai was highly suspicious of "anything which might bring a preponderance of foreign influence." Adams did not see any pragmatic grounds for Kawai's perspective but instead read these priorities as inimical prejudices tied to broader racial characteristics. She thought that Kawai had inherited from her father's "aristocratic bloodline . . . the pride and sensitiveness and the autocratic qualities of the high class Japanese." Kawai "did not love foreigners" and was "jealous of any assumption by them of leadership which is either aggressive or superimposed. She does not enjoy the feeling that the Japanese need foreign help."[40] In effect, Adams faulted Kawai because Kawai rejected the premises of Western women's Christian internationalism. Her attention to institutional power imbalances and her confidence in the capacities of indigenous leadership signaled an unwillingness to view national borders as inconsequential and Western stewardship as beneficial.

In fact, Kawai was quite willing to ask for foreign help, and in the speeches, writings, and private communications in which she made these requests, she used the missionary's rhetoric of sentimental attachment and emotional reciprocity to militate against institutional inequities. While Adams was assisting the Japanese association, Kawai attended the 1920 convention of the US YWCA. There, she asked for international friendship and intercessory prayers—and funds. She gave many such talks, and her convention speech can be interpreted as a strategic appeal to orientalist sensibilities of the audience that pushed against the power dynamics of mission relationships. In previous speeches, she had drawn on themes of infantilization. Kawai described Japan as an "unlovely" adolescent, "not old enough . . . to lead others" but "full of curiosity," to explain Japan's need for Western influence, an assertion that American association women were fond of citing.[41] At the 1920 convention, Kawai subtly veered away from this narrative while still playing to paternalist longings. She asked US women to help Japanese build up their own work by giving material and spiritual support rather than directives. Japanese association work was not an adolescent endeavor, she explained, but one now fully realized and in need of reinforcement.

Kawai opened by expressing "humble penitence" for the national weaknesses of Japan: "our militarism, our commercialism, our immorality." She urged a similar spirit of renunciation on the part of American women. Citing critiques of Japanese industrial life, which caused workers to live "in ignorance, disease, sin, superstition," Kawai pointed out the transnational economic relationships underlying such labor conditions. She instructed her audience to "turn back your hat, the lining of your hat. Our women are making that silk . . . , working thirteen hours a day." Instead of giving the West the responsibility for the uplift of the East, her speech called for Westerners to take responsibility for problems to which they contributed. To address such circumstances, she asked the YWCA to demonstrate "true Americanism, which is not self-aggrandizement or materialism," suggesting that audience members might scrutinize their own national weaknesses. Americanism at its best, she encouraged them, was a disinterested sentiment marked by "the spirit of Jesus, who said, 'I came to this world not to be ministered unto, but to minister and give life to many.'"[42] This Christ-like spirit was not messianic but self-sacrificing. Such reminders of the cooperative thrust of Christian principles posed a rhetorical challenge to the presumptuousness of the US partners in Japanese work at the same time as they reinforced a sense of bonds connecting women of the West and East.

Ultimately, Kawai's practical success as an administrator was most critical in thwarting the US leadership's inclination to make heavy-handed interventions. Adams's recommendation that a US executive assume leadership in Japan went unheeded. During her tenure, Kawai achieved many of her goals: she secured a staff of Japanese women and made the YWCA of Japan a lively center of evangelical Protestant religious life. Her departure from the YWCA of Japan was also an assertion of autonomy. The US YWCA had pinned its hopes on Kawai leading the association for the rest of her career, but she did not. When she resigned in 1926, an American hinted that this act endangered the future of the association, which otherwise would "have seemed full of promise." While citing her twenty-year tenure as evidence of ample service to the movement, Kawai maintained that her resignation came at a time when competent Japanese leadership assured the future of the association. She trusted that her successors "might dream greater dreams and aspire to still greater heights in the service . . . for the girlhood of Japan."[43] The YWCA of Japan's growth over the coming decades substantiated her prophecy. Another Japanese woman, Yamamoto Koto, succeeded her as general secretary. Because Kawai rebuffed American secretaries' attempts to reserve positions of the authority for themselves, she ensured that the YWCA was well-rooted in Japanese soil. She had a post-YWCA career of distinction. Following the examples of Tsuda and the Hokkaido missionaries who had provided her education, Kawai opened a women's institute of higher education in 1929 now known as Keisen University, whose curriculum emphasized Christianity, international understanding, and horticulture while matching the educational standards of men's schools.

The US staff's muted petulance at Kawai's departure indicates that although they increasingly affirmed "respect for the rights of others" as crucial to international relations, they were unable to recognize paternalism in their own practices. Still, in the 1920s, the US and world organizations phased out affirmations of Western civilization in recognition "that in the bringing in of the Kingdom of God each nation and race has its unique contribution to make."[44] "World friendship" came to replace "woman's work for woman" as the watchword of international outreach, signaling recognition that the era of stewardship had come to a close and that its inequalities were un-Christian. As documented by the historian Karen Seat, such changes reverberated more widely in women's mission circles. Rejecting a mission movement in which Westerners positioned themselves as the saviors to benighted people, the younger generation of Protestant women internationalists prodded "Americans themselves to reexamine their ideological assumptions about gender, race, Christianity, and civilization."[45] YWCA leaders had celebrated the heritage of the "Anglo Saxon races" as the root of association success, but in 1924, they acknowledged that associations were "too few and too Anglo-Saxon." A more pluralistic movement was integral for discerning "God's will in the complexity of modern life."[46]

"I AM PRO-GIRLS, ALL RELIGIONS": FROM MISSION TO SERVICE IN TURKEY

While Kawai's story fleshes out the types of interpersonal encounters that could check the colonialist designs of overseas mission organizations, the evolution of the YWCA in Turkey provides a look at the ways in which nationalist and anti-Western movements provoked American women to make dramatic transformations in their work. In laboring to build associations appropriate for local contexts, US secretaries adjusted their organizational practices and spiritual commitments alike. As Turks secularized their civic life while waging anticolonial cultural battles directed at Christian missionaries, the YWCA in Istanbul evolved into a markedly interfaith and interethnic community center.

This evolution might seem unlikely given the origins of this association. Kawai had assured the 1910 World's YWCA convention that Asian countries were extending "open doors and earnest invitations" to missionaries, and, presuming this to be true, the organization initiated expansion work in the "Near East" following a 1911 student missionary conference in what was then Constantinople. There, in the words of the organization's magazine, delegates witnessed "glittering mosques and minarets, proclaiming here that Mohamed, and not Christ, was the ruling Spirit." The World's YWCA planned for a "more glorious future, when, in spite of every opposing enemy, every knee shall bow, and every tongue confess the Crucified to be the Lord of all."[47] It strengthened association presence in the contested terrain in and around the former Ottoman Empire: in Greece, the Anatolian peninsula, Syria (which included what would come to be Lebanon and Palestine), and Egypt. While British women oversaw work in Syria and Egypt, US women had charge of Turkey. There, they established associations called "service centers" in three cities, Izmir (Smyrna), Adana, and Istanbul. Unlike some associations, these operated more as community centers than as boarding facilities. Clubs, vocational and physical education, and a particularly popular summer camp—"the Garden of Happiness" on the Marmara Sea—attracted an active, religiously and ethnically heterogeneous membership. Religious programming had a special importance because Eastern Rite Christians sought out the YWCA for worship activities. Young Greek and Armenian women, communicants of the Orthodox and Gregorian churches, represented the largest contingent of the membership, but the associations drew a cosmopolitan mix. Istanbul secretaries recorded twenty-six nationalities and eight religious creeds among program participants in 1925.[48]

Amid the crises of war and revolution that erupted after World War I, YWCA women were unclear about the role Islam would play in the lives of Turkish women and association programming. But they had already realized that the religious life of the territory was not theirs for the taking. While making an initial survey of the field in 1911, an American secretary noted that "the question of race and religion is so hopelessly mixed in people's minds that for a Turk to give up Mohammedanism, or an Armenian to leave the Gregorian Church . . . would seem to many equivalent to shameful desertion of his race and its traditions." She doubted the prospects for evangelization: "I did not see one baptised convert from Islam, though the Christian Church has been in Turkey for centuries."[49]

When the Turkish republic was established in the early 1920s, US secretaries endeavored to adapt the service centers to the needs of the new nation. The

FIGURE 2.1. "Now I vant explanations from bot' sides." Dramatics at the Istanbul YWCA's Garden of Happiness camp, 1921. Credit: Sophia Smith Collection, Smith College

association voiced approval of the democratic ideals under which the revolution had been carried out. After all, effused US YWCA publicity, "wherever the watchword of a country becomes 'Liberty, Equality, Justice,' the emancipation of women is inevitable." Turkey, it seemed, was on the path toward Western civilization, and the US group confidently predicted that political revolution had created a favorable climate for a religious revolution: "the Moslem faith, although the religion of the rulers, has been superimposed upon the people and not assimilated." Accordingly, "many Moslems are turning to Christianity [in recognition that it] has a higher type of civilization to offer than that which they have known." The association, "the handmaid of the church in every place where women are coming to a new life," was ready to show the way to evangelization and emancipation.[50]

Perhaps the glory of such a crusade lost its luster as YWCA women witnessed the toll of religious animosity on the front lines of the Greco-Turkish War (1919–22). Secretary Margaret Stewart did not know what to make of the somber mood of service center members in 1921 until a young woman pointed out the disjuncture between the YWCA's sunny ideals and her difficult circumstances. The woman told Stewart that "it is easy for Americans to talk of cooperation, the common good, economic progress and forgiveness for [they] have no deportations to remember." Stewart reported the pall cast over recreational activities. In arts and crafts, "pictures of storm and stress at sea or lonely coasts were first place, [and one young woman] expressed 'muses' that make me shiver with sadness." She concluded, "the girls here are old in sadness."[51]

Turkey YWCAs were conduits for war relief. They sheltered refugees and carried on programming in the service centers as Mustafa Kemal's army drove out the Greek military occupation, bringing devastation to Greek and Armenian communities. Protected by a guard of US soldiers ordered to protect American property, the Izmir Service Center took in hundreds of refugees as the Greek army abandoned the city as the Turks advanced on it in 1922. When the city began to burn, association staff members helped lead more than a thousand refugees to safety on a US freighter, which transported them to Greece.[52]

The YWCA attempted both to conduct its usual programming and to demonstrate that it was not an institution for Christians alone. The Kemalist regime ordered Christians to evacuate Adana in late 1921, but even though only ten of the YWCA's five hundred members remained in the city, secretaries decided it "unwise to discontinue the center." They attempted to refute Turkish accusations that YWCAs were "interested primarily in serving the Armenians and Greeks."[53] After the great fire in Izmir, accusations flew as to whether the retreating Greek army set the fires to ruin the city for the Turks or the advancing Turks burned the city to drive out Christians. Service center secretary Jean Christie stated her allegiances: "I do not know who set the fires. When people ask me if I am pro-Turk, or pro-Armenian, or pro-Greek, I answer that I am pro-all-of-them. I am pro-girls, all religions."[54] The association had once hopefully envisioned a martial-like subjugation of Islam in Istanbul where, "in spite of every opposing enemy, every knee shall bow" before Jesus. After the revolution, it sought peace.

Closing all but the Istanbul service center, US administrators attempted to adjust to the new republic. They did not predict that these new conditions would require them to choose between the YWCA's religious identity and its commitment to a global women's movement; before, the two had gone hand in hand. As a foreign, religiously affiliated educational institution, the YWCA was caught in the crosshairs of national secularization and modernization. While in Japan, the association could draw on the state's tolerance of the Christian minority, in Turkey, because of state pressure, the organization had to revise the ideological foundations of its work and rehabilitate its image as a missionary interloper.

Although secular republican ideals guided the founding of the state, Islam had central importance as a constitutive element of national identity, and Turkish press and officials took the occasion of the revolution to vent their hostility toward the predatory designs of missionary organizations. One official accurately pointed out to the YWCA that "Young Christians' Organizations were opened for the purpose of making Christians of our Moslem young people, and that having spent thousands of liras they have not been able to do this."[55] By the mid-1920s, the republic's policies toward religious education forced the YWCA to decide whether it was a religious organization for Christians, offering Bible study and worship alongside secular activities, or a service organization for all, in which case religious instruction could not be provided. In weighing the future of the work under these circumstances, the US executive in Turkey, Ruth Woodsmall, asserted that the intrinsic religious mission of the YWCA depended on the participation of Muslim women, and the participation of Muslim women in turn depended on the YWCA's relinquishing its ambitions for their conversion. She recommended: "If it is really desired that the YWCA should be broadly effective, a true force for the interpenetration of Christian ideals, the YWCA must avoid the danger of being too distinctly identified with the Christian races. Otherwise the Moslems will be alienated from its influence."[56] The YWCA would not be able to bring a Christian message to Muslim women if Muslim women stayed away from the association altogether.

Woodsmall—who would later receive support from the Rockefeller Foundation to produce a scholarly interpretation of the Middle East, titled *Moslem Women Enter a New World* (1936)—was not intent on overt proselytizing. She put to rest fantasies of the Christianization of this strategic gateway to the East and made clear to the administrators of the World's YWCA what many missionaries had refused to understand: Istanbul was a Muslim city, and "the Christian races . . . will continue to be a minority with no hope of having the controlling power or influence." Association activities instead needed to be "practical demonstrations of the value to Turkey of life and institutions dominated by the spirit of Jesus." She wanted to assure Turks that "we are not interested in criticizing Islam," yet she hoped to call attention to "the creative values . . . which can be found in any understanding and serious observance of Jesus' way of life."[57] Here, she turned toward the sentiment underlying the New Testament version of the YWCA motto: "By love, serve one another." The Christian spirit was manifested through solicitousness and service, not through a triumphal fight for the kingdom.

To attract Turkish participants and avoid harassment at the hands of Turkish authorities, the YWCA registered itself as a secular educational institution in 1925, and it renamed itself the American Girls' Service Center, taking seriously the opinion of a consultant who warned "that the word 'Christian' stands out as a red flag before the people; it offends their national as well as their religious sensibilities; it connotes enmity and all the hateful things that have come down through history."[58] While it was still affiliated with the World's YWCA and the Foreign Division of the YWCA of the USA supplied many of its secretaries, the Turkish YWCA "no longer functions in the minds of the police." The staff made a firm decision "not to have any Christian teaching for Christian girls because it separates the girls into Christian and non-Christian groups." Instead of carrying out a narrowly religious program for the Christian minority, they pursued fellowship across creedal lines. This change in policy elicited a "constant increase in Moslem membership," according to a 1929 report.[59]

Grappling with these challenges, staff members gained a more ecumenical sense of evangelization, reasoning that spreading the message of Christianity did not hinge on inducing conversion. In their ethos, if not in the governing documents, leaders remained convinced that their response was not a capitulation to an outside religion but instead a mark of Christian ethics. They expressed their interpretation of the Gospel message of human unity by creating a more Turkish and Muslim association. The secretaries identified members' individual growth, as well as ethnic and religious cooperation, as the expression of the Christian spirit undergirding the service center. Through such activities as charity work and educational discussions, girls' clubs aimed to develop "fellowship, cooperation, helpfulness, real understanding of each other, [and] free and fearless self-expression." The programs promoted Christian ideals without demanding religious allegiance. The YWCA of the USA's magazine touted these "character building ideals which are held in common" across creedal lines as the "spirit which leavens the whole," a New Testament quote.[60]

Most poignantly, the service center had become a place for ethnic and religious rapprochement. Its publicity described the YWCA as an "international safety zone." The Izmir service center had once served as a safety zone when it delivered refugees from danger. Now the multiethnic Istanbul service center could help young women move forward from the trauma of war and learn how to coexist. One pamphlet claimed that "girls check their . . . prejudices at the door and enter on neutral ground, brought together by common needs and common desires—the love of self-expression through service; the desire for mental improvement . . . ; or for association and fellowship." The center served as "living proof of the fact that the individuals of the Near East, belonging to antagonistic races, can come into sympathetic understanding with each other." The pamphlet's conclusion "that peace is after all, more fundamental than war, if built on the basis of mutual understanding and friendship" served as the cornerstone of the secular service center's mission. The structural change predicted by the YWCA—a transition from a warlike to a peaceful, and hence Christian, society—would be built on the foundation of interpersonal connections. The association, the pamphlet asserted, could have an instrumental role in healing historical divides: "by steadily increasing the number of personal friendships . . . , the YWCA is widening their horizon beyond narrow racial, nationality, and religious antagonisms into the common ground of international friendship and understanding."[61]

Leaders cited anecdotes that demonstrated the effectiveness of the new approach. A Turkish educator pointed out the importance of dropping the language of Christianity: "there used to be a good deal of suspicion of your work because of your name YWCA . . . but now there is no longer so much suspicion. You are gradually proving to them what you are trying to do in this country." An "old Turkish woman" noted the convergences between the service center's dedication to character development in a single-sex setting and the Islamic value of gendered spheres of activity. She told a secretary: "Your center is doing a good work here. Now we have found the place where my daughter will be away from men and I myself might come to your . . . programs. This is a safe place to send my daughter."[62]

The service center's decision to prioritize having a heterogeneous membership over focusing on Christian community eventually placed it at odds with the World's YWCA. The Turkish situation challenged the international organization's religious requirements, which stipulated that affiliated associations affirm a profession of faith in Christian salvation. When members of the executive board of the Istanbul service center had all been Christians, several of whom were European and American, this had not posed difficulties. However, as the service center began actively recruiting Turkish Muslims to serve on the board in the early 1930s, it eliminated religious pledges. The World's YWCA decided that, although it offered "sympathetic interest," it would not align itself with the novel endeavor. The executive committee determined that "in view of the development toward indigenous control involving the entrance of Moslem women into the directing committee, the Service Centre work in Istanbul could no longer be recognised as having an organic relationship to the World's Young Women's Christian Organization."[63] The interfaith spirit of fellowship promoted by the service center's staff members did not align with the still-evangelical purpose of the world organization.

Overall, the religious rhetoric of the World's YWCA followed a trajectory similar to that of the US YWCA, which grew more liberal and ecumenical after World War I. However, in the 1930s, the World's YWCA attempted to reassert evangelical priorities. It faced discontent in some quarters over the extent to which social reform and religious pluralism occupied the agenda; the national associations of Finland and South Africa disaffiliated themselves from the world group for these reasons in 1931. While the World's YWCA still endorsed the use of Christian principles to solve social problems, it feared that "the very variety of our modes of expression [have] given an impression of dispersion of energy." In response, the governing board determined that "the religious needs of existing groups of Protestant girls [should] be safeguarded," and it "re-affirmed that a dynamic Christian conviction should be at the heart of all our work."[64] To promote Protestant religiosity anew, it turned to religious education as a major area of programming until leadership changes and World War II brought revived interest in social issues.

For decades, the US YWCA continued to have a relationship with the Istanbul service center. A US secretary, Phoebe Clary, stayed at the helm from the 1930s until the 1960s, but most staff and board positions were turned over to local women. In 1968, the organization changed its name to the Genclik Kultur ve Hizmet Vakfi (Youth Cultural and Service Foundation) and continued to offer programming that had long been part of the service center, such as clerical training and English-language instruction. In the late 1980s, the US group turned over remaining funds designated for Turkish work to the foundation, which continues to operate as a community center and educational facility.[65]

THE END OF THE EXPANSION ERA

By the late 1920s, two of the crown jewels in the association empire, the YWCAs of China and Japan, were operating primarily under local control. Although new associations continued to be formed, the World's YWCA no longer had the funding or millennial ambitions that had sparked its early success. Still, the international movement flourished as a federation of independently operating organizations, some linked to each other in transnational partnerships.

US and European women once envisioned the internationalization of the YWCA through the distorting lens of an orientalist evangelicalism. They saw headway made in non-Protestant countries as a demonstration of the success of leadership based on the guiding forces of Christianity and Western civilization. They interpreted the participation of women native to those countries as a sign that the pull of the kingdom of God was effecting a revolution in women's lives. From World War I on, this vision faced a growing set of challenges. Women in missionary-receiving countries ably took over the leadership of their associations and proposed their own plans for the movement.

Early leaders may have misunderstood the reasons behind the YWCA's successful expansion, but one piece of the rhetoric of the international movement seems accurate: women in many parts of the world faced "the same dangers, the same sins, the same temptations, the same aspirations, the same human nature, with increased freedom from restraints."[66] Or, rather, industrialization, nation and empire building, and growing educational opportunities elicited an outpouring of women's activism in many places around the globe. Middle- and working-class women in a variety of countries joined YWCA efforts to cope with these changes. They believed that uplift could transform the conditions of women's lives, and they found promise in an international movement that could create leverage for women's issues that otherwise had a marginal place in national political agendas.

European and US women's vision of the global YWCA movement was rife with contradictions. They yearned for unity but created racial and national hierarchies. They sought peace in the realms of labor and international relations but made only incremental reforms in their own operating practices. They pursued the indigenization of the association while making it difficult for YWCAs in missionary-receiving communities to gain autonomy. As the US YWCA learned in Japan and Turkey, those contradictions were ultimately untenable. Even as they struggled with the presumptions of US administrators, local women used the associations as vehicles to promote their own ideas of development and social change. They elaborated on the strands of progressive internationalism that drove world expansion, but they discarded the orientalist feminist ideologies that accompanied this impulse. The stories of the YWCAs of Japan, Turkey, and the United States impart an important lesson about the type of everyday exchanges of power involved in the practical work of transnational institution building. The YWCA's pledge to love and serve was a lesson learned, in some ways, through the evangelization of the evangelizers: the refusal of women in places designated as mission destinations to brook the coercive presumptions built into the idea of Christian sisterhood.

3 · "HIDDEN AND EFFECTIVE SERVICE"

The Maryknoll Sisters Enter the Mission Field

When asked why she chose a religious vocation, Sister Virginia Flagg, who joined the Maryknoll Sisters of St. Dominic in 1930, described the emotional pull of faith and community life: "I really fell in love with God. . . . I wanted to spend my life doing whatever God wanted. I knew that Maryknoll was the place for me. Everybody was so friendly. All the sisters were fun-loving, and they loved each other." In the twenty-six years since a student volunteer celebration at Smith College sent Mary Josephine Rogers—widely known by her religious name, Mother Mary Joseph, after 1913—on a missionary journey, some four hundred women had joined Flagg in responding to the call of religious service and the unique environment of this new community.[1]

The turn-of-the-century missionary movement that initiated the foreign work of the YWCA of the USA inspired the Maryknoll Sisters to make the first concerted effort to populate the mission field by US Catholic women. As the Foreign Division of the YWCA of the USA labored to transfer overseas associations to local control, the Maryknoll Sisters adapted the Protestant mission model of "woman's work for woman" to their own purposes.[2] While a progressive sensibility about women's capacities and a longing for international connections prevailed in both organizations, their approaches to evangelization diverged not only in creed but in method when the Maryknoll Sisters received Vatican recognition as a religious institute in 1920. Hearkening to a mission era that had preceded the professionally oriented YWCA's late-nineteenth-century expansion, the Maryknoll Sisters pursued a "domestic empire" overseas.[3] However, the infantry of this domestic empire was not the transplanted conjugal household modeled by Protestant missionaries; instead, it was the regimented community of women religious. Maryknoll women did not reinforce the US heritage of Protestantism but rather showcased new developments in a distinctly American Catholicism. They did not represent a young nation jockeying for a place among European imperial powers but worked under the aegis of the leading agent of global capitalism.

The US Catholic Church came late to the foreign mission scene, but when it arrived, women figured centrally because of Rogers and Maryknoll. In terms of the number of entrants and professed sisters, as well as of their media presence, the Maryknoll Sisters became one of the largest and most influential Catholic women's missionary organizations. They developed a religious vocation that transformed Catholic conceptions not only of mission but also of the value and purview of women's work. The sisters carved out a distinct place through their subtle reform of the strictures that circumscribed women's place in the institutional church. The group adopted a pose of submission as it made ever more prominent contributions to the global growth of Catholicism. However progressive the congregation was in regard to its members, Maryknoll, like the larger church, was slow to question the domineering drive to proselytize that underwrote its missiology. Mission methods clashed with pluralist longings. From a subordinate station, sisters established themselves as a powerful—and power-wielding—missionary presence. Nevertheless, the communal identity and enduring institutions they established in these years laid the groundwork for a person-to-person model of social change that would ultimately be put into service in the transnational human rights movement.

MARYKNOLL ORIGINS

Mary Josephine Rogers's avowed esteem for the Protestant missionary movement was unusual among Catholics in religious life. While the Catholic Church viewed Protestantism as a threat, Rogers credited the missionary enthusiasm at turn-of-the-century Smith College with sparking her life's work. Looking back at her Smith days, she judged the students who volunteered for mission to be "the college's best," and she longed to bring out the same spirit among American Catholics. "Protestant activity has wonderfully increased till today," she wrote, but "America, as a nation, had done next to nothing [to fulfill] the Saviour's command: 'Go, teach all nations.'"[4] She hoped to make the United States a force in the global growth of the Catholic Church, and she saw women as indispensable in this task.

Her determination to infuse the labor of women religious with evangelical zeal contrasted with the prevailing sensibilities of the Catholic hierarchy. In fact, in 1928 the Jesuit magazine *America* rebuked Rogers for her favorable appraisal of the religious atmosphere at Smith. It perceived her comments as an insult to

Catholic education, a challenge to the self-contained institutional life that commanded the loyalty of the faithful. An editorial instructed her to review church doctrine and repent, lest she encourage students to abandon Catholic universities.[5] Unintentionally, Rogers's conception of women's evangelization militated against the church's insularity. She not only acknowledged Protestant influence, but she also resisted the marginalization of women's labor. The success of her vision compelled members of the clerical hierarchy to reassess their resistance to such influences.

Throughout the latter half of the nineteenth century, the US Catholic Church had been in no position to respond to the lively mission activities of Protestant colleges and voluntary organizations. A few Catholic orders supplied missionaries to overseas efforts; larger numbers embarked on "home" missions among immigrants, African Americans, and American Indians. The Catholic Church's embattled place in US culture militated against an emphasis on expansion and proselytizing. Subject to the distrust and occasionally repressive measures of the Protestant majority, Catholics and their institutions turned inward for support. The position of the US church in respect to the Eurocentric Vatican also initially hampered program building. In 1899, Pope Leo XIII condemned the "Americanist" heresy, which was in part a proposal to co-opt the evangelical spirit of Protestant revivalism to proselytize on behalf of Catholic Church. The pope's rejection of Americanism was offset in the long run by a liberalizing body of papal social teachings, but the church's antimodernism created obstructions for Maryknoll's founders.[6]

In spite of the Vatican's truculence, the momentum of the US church grew quickly in the early twentieth century. Catholic institutions incorporated themselves into the body politic, particularly as immigration swelled Catholic constituencies in urban centers. Decreasingly segregated and ghettoized, the socially mobile children of immigrants gained access to political and economic power. The strengthening of group identity and institutions, Catholics' economic success, and their acceptance into a religiously pluralistic nation fostered a belief that US Catholicism had unique value in the broader work of the church. In 1908, the Vatican removed the United States from the status of mission church, a church administered in Rome rather than by native ecclesiastical structures.[7]

After college, Rogers sought out Father James A. Walsh, a mission enthusiast engaged in a long struggle to enlist the support of the Vatican and Catholic laity in sending Americans into foreign mission. In 1907, he founded a successful magazine, *The Field Afar*, to publicize missions and raise funds, stressing the potential for American largesse, labor, and prayers to Christianize and civilize East Asia. Driving home the need for US intervention in foreign lands against enemies of the "True Faith," *The Field Afar* combined appeals to American imperialism with insistence on Catholic righteousness. In such fashion, contributor Alex Doyle invoked national and religious triumphalism to stimulate a sense of responsibility among readers for spreading the faith: "America is already in the forefront of world powers, and the Church in the United States must not only follow the American flag, with its helpfulness, but it must push even beyond into the heathen lands to help the soul that is lying prostrate under the domination of heathen error."[8] The magazine warned that the spread of Protestantism as well as paganism threatened foreign lands, and Catholic missions provided means by which Americans could address these dangers—whether through making financial contributions or dedicating their lives to missionary work.

Rogers became Walsh's helpmeet and a tireless worker for the mission cause. The two established a property named Maryknoll in Westchester County, New York, for a seminary. Rogers supervised a small group of devout single laywomen who provided the behind-the-scenes labor necessary to put out the magazine and maintain the seminary. A *Field Afar* article assessed the women's work with a simple sentence in praise of their submissive labors: "To their hidden and effective service we owe much." In 1912 the Catholic Foreign Missionary Society, known popularly as the Maryknoll Fathers, received Vatican approval to train priests for mission, and six years later, it established missions in China.[9]

The sharply subordinated position of women in the Catholic Church led to a more tangled route for the establishment of the Maryknoll Sisters. First called secretaries and then "Teresians" in reference to their devotion to Saint Teresa of Avila, the laywomen who helped launch the Maryknoll Fathers entered into communal life with no formal status in the church. They lived together at Maryknoll and offered their unpaid service to the fledging effort. With little precedent for a women's missionary religious order, they initially did not seek Vatican recognition.

Walsh had been content to leave Maryknoll's women workers as the support staff for the seminary. But Rogers, fascinated with the student missionary movement, "always nurtured the hope that young women would go overseas." Eventually Rogers's view prevailed, but arranging Vatican approval required years of petitioning. In 1920, the Teresian volunteers received this recognition and became legally established as the Foreign Mission Sisters of St. Dominic (the name was later changed to the Maryknoll Sisters of St. Dominic). Under the training of the Sinsinawa Dominican Sisters, Rogers and several Teresians took religious vows the same year. Rogers became Mother Mary Joseph, the mother general responsible for all manners of leadership. Her congenial, gentle temperament fostered an energetic atmosphere that contrasted with the typical severity of Catholic religious orders.[10]

FIGURE 3.1. "Our Marys Take Their Turn as Marthas," *The Field Afar*, June 1931, 177. Credit: Maryknoll Mission Archives

Sisters continued to carry out support work for the seminary, cooking and washing the laundry. In fact, they had such responsibilities through the 1950s. But they wasted no time in establishing more ambitious mission projects. In 1920, small groups of sisters set out for Los Angeles and Seattle to staff orphanages, schools, and a tuberculosis asylum serving Japanese American communities. Such tasks echoed the responsibilities assumed by other US women religious, who engaged in teaching, child care, and medical care, but the Maryknoll Sisters designated their work as mission oriented. They dedicated themselves to the "conversion of pagans in heathen lands and of Asiatics in Christian countries."[11] In medical and educational settings, they sought cross-cultural encounters to fulfill their call to evangelization, and their ministry reached out to underserved populations in emulation of Jesus's care of outcasts and the unloved.

In 1921, the sisters sent their first overseas group to Hong Kong, where they started a kindergarten and an industrial school that produced religious vestments to be sold in the United States. Attendant to the preponderance of Protestant missionaries in East Asia, Maryknoll Fathers and Sisters selected China as their main mission field, first establishing missions in the ports and then moving to the interior. Before long, they fanned out to Korea, Japan, and the Philippines. Maryknoll sisters were usually assigned to mission stations alongside the priests, but while the groups worked in association, they were administered independently.[12]

In the 1920s and 1930s, the sisters primarily staffed small schools and medical dispensaries. They offered catechumenal training (teaching the catechism of the church to those who wished to become members) and started leprosariums, orphanages, and homes for the elderly and blind. In 1926, the first group of Chinese women took instruction with the sisters to enter religious life, forming a so-called native novitiate. Other such novitiates followed. In Hong Kong, Maryknoll started larger institutions: two schools designed to prepare students for university, which attracted prosperous multinational student bodies; and a hospital. Although the sisters desired to reach into the provinces and address those whom they understood to belong to the most benighted populations, their services were much in demand in cosmopolitan areas like Hong Kong and Manila. With English as a lingua franca and professional educational opportunities rare, the local middle classes availed themselves of Maryknoll's private schools.[13]

The congregation distinguished itself from Protestant women's groups with its distinctly Catholic conception of women's work. As a voluntary association that operated independently from denominational control, the YWCA had considerable latitude in crafting its institutional identity. As a religious institute governed by canon law, Maryknoll contended with the restrictive traditions of cloister and the patriarchal structures of the Catholic Church. Still, much as the nineteenth-century discourse of separate spheres gave rise to the women's culture of the YWCA, a gendered conception of religious life gave Maryknoll women freedom to craft their own vision of community and evangelization. While they embraced new opportunities, the women did not challenge the precepts of the church, nor did they interrogate the power dynamics of foreign mission.

"ECCE ANCILLA DOMINI"

The Maryknoll Sisters secured a position of both strength and subordination by identifying with the biblical handmaid. Modeled on Mary, the mother of Jesus, the handmaid figure served as a model of unobtrusive assistant rather than primary actor in the work of the church. The Gospel of Luke provided the terms for this relationship in the story of the Annunciation, when an angel tells Mary that she will conceive the son of God. Mary accepts her station and says, "behold the handmaid of the Lord; be it done to me according to thy word." The sisters adopted the first clause of the Latin verse, "*ecce ancilla domini*," as their motto.[14] Not only did it mark their devotion to Mary, but it also was a proclamation of womanly servitude to God and the church. The sentiment diverged from the expansive restatement of Jesus's promise of fulfillment given in the "Christian purpose" of the YWCA of the USA. In this statement of institutional identity, YWCA women interpreted Jesus's declaration "I am come that they might have life . . . abundantly" as a directive to assist young women in finding "fullness of life."[15] This served as a touchstone for the YWCA's efforts to promote individual development and seek social change. In contrast, the Maryknoll Sisters emphasized feminine service to the masculine authority of the church in their reference to the handmaid.

In some ways, the Maryknoll Sisters maintained their integrity as a single-sex organization through submitting to the church hierarchy. Using an unthreatening pose of religious obedience, the congregation proved the value of women's culture and labor. Catholics designated the religious order the most sanctified means for women to pursue spiritual callings, and this regimented life emphasized self-abnegation and effacement. From the medieval period until a revision in canon law in 1918, the church insisted on the cloister as the singular domain of women religious. The enclosure of the cloister was manifested not only through the symbolic separation of nuns from the community at large, setting them apart as an inviolable and unknowable population, but also through conspicuous physical barriers: heavy cloaks and veils that obscured the sisters' appearance, chapels that separated them from parishioners, and physical barriers in living spaces that mediated necessary transactions with the outside world. Barred from the sacred space of the altar and excluded from a relationship to the sacramental embodiment of Jesus available only to the male priest, women religious performed spiritual labors of prayer and penance. They dedicated their work to God and invisibly facilitated the work of his earthly clerical messengers.[16]

The nineteenth century saw the growth of apostolic, or active, religious communities, which gave women a new visibility and an expanding set of responsibilities in the church. In contrast to cloistered orders, in which nuns lived in seclusion, apostolic congregations engaged with the outside world through teaching, nursing, and caring for society's marginalized people—orphans, the elderly, and the disabled. Women in active service still lived communally and participated in the spiritual labors of Catholic life. The frontier conditions of the church in the United States created a gulf between the Vatican's insistence on the cloister and the demands for women religious: it was difficult to justify the cloister rule when most dioceses desperately needed personnel to propagate Catholic traditions.[17]

Apostolic sisters still fit within a framework that valued women's self-denial. This selflessness placed them at the disposal not of family or husband but instead of the populations they served and the ecclesiastical officials who determined their assignments. The convent had long provided a respected occupation that evaded the demands of the patriarchal family. It gave a Catholic gloss to the shifting terrain of women's authority in the late nineteenth century. As the historian Maureen Fitzgerald notes, in contrast to Protestant women's "claims to public voice, especially through their roles as mothers," the effectiveness of women religious "was based on the ability to live together and organize themselves as large bodies of single women who lived apart from marriage and domesticity."[18] Mary Josephine Rogers created the Maryknoll Sisters to give such single women a role in the global stewardship of the Catholic Church.

Rogers adapted the Protestant call for women missionaries to a community structure based on strict regimentation. Though she still established community bonds through rituals of initiation and discipline, she felt that many rules needed adjustment. Without rejecting the ascetic, disciplinarian traditions of European religious communities, she wanted the congregation to be distinctively American. A national character of pragmatism, friendliness, and exuberance would be new tools in the evangelization of the world.

Maryknoll community life embodied two contradictory impulses: first, an emphasis on spontaneity, individuality, and lightheartedness that Rogers identified as crucial to the congregation's success; and second, an affirmation of the church's ancient priorities and practices. These impulses remained at the core of the sisters' training from the inception of the congregation in the 1920s until the reforms introduced during the Second Vatican Council. Though the sisters amended and revised their constitution periodically, much of what was codified in the 1920s remained in practice through the 1950s.

Religious orders were predicated on vows of poverty, chastity, and obedience, and Rogers affirmed the hierarchical order of the church in her emphasis on the vow of obedience as the "supreme vow." She underscored that obedience to superiors—not only women in a supervisory capacity in the order but "all those" in the chain of ecclesiastical authority "who have a right to command us"—was "the visible manifestation of conforming our will" to God's. She affirmed the apostolic order of the church, the so-called grace of office that enabled those with managerial positions in the religious hierarchy "to act as God's representatives," in the words of scholar Helen Rose Ebaugh.[19]

As founder, Rogers was responsible for discerning and cultivating the congregation's charism, a theological term designating a unique gift conferred by the Holy Spirit to further the work of the church. She named this charism the "Maryknoll spirit," a positive force of personality that missionaries would use to make converts. The Maryknoll spirit balanced Catholic disciplinary structures with the openness that Rogers associated with the American national character. While emphasizing obedience, Rogers sought "to have the Sisters preserve their naturalness."[20] Individuality and forthrightness, two qualities usually discouraged in religious communities, would be assets in Maryknoll's missionary work.

In describing the Maryknoll spirit, Rogers listed a host of traits that would attract people to Catholicism. The traits would contrast with the conventional perception of religious orders as dour and rigid. She encouraged sisters to "be open and frank, ready with their smile," "happy and joyous," and "open to . . . truth, and justice, and peace." They should "act as magnets drawing people to them."[21] She described this magnetism as the ineluctable pull of Christian love, a selfless dedication that undergirded the bonds of Maryknoll community life. When outsiders encountered the sisters, Rogers wanted them to "see in us the spirit of mutual love and tenderness which certainly existed in the early ages of the church, when the pagans were forced to say, 'See how they love one another.'"[22] She sought to create a community that radiated joy from dedication to God. At the same time, "true American adaptability" would be the most useful quality Maryknoll women could bring to mission. The "endurance, the zeal, the buoyancy . . . of our girls" would enable them to withstand hardships and win friends in foreign lands.[23]

The Maryknoll spirit indeed stood out as a charism. Themes of sorrow, suffering, and sin predominated in Catholicism. Many orders had been founded as penitential, their prayers intended to compensate for humanity's degraded state. Apostolic groups modeled their work among the ill and the outcast on the selflessness and suffering of Christ. Although Maryknoll women did not stray entirely from the cult of suffering, they also hoped to win souls through the transformative power of God's love and by outwardly demonstrating the positive effects of God's grace on his believers. Instead of threatening nonbelievers with invocations of divine power and punishment, "we need winsomeness and magnetism to invite people to us," Rogers instructed the sisters. Nonbelievers would reject Christianity "if they are not attracted by us." This winsomeness could not be a performance; rather, it must come from the exacting cultivation of godliness to which religious aspired. To serve as a vessel of God's love to nonbelievers, sisters had to "be sure that the smile on our lips is [God's] joy that is being shown forth," for only the disciplined life allowed Christians to experience the true fulfillment that came from God's grace. Sharing this joy was the purpose of their work and the mark of its success.[24]

Rogers endeavored to create a communal life that fostered pious cheerfulness. Although sisters had full schedules of work and prayer, she encouraged fun in times of recreation and a sense of humor in labor. To enliven religious routines, she introduced to convent life "activities that were taken for granted during her college days." The Maryknoll historian Penny Lernoux notes how simple diversions imported from Rogers's school days—"long walks, free afternoons on Wednesday, simple family entertainments [like games and dramatics], and home vacations"—were "highly unorthodox for women's religious communities of the time."[25]

Reinventing rituals of recreation and friendship that peppered the lively single-sex culture of Smith College, sisters celebrated holidays and saints' feast days with ice cream, homemade presents, and pageants as well as their more traditional masses and devotions. A 1921 account from a Los Angeles mission school suggests the schoolgirl levity that Rogers made possible. A sister described with mock horror a Christmas banquet of Maryknoll sisters and priests: "The first [phonograph] record proved to be unfortunate. It sounded too jazzy—too utterly jazzy—and before one knew what was happening, two of our oldest [sisters] were fox-trotting. Fr. Kress saw them, too, but he held his hand over his eyes to hide the awful sight. They continued to misbehave in this manner all evening."[26]

Such activities softened the rigors of religious life and created a congenial community atmosphere. Virginia Flagg reminisced about the appeal: "Other communities were . . . stringent, they didn't seem to laugh as much. . . . I liked the attitude of the Sisters. I liked Mother's wholeness." Many shared this sentiment. Religious life was understood to be purposefully joyless. In many orders, harsh disciplinary measures perpetuated ascetic traditions. The most extreme practiced flagellation, required sisters to kiss the feet of superiors, or mandated that members go barefoot. More common strictures forbade reading outside of required prayer books, prohibited communication with the outside world, or required obeisance to superiors. They might restrict sisters' material possessions to the barest necessities and mandate fasting. Maryknoll eschewed such privations.[27]

Rogers did not want community rules to hamper the Maryknoll spirit. She rejected severe traditions she believed to be outdated. Sister Agnes Donovan's assessment echoed Flagg's: "Our community was quite free because of Mother Mary Joseph." Donovan noted this freedom in regard to sisters' access to life outside the convent, contrasting Maryknoll with congregations that strictly segregated women from their families: "I used to see some sisters . . . who could not enter their homes, and they were . . . from local communities with families all around, and they could only go and sit in the car outside their home and talk to [relatives]." In religious life, "you were supposed to be detached, [but] Mother Mary Joseph said your family is your family, and you love your family and you should write to them."[28]

Flagg appreciated Rogers's flexible interpretation of the vow of poverty. Without reveling in luxury, members of the congregation were encouraged to enjoy material goods: "Mother loved beauty, and she said beauty was not against poverty. At Maryknoll, we try to have beautiful things even though these things are simple. God has filled the world with beautiful things. Why then pick out ugly ones?" Whereas some communities constructed their identities around material deprivation, Rogers encouraged openness to innovation: "She wasn't stultified, and if there was something modern . . . , use it for goodness sakes. Just because it's new and looks good don't think you can't use it for the help of the work."[29]

Irrespective of the salutary effects of the Maryknoll spirit, Rogers's openness did not prevent enforcement of the discipline that was a bedrock of religious orders and the key to God's grace. Sisters bound themselves to rigorous self-control and a limited emotional life to become channels of God's work. Entering religious life was a true ritual transformation that removed individuals from the social order they had once inhabited and remade them in the mold of the community.[30] Entrants to Maryknoll learned the trade of the handmaid in a multistage process of religious formation, which culminated in the profession of final vows. Final vows established a permanent commitment to religious life and could be dissolved only by excommunication or petitioning the Vatican. Rules of initiation limited connection to the life left behind to bring entrants more fully into the self-contained environment of the congregation. Though Maryknoll did not forbid contact with outsiders through visits or correspondence, it designated a limited number of days for such activities. Novices—those in the first stage of religious life—were largely sequestered in the convent where they undertook their training. They abandoned most of the material possessions of their outside lives to conform to the congregation's regulations about the accumulation and distribution of goods. The convent held personal care items like soap in common, and it was necessary to ask superiors for permission to use them—and to give thanks to God when permission was granted.[31] This mode of surveillance instilled a sense of the sacrifices necessary to honor the vow of poverty.

Rules compelled novices and professed sisters alike to cast out "what is objectionable [in] our individuality" to distill their holiest qualities. They also experienced limits on their ties to the world beyond the community. Maryknoll required that sisters travel with a companion, including when they visited their homes. On the street, they were enjoined to adopt an unapproachable attitude befitting the spiritually elevated. Instructions outlined that sisters "should not readily enter into conversation with others; they should answer with prudence and charity those who address them, and not speak with familiarity or freedom, especially to those of the opposite sex." Even though they could partake in such diversions as knitting and radio in their recreational moments, they could not do so in situations in which "outsiders" might be given "the impression that our Sisters are free" to engage in nonspiritual matters.[32]

Though Rogers celebrated friendliness as crucial to the Maryknoll spirit, she keenly felt the need to place restrictions on sisters' interpersonal relationships to guard against the excessive familiarity fostered by communal living conditions. Sisters followed a rule of silence that designated when and where they could converse. They could not talk or gather in groups of two. They were forbidden to engage in conversation with those outside their own stage of profession: that is, novices could speak only to novices, and professed sisters only to each other. They could mingle freely only on special days of "Fusion"—often feast days, when rules were suspended.[33]

These restrictions were rooted in the perceived danger of intimacy. Rogers understood friendship as vital to community and saw love as the root of friendship. She told the sisters, "If you know that between two souls there is a tender, helpful friendship, let us thank God." Yet danger lurked in friendships that strayed from the discipline of religious life. The all-consuming process of sanctification demanded restraint in interpersonal attachments: "We must remember that . . . God has given us the ability to love, and it is right for us to love one another so long as the affection does not detract from our love for God nor injure others."[34] The community held women together in common purpose and mutual support, but it was carefully structured to divert uninhibited emotional expressiveness into spiritual avenues.

Rogers had been immersed in a culture of same-sex romance that thrived at Smith College, but this element of college life was not allowed at Maryknoll. She prohibited close friendships, physicality, and crushes among the sisters. It was commonly understood that relationships between the sexes served as the foundation for the vow of chastity, but "particular friendships" historically had been forbidden within religious orders. The desire to attract and cultivate deep friendships reflected a sinful glorification of self, a desire to be appreciated and valued through the attention of others. Moreover, such intimacy, Rogers explicitly acknowledged, could lead young women toward a sensuality that violated vows of chastity. The sisters were "not to handle one another," for in these contacts, "if we will examine a little more closely into our own souls, we will realize the pleasurable reaction we get . . . and the dangers that are inherent." She warned of intense emotional attachments: "We know there are times when the face of some Sister whom we love rises before us, even in Chapel. It creates a sort of veil between us and God. We know how, when recreation comes we try to get close to this particular Sister and we make for that seat." She added an admonition that sounded a more ominous tone than most of her theological meditations: "Remember that God is a jealous God."[35]

Maryknoll sisters were subject to further controls to resist temptations and improprieties in their encounters with outsiders. In contacts with men, the congregation mandated an abiding modesty aimed at giving the impression of untouchability and asexuality. This undergirded such injunctions as "*Modess cartons* should always be *torn up* and put down the *incinerator chute* and never left around for the men to dispose of," as though by doing so workmen would be given the impression that sisters did not menstruate.[36] Judging from the frequency with which the sisters had to be reminded not to become friendly with the seminarians who trained with the Maryknoll Fathers, Rogers could not depend on her vision of "a nice appreciation of propriety, and a deep sense of religious modesty" to regulate behavior. Superiors had to watch closely when seminarians worked with sisters so that no superfluous socialization would occur. After discovering that visiting priests had been committing the intolerable familiarity of kissing sisters, presumably on the cheek, Rogers was livid: "A Sister who allows this to happen has a very warped moral sense. And the Priest who does it is absolutely inexcusable." The constitution reiterated that prohibitions against familiarity were particularly crucial in the mission field: "Because of native customs, the mentality of the Oriental, and his usual interpretation of the association of men and women, it is of supreme importance that Sisters shall not go into the house of a priest, nor be in any place whatsoever with a priest or Brother, or any man, unless in the company of others."[37]

The rules and rituals that brought women into the Maryknoll sisterhood were not simply the arcane processes of an antediluvian institution. Rather, they cemented the collective identity that mobilized members of an American religious community to make a lifetime commitment to an exotic vocation. Respectable and respected, sisters conformed to the strictures of their vocation. Still, Maryknoll ushered in reform in women's religious life—albeit a reform both tentative and conflicted—by proposing that the community be defined by both traditional submissiveness and the unique Maryknoll spirit of pious joy. If the outward identity of the congregation can be understood as an amalgamation of restrictive gender structures with a modern sensibility regarding women's abilities, its approach to mission can be understood as embodying similarly contrasting impulses. Maryknoll sought a more unified, cooperative humanity but established domineering, ethnocentric methods of religious outreach. Minimally concerned with the social and political context of mission, the group aimed to win converts and establish ecclesiastical authority, an authority that was white and Euro-American.

SOCIAL TEACHINGS AND CATHOLIC FOREIGN MISSION

In the years before the Second Vatican Council, the substance of the Maryknoll Sisters' work did not differ significantly from the apostolic social services that engaged women of other congregations. The circumstances of foreign mission, however, created an air of novelty and importance. Although Maryknoll emphasized priests' activities as the most important element of mission, sisters' labors made those activities possible. Working at the behest of a local bishop or in concert with the Maryknoll Fathers, sisters staffed institutions designed to raise the church's profile and to establish contact with non-Christians. In these settings, sisters attempted to use their authority as church representatives to establish control over those not yet under its sway. The handmaid identity may have emphasized submissiveness, but in the field it did not engender subordination.

In missions, sisters lived together in convents that might house as many as two dozen women or as few as three. Some sisters secured their upkeep by teaching tuition-paying middle-class and affluent students in large cities. Others operated modest medical facilities, and they found no shortage of places, both rural and urban, where health care was lacking and non-Christians were willing to avail themselves of the facilities. Though English-language instruction was an especially popular service in pioneer missions, stories of exotic dangers and travels loomed large in the missionary literature and in the minds of those hoping for overseas assignments. In the 1930s, Flagg taught English in Dairen (Dalian), Manchuria. She reflected, "oh, we really envied the sisters that were working in the little clinics and directly with the poor." Longing to immerse herself in the most demanding tasks, Flagg worked in the clinic in her off time and relished the rugged conditions: "Loved it. This nurse taught me everything, we could do everything. No licenses, you didn't need a thing. Oh, you cut off frozen toes if they were there. But it was wonderful."[38]

Sisters assigned to stations in the United States—which accounted for roughly eighty of the two hundred sisters in mission in 1933—likewise approached their task in the spirit of adventure. Pursuing what its constitution referred to as the "conversion of pagans in heathen lands and of Asiatics in Christian countries," Maryknoll cast Asian Americans as immutable outsiders, the pagans within the United States. Maryknoll publicity portrayed US Asian communities as unassimilated colonies, emphasizing that such work still counted as foreign mission. "Our priests and Sisters in Honolulu have the Far East at their doors," *The Field Afar* enthused. Hawaii offered a multitude of outsiders to assimilate into Catholicism: "There are more than 125,000 Japanese, 50,000 Filipinos, and 30,000 Chinese and other Asiatics."[39] Throughout Maryknoll's stateside endeavors, sisters interacted with Asian students, patients, and parishioners as though they were encountering a distant, alien culture. Sisters came to one of their earliest projects, a school for Japanese in Los Angeles, with a strong sense of boundaries. They seemed to tolerate rather than embrace their surroundings: "While we like the Japanese and do not mind many of their ways and customs, we do draw the line on eating our meals with a chop stick."[40] With this exoticizing mentality, Maryknoll women did not have to leave the country to experience foreign cultures—and to appraise their own favorably in comparison.

Exotic locales and people were not the only novel features of mission. As they established outposts among non-Christians, Maryknoll sisters had considerable responsibility for spiritual ministry, a domain normally reserved for priests. Women religious had an influential, if underappreciated, pastoral responsibility as providers of catechumenal instruction, a labor-intensive process. Sisters provided this instruction in their schools, and they attempted to persuade those who sought out charitable services to become catechumens.

Mission conditions gave sisters the unusual opportunity to administer sacraments, the liturgical rites foundational to Roman Catholicism. Normally, priests alone administered sacraments. But in emergencies, sisters could administer baptisms and last rites. They sought out these moments when they could participate most directly in the quest to deliver souls to the Catholic Church and demonstrate their own importance to mission work. In *The Field Afar* of the 1920s and 1930s, sisters frequently relayed tales of baptizing dying children in Chinese orphanages. The magazine celebrated sisters' emergency interventions, reasoning that the Christian salvation thus conferred would bring the children's troubles to an end in the afterlife. In one account, sisters reported: "On a shelf, very similar to display counters in a department store, there were bundles of rags [infants]. Two were found and baptized; and then we had to leave the poor little things. But not for long would they be in suffering!" This pursuit had shades of subterfuge. Did the staff of the "pagan orphanages" know the intentions of two other sisters, who came away disappointed that "there were no babies to be baptized"?[41] Frequent encounters with illness and death in impoverished areas gave sisters a sense of urgency in exercising their sacramental privileges and a strong desire to bring what they believed to be the peace of God to the suffering. But it also gave rise to an opportunistic approach to evangelization.

The most distinctive ministerial task undertaken by Maryknoll women became known as the Kaying method of proselytization.[42] While most sisters in mission staffed Catholic institutions in cities, a few of them worked in small, peripatetic teams. Named for the Chinese region (Meizhou) in which this activity was pioneered, the Kaying method involved house visits, including overnight trips, to distant settlements to provide religious training to Chinese women.

The Kaying method was the Maryknoll activity that most resembled Protestant "woman's work for woman." Francis Ford, the Maryknoll bishop who authorized it, reasoned that common conditions of womanhood would give the sisters a "hold" on the hearts of Chinese women and access to their homes. He wrote: "The Chinese mother, despite her low esteem outside the home, is the real molder of the faith of her children, and an enduring Church is founded on her conversion." While this maternalist logic was commonplace in the Protestant missionary movement, it was difficult for the Catholic hierarchy to imagine religious instruction without priests. In a 1956 history, Sister M. Marcelline, a Dominican sister who worked with Maryknollers in China, affirmed the patriarchal logic that made such ministry seem so unusual. She explained that women's direct evangelization supported rather than subverted clerical hierarchy: "the priest is Christ's official representative in the strict sense . . . ; the missionary

Sister . . . , an auxiliary worker in the gigantic task of reaching 'every creature . . . ,' is not indispensable as the priest." Though only a handful of sisters participated in the Kaying venture, Rogers found satisfaction in finally having work parallel to that of the missionaries she had admired at Smith. She told Ford: "This particular phase of work has always been dearest to my heart. I believe it is our essential missionary work."[43] Over time, as Maryknoll revisited the charism that gave it purpose, the sisters would identify the Kaying initiative as the germ of a more active women's ministry.

A nascent vision of the social responsibility of the church guided the sisters as they first entered mission work. The foremost task was bolstering the reach of the church, to which the sisters dedicated themselves wholly. Still, within efforts to elicit Catholic piety, church leaders responded to global economic and political change. Catholic mission enthusiasts' vision of the perfecting of the social order differed significantly from the kingdom of God pursued by both millennial Protestant evangelicals and Social Gospel advocates. Still, in the early twentieth century, the creeds found common ground in their dismay about class friction, dedication to the salutary benefits of Christian salvation to the non-Christian world, and halting repudiation of doctrines of racial and national superiority. As had been the case for the evangelical Protestants of the early YWCA, the Maryknoll Sisters insisted that social progress began with Christianization.

Two popes, Leo XIII (papacy, 1878–1903) and Pius XI (1922–39), advanced the teachings that most affected the Maryknoll Sisters' early years of mission. Leo XIII introduced a more socially invested church in the 1891 encyclical *Rerum Novarum*. This document laid out three major principles that affected mission theory. First, it established devout religious practice as the basis of a harmonious Christian society. Designed to mediate growing class struggle, it set the pace for Catholic reform with the conclusion that "if human society is to be healed now, in no other way can it be healed save by a return to Christian life and Christian institutions." The church presented itself as the only force capable of eliciting cooperation between rich and poor, "reminding each of its duties to the other, and especially of the obligations of justice."[44] Motivated by piety, the groups would respect each other's right to sustenance and property. Second, the encyclical affirmed that charity was the engine of social change. Those who had been blessed with spiritual and material resources had a moral obligation to give selflessly to those without. Finally, it designated religious communities as the primary source of charity. Completely devoted to sacralizing works of charity and mercy, religious communities were the proper providers of social services. The pope repudiated any assumption of state responsibility for social welfare.

Pius XI's 1926 encyclical, *Rerum Ecclesiae*, affirmed these conclusions in a call for support for foreign mission work. His appeal to "spread the light of the Gospel and the benefits of Christian culture and civilization" advanced the notion of a united world church but couched the task in terms of the enlightenment of degraded people. Citing the doctrine of agape, he asked, "can we give a mark of greater love for our neighbors than to assist them in putting behind themselves the darkness of error by instructing them in the true faith of Christ?"[45] The Maryknoll Sisters concurred, framing their missionary task as an outpouring of the Maryknoll spirit: sanctified love, purified through the discipline of religious life.

Though the Protestant mission movement emerged from World War I chastened, Maryknoll began its work with full confidence in the eventual Christianization of East Asia. Maryknoll's constitution stated that all assignments, including medical and educational, were opportunities to evangelize: "Sisters should never lose sight of their desire to attract to God each individual soul that comes within the sphere of their influence; students, patients, employees, or guests. No matter what their occupation, they should lovingly cultivate their own souls and minds, that they may by word, example, and personal holiness realize that end."[46] The women indeed used their charitable interventions to advance a religious agenda. This could be a self-serving sensibility, as when *The Field Afar* reported in 1938 the "great good [that] is done in . . . our Sisters' visits to pagan homes." It explained: "The pagans usually have some temporal motive for inviting these visits, such as medicine, money, education for their children; or perhaps if some member of the family is a burden . . . , they invite us expecting help." Maryknoll was willing to provide such help because "any of these serves as a means for contact. . . . This activity breaks down prejudice, secures the confidence and interest of the people, and gives [them] a chance to hear the doctrines of the Church." Meeting the temporal desires for which the author expressed some disdain gained Maryknoll an audience for doctrinal instruction. Even when this emphasis was not expressed in such a mercenary fashion, sisters made evangelization a priority in their labors. Sister Marya Thyne relayed the spiritual underpinnings of her clinic work in *The Field Afar*: "I clipped off two fingers [of the patient's crushed hand], set the bones in the other three, and prayed, while dressing it, that the hand might be saved. If not, I could try at least to reach the soul of this young man, as he would return daily for treatment."[47]

Maryknoll measured the progress of evangelization in a social-scientific quantification of its efforts. This quantification permeated the diaries sent monthly from missions to the motherhouse in Westchester County. The diaries were not personal reflections but an official record of work and community life, tabulating conversions made, visits to non-Christian homes, religious instruction given, medicines dispensed, and students taught. The numbers conveyed the cumulative growth of the church as measured by the missionaries' successful incursions into "pagan" communities. Maryknoll used this quantification to drum up donations. In its first few decades, it solicited funds to "ransom pagan babies," an effort to purchase unwanted children from Chinese parents to raise them as Catholics. The campaign portrayed Maryknoll's work as a shrewd, albeit charitable, business venture. It promised US Catholics that their donations would yield tangible dividends in the souls delivered to the church.

Sisters could show a striking lack of empathy, as suggested by an account of missionary outreach in Hong Kong. During a charitable visitation to the dying brother of one of their students, sisters took the opportunity to proselytize aggressively. They went to the hospital "hoping to baptize the child, only to find the crisis had passed and hopes of his recovery high. They pinned a small

FIGURE 3.2. "Buying Pagan Babies into the Bondage of Christ," *The Field Afar*, October 1921, 297. Credit: Maryknoll Mission Archives

miraculous medal on his clothes and asked to be called if he got any worse."[48]
Their hopes of baptism seemed to be succeeded by disappointment in his recovery and perhaps even anticipation of another chance to administer a deathbed
baptism. The diarist gave priority to the opportunity to harvest a soul over charitable compassion to those affected by the child's illness.

Though the Maryknoll Sisters did not devise a social agenda much beyond
the quest to win conversions and inculcate piety, in the 1930s there were rumblings of a politicized ideological battle that would become the central Catholic
preoccupation of the midcentury: the threat of communism. To a significant
extent, *Rerum Novarum* had been directed against socialist agitation, and Maryknoll witnessed the rise of communism in China. On occasion in its early mission years, the congregation vaunted the potential for sisters to ward off these
dangers. Recounting a tale in which religious instruction won a Russian student
to Catholicism, *The Field Afar* rejoiced that "the boy was ruined for Bolshevism
because of the time he had spent in the Catholic school!" It projected an active
role for teachers in the eradication of communism: "God grant that many a one
may be ruined for Bolshevism, and that all of them may think, and think, and
think themselves into the Kingdom of God."[49]

Given this facile confidence, the church did not address the structural conditions underlying the poverty and political struggles inevitably encountered in
mission. In 1922, while the YWCA of the USA was lobbying for labor reform,
Sister Mary Paul McKenna revealed Maryknoll's divergent priorities as she
observed the labor of Chinese women, "their heads bent under the heavy load."
While decrying their drudgery, she emphasized the tragedy of their ignorance of
redemptive struggle, the Jesus-like sacrifice valued in Catholicism, rather than
the possibility of social change. "All day long these poor creatures work," she
lamented. "They know nothing of an 'eight hour day,' and, saddest of all, they
know nothing of the Christ who sanctified labor." A 1940 account of charitable
outreach to children in the Philippines indicated that the sisters believed they
had little power over temporal conditions. "If this vast problem of poverty is
beyond the Sisters, they can at least prepare these little ones for the sacraments,"
The Field Afar reported.[50] Their domain was fundamentally spiritual.

In the 1930s, the sisters declared that "mission work is social work," but
they named religious fidelity as the root of community development. Their
social work expert, Sister Victoria Francis Larmour, took pains to differentiate
Catholic social teachings from the secular professional curriculum, dismissing
its insights as nothing more than a weak variation on Catholic principles. She
wrote that Maryknoll had "not been directly influenced by modern social service to any appreciable degree," but the resources of its "rich heritage" elicited
a superior model of intervention: the centuries-old prescriptions of the "Rule
of St. Augustine, the Dominican constitution, canon law, and the tradition and

experience of the older European foreign mission orders." Larmour detailed the advantages of sisters' caring service over the supposedly pedantic and indifferent professional pursuits: "Few Maryknoll Sisters know all of the social worker's jargon. . . . But they do know how to meet others as equals . . . ; they do know that sympathetic understanding and unselfish service are better methods than precept and preaching."[51] Maryknoll's model, she argued, was guided by the selfless and depoliticized contacts of Christian love rather than by spiritually barren academic training.

"THE WORLD FOR OUR USE"

In theory, the Maryknoll sisters' dedication to love positioned them to become agents of international cooperation. They did win many admirers and provide much-needed services in their humanitarian outreach. However, in practice, the church's emphasis on piety overlaid Christian ideals of social harmony with a domineering drive to elicit allegiance. While the sisters subscribed to the subordination inherent in the religious order, they also sought obedience from mission populations in a single-minded dedication to proselytization. Although they proclaimed ideals of pluralism, a racialized sense of cultural superiority informed their sensibilities. When fervent prayers and good intentions yielded fewer converts than expected, Maryknoll women, envisioning themselves as divinely ordained heroes fighting pagan belligerence, were not above responding with coercion and contempt. The sisters professed great love for the people of the world, but just as love for God compelled them to submit to ecclesiastical authority, they likewise expected people in mission territories to submit to their authority as representatives of God.

From the beginning, Maryknoll sought to distinguish its theory of mission from imperialism by emphasizing indigenization—what the Catholic Church described as the development of a native church and native clergy. In this pursuit, the sisters and fathers echoed the mission priorities that guided turn-of-the-century Protestant groups. This objective also proceeded from the internationalism advanced by the Vatican in the 1920s—particularly *Rerum Ecclesiae*, which doubled the number of Catholic personnel assigned to foreign mission. Pius XI's guidelines to "make easy for heathen nations the way unto salvation" reminded the clergy of the effectiveness of indigenization. The native priest was "by birth, temper, sentiment, and interests . . . in close touch with his own people" and thus uniquely poised to instill "the Faith into the minds of his people." To bolster the case for a native clergy, Pius XI issued a warning that marked the church's growing, if fitful, attention to racial inequality: "Anyone who looks upon these natives as members of an inferior race or as men of low mentality makes a grievous mistake."[52]

Both the Vatican and Maryknoll held to the liberal view that culture, rather than nature, was at the root of racial difference, with Pius XI generously noting that "inhabitants of those remote regions of the East and of the South frequently are not inferior to us at all, and are capable of holding their own with us, even in mental ability."[53] They rejected scientific hierarchies of race, even if they showed no recognition of racial hierarchies embedded in ecclesiastical structures. Maryknoll had the task of the practical application of pluralistic ideals. This produced often competing objectives: on one hand, an expectation of submission to a European and US Catholic culture; and on the other hand, a desire to foster respectful interaction across racial and national divides.

The tension between these ideas was embodied in the Maryknoll Sisters' constitution, which affirmed that sisters should not "try to impose on native people our customs" but included the caveat "except such as make for better moral and health conditions." This gave wide latitude for criticizing disagreeable practices. Sisters went into the field assured that the customs of their nation and religion were pivotal to raising standards of morality and health. Accordingly, as a sister later reflected, Maryknoll sisters initially "travelled to . . . mission areas on the wings of the American eagle [and believed]—unconsciously perhaps—that a person could not be truly Catholic unless they also picked up the trappings of Western culture."[54]

Sisters in the field had difficulty seeing cultural difference as less than an affront to the church. Sacraments, the path to participation and salvation in the Catholic Church, peppered daily routines and defined pivotal moments in the life cycle. Given such expectations, non-Catholics inevitably came up short. Sisters nevertheless attempted to create respectful connections across cultural divides, and they believed that they succeeded in doing so. The congregation's constitution stipulated that sisters "shall be very careful to do and say nothing that might be construed as disparagement of native customs and manners." Sister Virginia Flagg explained that religious tolerance was among the ways they expressed this consideration: "We deeply respected them and their religious practices. At the Buddhists', we'd go to the temple and bow and do everything they did."[55] Cognizant of the hostility that many Christian missionaries expressed toward local folkways, Maryknoll encouraged sisters to gain an understanding and appreciation of native cultures. This served Rogers's vision of friendly openness as a missionary tool.

Drawing on egalitarian rhetoric of the "universal brotherhood" of all as children of God, Maryknoll found occasion to criticize racism in the United States. *The Field Afar* highlighted racial tolerance as a Catholic principle and projected a sanguine expectation that piety would eliminate prejudiced behavior. Noting widespread anti-Asian sentiment in the United States, a 1928 editorial described xenophobia as a regrettable but transitory trend. The editorial concluded

that "some Catholics have doubtless been influenced by political or errone-
ous considerations which have made them . . . unfriendly . . . in their attitude
toward foreigners." A later article made a more explicit endorsement of cultural
pluralism—and of the attributes of Asian culture—as it defended West Coast
mission projects against those "who may criticize the activities of the Maryknoll
Sisters on behalf of an alien race." It argued that Maryknoll's work promoted
civic values and helped the assimilation of these aliens. The sisters provided
"great service to their country by establishing interracial understanding and by
training good citizens among a people who even the prejudiced admit are thrifty
and law-abiding."[56]

Maryknoll also made efforts to promote interracialism in the sisters' day-to-
day activities. One sister stationed in California reported to the motherhouse
her encounter with signs that read, "Japs, *keep moving! don't let the sun set on you
here—this is Rose Hill*!" She expressed her disappointment in the prevailing anti-
Asian environment with an affirmation of a Gospel message of equality: "Poor
foolish white folk, who have heard the word of God, and do not keep it!" Her
dismay over white Christians' faithlessness did not shake her racial paternalism
or religious self-righteousness, as she predicted the Catholic triumph over the
infantilized Japanese: "May it not be true of our little brown brethren when they
receive the Faith."[57]

Such gestures did not overcome the chauvinism that underwrote Catholic
mission. The pages of *The Field Afar* decried "superstitious" religious practices far
more than they respectfully recounted them—singling out ancestor totems and
"joss sticks" with no irony, considering their similarity to the icons and incense
of Catholic practice. Despite her profession of love for all people, Rogers excori-
ated the "underlying superstitions" that guided the "pagan" cosmic order while
lecturing on the degradation inherent to those outside of Christianity. She contrasted the "darkness and despair and fearful ignorance" of paganism with the
"light and courage from the knowledge of [God] who gives us the world for our
use."[58] Certain that God wanted communicants of the Catholic Church to shape
the world as they saw best, Maryknoll sisters' sense of service remained entan-
gled in discourses of Western superiority.

Day-to-day practices also betrayed the difficulty of casting off ethno-
centrism. In Maui, a sister described a donation presented by a group of
indigenous Hawaiian church members as an unpleasant culture clash. She
complained of their unwillingness to speak English and "a few more minor
objections—namely—they all dress in white the Sunday they go to Communion, wear loose fitting gowns, straight lines, straight from the shoulders [and]
tall white panama stove pipe hats." The Hawaiian women's disinclination to speak
English and dress in a sober style at church chaffed missionaries, who expected
docility in their spiritual charges. (The irony of fashion critiques dispensed by

sisters who wore full habits in a tropical climate was lost on the diarist.) The sister concluded that in light of the Hawaiian women's generosity, "we've forgiven them for all that," but such petty offenses struck at Maryknoll sisters' expectations of deference.[59]

By World War II, the missionary efforts of US religious congregations had come of age largely because of the personnel and publicity supplied by the Maryknoll Sisters and Fathers. The groups advanced the Vatican's quest to build a world church as well as their own agenda to increase the US share in this work. By the war's end, mission territories had expanded from China, the initial focus of Maryknoll's attention, into other East Asian countries, throughout Latin America, and to a lesser extent to the Pacific Islands and Africa. The sisters had distanced themselves more and more from the cloister tradition, positioning themselves as one of many groups of women defying the postwar call for domesticity. They were a socially engaged community distinguished by expertise and profound moral commitments.

Before World War II, the Maryknoll Sisters' temporal political goals may not have been as well-developed as those of the YWCA, but the congregation's yearning to foster caring personal contact, mutual service, and a faith in a God of love planted seeds of social consciousness that would germinate in the coming decades. This social consciousness caused an evolution in the premises guiding the first two decades of mission: women missionaries as handmaids rather than central actors; charity as a panacea; and the belief that cross-cultural interventions constituted the solution to, rather than the reinscription of, racial and national hierarchies. As the Age of Empire gave way to the American Century, the Cold War years created a dramatic crucible for this evolution.

PART II

FROM THE POPULAR FRONT AND AMERICAN CENTURY TO THE NEW FRONTIER

On the brink of World War II, the Maryknoll Sisters proclaimed themselves handmaids to the Catholic Church's increasingly ambitious foreign mission project. Owing to the sisters' labor, a growing number of educational and medical facilities reached into communities that had not, in the estimation of the ecclesiastical hierarchy, been sufficiently reached by the institutional church: primarily East Asia and enclaves of racial minorities in Hawaii, California, Washington, and New York. Much as the pose of submissive service sat in tension with the instrumentality of the sisters' efforts to establish and sustain mission outposts, the canonical rules that circumscribed the behavior of women religious contrasted the light-hearted Maryknoll spirit cultivated by Maryknoll founder Mary Josephine Rogers. It was a productive tension. Early outreach earned the favor of clerics and bishops, as the institutional church benefited from the women's contributions, and the congregation created a community life that thrived because of women's leadership. Though the sisters had not yet achieved wide visibility, they brought a combination of tradition and innovation to the religious vocation, which positioned them to be well-respected foot soldiers in the incipient American Century. Heeding Henry Luce's 1941 call for Americans "to accept wholeheartedly our duty and our opportunity as the most powerful and vital nation in the world . . . to exert . . . the full impact of our influence,"

Maryknoll assumed the "manifest duty" to be the "Good Samaritan of the entire world."[1] With a well-honed sense of the United States' rightful place as a world power, the Maryknoll Sisters joined the front lines of postwar cultural and geopolitical battles for spheres of influence.

While the sisters established a place for themselves in the Catholic missionary enterprise in the 1920s, the YWCA of the USA reached a peak in terms of membership and institutional presence. It came to maturity as a national center of women's intellectual and professional activities, a cornerstone of community and campus life, and a major player in the realm of women's transnational organizing. This growth of influence was marked by a diversification of programming and membership recruitment, as lines of work emerged to address constituent groups of immigrants, women of color, and wage earners. National Board professionals asserted themselves as leaders in their fields, making a particular mark, as the following chapters describe, in social work and theological and political thought.

When the YWCA formalized a politicized vision of Christian fellowship at its 1920 convention, its leaders came away convinced of the unstoppable momentum of the association movement. The decade's new initiatives held promise for addressing postwar needs. The association followed the US military in establishing a presence in the Philippines and Panama Canal Zone. The wartime housing crisis sparked the YWCA's construction of the Grace Dodge Hotel in Washington, D.C.; after the war, this was converted into a whites-only, income-generating tourist hotel. The National Board successfully expanded the Hollywood Studio Club, which provided housing and club activities to the aspiring actresses who descended on Los Angeles. The number of staff members sent overseas by the Foreign Division went into precipitous decline under drastic funding reductions, but, as portended by the circumstances of US association's involvement with the YWCAs of Japan and Turkey, the reduced budget for secretaries hastened the implementation of a "partnering" model of transnational organizing. The US secretary no longer functioned as the foundation of an overseas association staff but instead was imagined as advisor and coworker in the creation of indigenized YWCAs.

Although the spider web controversy (see chapter 1) brought unfavorable attention to the YWCA, quotidian matters of finances proved to be the most daunting obstacle to face the national organization. In 1926, at the third convention of the decade, the National Board had to acknowledge that while World War I had produced great expectations for association growth, its financial means had not expanded at all. Before long, the Great Depression magnified its financial and administrative woes. The organization cut back on new commitments and economized in established programs. The Foreign Division experienced these effects most dramatically, but cuts affected every level of the organization.

At the same time that association leaders were compelled to scale back some of their aspirations, they advanced an ever-ambitious vision of social change. Traditionally defined religious activities such as worship services receded in prominence in programming, but evolving Christian ideals of fellowship, the abundant life, and the kingdom of God continued to impart spiritual significance to everyday association activities. The YWCA's religious life followed the modernist turn in liberal Protestantism and progressive thought. With the Great Depression, the group's interest in political issues intensified markedly, and in both international and domestic contexts, the National Board prioritized advocacy work.

Though there are few obvious convergences in the organizational histories of the YWCA and Maryknoll Sisters in the first half of the twentieth century, underlying similarities can be detected. Three continuing features stand out as particularly relevant for the story of religious politics narrated in this part of the book: first, the degree to which both groups continued to flourish as single-sex organizations; second, the groups' evolving assertion of institutional ethics that tied interpersonal interaction to broad social transformation; and finally, their abiding commitment to the creation of global community. The principles guiding this outreach remained centered on New Testament ideals of love and fellowship as the root of Christian practice.

The divergences between the groups from the 1920s to the 1960s pose an interesting set of challenges to commonplace periodizations of women's history, which highlight the eras of the suffrage victory and World War II as crests in women's organizing, and write off the 1920s, 1930s, and 1950s as troughs. An examination of the complexity of YWCA and Maryknoll histories provides something more than the well-rehearsed challenge to the wave metaphor of feminism: it gives a glimpse into the ways in which antiradical movements from the 1920s to the 1950s fed off the robustness of women's participation in the public sphere. It also provides a prehistory of the feminist insurgency in religious life that has thus far been identified with the 1970s, demonstrating that a woman-centered faith took center stage in these groups well before it infiltrated denominational life. In doctrinal points, the YWCA's turn toward therapeutic and realist schools of Protestant theology does not resemble the Maryknoll approach to evangelization, in which Catholic dogma and US women's supposed know-how both figured centrally. Still, as both groups developed their distinctive approaches to faith in action through interpretations of agape, they created ethical interests that would converge in their later histories.

The midcentury Cold War context provides an illuminating vantage point on the two organizations because in these decades they occupied markedly different points on a spectrum of political and religious liberalism. Both sought transformations in an age that seemed charged with great danger as well as great possibility, but they set out in opposite directions as they pursued ideals of cooperative global democracy. Professionals overseeing the YWCA's religious activities pushed at the outer edges of liberal Christianity, grafting Social Gospel principles onto the Popular Front, interracial activism, and world fellowship. Consequently, they were visited by the types of antiradical attacks that had accompanied the National Board's first advocacy work. In contrast, Maryknoll leaders connected Catholic triumphalism with the American Century impulse, sending sisters into the mission field as soft power agents of the struggle for the free world. The congregation gained considerable esteem within and beyond US Catholic circles. The institutional differences between the groups also stand out, with the YWCA's flexible religious ethos contrasting with Maryknoll's continued adherence to the framework of religious life as a total institution. Still, the Maryknoll Sisters' exploration of an expanding body of Catholic social teachings and their autonomy in the mission field placed them in a liberal wing of their faith tradition.

The following chapters will examine these different points at which liberal Christian practice met liberal approaches to social change. In the story of the YWCA, the tenacity of a long Red Scare makes clear the obstacles the association faced in advancing an experimental religious politics, but the organization's refusal to capitulate reveals the depth of its commitment to a diverse membership and audacious advocacy interests. In contrast, the Maryknoll Sisters reaped acclaim for their service to ideals of Americanism and Catholicism at the same time that they struggled to face the divides of race, socioeconomic status, and nationality that determined the contours of foreign mission.

4 · "DARE WE BE AS RADICAL AS OUR RELIGION DEMANDS?"

Christian Activism and the Long Red Scare

A pivotal turning point in the religious orientation of the YWCA of the USA occurred at the 1920 national convention, when Helen Gould Shepard made headlines with her sudden, indignant resignation from the National Board. Aghast at the YWCA's support of organized labor and its relaxation of religious requirements for membership, Shepard believed that the association had been commandeered by anti-Christian forces moving toward "the political movements for subversion of our government." She identified the malevolent influence in the YWCA not as socialism itself but rather as the expansive quest for fellowship. The starting point of subversion, she warned, was the "emphasizing of brotherhood instead of the atonement of Jesus Christ and his divinity." As student groups reached out to nonevangelical members and the association endorsed political advocacy in service of the Social Gospel, the YWCA migrated away from its founding evangelical vision.[1] To Shepard, this led away from Christianity itself.

Over the coming decades, critics from outside the organization issued similar warnings. Contingents of reactionaries warned of the "anti-Christian Communistic activities going on in the 'Y's.'" Evolving beyond the Social Gospel, the YWCA's religious life became indecipherable to conservative Christians. How could a Christian organization circulate such "red literature" as song sheets of workers' music or "inter-racial propaganda" that followed the "Party 'line' [of] social intercourse and interbreeding . . . between Negroes and whites"?[2] Detractors argued that the YWCA had clearly been infiltrated.

Activists working through the National Board insisted that these interests were organic Christian developments. In the midst of the Great Depression, one secretary made the provocation, "dare we be as radical as our religion demands?"[3] As unlikely as it may seem, given the organization's attenuated relationship with denominational life, the YWCA of the USA was compelled to navigate waves of antiradical movements because of the strength of the religious resolve of its leaders. Though its religious programming bore little resemblance to that of its early years, the National Board promoted a Christian social consciousness that challenged YWCA members to confront the everyday injustices that touched their communities. The association looked not to tradition but to modernity as the wellspring of its spiritual principles.

By midcentury, the religious ideals advanced by the YWCA of the USA stood near the vanguard of mainstream liberal Protestantism. Despite alarms raised by the far right, the association's public affairs programming endorsed a slate of reforms that overlapped with the Popular Front and gently challenged the orthodoxies of the Cold War. This position in the vanguard was undeniably more evident in rhetoric than it was in action. But even if the National Board did not foment revolution, the tenacity of charges of radicalism indicate the challenges posed by its activist contingent, as does the degree to which YWCA women became an organizing force in Protestant intellectual life and the labor and civil rights movements. The religious discourse developed by the US YWCA in the 1930s and 1940s uniquely articulated a Christianity borne of women's commitment to progressive, and sometimes even leftist, forms of social change.

"A NEW TECHNIQUE FOR FINDING GOD"

Writing in the association's magazine in 1927, Mary Ely Lyman, a former secretary who had become a religious scholar, noted young members' pronounced discontent with organized religion. She found in this a revival spirit, detecting that "in our very restlessness, our dissatisfaction with the old uniformity in worship, there is a hopeful indication that this generation is working out, painfully and gropingly, a new technique for finding God." The association was primed to nurture these impulses, for "new freedom from set forms" was the YWCA's "greatest asset." Similarly, Anna Rice, a mainstay of the National Board, offered a positive evaluation of the "religious situation in the association" in a 1928 board report. She too noted that once-popular activities such as "Bible study and vesper services . . . no longer . . . give to the Association its dynamic for living." She was not discouraged, nor did she propose reasserting evangelical priorities. She encouraged association leaders to answer young women's "increasing hunger for an expression of religious faith and purpose more positive, more rich in content" by presenting a message of Christianity relevant to contemporary life.[4]

Looking back to these decades in her 1950 association history, secretary Mary Sims located changes in the YWCA's religious life in the theological split between fundamentalists and modernists—or, as she termed it, Protestantism's division into "orthodox" and "liberal" camps. Though she conceded that women in the association expressed a "wide gamut of opinion" about this split, she concluded that the liberal turn clearly prevailed in programming, with an emphasis on "individual inquiry into religious matters, directed by no recognized authority, not even that of Christian experiences."[5] Because churches still confined women to "housekeeping activities," Sims noted, the YWCA was well positioned to create opportunities "for constructive religious leadership," which provided "satisfactions [in members'] own personal religious life."[6] The association became a space in which people could question social and religious orthodoxies in ways that were often not possible in churches or other voluntary organizations.

Though the Protestant schisms that came to a head in the 1920s are generally traced to theological disputes, the YWCA's exploratory approaches to spirituality reveal a cluster of influences that pushed liberal Christianity in new directions. The YWCA's religious thinkers were indeed affected by theological developments, incorporating aspects of liberal academic theology such as historical criticism into their publications and programming. More generally, though, the ostensibly secular social sciences fundamentally reshaped the association's spirituality, informing its religious purpose and theories of pastoral practice. The National Board articulated a spirituality aimed at psychological growth and community development. With optimism about emerging avenues of international cooperation and concerns about the dislocations of economic depression and war, it redoubled its language of global Christian citizenship. Though breezy confidence in the power of love to bring about a kingdom of God on earth had been checked by World War I, YWCA thinkers maintained their faith that modernity could bring a more perfect social order.

A social-scientific influence of particular note was the pedagogical methods of John Dewey, which impelled YWCA clubs and conferences away from hierarchically structured activities and toward self-exploration. One secretary used biblical language to describe Dewey, calling him "a prophet of a new day in education [who] led this country out of much ignorance and dogmatism about human nature." Applying "his discoveries about the learning process" to young women's spirituality, the association promoted club meetings as a democratic space where members collectively would ponder the philosophical and social questions affecting their lives, a configuration that bears some resemblance to feminist consciousness-raising circles in the 1970s.[7] To guide members through inquiries into the ethical and spiritual bonds linking humanity, discussion leaders used YWCA handbooks such as secretary Helen Thoburn's *Christian Citizenship for Girls* (1924) and Winnifred Wygal's *The Superb Adventure: Acquiring a Theory of Living* (1934). This search for meaning highlighted faith as an experiential process that permeated everyday life, in contrast to a religiosity centered on church and ritual.

Dewey's pedagogy had a particularly important impact on the specialized constituency groups that were formed as self-governing units in the YWCA membership in the late 1910s. Concluding that "different groups—such as industrial girls, Negroes, and the foreign-born—would not be reached . . . without special efforts related to their own life-experiences and cultural back-grounds," departments and clubs were organized to target those populations, as well as "business and professional" (that is, clerical and white-collar) workers, American Indian women in boarding schools, rural women, and adolescents. Campus groups functioned in a similar manner. This style of organizing served, in Sims's opinion, "to make the Association a true cross-section movement of all kinds of women and girls in the community, the nation and the world." Admin-istered separately from general community association work, constituent groups determined the directions of their own programming and articulated their con-cerns to the larger association.[8]

While the association at large moved slowly on interracial and pro-labor ini-tiatives, the constituent groups gave such issues a prominent place in their agen-das. The interpersonal politics devised in these settings would eventually prove to be the YWCA's most distinctive contribution to the civil rights movement. However, the YWCA's path to becoming a civil rights pioneer continued to be complicated by internal racial inequalities. In 1921, the National Board cre-ated a Council on Colored Work that—like the student and industrial assem-blies, which had become autonomously administered—served as an interface between specialized programming ventures and the national association. But the council was composed of equal numbers of black and white women who were appointed, not elected. It did not have convention privileges or represent members. It gave black secretaries less of a forum to articulate the needs of their constituencies and more of a bureaucratic structure that mediated their input into the national organization. It was a hard-won and frequently unsatisfactory compromise that slowly reshaped the consciousness of white administrators.[9]

Yearnings to heal social divisions nevertheless clearly affected the work of membership groups. The YWCA's approach to social transformation contin-ued to emphasize the application of New Testament ethics in individual rela-tionships as the starting point for structural change. Interrelationships among humanity demanded that Christians could not simultaneously obey the com-mandment of love and perpetuate social stratification. One student delegate to the 1924 national convention reported how conferences that brought together white and African American students made tangible the fundamental bonds connecting humanity. After collective deliberation, the delegates concluded that "world fellowship, to white students, can no longer mean fellowship with the foreign students only, but must mean fellowship with the Negro student at the door. World peace can no longer mean to the colored student a matter of concern only to the white world; the colored student must realize that she must join hands with the rest of the world to bring peace about." The constituency groups were most responsible for devising activities that brought women of diverse circumstances into closer contact. The national staff asserted that such interactions struck at the heart of social problems: "the greatest need of the world to-day is for direct contact and understanding between similar groups"—groups such as the ones "all bound together in our national membership." Providing occasions for this direct contact "could be the best contribution [the YWCA] can make to society."[10]

While the democratizing impulse of Deweyan pedagogy marked one important area in which social science reconfigured the meaning of fellowship, the "New Psychology" of psychodynamic development contributed a therapeutic ethos that came to suffuse the association's religious vocabulary. Liberal Protestantism at large handily incorporated the "therapeutic gospel" of psychological fulfillment that took hold in the 1920s. Concerned with adjustment, maturity, and socialization, this popular psychological discourse emphasized "individual well-being" as a foundation for "social stability."[11] Supplanting an older language of moral injunctions and standards of virtue, the therapeutic gospel provided religious thinkers with modern terms to describe the task of building Christian character. YWCA authors translated long-standing categories of Christian behavior such as will, character, and virtue into Freudian and psychodynamic terminology. With this gloss, the Gospel message of Jesus would continue to provide, according to a National Board convention report, an "infinitely attractive" model for young women "seeking for help on the meaning of life."[12]

The promise of "fullness of life" had once guided the YWCA's evangelical quest to win allegiance to Jesus, and it later served as a reference point for the association's Social Gospel efforts to improve the material conditions of female workers' lives. In the 1920s, YWCA thinkers put a therapeutic connotation on Jesus's injunction to live life abundantly, portraying abundance as the realization of "personality and a fair chance for self-fulfillment for every member of the community." Personality was a watchword throughout the association as it was in the field of psychology.[13] In the YWCA magazine, National Board secretary Margaret Burton elaborated the religious dimensions of the development of well-adjusted personality. The abundant life for "women everywhere . . . can be found only as, person by person, human capacities for achievement are released by Jesus Christ." She explained that "personality is not the whole body, nor the mind, nor the spirit, but the entire person," in whom these spheres were necessarily interdependent. The integrated personality, "wholeness," necessarily had a spiritual element.[14]

As much as therapeutics and the language of personality could promote a self-involved individualism, the association's religious texts in the 1920s and 1930s foregrounded the ethical dimensions of personal development. In contrast to critical accounts of therapeutic culture that underscore tendencies toward complacency and narcissism, YWCA thinkers argued that social consciousness played a pivotal part in personal fulfillment, and they asserted that boundary-crossing fellowship was the measure of individual maturity and a healthy community.[15] Therapeutic religion was another dimension of the YWCA's activist discourse. In this vein, in the mid-1920s the Division of Education and Research identified club life as a source of social ethics. YWCA settings promoted the "development of personality," which enabled "young women . . . to adapt themselves to their social environment, to appreciate the world in which they live, and to be intelligent and creative citizens in the social order of their day."[16] Sketched out in this method was a progression from personal growth through small-group socialization to a place of maturity in the assumption of social responsibility. In "conferences large and small, program activities as varied as the women, [and] committee groups concerned with fulfilling the historic purpose of the association," members discovered "the present day significance of the YWCA as a nation-wide act of fellowship in discovering the meaning of life." Religion remained crucial to this quest as it took "on a meaning as a way of life in [YWCA] fellowship—a meaning much more creative than that of the old word 'tolerance.'" Fellowship that went beyond the tolerance of difference was based on honoring "the need of women to find full, free, and understanding adjustment" to modern conditions.[17]

The therapeutic ethos surfaced in multiple ways beyond conference and club gatherings. Jane Bellows, a physical educator at the association, could point to the religious benefits of physical fitness, the gateway to the "efficient functioning of the whole personality," when she described stretching exercises designed to "attain efficiency in mental, social, and spiritual life."[18] A "service of worship to be used at the initial meetings of a board of directors" would issue a charge to the assembled volunteer leaders "to turn to account the inherent worth of every person, her capacity to think, to work, to contribute to the common life."[19] Programming materials emphasized that the process of personal development had to be undertaken in cognizance of women's differing needs, and it could be achieved only through the mutual respect and affection mandated in the Gospels.

If the ideological foundations of the activist religion of the YWCA rested largely on Protestant therapeutics, National Board professionals established pragmatic architecture for outreach through their pioneering contributions to the field of social work. This extended to the founding of a university-level program. In partnership with the YWCA of India, Burma, and Ceylon, the YWCA of the USA had a hand in creating what would eventually become the University of Delhi's School for Social Work. In the late 1940s, the US YWCA provided funding and technical assistance to found the National YWCA School of Social Work in Delhi. The school had an explicitly Christian curriculum of humanitarian service, and its first students pledged to serve "my countrymen with all my heart, with all my mind and with all my might, realising the need of each one for social security and those opportunities which build for the good life." Resonating with the optimism of the Indian national independence movement, this affirmation of the Christian abundant life announced an intention to assist the "depressed, the handicapped and the needy [with no distinction] as to creed or colour or position of people in any personal or professional relationship."[20] Paying particular attention to issues of labor, health, and community cooperation, the school's inclusive vision of the "welfare needs of the New India" was closely influenced by the methodology of the US association. Dorothy Height, a former social worker and stalwart US YWCA executive, served on the faculty in the early 1950s. Demonstrating the YWCA's fondness for pageantry, Height introduced educational dramatic productions to social work students as they led health demonstrations in outlying villages. She worked in collaboration with Indira Gandhi, who was then chair of the Indian YWCA Committee on Volunteer Training. Despite its strongly Christian character, the Indian association piqued Gandhi's interest in advancing humanitarian civic service in the early years of independence. According to Height, Gandhi valued "what could be learned from [the] dedication to human service and [Christians'] devotion to each other."[21]

Based on their experience in advising constituent groups, US YWCA secretaries supplied a more diffuse, but highly instrumental, innovation to the social work field as they devised an approach to individual and community development that came to be called group work. The YWCA's social work theorists saw association activities as a way to foster community values, and they tied the search for Christian fellowship to a civic project of disseminating democratic values in small-group settings. Through group work, the YWCA and other volunteer agencies could create the foundations for a moral social order on a national scale. In the 1930s and 1940s, this body of thought gained currency in the wider social work profession, providing a collective-oriented alternative to the casework model of community intervention.

As a secretary employed by the National Board for roughly a decade, and later as a professor of group work at Case Western University's School of Applied Social Science, Grace Coyle played a central role in the creation of group work theory. Based on her tenure with the YWCA's employed women's clubs, she centered group work around the "growth and adjustment of the individual," which was the springboard to "social responsibility for the making of citizens." Group work, she argued, could stimulate "the production in individuals of those attitudes and accomplishments which will contribute to the kind of society we desire." This process of personal development was interwoven with the search for religious meaning. In an address to the 1934 YWCA national convention, she mused: "God is sometimes defined as the movement throughout the universe for justice, righteousness, love. Many of us who seek the meaning of life today cannot be satisfied until we see our own lives in the setting of some such cosmic process."[22] Her approach also had links to a developing antifascist movement. Since "group pressures" exerted a controlling force on political life, group settings could teach skills like "compromise, debate, self-government, resistance to illegitimate authority, and democratic leadership," according to the social work historians Janice Andrews and Michael Reisch.[23] These skills might answer the threats to democracy surfacing in US communities and around the globe. The group work process centered on fostering constructive approaches to conflict, mutual respect, and collective commitments—the indispensable skills of a functioning democracy.

With group work, club life created a forum in which the culture of therapeutics converged with a politicized interpretation of Christian fellowship. The personal language of friendship across barriers was the metaphor predominantly used to explain the obligations and mechanisms of social Christianity. YWCA authors invoked the "Kingdom of Friendly Citizens," a reworking of the kingdom of God on earth. This described a law of love that straddled the private and public spheres, emphasizing both civic responsibilities and caring, emotional connections.[24] In addition, group work added a civic spin to small gatherings, directing groups toward action on contemporary social issues. In the YWCA, this usually meant dramatic productions and letters to the editor, not sit-down strikes and "don't buy where you can't work" campaigns. But as Coyle argued, "when a club of business girls has discussed unemployment, studied a bill before the state legislature and taken action on it, the group has learned how to participate in our society." In recognition that cultural life could not "avoid the great molten stream of social discontent and social injustice," group work also involved the recreational side of club activities. "Music, dramatics, dancing, writing, and painting" could be used to constructively express the "tragic experiences of modern youth," Coyle pointed out.[25] To such effect, industrial workers expressed their hopes for an empowered future by singing the "Internationale" at conferences, while a public affairs committee educated audiences about world governance by performing skits from the YWCA's tract "Uncle Sam at Geneva: The United States and the League of Nations." Perhaps young Japanese American women tried to make sense of their incarceration in World War II internment camps using these materials as they re-formed the YWCA clubs that had been such a lively part of community life back home.[26]

FIGURE 4.1. "'Forget-Me-Nots' Junior Girl Reserves installation." From an unknown YWCA internment camp project, Manzanar, California, undated. Credit: Sophia Smith Collection, Smith College

The YWCA encouraged members to put fellowship into motion with modest, personal gestures. For example, it conducted a successful fund-raising campaign in 1923 for earthquake-devastated Japan, and although this money was earmarked to rebuild the YWCA itself, US women understood the effort as a sign of "good-will much appreciated at the time the Japanese Exclusion Bill was passed."[27] In 1920, the student contingent pledged to combat prejudice by making their "attitude toward the foreign students . . . one of real sisterhood" and taking "advantage of what they have to give us in personal friendship." The YWCA magazine likewise encouraged foreign-born students to give "talks about [their] homelands" in clubs to close geographic distances and promote mutual understanding. When interpersonal contact was not possible, a broadly conceived friendship could be approached in other ways. "True world fellowship," the article instructed association members, meant that "we must love the girls of other lands, and to love them, we must know and understand them." How was that possible when none of these girls were on hand? *Imagination.* World friendship was frequently expressed through performances of the assumed experience of the foreigner, conveyed in tableaux with "realistic scenery . . . created from ordinary wrapping paper," costume parties, ethnic meals, and plays.[28] YWCA women might sing spirituals as a gesture of affinity with African

American culture, stage a folk dance in national costume to walk in the shoes of Eastern European women, or read about American Indian *Women of Trail and Wigwam* in a 1930 Womans Press publication.

The national organization had resources other than imagination to bring members together across geographic and social distances. The popular YWCA camps and conferences offered venues for staging personal, therapeutic attempts at social change, as secretaries encouraged participants to establish solidarities built on Christian fellowship. An interracial gathering of industrial workers examined "the kinship of labor" from the perspective of caring for one's neighbor. The group resolved "to make every girl conscious of the fact that every girl is her neighbor and no girl can be overworked, underpaid, segregated and unemployed without affecting every other industrial woman." The announcement for the 1922 student assembly similarly explained its pacifist, internationalist agenda as an outgrowth of the interpersonal bonds of Christianity. The event would cultivate "our relationship to the students of the world, that we may stand together in a fellowship for righteousness and justice and peace in the earth."[29]

YWCA groups explored several permutations of these cooperative relationships in club life, and in hosting joint conferences of student and industrial members, it continued to promote cross-class coalition in the women's labor movement. The YWCA publicized, lent staff to, and recruited participants for the pioneering summer schools for workers conducted at Bryn Mawr College and the University of Wisconsin. The National Board report of 1926 noted the success of its efforts: "More than half of the students at the Bryn Mawr Summer School in 1924 . . . were connected with the [YWCA]." Worker-students had not only opportunities for education but also had a space for creative expression, with the *Womans Press* publishing their poems and essays. In "student-in-industry" projects conducted in community settings, interracial groups of students took an experimental approach to understanding the lives of factory workers. They took jobs where they experienced layoffs and unhealthy working conditions, and they learned the skills necessary to maintain employment.[30]

Interracial club programs and conferences, which began to be conducted in the 1920s among black and white women of the student and worker contingents, posed unique difficulties and unique rewards. An interracial group might not have been able to form under everyday circumstances where racial lines were sharply drawn, but YWCA clubs and assemblies supplied a specially demarcated space for questioning and experimentation. Racial divisions permeated everyday moments of conference and program life, but the YWCA's interracial programming provided a temporary, tentative challenge to the extant racial order. Amid a wider culture of segregation, the association offered young women opportunities to explore progressive principles of integration.

Dorothea Browder notes the significance of the small-scale encounters initiated by the YWCA's Industrial Division, which "provided rare spaces and communication lines that facilitated working women's interracial organizing" in a nation and an organization that were racially segregated. Activist secretaries and group leaders focused activities on encouraging solidarity among working-class white, black, and immigrant women. The Student Division joined industrial members in highlighting the association's potential for promoting interracial and interethnic harmony in recognition of both the "growing desire of colored students to share in all activities [and] the contradiction between student standards of action and the principles of Christ as embodied in our purpose"—the pursuit of the abundant life and the kingdom of God.[31]

Students' explicitly interracial activities consisted of personal encounters engineered to bring about racial rapprochement. "We began with the active participation by colored students in . . . the councils . . . and commissions of the national movement," noted a 1924 report from the Student Division. White and black secretaries together visited "mixed campuses . . . in the interest of interracial understanding," and they arranged discussions among "students from white and colored colleges." In raising awareness of racial issues, the division concluded that "our movement is touching one of the most important American problems and a question greater than America." It portrayed its interventions as part of an international mission, designating this pursuit a religious quest "to find Christ's way for all races."[32]

In the interracial efforts initiated by the constituent groups, activist principles of religion were explored most directly within rather than beyond the association. That is, members discussed and studied questions of interracial relations and international fellowship in clubs with greater frequency than they posed challenges to their communities. Browder recounts a particularly startling example of white members' reluctance to act on the interracial agenda: an interracial group ventured out from a YWCA conference to a dance hall in town, where "white members were unduly surprised or did not seem sufficiently concerned when their African American companions were refused admission."[33]

Interracial shared meals, physical proximity, and discussion of sensitive topics generated discomfort as well as inspiration. Not surprisingly, the association emphasized the latter in reports, interpreting the encounters as momentous. In an account of "unity in diversity," for instance, the National Board lauded the simple face-to-face interactions of conferences where "colored secretaries and girls" created a "fellowship incidental to the togetherness [which] has broken down the most deep-rooted barriers of racial prejudice." The secretaries privately mulled over the frustrations of the less-than-transformative, truculent paternalism and racial hierarchy that belied the National Board's confident proclamations of harmony.[34]

Although National Board advocates of interracialism sought to bring issues of racial prejudice home to the association, the organization frequently reinforced segregation in its practices. "If you were an educated Negro, Japanese, or Jew," the YWCA's magazine asked students, "how would you feel about the discrimination against your race in educational opportunity? In housing?" Only pages away, in an announcement for summer conferences, the magazine listed several segregated sessions.[35] The successful Grace Dodge Hotel in the District of Columbia remained exclusively for the use of white customers at least through the mid-1940s, though secretary Lucy Carner complained that the YWCA "was put in an embarrassing position before the other social agencies" when it hosted the National Conference of Social Work at the whites-only facility in 1935.[36]

The YWCA regularly commended itself for making "progress toward a world more decent for human beings to live" and promoting fellowship between "women and girls of different backgrounds, races, nationalities, and religions." It was loath to hasten the pace of this progress. During the 1930s, the National Board took steps toward remedying the administrative structures that placed black YWCA branches in subordinate positions to white associations. It also occasionally acknowledged that the segregation of YWCA facilities contradicted its much-vaunted endorsement of interracial fellowship. But it took years of pressure to bring these questions to the forefront. This culminated in the 1946 "Interracial Charter," which committed the organization to making "the inclusion of Negro women and girls in the mainstream of association life . . . a conscious goal." Association staff then made a more deliberate effort to integrate YWCAs. From these foundations, Dorothy Height came to maturity as a civil rights leader producing programming and conducting fieldwork to raise antiracist consciousness in local associations. Still, twenty-one years after the charter was adopted, a handful of community associations in the Deep South remained segregated. Only under the impetus of the 1964 Civil Rights Act did the National Board finally disaffiliate noncompliant associations.[37]

Such ambivalences were not as evident in the advocacy work administered by the National Board's Public Affairs Committee, which embraced the 1920 convention charge to "use its resources and influence to help secure such legislation as shall promote the welfare of young women." The membership as a whole may not have united behind the committee's agenda, with some local associations airing doubts about whether the association, "taking gifts of money from the public in general, had a right to act on controversial matters in the field of politics."[38] The national leadership, however, continued to insist that a collective Christian civic mentality was essential to association life. A number of public affairs mobilizations aroused significant interest among members, particularly peace initiatives and maternal health efforts. While some associations reported scant member interest in political issues, a dedicated core of National Board secretaries and local leaders ensured that public affairs retained a central place in programming. They did this by distributing thoroughly researched informational packets on impending legislation and urging members to petition, vote, and raise public awareness. The National Board and national conventions regularly issued statements on policy issues. In addition, public affairs secretaries networked with representatives of advocacy organizations, and the association engaged the services of a Washington lobbyist.

The National Board's vision of world fellowship extended beyond the on-the-ground work of the Foreign Division. When extraterritorial rights, which gave foreign settlers exemptions from local laws, became a flashpoint of the Chinese revolution in the mid-1920s, the National Board made a formal anti-imperialist gesture by signing over ownership of its real estate in China to the Chinese YWCA. Foreign Division secretaries stationed in China attempted to renounce their extraterritorial privileges before the US State Department.[39] Joining other women's organizations seeking to turn the tide against militarism, the US YWCA looked to the intergovernmental organizations established by the Treaty of Versailles as vehicles for achieving global unity. In the 1920s, it rallied behind the pacifist cause. "Belief in the achievement of a world at peace is implicit in the faith and purpose of the YWCA," the association's president, Emma Bailey Speer, wrote to the US Senate Foreign Relations Committee in 1924. Referring to the World Court, Speer impressed on the committee the widespread sentiment that the country needed to stand behind this "practical step toward peace. . . . No other subject in our legislative study program, with the possible exception of the Child Labor Amendment, has been of such universal interest among our six hundred thousand members." Furthermore, from "its own experiences in cooperation with peoples of other nations," the YWCA had a valuable perspective on the promise of "international cooperation through governmental agencies."[40]

Like Speer, Lucy Randolph Mason, a secretary who would become one of the most prominent labor activists in the South, interpreted the 1924 YWCA convention's endorsement of the League of Nations as a clear application of the Gospels. Mason suggested that the spirit of Jesus's caring ministry could best be captured in the cooperative compact of the League: "We believe in a God of love and of goodness . . . , and we also believe that a practical solution of the troubles of mankind is to be found by making the way of Jesus a reality."[41] YWCA policy endorsements were frequently at odds with the priorities of those holding political office. Still, the membership expressed its collective support of world peace and international governance initiatives. Setbacks such as the US failure to participate in the League of Nations and the World Court, despite the flood of telegrams and petitions members sent to legislators, could be weighed against victories such as the symbolic commitment of the Kellogg-Briand pact outlawing war.

In lending practical support to the League of Nations, the YWCA became part of the emerging network of international nongovernmental organizations. The World's YWCA was a corresponding member of the League's Advisory Committee on Social Questions, and the International Labor Organization (ILO) provided a productive forum for national associations to pursue women's labor issues. The ILO built collaborative relationships with international women's groups, much like those that developed between the Women's Bureau of the US Department of Labor and US women's organizations. Showing a receptiveness to women's labor reform that was lacking in many unions and national governments, the ILO solicited the participation of women's groups, asserting that both it and they stood "to gain considerably by the constant interchange of information and pooling of experience, as well as by the cultivation of close personal relations between their representatives." Women's groups offered their support to the ILO in a variety of contexts, such as carrying out investigations and providing an attentive audience for ILO officials. When the ILO enlisted the YWCA to report on "the intimate knowledge of industrial conditions which the association has through its industrial members," the World's YWCA gave national associations the task of collecting employment data.[42] Responding to calls for equal pay, the minimum wage, and the abolition of child labor, YWCAs in the United States and several other countries lobbied for the adoption of ILO labor standards.

Over the course of the 1930s, the National Board's Public Affairs Committee and convention assemblies came to see an ever-widening array of political issues as relevant to the YWCA. The board supported social welfare measures that went beyond those of the New Deal. It vigorously criticized free market capitalism, even boldly calling for income redistribution in a 1936 convention resolution supporting "the adjustment of the economic life of our nation as shall make for a more just distribution of wealth in the interests of all people." National conventions consistently presented liberal messages in public statements on controversial issues, ranging from race to sex and from civil liberties to the "special problems of youth." The 1934 convention issued a statement supporting the medical dissemination of birth control information just as Margaret Sanger's legal challenge to federal contraception prohibitions gained momentum. The regular "Citizenship and Legislation" column of the association's magazine kept members apprised of the antilynching campaign, publicizing the work of the Association of Southern Women for the Prevention of Lynching and the National Association for the Advancement of Colored People alike.[43]

Still, as much as the US YWCA trumpeted its social consciousness, its political gestures were circumscribed by its cautiousness as a majority-white, largely middle-class organization and by the prejudices of the individuals within it. YWCA assemblies affirmed bold legislative agendas, but as Anne Firor Scott explains, "a gap developed between . . . what the most articulate leaders wanted to accomplish and what timid members of local groups were willing to undertake."[44] This was evident in the slow progress on racial integration and in the association's tepid reaction to Nazi Germany. In particular, the US YWCA's refusal to protest Jewish persecution revealed that despite its flexibility in places like Turkey, creedal allegiances still shaped its political advocacy.

Joining the "large body of decent and normally considerate people" whom the historian David Wyman argues were "predisposed to not care . . . whether the government did anything to help save" Europeans Jews, the National Board evaded a call to respond to Third Reich policy.[45] From 1933 onward, it received repeated requests from the National Council of Jewish Women (NCJW) to denounce publicly the turn of events in Germany. Rather than issuing one of the political resolutions that hardly made for a radical entry into international politics, YWCA leadership temporized. When US YWCA executive secretary Henrietta Roelofs explained to Mary Schonberg, executive secretary of the NCJW, that a statement of protest from the US association could bring reprisals against the German YWCA, Schonberg questioned the association's diffidence. She asked whether association allegiances "ought not to prevent the Y's in the other important countries . . . and even in this country from expressing its opposition to racial discrimination." She added, "your organization has certainly had a long and distinguished record in that direction." Roelofs referred Schonberg's repeated requests to various committees, which promised to give "the matter serious consideration." Internal correspondence revealed staff ambivalence over addressing anti-Semitic violence. Committees resisted action under the pretext that the "dangers of a public pronouncement were very great unless the statement could be very carefully worded." They cited the growth of anti-Semitism in the United States, where associations reported "many incidents [in which] racial intolerance in their own communities was growing." YWCA women did not want "to run the risk of doing something which would fail of being just right."[46] Whether this risk meant fear of stirring up a backlash or a reluctance to have the YWCA so closely associated with Jewish issues is unclear.

Sentiments that Roelofs expressed privately suggested a "passive anti-Semitism," which characterized the broader American response to the Holocaust. Referring to a proposal to endorse giving asylum to German political refugees, she questioned quality of their character. She wondered "whether the United States can absorb these people—whether they are the type that we want to have come over here." It took the Anschluss in early 1938 to prompt the National Board to issue an anodyne resolution in support of refugee asylum that did not explicitly name Jewish persecution. Its refusal to respond to the NCJW—or even to sign Carrie Chapman Catt's "Protest Committee of Non-Jewish Women against the Persecution of the Jews in Germany" petition (which boasted that "among the 5000 signers of this petition, there is no Jewess")—made clear that Christians still held a privileged position in the YWCA's vision of a better world.[47]

RELIGION IN YEARS OF CRISIS: SIN, STRUGGLE, AND THE REDEMPTIVE POWER OF LOVE

The atmosphere of crisis in the 1930s could not help complicating therapeutic perspectives on personal development and self-realization. The challenges of the Great Depression intensified the political thrust of YWCA religious thought, and ideas generated in YWCA settings were significant enough (to some, dangerous enough) to subject the organization to attacks that would prove to be the most debilitating of its several brushes with antiradical agitation. This scare did not abate until the civil rights movement lent liberal religion new legitimacy. The resolve with which the National Board stood behind its activist religion testified to the significance of women's voluntary clubs as vehicles for resisting anticommunist suppression of dissent.[48]

The religious discourses circulating in the YWCA in the 1930s indicate a transition in Protestant thought that brought together the lingering influence of the Social Gospel with Protestant therapeutics and the revolution-minded ethos of the Popular Front. The latter theme had roots in the upstart Christian realist movement in Protestant theology, which aimed at roiling the waters of ineffectual liberalism amid the exigencies of the Great Depression. Christian realism inspired a new sense of urgency among progressive activists employed by the National Board. These activists called for commitments that went beyond the comfort zone of mainstream Protestantism, but as the architects of the YWCA's religious life as well as the targets of right-wing attack, the relatively small realist contingent had a disproportionate impact in association life.

Christian realism, a movement associated with Reinhold Niebuhr, Paul Tillich, and their colleagues at Union Theological Seminary, straddled a fissure running between liberal and radical Protestantism in the 1930s. Formed in reaction to the Social Gospel's Whiggish confidence in nonconfrontational social change, realist theology focused on the intractability of humanity's sinfulness and the necessity for conflict to bring society in line with the Gospel. In its more radical guises, realism considered the possibilities—even the likelihood—of Marxist proletarian revolution. Less inflammatory but still controversial realist theologians took as axiomatic the need for socialist reform.[49]

Scholars treat Christian realism as equivalent to the academic theology of the men of Union Theological Seminary, but two National Board secretaries had equally important roles, particularly in making these ideas accessible to popular audiences. Winnifred Wygal and Rose Terlin came in on the ground floor of realism. They both studied under Niebuhr at Union, and they were founding members of his Fellowship of Socialist Christians (FSC), established in 1931. The FSC's quarterly journal *Radical Religion*—whose masthead pledged devotion "to Christianity and radical social change"—explored various avenues for advancing realist principles. Wygal and Terlin had posts on the FSC's executive committee and the editorial board of *Radical Religion* for much of the organization's twenty-five-year existence. Wygal helped organize the FSC conferences that, with the magazine, were the organization's primary activities. In short, Wygal and Terlin performed many crucial behind-the-scenes tasks that enabled Niebuhr to make *Radical Religion* "his personal megaphone."[50]

Wygal and Terlin were the National Board's foremost religious thinkers in the 1930s and 1940s, and though they the smoothed out the rough edges of revolutionary sentiment, they integrated realist innovations into their writings and group work efforts. Wygal's publications expanded the association's psychological vocabulary as she drew links among personal fulfillment, Christian fellowship, and social justice. She touched on themes of liberation and self-realization that foreshadowed theological and psychological thought of subsequent generations. Tending more toward concrete terms of social reform, Terlin insisted that a demanding Christian ethics serve as a force of political change.

During her lengthy YWCA tenure, Wygal worked primarily as an author and advisor. In 1913, shortly after her graduation from Missouri's Drury College, she began her career as a student secretary. She ascended through the ranks of the Student Division, then had charge of religious programming from 1934 to 1944. Drawing on her advanced training in ethics at Union and in sociology at Columbia University, Wygal's writings advocated the psychological and social benefits of immersion in the higher purposes of God. Infusing the therapeutic ethos of YWCA religion with the critical edge of realism, she found that the lessons of the Gospel were far from irrelevant in troubled times. The Gospel message, she argued, gave weight to secular theories of psychology. "Modern psychologists have begun to catch up with [the] insight of Jesus," she wrote. What psychologists "called . . . consciousness, freedom, maturity, clarification, integration, socialization of the individual" echoed Jesus's promise of abundant life.[51] Wygal may have parted ways with modern psychologists when she argued that transcendent fulfillment was won through submission to God's will.

Wygal's description of the fullness of life affirmed that the principle of Christian love, expressed through the reciprocal bonds of fellowship, was at the center of a moral social order. Eschewing obsessions with gender norms that predominated in psychological thought, Wygal emphasized the diverse spheres of a woman's life. Religion could not be kept apart from everyday interactions: "It is in the way one lives in one's family, deals with friends in the sorority house, works in the physics laboratory, participates in the political and economic struggles of America today, faces insecurity in the form of low wages or unemployment, views industrial standards and racial tensions across the United States." Navigating this "inter-relatedness of life" called for a value system that took account of the "inner relationship between oneself and God and oneself and other men." Placing God's will at the center of that relationship, which demanded selfless generosity and care, opened the path to fulfillment. It made it "possible to be so realized, so open to adventure, so secure in one's relationship to the best one can imagine" that personal and social constraints "can change or disappear." Quoting a popular hymn, Wygal identified the Gospel message as one of liberation: "'Make me a captive, Lord, and then I shall be free.'"[52]

In Wygal's scheme, as in other examples of YWCA therapeutic culture, fellowship could not be a solipsistic exercise; instead, it followed from the renunciation of self-interest. Moreover, caring for one's neighbors meant confronting the conditions that hampered the formation of a Christian social order. Identifying the psychological "longing for integrity, wholeness," Wygal located the "vital religion" that answered these longings in a "social philosophy" that addressed injustice.[53] Individual-oriented doctrine—"personal religion"—did not apprehend God's living presence in human relationships. To bear witness to God's presence on earth, she advised YWCA audiences to pay attention to activist efforts: "whenever you see a person or a group that behaves with any degree of love and justice, there you see evidence of God struggling against human interest [and] greed." She encouraged solidarity, instructing them to "jump into the struggle . . . , give yourself to creating more love and justice and freedom." Her examples of the Christian struggle were a familiar litany to YWCA audiences: "men and women who work intelligently for world peace, or better labor laws . . . , or right race relations."[54]

In keeping with a therapeutic emphasis, such activities had social significance, but they also wrought personal transformations. Wygal advised the unemployed "if you can't get a job," join others and "see what a group of intelligent young citizens can do." And she encouraged the demoralized to "think about those whose sufferings are far greater than your own. . . . Learn to care deeply about them." She offered a YWCA-style solution to racial and ethnic strife, proposing that friendly contacts could overcome social barriers: "Develop your own powers of brotherhood by . . . perhaps knowing some of the Polish girls at the mill, or really knowing the Negroes."[55] Though these suggestions constituted a facile response to xenophobia and racism, Wygal and other religious thinkers urged activist outreach as a consequence of Christian commitment. Therapeutic religion in the YWCA was not a religion of self-satisfaction, even if it might be one of self-realization.

The realist influence on religious thought prompted a new concern about sinfulness embedded in the social order, in this case the persistence of the structural inequalities. When Wygal offered a definition of sin, she reiterated a realist interpretation of social sin: "At root there is but one sin. . . . Sin is devotion to self. Sin is putting oneself in the center instead of putting God . . . in the center of one's life."[56] The interconnected realms of sin moved from the internal, in which sin "is any act or attitude that closes the channel of communication between oneself and God or between oneself and one's fellow men," to the interpersonal and structural, in which sin occurs through the "exploitation of people, using them as if they were . . . objects rather than subjects, free moral beings of purpose and dignity." Ultimately, sin became political, a dedication to self "rather than devotion to the highest good for oneself and for all men—God, love, and justice." "One's country, or the white race, or, on the individual level, business success and even a happy marriage, viewed as ends in themselves" represented social forms in which humanity projected its selfish nature over the will of God, creating conditions of complacency and injustice.[57]

While Wygal added a realist influence to therapeutic Christianity, a realist approach to economics characterized Rose Terlin's writings. After graduate work in economics at the University of California, Berkeley, and ethics at Union, Terlin began her employment with the National Board in 1934 as the Student Division's economic secretary. In addition to her duties with the FSC and the Student Division, she served as a secretary of social and economic studies for the World Christian Student Federation and was employed by the World's YWCA in the 1940s. Through her unapologetic indictments of economic injustice, Terlin was the most exacting of the YWCA's religious thinkers, and she advocated for social planning and the redistribution of wealth—two themes that fit comfortably in the mainstream of Depression-era thought but became highly suspect as the 1930s wore on. Terlin framed her economic analyses not in terms of class struggle but with reference to Christian ethics. For her, the alienation of labor, a central tenet of Marxist thought, violated God's provision of the "fruits of the earth" to meet the needs of "every living creature." Labor and production materials were not commodities, they were divine gifts. She trod lightly around the language of class, criticizing not the "individuals who are on the ownership end of our economic stick" but rather the "*organization* of our economic life." The exploitive desecration of God's gifts challenged Christians to "be as radical as our religion demands."[58]

Terlin's work supplied both economic education and moral exhortation. With a desire to provoke "intelligent, democratic change," she castigated Christians who, despite the demands of God's law of love, behaved no differently than non-Christians in perpetuating inequality and debasement. She tacitly praised the insights of communism, asking "why is it that the voices that cry out in indignation at the sufferings of the whole basis of our senseless economic 'order' are so rarely Christian voices?"[59] She did not urge YWCA women to adopt Marxist determinism, but she called for a thorough repudiation of the economic status quo.

In contrast to visions of revolution that circulated among realist theologians, YWCA thinkers maintained that democratic governance in the association and the nation could be wielded effectively in the struggle against a sinful society. As a long-term member of the Public Affairs Committee, Terlin viewed civic participation as a necessary outgrowth of Christian ethics. Public affairs, she declared, was "not a political task but a religious one—the inevitable expression of a Christian faith."[60] The YWCA's Christian purpose was connected to structural reforms that could "create the kind of economic conditions, social institutions and political patterns that make it impossible for human life to be degraded by causes beyond the individual's control." She listed the targets of such reforms: the industrial worker "feeding his own life into the machine"; African Americans, who "constitute . . . a separate nation, stunted, stripped and held captive within this nation, devoid of . . . human rights"; Jewish people, "hounded from land to land, pursued by a ruthless violence . . . dumped in the grim . . . wastes of Poland"; as well as the "middle-class Christian . . . complacent before his own meager success."[61]

In her writings and public affairs leadership, Terlin addressed areas of traditional YWCA interest but challenged members to pursue more audacious solutions. While national convention assemblies expressed support of the League of Nations, Terlin called for binding world governance. The US YWCA promoted progressive race relations; Terlin demanded civil rights legislation. The National Board encouraged Americans to make gestures for world friendship; Terlin asked them to support refugee settlement.

Given such provocations, it is hardly surprising that the reactionaries who had set their sights on the YWCA during the 1924 spider web controversy continued to attack the association. Its socially conscious approach to recreation prompted Elizabeth Dilling to count the YWCA among the "more than 460 Communist, Anarchist, Socialist, IWW, or Radical-Pacifist controlled or infiltrated organizations" profiled in a 1935 exposé of a "Communist-Socialist" world conspiracy titled *Red Network: A "Who's Who" and Handbook of Radicalism for Patriots*. Dilling, whom the historian Glen Jeansonne calls "the most important woman to emerge on the far right in the 1930s," cataloged 1,300 Communist infiltrators controlling liberal and left-wing organizations in a self-published update of the spider web of subversive organizations. Dilling listed groups that ranged from the Federal Council of Churches and League of Women Voters to the Workers Philatelic Society and League for Industrial Democracy. Despite Dilling's position on the radical fringe, her accusations received considerable exposure through manufacturers' organizations and patriot groups.[62]

Dilling warned that "four horsemen, Atheism, Immorality, Class Hatred, and Pacifism-for-the-sake-of-Red-revolution" led the charge of communist conspiracy, and liberal Christian organizations furthered the advance of all four. YWCA sing-alongs prompted Dilling to dispute whether the "'C' in YWCA . . . stands for 'Christian,' not 'Communist.'" She deemed the musical selections of an industrial workers' conference to be songs of "class-hate," citing the labor anthems "Solidarity Forever" and the "Internationale." With disdain, she reported that "two Negro spirituals [were] the *only* songs that mention . . . 'God,'" signaling that religious music from the African American tradition registered a lesser Christianity.[63]

Reflecting the YWCA's commitment to advocacy and resistance to the pressures of red baiting, Theresa Paist, the National Board president, responded to Dilling's charges by distributing a communiqué to local associations that explained why a "Christian Association . . . inevitably must be concerned with social and economic issues." These issues, she maintained, were crucial to fulfilling the YWCA's mission "to build a fellowship of women and girls devoted to the task of realizing in our common life those ideals of personal and social living to which we are committed by our faith as Christians." Such commitment drove the "fearless progress" that had been made by the association, Paist insisted, and she urged local groups to renew their efforts to educate the public about Christian social responsibility.[64]

BEHIND THE LACE CURTAINS

YWCA audiences would have encountered the organization's public affairs efforts in the libraries of their local associations, at talks given by traveling National Board lecturers, and at conferences where groups would be instructed to study and discuss the material. But the penumbra of leftist Popular Front influences would touch the association most closely through its involvement with the American Youth Congress (AYC). In the mid-1930s, the constituency assemblies of students, industrial workers, and business and professional women voted to affiliate with the AYC, a confederation that encompassed the Young Communist League and the Woman's Christian Temperance Union alike.

Because of its vocal factions of socialists, Bolshevists, and Trotskyites, a cloud of subversion hung over the AYC from its inception. Many saw the group as the consummate Communist front.

To the YWCA's ultimate detriment, its constituent groups lent considerable support to the AYC. From an early point in its history, the National Board identified cooperation with other organizations as an extension of public affairs, and it lent its name and womanpower to other voluntary groups. While it courted criticism from some quarters because of its affiliation with organizations like the Federal Council of Churches and the Women's Joint Congressional Committee, these were hardly radical outfits. From that perspective, the AYC was not substantively different than other affiliated organizations. Nor did the AYC pursue a course of action that deviated from the YWCA's scope of concerns, focusing much of its energies on New Deal legislation for youth. However, the AYC was among the first organizations investigated by the House Committee to Investigate Un-American Activities chaired by Martin Dies Jr., convened in 1938. Because of guilt by association, the National Board would come to experience a full measure of the persecution of the left. Rose Terlin bore the brunt of this attack.

The AYC endeavored to represent the numerous segments of dissatisfied youth—rural, working, and student—that New Deal measures had failed to reach. University groups predominated, but the AYC attracted the participation of a wide range of political, labor, farm, and religious affiliates. The core leadership of socialists and Communist Party members labored in the spirit of the united front, willing to mute their doctrinal antimonies in "reformist campaigns to first mobilize and then radicalize" the liberals they sought to enlist in a revolutionary struggle. The wide scope of concerns and united front strategy paid off. Already upon its second convention in 1935, the AYC caught the attention of Eleanor and Franklin Roosevelt.[65] Though delegates to YWCA conventions questioned the wisdom of affiliating with the AYC, constituent groups were authorized to send representatives to the AYC governing council in 1936, where they would hold positions until the organization disintegrated five years later.

The AYC provided a forum for the practice of Christian citizenship, and YWCA constituency groups enthusiastically worked to shape its agenda. Involvement in the united front was self-consciously approached as a means to bridge the liberal-radical divide. Association participation could even be described as a strategy of Christian infiltration. At its 1936 convention, the YWCA pledged to "work for the building of a society nearer to the Kingdom of God [where] barriers are broken down in the common objective of a better life." Although it usually cited barriers of nation, religion, and race, the association cited the need to breach the barrier between religious and secular organizations "to the end that those groups holding Christian convictions and having Christian programs shall be able to . . . demonstrate their methods in this wider group of people."[66] This cooperation served two purposes: it thrust the YWCA out of a religious ghetto, and it proved the value of social Christianity in political struggle, asserting the value of democratic fellowship and moral sincerity as an activist force.

Terlin served as a National Board advisor on the AYC governing board. Recognizing that the AYC's radical reputation hampered its effectiveness as a political voice, she encouraged the group to advance a reform agenda centered on civic participation. The AYC adopted her suggested theme for its 1937 convention: a model congress that demonstrated what youth delegates "would do if control of the Nation's political affairs were vested in their hands." Touted as "practical training for the future leaders of our democratic society," the model congress was an exercise in good citizenship that drew endorsements from congressmen. Franklin Roosevelt sent a letter of commendation, finding it "reassuring to know that the future of our democracy rests in the hands of a generation which is alive to the responsibilities which democratic government involves."[67]

With its civic orientation, the model congress put many of the principles of group work into action. Given Terlin's input on its structure, the YWCA deserves a measure of credit for the congress's success. Between 1937 and 1939, the AYC put forward a conciliatory social program, turning what had been campus strikes for peace and free speech into calm demonstrations "in which political ideas were dropped from view allowing vague and virtuous froth and ambiguities to come to the fore," according to historian George Rawick's dyspeptic evaluation. Rawick, who dismissed the group as a front, also noted that a "social-work emphasis" increased after the 1937 model congress. "In fact," he wrote, "the AYC was to become in a sense an appendage of the social work movement." Negatively appraising the AYC's New Deal enthusiasm and such reform interests as sex education, community centers, and the prevention of juvenile delinquency, Rawick concluded that "this type of activity was, of course, unexceptionable [and] provided the AYC with useful protective coloration."[68] Such activity also suggested the moderating influence of the YWCA.

For most of its existence, the AYC advanced an unremarkable liberal agenda, but anticommunists made reference to its undeniably radical elements in a successful effort to paint it as subversive. These efforts gained legitimacy and power by virtue of the Dies Committee. In October 1939, Kenneth Goff, an informer who claimed to have ties to the Young Communist League, recounted the radical operations of the AYC before the committee, and he identified its advisor, Rose Terlin, as a Communist Party member.[69] Terlin testified to refute the charges, armed with proof that she had been out of the country at the time of the alleged offenses, and the committee took no further action on her case. Still, accusations initiated by Goff were recycled for twenty years by right-wing groups.

Soon after Goff's testimony—as well as the 1939 Nazi-Soviet Pact—an indeed domineering bloc of Communist Party affiliates steered the AYC into ruin. Most organizations involved with the AYC defected after a chaotic 1940 citizenship conference held at the White House, where participants heckled Roosevelt. Notably, YWCA constituent groups did not. Paternalist critics would unfairly come to tag YWCA women as communist dupes, but in this case, the association was slow to recognize the AYC's shortcomings. Perhaps because they had been part of the nominal leadership for so long, YWCA members felt invested in redeeming the AYC. Constituent groups' resistance to attacks on civil liberties might have inspired their defiant support.[70]

Only in the AYC's death throes did YWCA women acknowledge its deceitful operating practices. A representative to the AYC's governing body finally concluded in 1941 that it was time to end the affiliation: "They don't care about the YWCA in itself but they do need it to sell themselves to other organizations, now more than ever before. . . . We are always left out in the cold . . . , when we offer constructive criticism, we are always disregarded."[71] As National Board leaders struggled to disentangle the YWCA from these troubles, they discovered that Communist youth groups had labored to gain power in the association more generally. Staff members found credible evidence that the "Young Communist League and Communist Party made a concerted effort to infiltrate the YWCA in every possible way between 1936 and 1940." The YWCA was mentioned in meeting minutes of the organizations "many more times . . . than we have any idea," a secretary reported.[72]

Communists' inability to bring the YWCA under its sway mattered little given the anticommunist panic that followed World War II. In June 1946, Representative George Dondero of Michigan revived many of the 1939 accusations against those who "rendered yeoman service to the Communist Party and its front organizations." He singled Terlin out, which inspired publications like *Counterattack: The Newsletter of Facts on Communism* and the Hearst newspapers to publicize her subversive presence on the National Board staff. The coverage prompted two board members of the Queens, New York, YWCA to resign, citing the YWCA's treasonous internationalist advocacy. News of this defection circulated among Community Chests, some of which cut their funding for local YWCAs.[73]

The attacks on the YWCA in the Cold War era generally followed the pattern set by those that occurred in wake of the Palmer Raids after World War I. Obscure reactionary publications and speakers started whisper campaigns like those once conducted by manufacturers' organizations. Professional anticommunists and an enduring network of female right-wing activists rehashed a litany of accusations. Echoing the 1924 spider web, they exposed supposed infiltrators who controlled a vast network of seemingly legitimate front organizations.

The YWCA was among the peculiar communist religious groups paradoxically reported to be Christian organizations that spread atheism.

The House Un-American Activities Committee (HUAC) itself highlighted the Christian-communist connection in a 1949 pamphlet titled *100 Things You Should Know about Communism and Religion*. It revealed the leftist influence in the churches as nothing more complex than duplicitous machinations: "Two-faced" communists made "plans to destroy religion [in their] secret Party meetings, [but] in public, they say religion and Communism should be friends and that both are working for the same goals." Easily manipulated liberals could not detect the apostates in their midst, who tailored the social agenda of groups such as "the Ys" to advance their revolutionary ambitions.[74]

Two notable incidents of Cold War red baiting, Joseph Kamp's 1948 pamphlet *Behind the Lace Curtains of the YWCA* and a 1951 ruckus instigated in the Alton, Illinois, YWCA, collectively served as the closing chapter of the YWCA's long Red Scare. Though these flare-ups had many continuities with those of the previous decades, the persistence and intensity of the McCarthy-era attacks put the YWCA in a vulnerable position. The National Board responded by softening—but not eliminating—its advocacy.

Kamp launched the most eye-catching attack when he devoted an entire tract to uncovering YWCA subversion. *Behind the Lace Curtains of the YWCA* was one of several pamphlets that he published under the auspices of the Constitutional Educational League (others included *High Taxes . . . the Quick Way to Communism* and *Vote CIO . . . and Get a Soviet America*). In it, he promised to reveal a comprehensive infiltration of the association by communists. The pamphlet had an intriguing cover, with a lacy overlay on top of the YWCA's blue triangle insignia. The "C" of the insignia was replaced with a red hammer and sickle. Though Kamp framed the book as a challenge to the National Board to prove "that it has no sympathy for any Communist, Socialist, or Left Wing philosophy and that it believes in . . . the American way of life," he preempted the board's defense by piling on evidence of communist allegiance. YWCA interracialism, he argued, promoted the communist party line of miscegenation. The National Board recommended revolutionary authors like Richard Wright, who promoted "social racial equality, no doubt," in books that no "decent, self-respecting parents would select for their daughters to read." It disseminated "music . . . with Marxist Overtones," the workers' songs that had so incensed Elizabeth Dilling.[75]

Kamp singled out "poisonous paragraphs on public affairs" and the YWCA's religious writers as fonts of radical ideas. He summarized the theme of the public affairs program as "hurrah for Russia . . . down with the USA." Similarly, he viewed Winnifred Wygal's "religion . . . with a revolutionary flavor" as a "deliberate subterfuge" that injected "anti-capitalist, anti-Christian, and anti-American" propaganda into purportedly Christian services. Wygal's offenses included her

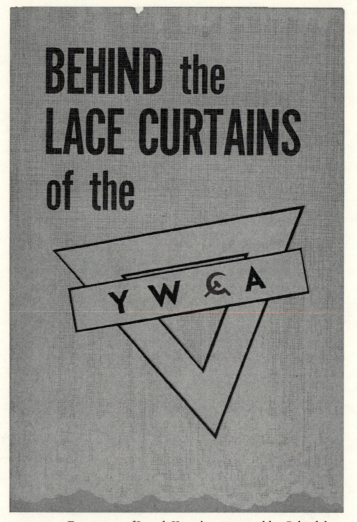

FIGURE 4.2. Front cover of Joseph Kamp's 1948 pamphlet, *Behind the Lace Curtains of the YWCA.*

suggestion that worship services use "modern dance [and] rhythmic motions" and her reading recommendations, which included the "vicious and blasphemous" Langston Hughes poem titled "Goodbye Christ."[76]

Kamp's assessment of Rose Terlin as "some kind of Communist—a little muddled, perhaps," evoked the paternalism of the anticommunists of the 1920s who set out to educate the YWCA "amateurs who . . . know nothing" about the subversion in their midst.[77] This theme was built on the presumption that guileless women in particular lacked the political consciousness either to recognize revolutionary operatives or to join them deliberately. They were pawns in the male political sphere. Kamp hoped that the women of "outstanding position and intelligence" in control of the YWCA would come to their senses and extirpate the "clever and subtle" propagandists who had taken control of programming. Regardless of their outstanding intelligence, these women had been so oblivious as to both overlook and apologize for the communist influences in the organization. Kamp and the "courageous leadership" of the military men of the Constitutional Educational League had come to the rescue.[78]

The overblown rhetoric of *Behind the Lace Curtains of the YWCA* betrays the absurdity of Cold War hysteria, which made the slightest deviation from anticommunist orthodoxy equivalent to a Bolshevik uprising. But Kamp was onto something with his lace curtain imagery. The YWCA no doubt made an appealing target for him because the association was so mundane, part of the landscape of hundreds of cities, towns, and campuses. The upright, bourgeois Protestant women most associated with the leadership of the organization promoted a lace curtain atmosphere—a place where "every good, right-minded woman, however adverse her fate, shall . . . be surrounded by every means of . . . the development of a gracious Christian womanhood," a secretary wrote in 1907.[79] Exposing their secret iniquities provided an undoubtable narrative hook. There may not have been much of the hammer-and-sickle variety of subversion happening behind those curtains, but such women did allow dangerous ideas to circulate in association settings: challenges to the status quo that called for women's empowerment, racial cooperation, economic justice, and the development of a loving community in the face of self-satisfied individualism.

The gulf that existed at times between YWCA members and the national leaders could be detected in a local association controversy of the early 1950s. These charges of radicalism showcased both the distaff side of the red-baiting tradition and the political diversity of women's movements. In November 1951, Dorothy Nossett, a fund-raising secretary of the National Board, traveled to the Alton, Illinois, YWCA to smooth over a controversy. "I do not believe I have spent a harder two days than those in Alton," she wrote in a confidential dispatch to the US YWCA's president. Nossett reported troubles with the volunteer board: "Mrs. J. F. Schlafly, Jr., Finance Chairman, young—in her late twenties—attacked the YWCA because we were 'pink,' we had communists on our staff and . . . Alton did not want to send money when it was spent that way." The source of the hard time was the future "sweetheart of the Silent Majority," Phyllis Schlafly, whom Nossett derisively described as Catholic, "pleasant, but cold and brittle," and a social climber.[80]

During the visit, Schlafly grilled Nossett about Terlin and National Board advocacy. She insisted that the Alton YWCA institute a "loyalty oath" that pledged belief in the "American system of individual opportunity, private property and

an economy free from government control and ownership." Swayed by the tenacious arguments of Schlafly, who Nossett called a "convincing speaker," the local
board approved a compromise oath, less strident but still patriotic and adamantly capitalist. The pledge "affirmed . . . belief in the American philosophy
of individual opportunity, private property, and free-enterprise." It effectively
repudiated the collectivist social Christianity of the 1930s and 1940s. Though
two Alton staff members refused to add such language to their employment contracts, Nossett felt that the overall consensus achieved by the compromise oath
had settled the matter.[81]

Schlafly was temporarily placated. The next year, 1952, she found more
opportunities to stake her claim in the civic sphere. She embarked on an unsuccessful campaign for the Illinois state legislature, attended the Republican
National Convention, and weighed in on YWCA public affairs during the association's national convention. The National Board proposed public affairs planks
promoting greater US support of postwar reconstruction, the United Nations,
and participation in the World Court, and Schlafly took the floor multiple times
during the debate period. Identified in the convention proceedings not by her
husband's name, like Mrs. Theodore Blegen and many other delegates, but
instead as Mrs. Phyllis Schlafly, she objected to resolution language that would,
in her interpretation, endorse sending development aid "to Red China, to
the North Korean Communists, who are killing our boys." In light of resolutions that had been passed in support of public housing, federal health care
interventions, and other measures that "probably advocate more taxation," she
suggested that a resolution be drafted in praise of the "individual initiative which
has made our country great." Her reasoning hearkened to the self-positioning
that would make her such an effective voice of the New Right: "Speaking as a
housewife and a mother . . . , my life has been made very pleasant by my use of
automatic machinery—my dryer and my dishwasher; and that it is that kind
of inventive genius that is going to raise the standard of living for all the people."[82]
Though she was not the only delegate who objected to Public Affairs Committee
proposals that promoted world governance and social democratic policy, hers
was a minority perspective at the convention.

Made in a forum governed by *Robert's Rules of Order*, where civic debate played
out calmly among women seeking consensus, Schlafly's time on the YWCA convention stage betrayed none of the sharp-edged needling that would characterize
her responses to Republican Party moderates and 1970s feminists. A condemna-
tion of the YWCA delivered in 1953 gave a better sense of her evolution as a pro-
vocateur. She distributed a paper among the Alton YWCA and Community Chest
that asked, "what's happened to the C in YWCA?" Targeting the public affairs
articles in the *YWCA Magazine* (which had changed its name from the *Womans*

Press in 1951), Schlafly indicted the YWCA's liberalism: its call for the diplomatic recognition of "Red China," support of government spending, and—most damning—persistent "indoctrination for Socialism." She argued that the YWCA's endeavor to make cooperative Christian love a guiding force in political and economic life contradicted the true "teaching of Jesus," which emphasized the individual over the collective. Schlafly wrote that the public affairs program "purports to show that Jesus favored Government-guaranteed cradle-to-the-grave security," but state-sponsored social services in fact weakened rather than reflected the spirit of fellowship: "the Good Samaritan can pass by his wounded neighbor with impunity; a Government bureaucrat will do the job for him."[83]

When asked about her experiences sixty-one years after she circulated her concerns about the "C" in the YWCA, Schlafly did not recall her tenure as volunteer chair of the Finance Committee as being marked by controversy or discontent. She explained that her "husband's prominence" had first drawn her into the YWCA. "They asked me to be on all kinds of boards," she noted. "It was just kind of the thing to do, I guess." The organization held some attraction for her, she pointed out, because "the YWCA was a factor in Alton. It was well thought of, and a lot of the important people in town, the important women, did serve on the board." When told about documentation of her dissatisfaction with the national organization, particularly its endorsement of the diplomatic recognition of the People's Republic of China, she gave a lighthearted response: "Well, that sounds legitimate. That sounds like something I would do." The discussion triggered a memory that she had spoken up as a convention delegate, but unsurprisingly—given the bustling activist career that followed the period in which volunteer boards consumed her time—the commotion addressed by Dorothy Nossett had not left a lasting impression on Schlafly. Though Nossett felt compelled to point out Schlafly's religious affiliation, Schlafly thought this had never been a point of interest. "I don't think the subject of my Catholicism ever came up in connection with the YWCA," she concluded. She described her departure from the organization as the simple expiration of her term as chair of the Finance Committee. In fact, the troubles raised by Schlafly may have been more a concern to the National Board than they were to Schlafly herself or other leaders of the Alton association. Still, shortly thereafter, Schlafly shifted her volunteer energies to the Daughters of the American Revolution, which likely provided a political atmosphere more closely aligned to her sensibilities.[84]

In the period of Kamp's and Schlafly's charges, the National Board steeled itself to outlast the wave of attacks, but it made adjustments that betrayed anxieties over McCarthyism. It discontinued the *Public Affairs News Service*, a serial political education publication. Though the 1952 sale of its publishing department, the Woman's Press, was no doubt a cost-cutting measure, the loss meant that there was no longer a venue for the mass distribution of so many YWCA-oriented texts influenced by liberal social Christianity.

Rose Terlin resigned from the National Board in 1950. No official correspondence indicates that allegations of communism prompted her departure, but it seems probable that these pressures either directly or indirectly influenced the decision. The same year, professional HUAC witness Louis Budenz reported to an agent of the Federal Bureau of Investigation (FBI) that Terlin was a concealed communist, triggering an undercover investigation that stretched into 1954. After Terlin made herself available for an interview, agents made clear in their confidential reports that they paid little heed to her denial of radical associations, though informants such as Budenz and Kenneth Goff would ultimately be discredited. One agent indicated his allegiances in the report's conclusion: "It is the observation . . . that the subject was lying in approximately every statement she made."[85]

During the 1950s Terlin put together a career as an editor, advisor to the World Student Christian Federation, and publicity director for the Pittsburgh YWCA. But when she was appointed to a position as an economist in the Women's Bureau of the Department of Labor in 1960, the FBI was again at her heels. Agents interviewed everyone from her childhood neighbors to colleagues at all of her intervening jobs. They could find nothing more damning than revelations that she was "sincere," had a "progressive . . . approach to social problems," and served as an "irritant to more conservative members of the YWCA."[86]

More troubling, though, FBI interviewers noted again and again that Terlin had developed a drinking problem for which she had sought psychiatric help. Perhaps they hoped that her alcoholism would induce her to drunkenly reveal communist contacts, but the juxtaposition of this revelation to the hundreds of pages of interviews searching for derogatory information suggests the stress to which Terlin was subjected. Despite dogged investigation, the FBI could find no reason to bar Terlin from federal employment. She retired from the Women's Bureau in 1975. This journey from red-baited radical to civil servant evokes the career of Mary Dublin Keyserling, which historian Landon Storrs describes as evidence of the "persistence and diversity [of feminism] from the 1930s into the 1950s and the complex roots of the 1960s movement."[87] Through her YWCA service and her federal publications such as *Jobfinding Techniques for Mature Women* (1970) and *A Working Women's Guide to Her Job Rights* (1974), Terlin can be counted among the ranks of labor feminists. She brought the influence of the Christian left to bear on the women's movement of the 1960s.

The YWCA, too, was battered but survived the McCarthy period. The Public Affairs Committee resolved "to go forward without fear, [for] we are not alone the champions of justice, freedom, and civil liberty; great groups of tried and tested Christian leaders are with us in spirit."[88] The activist lawyer Dorothy Kenyon, who denounced Senator Joseph McCarthy as "a lowdown worm" when he

FIGURE 4.3. Board publicity, circa 1960: "Being part of the YWCA is a deep spiritual experience: board and staff in a traditional before-meeting prayer." Credit: Sophia Smith Collection, Smith College

called her before the Senate Foreign Relations Committee, served as the committee's advisor for some of this period. The YWCA made a perfunctory effort to add its voice to the chorus of liberal anticommunists, but at the same that it denounced "communism and any other ideology which denies . . . fundamental human rights to any individual," it called for civil liberties protections.[89]

The group weathered the Red Scare, but in some ways Schlafly and her colleagues emerged triumphant. The link Schlafly drew between conservative Christianity, free enterprise, and small government in her disagreements with the YWCA foretold the conservative revolt that her Barry Goldwater tract, *A Choice Not an Echo* (1964), would inaugurate a decade after the Alton skirmishes. Schlafly's YWCA crusade heralded the ascendancy of the New Right. Only as the Equal Rights Amendment gained momentum in the early 1970s would she orient her public identity primarily around antifeminism.[90] Far more legitimate than the occasionally fascist fringe of Elizabeth Dilling and her supporters, the New Right caused mainline liberals to "lose the institutional control of Protestantism" they once had.[91] In this changed environment, the US YWCA labored to stay solvent and relevant.

5 · A "FIFTH COLUMN FOR GOD"

The Maryknoll Sisters at Midcentury

The Maryknoll Sisters of St. Dominic experienced exceptional growth over the first twenty-five years of their existence. The congregation started in 1920 with 35 vowed women. By 1930, it had attracted 420 sisters, and it added another 200 over the next decade. But between 1945 and 1960, when vocations among American women hit their peak, the congregation had its widest appeal. Its numbers went from 760 to 1,430 women, an increase that well outpaced the 20 percent growth rate among US Catholic women's congregations more generally. In 1966, the congregation reached its peak membership of 1,675.[1] Though these numbers may not approach the hundreds of thousands of women who participated in the ventures of the YWCA of the USA, by midcentury, the Maryknoll Sisters had secured a comparably prominent place in the Catholic public imagination. A lively missionary press dramatized the work of Maryknoll priests and sisters, the church hierarchy cheered their charitable and spiritual exploits, and the mass media included them in their newfound fascination with religious vocations.

This expansion in renown accompanied an expansion in territory and in the ideological parameters of the sisters' mission. In the 1920s and 1930s, Maryknoll focused its efforts on the religious conversion of East Asia. In the 1940s and 1950s, the sisters established a presence in Africa and Latin America, while continuing their work in East Asia, the Pacific Islands, and US minority communities. While they still placed a premium on proselytizing, they embraced the sentiments of the American Century, carrying forward Henry Luce's call for the United States to become "Good Samaritan of the entire world."[2] While notions of evangelization had once centered on piety, the congregation came to emphasize the connections between spiritual and political commitments. Cloister traditions of discipline persisted, but the sisters by no means hid behind convent walls. Maryknoll was the most active of active orders, and its sisters constituted a specialized labor force with considerable pastoral responsibilities.

In a 1952 fund-raising appeal, the Maryknoll Sisters declared themselves a "Fifth Column for God," quietly undermining the impediments to his reign.[3] A threat more insidious than paganism—atheistic communism—now challenged missionaries, and Maryknoll's response to this danger straddled secular and spiritual approaches for creating global unity. Maryknoll's politicization had two main themes, which dovetailed with both the Vatican's social teachings and the concerns of internationalist American liberalism: first, the defeat of communism; and second, racial and national cooperation. It was a cautious liberalism, aggressively anticommunist but weak in addressing the structural inequalities underlying racial, national, and economic divisions.

During the height of the Cold War, the Maryknoll Sisters were as popular and populous as they would ever be. The congregation offered women opportunities, adventure, and sanctification. It promised to transform the world into a more Christian place through the dissemination of US Catholic values and services. But this period of synergy between American exceptionalism and Maryknoll missiology did not last. The ruptures in the anticommunist consensus and in the institutional identity of Catholicism that came to the fore in the 1960s brought a reckoning to the Maryknoll Sisters.

WORLD WAR II AND THE HEROIC MISSIONARY

World War II stoked a sense of responsibility for global stewardship among US Catholics and bolstered the Maryknoll Sisters' distinction as a body of skilled, sanctified women. Well before the United States entered the war, Maryknoll missionaries stood witness to growing militarization in East Asia. With an eye to avoiding the political entanglements that might endanger their presence in China, they attempted to maintain a studied neutrality amid decades of civil unrest and after Japanese occupation of Manchuria (Manchukuo, 1932–45). This pose of neutrality was belied by Maryknoll's invocation of extraterritorial privileges, which undermined Chinese nationalism, and its cooperation with the Japanese occupation in the face of Chinese resistance, which Maryknollers dismissed as communism and banditry.[4]

The wartime Pacific made such pretenses impossible. Some 120 of the 450 Maryknoll priests and sisters assigned to the Pacific (including Hawaii) remained at their stations in Japanese-occupied China, Korea, and the Philippines after the attack on Pearl Harbor. To Catholics, this perseverance made them heroes of the faith and the Allied cause. "With humility and envy we [watched] the Maryknollers carry the spirit of their vocation into their unchosen wartime service," observed Richard Cushing, the cardinal of Boston.[5] US missionaries, including more than 60 Maryknoll sisters, endured the hardships of siege and internment at the hands of the Japanese during the Sino-Japanese War and World War II. Such experiences gave substance to the cult of martyrdom that had always been part of Maryknoll's publicity and devotional life. Théophane Vénard, a French missionary priest killed in East Asia in the 1870s, had been the most prominent "modern martyr" celebrated in Maryknoll's devotions. Vénard set the bar for the highest mission accomplishment with the vow: "I have come to the conclusion that nothing can be done [here] until some man's blood has been spilled. [If] I were called upon to meet death for Christ and souls, I should be the happiest of men."[6] With the onset of war, the sisters could look to their own ranks for models of redemptive sacrifice.

One set of sisters who remained in Asia after the declaration of war was repatriated in a well-publicized exchange of Japanese and American nationals in 1942. In the wake of the exchange, a New York priest used the platform of the *New York Times* to remind Catholics of the connection between patriotism and foreign mission: "Your interest in the missions will strengthen the country's spiritual stamina. . . . Your effort to spread religion will help . . . the spread of democracy in the world."[7] A Maryknoll group carried on in Manila until they were sent to the brutal Los Baños internment camp in 1944. Throughout the Pacific, as priests and sisters experienced the meager rations, imprisonment, and forced marches of war, they joined the ranks of rugged mission heroes, and when Communist regimes targeted the church in postwar China and Korea, the martyrs.

Maryknoll sister Mary Concepcion described her Philippine internment not as a military struggle but instead as redemption: "We accepted death and offered our lives for the conversion of the Japanese."[8] The battle against the Japanese had become a battle for the Catholic Church. At the conclusion of the war, mainland China and North Korea, "buried under the ice of forbidding communism," posed new challenges. Maryknoll publicity predicted that "the blood of martyrs shall . . . fructify the seeds of the church" and yield conversions.[9] Yet as Allied occupation of the Pacific came to a close, China and North Korea expelled Maryknoll personnel, with the exception of Sister Agneta Chang, a Korean national executed in 1950, and imprisoned bishop James E. Walsh, who was released in 1970.

An ambiguous response to battles on the home front during World War II contrasted Maryknoll's prideful embrace of overseas sacrifice to faith and nation. Before the 1950s, more sisters in mission were stationed in the United States than in foreign countries. In early 1942, while the Japanese military gathered US missionaries for internment, Maryknoll sisters in the Boyle Heights section of Los Angeles observed the forced removal and internment of civilian Japanese Americans. There, in one of their oldest mission projects, the sisters operated a school and orphanage for Japanese American children. With news of the attack on Pearl Harbor, a Los Angeles diarist reported the intensification of the anti-Japanese sentiment that had long surrounded them: "We prayed fervently that our Sisters would be safe and our work with the Japanese here would not be handicapped." In the days that followed, she recorded forbidding repercussions: frozen assets, job losses, and then the evacuation decree. As their neighbors were sent to internment facilities in March and April, sisters felt the impact in immediate ways. Not only did the families of their students leave, but the children in their orphanage—some of whom reported that they "did not know they were Japs" until the evacuation—were removed to the Manzanar camp. The diarist reflected on the quick turn of events: "It doesn't seem possible to believe that slowly but surely, our house is being deserted as one by one, our children are leaving us."[10]

Despite this feeling of loss, even the loss of "our children," the sisters could afford a certain equanimity. "For some reason," the diarist noted after the sisters visited an internment camp, "they found everyone very blue"—as though the internees' dejection was puzzling. Two Japanese-born Maryknoll sisters, Susanna and Bernadette, accompanied "their own countrymen" to Manzanar. Reporting in a Maryknoll brochure that "well over a hundred" had been baptized there, one of the women told of the "good in war": "It is wonderful to see these people turning to the One True God."[11] Though mournful, the Maryknoll Sisters could take the displacement of Japanese Americans in stride. They did not question the racial logic that made internment a reasonable response to war. Perhaps not ready to classify their parishioners, students, and wards as enemy aliens, they still understood them as a foreign race, in America but not American.

"A NEW KIND OF FULFILLMENT"

With the conclusion of the war, Maryknoll recovered from its expulsion from Communist-controlled lands. Sisters returned to the Philippines, Hong Kong, South Korea, and Japan. They increased their work among US racial minority groups, branching out to African American and Latino neighborhoods. They established stations in protectorates and colonial territories that included the Pacific Islands, Ceylon (Sri Lanka), British East Africa (Tanzania), Macau, and Mauritius. Above all, they heeded the appeal of Latin American bishops, who asked for "help in preserving the faith of their people" by inviting missionaries to expand the reach of the institutional church.[12] During the 1950s, Maryknoll shifted its attention from East Asia to Central and South America, where priests and sisters aimed to root out a syncretic Catholicism that had strayed from orthodoxy. They also sought to calm social unrest that threatened the authority of the church and the ruling classes who ensured this authority. The task of helping Latin American Catholics reach a "better knowledge and appreciation of the rich heritage of their Faith" now ranked with the sisters' founding purpose of "the conversion of pagans in heathen lands."[13]

With territorial and demographic expansiveness came an expansiveness in conceptions of women's religious community. As sisters continued to prove their value in the field, they became decreasingly defined by the cloister heritage of effacement and submissiveness. The religious vocation was a domain that resisted the postwar cult of domesticity. With global horizons, the sisters strayed far from what Betty Friedan notoriously referred to as the "comfortable concentration camp" of suburbia in *The Feminine Mystique* (1963). "'Motherhood is woman's highest calling,' was the protest encountered by a Maryknoll Sister before she entered the community," read a 1947 financial appeal. The sisters answered the protest: "'And who will be mother to the orphans?'" The solicitation suggested that sisters responded to a higher calling than family with their capacity to dispense loving charity beyond kin. No household drudges, Maryknoll women cultivated a specialized set of skills. "Maryknoll believes in turning talents or training completely to the service of God and men," the appeal continued, and missions needed professional talent: "social workers, teachers, cooks, seamstresses, office workers, librarians, nurses, pharmacists, doctors, technicians."[14] During the 1940s and 1950s, most Maryknoll women entered with a high school education and received their training in the novitiate or on the job. Only a few would be selected from their cohort to attend college or graduate school. But the young white women of working- and lower-middle-class backgrounds who formed the majority of new entrants nevertheless found in Maryknoll the means of developing professional skills in challenging, far-flung settings. As Kathleen Sprows Cummings argues, before the feminist movement of the 1960s, US Catholic women generally found "more opportunities for education, meaningful work, and leadership" in religious vocations than they did in secular contexts. Shielded by the respectability of religious life, they did not draw censure for centering their lives on a career.[15]

Between the 1940s and the mid-1960s, religious vocations attracted recruits like never before (or since), and the wider culture expressed fascination with the idealistic service and baroque costumes of priests and nuns. From *The Flying Nun* and the singing nun to *The Nun's Story*, popular portrayals of religious life appealed to Catholics and non-Catholics alike. Images of women religious revealed and contained percolating conflicts over gender and sexuality. They celebrated, in the words of scholar Rebecca Sullivan, "educated, professional women unencumbered by husbands or children" who remained "sexually contained and subservient to male authority figures."[16] Portrayals of women's religious life disrupted the perceived dichotomy of ideals of traditional domesticity and a modernity characterized by women's sexual and economic liberation. For young Catholic women, the vocation provided a way to navigate the shifting terrain of gender roles, allowing them to be independent yet deferential, and single but respectable. It offered women who had no desire to follow a heteronormative path an option that bridged the domains of traditional and progressive in an unthreatening manner. Religious life opened avenues for personal fulfillment and professional advancement distinct from those available to single women at a time of restrictive gender norms and limited job opportunities.

In addition, demographic factors were pivotal to the increase in the number of vocations at midcentury. The historian Patricia Byrne explains: "The entire period was characterized by the apparent cohesion of Catholic culture . . . and the euphoria of success." The population of Catholics in the United States doubled between 1940 and 1960, from twenty-one to forty-two million. The parochial school system expanded accordingly. It created a demand for sister-teachers, and it facilitated intensive recruitment among students for religious life.[17]

The opportunity to embark on foreign mission work distinguished Maryknoll from other US Catholic congregations. The sisters' ministry was uniquely suited to an internationalist age. Even before Luce's "American Century," the sisters spent their days in charitable ministrations around the world. Much like the People-to-People program of the Eisenhower White House, which linked interpersonal interactions to international relations, Maryknoll sisters could informally assist in the struggle for spheres of cultural and political influence. A public health official in the Office of Coordinator of Inter-American Affairs, a US wartime propaganda agency, praised the sisters' efforts: "While helping these needy people spiritually and physically, these missioners are also, albeit unwittingly, serving their country as its best good-will ambassadors."[18]

Maryknoll appealed to many strains of liberal internationalism. By supplying donations and vocations, its supporters augmented the imagined helpfulness of their government in postwar reconstruction. Like United Nations relief agencies and private charities such as CARE, the sisters addressed the devastation of war as they worked among refugees and provided social services in ruined cities. They expected that US economic and technological assistance would spread democracy and prosperity. Still, Maryknoll had something unique to contribute to the pursuit of global stewardship: "America is generously sharing its material goods and scientific knowledge with the poor of alien lands. What a challenge to American Catholics to share their gift of the Faith." While YWCA internationalists looked to world government to secure peace, Maryknoll proposed a simpler, if predictable, solution: "only Christ's gospel, faithfully lived, will bring unity and concord to the world."[19]

Maryknoll publicity portrayed sisters as both special and typical: special in their expertise and God-centered selflessness and typical as attractive, friendly, and pragmatic American women—"a cross section of American womanhood."[20] The media reinforced these descriptions. The exceptional qualities of the sisters were highlighted in a spate of media appearances in the mid-1950s, when the Cold War accelerated and Catholics across the class spectrum benefited from a rising tide of economic and political power. *Nun in Red China,* a 1953 McGraw-Hill publication to which Cardinal Francis Spellman gave his imprimatur, was one of several best-selling fictionalizations of Maryknoll ministry written by the sisters' communications specialist, Sister Maria del Rey (Ethel Danforth).[21] The book was the basis of a 1955 episode of *The Jane Wyman Show,* "The Bamboo Cross." The famed director John Ford shot the episode as a "tribute" to Maryknoll missionaries, whom he "ardently supported," according to a biographer.[22] Wyman portrayed Sister Regina, who is persecuted by Chinese Communists while steering a Chinese pupil to Christian righteousness. In the same year, *Time* placed Maryknoll on the cover of its issue containing an account of women religious in "the age of fission." The article described the sisters as a winsome and capable "worldwide spiritual army" in a dangerous time. Its "young, remarkably handsome girls smiling under their black, pointed headdress" knew "how to drive jeeps (and repair them), how to administer hypodermics and do major surgery, how to teach Christian doctrine—and how to be gay." The sisters had not lost their feminine charms but rather had supplemented them with the rugged skills necessary to carry out their adventuresome vocation.[23]

Cosmopolitan (at that time a general interest magazine) highlighted the more everyday qualities of a Maryknoll sister, presenting her as a paradigm of American womanhood. The photo essay "Bernie Becomes a Nun" told the story of a woman's journey from postulant to professed sister. It described Bernie in terms of the contrast between her experience joining the Maryknoll community and the stereotypes about ascetic religious life. Bernie "had no emotional problems . . . no desire to give up the world." She "dated, danced, went to parties—then surprised her friends by entering the Maryknoll convent." She was set her apart from her peers by her devotion to a higher calling and her capacity to meet this calling's standards of labor and discipline. Bernie insisted: "I am not making any great sacrifice in giving up the world. . . . I am, instead, receiving a new kind of fulfillment." A reader cheered this spiritual journey with "congratulations on the most inspiring story you have ever printed."[24]

The essay's portrayal of Bernie—Sister Bernadette Lynch, who entered Maryknoll in 1949—matched her recollection that she had seemed to

Sister Mary Victoria

NUN in RED CHINA

A true and deeply moving account of the appalling experiences of a Maryknoll Sister and her confrères as prisoners of the Chinese Communists

FIGURE 5.1. The cover of the 1953 *Nun in Red China*, "a true and deeply moving account of the appalling experiences of a Maryknoll Sister and her confrères as prisoners of the Chinese Communists." Credit: Sister Mary Victoria, *Nun in Red China*, McGraw-Hill Education

outsiders an unlikely candidate for religious life: "If you believe this—maybe you won't—people were surprised when they found out I was entering the convent because I guess I didn't give the impression of the stereotype, 'she's pious'—I don't quite know what it is." A photo caption, "keeping silent was the hardest thing I had to learn," was no doubt true for the effervescent Brooklyn native. As much as religious life offered life beyond the cloister, disciplinary regimens such as prohibitions on friendship and rules of silence remained central to vocational training.[25]

Looking back at the *Cosmopolitan* article, Lynch described an encounter unusual in the preconciliar congregation. On the verge of taking her final vows, she had been asked to participate in the photo essay. She inquired of her superior how to respond to the request and recalled: "I was so surprised because she said, well, what do you want to do, what do you think about it? That surprised me because in those days, you didn't hear that too often." Maryknoll sisters were envisioned as cheerfully outgoing but were expected to be pliant and silent. There was an element of the vow of obedience in Lynch's decision: "Well, I just felt like it was another work assignment, and so I didn't even blink my eyes at all. If it's something I could do [for Maryknoll], fine." The photo essay was turned into a book, *Bernie Becomes a Nun*, in 1956. The photographer, George Barris, is better known for his images of Marilyn Monroe, but Bernie still receives fan letters.[26]

Though the image of the sisters had changed, the group held to methods of outreach that had marked its earlier years. It still measured success through the quantification of converts and sacraments. Maryknoll women continued to take opportunistic approaches to harvesting souls, as when a sister in Tanganyika hoped to baptize a dying girl whose mother "flatly refused . . . all Sister's coaxing and pleas" with the explanation, "'no, we're Islams.'" The sister secretly baptized the child and gave her the Christian name Helena. The diarist reported with some satisfaction that soon thereafter "Helena took her flight to Heaven," having gained by baptism and death access to the Christian afterlife. Such scheming made its way into medical ministry, which was "one of the foundation stones in building a successful mission" because it attracted potential converts. Through medical services, Maryknoll's magazine explained, "the pagan can see the charity of Christ in action . . . [and] is led to inquire about the doctrine which makes such work possible."[27]

In the early years of mission, priests and sisters usually worked in association. Priests might have charge of a mission church or vicariate while sisters ran a school. Associations continued to occur, but as the communities of both groups grew numerically, they also established projects independently from each other. Maryknoll publicity emphasized the autonomy of each religious institute, a strategic move meant to remind donors that they were "two separate ecclesiastical and civil organizations, [each] responsible for its own financing."[28] In so doing, public relations materials highlighted the value of complementary, gendered spheres of activity in religious life.

In the 1950s, the Maryknoll priest and missiologist John Considine offered a feminist explanation for separatist organizing: "By the law of the Church and the Church's long tradition, a community of women cannot and must not be subordinate to a body of men. It must possess its own vital fabric, its own complete self-sufficiency, its own religious spirit and its own spiritual and apostolic goals."[29] Even if Maryknoll fathers had no inherent authority over the sisters, informal gender hierarchies shaped the power dynamics of the relationship. Novice sisters who received their training in proximity to Maryknoll seminarians found themselves responsible for the seminary's laundry, and an expectation of female deference to male clerical authority prevailed.

The sisters secured a position of active participation in international humanitarian projects by accommodating such strictures. Religious discipline limited the sexual dangers posed by a body of single women and ensured compliancy. With these safeguards, Maryknoll sisters gained access to overseas communities, and they were given the autonomy to carry out their appointed tasks. Increasingly, the Vatican underscored a Catholic vision of social change as part of those tasks. Sisters' still feminized domains of labor—education, health, caregiving, and social work—served as the site to put the church's teachings into motion at the grassroots level.

THE MYSTICAL BODY AND CULTURAL PLURALISM

In the 1940s, the hierarchy of the Catholic Church initiated a discourse on racial and national difference that would gradually turn Maryknoll away from the dualisms underwriting the constructs of American and alien, West and East, and Christian and pagan. Pius XII's contribution to this discourse in a 1943 encyclical on the doctrine of the Mystical Body of Christ was prompted by factors internal to the church. The pope sought to clarify the authority of the ecclesiastical hierarchy over the laity's increased involvement in intellectual and pastoral life. But the encyclical went beyond these inward concerns at a time of heightened awareness of violent ideologies of racial superiority. It promoted ideals of democratic unity that resembled the Social Gospel's invocation of the kingdom of God on earth, yet it described the factors uniting humanity in the distinctly Catholic terms of the corporeality of Christ. That is, humanity was united by the living presence of Jesus in each soul. Humankind was the manifestation through which Jesus continued to exist on earth after his death, and those who had not been severed from God by "schism or heresy or apostasy" formed the Mystical Body of Christ.[30]

The doctrine marked, in the words of one scholar, a "less juridical definition of the nature of the church" as it affirmed the value not only of the clergy, but also of the body of believers, as conduits of God's grace.[31] Still, the encyclical reiterated the traditional apostolic order by stipulating that God governed the Mystical Body through the pope and bishops—"the divinely appointed successors" of Jesus's original apostles. The church hierarchy stood as the body's literal and figurative head. Some lay people found that the doctrine's emphasis on the sacredness in each individual presented a radical conception of equality. However, Pius XII maintained that the graces of God were limited to the faithful, shutting off the possibility that those who remained outside the church could achieve salvation. Maryknoll's response was aligned with the papal interpretation.[32]

The doctrine of the Mystical Body invested Maryknoll's identity as a cross-cultural and cross-racial organization with a new significance. Leaders concluded that the temporal project of unifying humanity had always been a part of their mission. "While others offer panaceas for political unity or economic unity," Albert Nevins told *Maryknoll* (formerly known as *The Field Afar*) readers in 1956, the popes "go to the heart of the matter and call for spiritual unity."[33] This gave the faithful a responsibility to bridge the social divisions that fragmented the Mystical Body. Much like the liberal Protestant quest to realize the fellowship of the kingdom of God on earth, the Catholic doctrine was used to counter scientific racism, racial antagonism, and ethnic separatism.

The Mystical Body doctrine affirmed many principles that undergirded Maryknoll's work: the impetus to reach neglected populations; the missionary's love for all people, which she showed by evangelization; and the rejection of racial superiority through respect of native cultures. But it also promoted an awareness of cultural pluralism that made new demands on the missionary. The doctrine gave Maryknoll a starting point for crafting a vision of mission appropriate to an age of decolonization. *Maryknoll* touted diversity as the church's strength as it highlighted the cultural richness of mission territories in *National Geographic*-style photo essays.

In promoting racial equality, the Maryknoll Sisters faced a more tangled set of power relations than did the YWCA of the USA. Maryknoll sisters tested doctrines of cultural pluralism in fraught circumstances where they attempted to exert authority: encounters between missionary and convert, teacher and student, and medic and patient. YWCA women approached interracialism in informal, voluntary ways, and from these incursions, the organization was challenged from within to act on its proclamations of unity. Women of color represented a significant contingent of YWCA membership and staff, and by the 1930s overseas work centered on the support of autonomous local associations.

In contrast, Maryknoll operated in an institutional context that promoted triumphal righteousness rather than self-scrutiny. The structures of religious life ensured that the priorities of ecclesiastical and congregational leadership would not be challenged from within. Maryknoll recruited sisters from missionary-receiving territories, but the dozens of women who joined from outside the United States did not exert an influence on the congregation's leadership. Hierarchical governance and the rigorous expectations of the vocation made it difficult for Maryknoll women to recognize how methods that insisted on religious allegiance and cultural conformity contradicted the church's message of human equality and cultural pluralism.

Still, changes could be apprehended in ministry. The Maryknoll Sisters increased outreach among US racial minorities, adding "other racial groups" to their purpose of spreading faith "among Asiatics" in their 1952 constitution.[34] They contracted with scattered dioceses to fulfill this call. Sisters taught and provided social services in the Chinatowns of Manhattan, Chicago, and Boston, the multiracial cities of Hawaii, and the black and Mexican American neighborhoods of New York City, St. Louis, Tucson, Houston, and Southern California.

The sisters made their most notable contribution to the US civil rights movement when sixteen women embarked in 1954 to administer an "alien novelty" in Kansas City, Missouri: the city's first interracial hospital, Queen of the World.

FIGURE 5.2. Sister and students in Boston, Massachusetts, undated. Credit: Maryknoll Mission Archives

The Catholic *Interracial Review* deemed the project "as much a missionary work as they might launch in foreign lands." The sisters set out "to ignore the color line . . . in a city with a high degree of race consciousness." One of the rare institutions that trained black doctors and allowed "White and Negro nurses [to] work together [with] patients of both races who lie side by side with no segregation," the hospital represented a "bombshell of an idea [that blew] to bits the notion that integration won't work in hospitals." With the Montgomery bus boycott in the headlines, the renowned physician Howard Rusk pointed to the hospital as "an example of tolerance, understanding and true spiritual motivation that could well be followed by many racially tense communities."[35] The sisters administered the hospital until it closed in 1965, when the city's health care system was desegregated.

By and large, the sisters remained on the cautious side of white liberalism as the civil rights campaign accelerated. Maryknoll stated its commitment to bringing "the Faith to Japanese, Chinese, Negroes and other racial groups" with self-importance: "Isolated by racial prejudice, [these groups] know little of Christ's love for all mankind." It also adopted the Cold War strategy of tethering interracialism and internationalism to the battle against communism. When a reader concluded from the new language of cultural pluralism in *Maryknoll* that the organization had been "duped by Communist propaganda," an editor issued the riposte: "It is unfortunate that Christians have allowed Communists to seize the initiative in preaching mankind's basic spiritual equality."[36]

The flashpoints of massive resistance induced the Maryknoll Sisters to stake a more forthright affiliation with the civil rights movement. In comparison to the YWCA's early involvement with church-based organizing, Maryknoll women, like the sisters documented by historian Amy Koehlinger, "came to the . . . movement quite late, riding the winds of the conclusive demonstrations and legislative developments of 1965 and 1966 when integration was well underway."[37] Still, at the 1965 march in Selma, Alabama, the congregation had a moment at center stage. A frequently reproduced Associated Press photograph showed two Maryknoll sisters at the front of the demonstration, plastic rain bonnets covering their distinctively peaked black veils. Captured in song, they were clasping hands with another white woman religious and two African American men in lay clothes. One of the Maryknollers, Madeline Dorsey, had traveled from her post at the Kansas City hospital to join Selma's Sisters of St. Joseph on the front lines. Dorsey recollected that this interracial configuration, heavy with representatives of the Catholic clergy, was staged to distract the police from the rear flank that was set to cross the Edmund Pettus Bridge.[38]

However important such a symbolic and tactical display of interracial solidarity may have been, paternalism tinged Maryknoll's interracial ministry. One project of that ministry was the administration of St. Anthony's school in the

Bronx, which, according to the convent's diary, had seen the neighborhood change from German to "negro" and then from the "better kind of negro to worse." As in East Asia, the sisters described their task as stewardship. Rendering in dialect a conversation with a neighbor, the Bronx diarist compared the work to training animals, even though she portrayed the sisters' presence as an act of love. The neighbor made a "profound remark that set us to thinking: 'Sistah, if you has a little puppy dog and you wants to train him, if you kicks him he'll be a cur all his life, but if you gives him a little love he'll be at your heels the rest of your life.'" The diarist concluded: "What a simple crystallization of what our attitude should be toward these colored people whom God has placed in our care for His glory!" The sisters conducted the school to "bring Christ's love" to those "isolated by racial prejudice," but they did not address the isolation of poverty and segregation in their ministrations.[39]

In overseas mission, the doctrine of the Mystical Body hit similar shoals owing to the premium placed on proselytizing. As much as the church promoted cultural pluralism, it was difficult to disengage from the heritage of mission as a drive to Westernize as well as Christianize. Despite a constitutional injunction to not "impose on native people our customs," sisters had difficulty distinguishing between cultural integrity and the violation of religious mandates.[40] Examples drawn from East Africa and Latin America indicate how the diversity of mission contexts brought many ambiguities to the surface.

The Maryknoll Sisters began work in Africa in 1949.[41] They joined a small mission in remote Musoma, Tanganyika (then a UN Trust Territory controlled by the United Kingdom, Tanganyika gained independence in 1961 and united with Zanzibar to become Tanzania in 1964). The sisters embarked for Musoma excited about their new assignment, the preparation of a group of African Luo women for religious life. Maryknoll delighted in the potentialities of these so-called native novitiates, seeing them as catalysts that might transform pagan territory into Catholic civilization. Deeming the novices "the objects of a miracle of grace," the Musoma diarist marveled at the coup: "Here in a new mission country where but ten years ago all but five hundred were pagans, we find children of pagan parents deciding to give their lives to God." A later account would add that the yield was all the more remarkable since "the area is one of the most backward in Africa."[42]

In publicity, Maryknoll celebrated its work in Tanganyika as both furthering the church and uplifting African women. A typical issue of *Maryknoll* in this era of decolonization included a cover image of a Quechua woman in a colorful skirt and derby and a photo feature of "Africa's Nonconformists" in ethnic dress. The images provided a lesson in the multicultural dimensions of God's people. "Without conforming to Western customs, ornaments, dress and hair styles," Africans still could know the "Western concepts of . . . freedom, unity

FIGURE 5.3. Sisters in Kowak, Tanganyika, 1956. Credit: Maryknoll Mission Archives

and progress." They cherished "their culture and [asserted] their individualism." The magazine instructed its readers that such "democratic ideals . . . enhance, rather than impair, the growth of the human family."[43]

African self-presentation demonstrated the visual richness of cultural diversity, but Maryknoll sources still maintained that these cultures stood to benefit from the "Western concepts" disseminated by missionaries. "Africans really do not want our Western ways," another article argued in an account of the obsolescence of imperialism. But as much as Maryknoll might try to pay heed to what Africans wanted, it was impossible not to identify what they needed: "Christianity makes the African a better man and a better African. . . . Christianity is a beautiful and sublime life that is meant to be the lasting possession of all peoples, of all races including the Africans."[44]

Ultimately, Maryknoll traced much of the progress made by Africans to the work of US religious personnel. Its magazine presented a novel interpretation of the fall of colonialism: "It was the education brought by the missioners that prepared the peoples for independence and self-rule." "'Uhuru, uhuru, na kazi' cry the people of Tanganyika," read the 1962 Maryknoll mission diary, as the territory became an independent nation. "'Freedom, freedom and work' is the familial greeting of independence heard throughout the country," the diarist translated for sisters who could not witness firsthand how the peaceful triumph of African self-governance affected the rural mission. This was an anticolonial revolt Maryknoll could comfortably stand behind. The sisters themselves might be the liberators of a postcolonial Africa: "freedom from ignorance, freedom from poverty, freedom from paganism. The Maryknoll Priests and Sisters of Kowak are taking part in helping their people rise to meet the challenging cry of 'Uhuru.'" Moreover, Julius Nyerere—"a hardheaded, clear thinking Catholic" in the estimation of John Considine—stood at the helm of the new country, and he was a friend, a teacher once employed by the Maryknoll Fathers who had translated the New Testament into the Kiznaki language.[45]

In Tanganyika, sisters struggled to accommodate local practices that clashed with Euro-American sensibilities. Working in a Luo village, the sisters felt a receptiveness that made for a pleasant, warm community life: "the people are kind and friendly, and seem to have an innate sense of the 'charity that ought to reign among men.'"[46] But, as in most mission settings, ways of life in East Africa did not accommodate the sacramental patterns of the institutional church. Sisters expected sinful customs to wither away in the face of the godly example of Catholicism. Such fundamental changes in the social order were not forthcoming.

Marriage and family structures violated the sisters' sense of Christian home life. A diarist bemoaned the resilience of trial marriage despite the missionaries' best efforts: "The Christian Luos realize the permanence of a Christian marriage and deem it imprudent to enter upon a life contract until they are sure they will get along with their partner. They need a revision of ideas in this regard although they have had plenty of instruction." The sisters decried the practices of polygyny and bride-price but tried to extend understanding. In one case, an angry husband attacked a priest who was hiding a runaway wife. The diarist reasoned: "You can't blame the husband entirely. He paid twenty cows for the girl, and a second, and even a third, fourth, and fifth wife is lawful and in full accord with custom among the Luos."[47]

The native novitiate provided Maryknoll the opportunity to celebrate African womanhood but do so on terms acceptable to institutional Catholicism. Midcentury Maryknoll publicity overlaid the new pluralism with the trope of women's uplift that had long characterized missionary efforts. *Maryknoll* explained the sisters' ministry among women as a feminist effort: "In this African mission area, women are traditionally little more than slaves or chattels. Christianity alone raises woman to her proper human dignity." Reporting on their work to the motherhouse, the sisters felt that they had a crucial role to play in winning "approval for the idea of education of girls, to slowly uplift the idea of womanhood . . . , and help to prove even to the girls themselves that they DO have God-given intelligence." The sisters were, in fact, pioneer educators in Tanganyika. When secondary schooling for women was almost nonexistent, they created the first Catholic girls' secondary school in 1957 and added two more over the next ten years. In the triumphalist atmosphere of the 1950s, Maryknoll liked to imagine that Tanganyikans' interest in its services could be attributed to the inexorable pull of Christian civilization. Certainly over time, sisters recognized that such an unmet demand for social services was linked to the deprivations of colonialism, but they started mission work in East Africa confident in the beneficence of their interventions.[48]

While sisters entered Tanganyika fully expecting to face the challenge of exotic folkways and non-Christian religions, the blend of indigenous and orthodox practices in syncretic Latin American Catholicism posed its own set of problems. The sisters had difficulty discerning cultural diversity in what they could regard only as sacrilegious defiance of the church's teachings. They bristled at divergences in standards of morality, personal comportment, and deference to clerical authority among those who shared their faith.

The sisters entered ministry in Latin America with the belief that traditional practices resulted from a dearth of clergy and proper religious instruction. One bishop warned: "There is still a strong Catholic tradition . . . , but behind the tradition, there is an ignorance of things spiritual that is appalling. . . . [Latin Americans] know very little about the doctrine of the Church, and have very little respect for its laws."[49] Sisters were disappointed to find that their presence was not always welcomed and that traditions underlying feasts, sacred objects, and family structures did not dissipate in spite of their strenuous and often strong-arm measures to impose sacramental regimens.

In Riberalta, Bolivia, a diarist complained that the community failed to respond to the sisters' charitable works with respect for the authority of the church: "Our people seem to take so much for granted—free medical and nursing care, free remedies, and the helpful home visits to those who cannot come to the dispensary. . . . This is characteristic of the attitude of indifference which is prevalent in regard to the practice of their religion too." Sisters interpreted boisterous feasts and unorthodox devotions, not to mention civil marriage and cohabitation, as indifference and paganism. The diarist found much to criticize in the emotional pageantry of the celebration of the Immaculate Conception. She acknowledged that God "understands the hearts of these people, who are such children . . . , and is pleased with their demonstrations of devotion," but the sisters did not share this indulgent response: "to us, the Procession seemed like an anti-climax to a very beautiful day."[50]

Even on the cusp of the Second Vatican Council, Maryknoll dismissed syncretic Catholicism as an impediment that could be solved with more missionaries. Financial appeals described the indigenous of Latin America, who practiced a mystical devotionalism, as an "able but unenlightened people." They burned incense to "the distant, pagan god" but were primed "to learn of the true God who would mean happiness." Even in mission among fellow Catholics, Maryknoll donors could exchange their money for souls, as they had in the days of ransoming pagan babies in China. The appeal promised potential donors that "you make a solid, spiritual investment when you send a Sister-missioner as your representative to teach, to nurse, and to instruct in doctrine."[51]

The sisters encountered racial and ethnic conflict in Latin America just as they did in their US ministry. This complicated the terrain of cultural difference because they decried racial antagonism more easily than they accepted defiance of orthodox practice. Such problems came to the fore in the Panama Canal Zone, where the sisters established missions during World War II. This US territory bisecting the Republic of Panama was the site of a number of military installations, including the Army Caribbean Training Center (known as the School of the Americas after 1963), that were busy training the military forces ascendant in governments throughout Central America. US settlers imported Jim Crow laws and customs to the Canal Zone, where sisters staffed a school for black children who were excluded from the Catholic schools attended by white North Americans and affluent mestizo Panamanians.[52]

In hospital work, a diarist expressed distress over the Zone's acute racial divisions: "The colored people are lovely to work with, but . . . they are mistreated by the whites here. . . . They can do the same work as the whites—in fact can work side by side—but the colored man receives only a third of the white man's salary." She recognized the injustice of segregation and economic oppression but upheld other racial boundaries, describing the horror of miscegenation in noting that sisters were "surprised and sickened" to see one of "our American boys"—an apparently white soldier—"paying too much attention to a girl who was the color of our black veil."[53]

In a more private account of the Canal Zone, another sister mulled over the moral ambiguities that emerged from the tangle of ideals—cultural equality, sexual order, and American benevolence—that Maryknoll brought to mission work. After meeting a young man who impressed her with his piety and goodness, Sister Loretta Kruegler wrote her family: "He and all his brothers and sisters are illegitimate, as is as frequent as not the case here. . . . This boy seems another Martin de Porres. You know, Martin was illegitimate, I never knew that 'til the other day." She expressed her esteem for an individual by linking him with the venerated Martin de Porres, a biracial Peruvian who ministered to African slaves and the poor in the early seventeenth century. Martin de Porres would be canonized in 1962, becoming a patron saint of interracial cooperation and people of color. The figure of Martin de Porres helped Kruegler recognize that racial prejudice hampered the work of the church and that the perceived grave sin of illegitimacy did not determine the value of an individual. She hoped to share this insight with her family but feared the intolerance of others back home, asking "please don't publicise this letter. People don't understand."[54]

Kruegler, the eleventh child of "a very religious family, a very Catholic family," struggled with reconciling illegitimacy, racialized stigma, and the sanctity of the individual, which had been so emphasized under the Mystical Body doctrine. Her task as a missionary was to act on the commandment of love, but she keenly perceived how Catholics who might support her vocation treated illegitimacy with contempt. In the end, when she asked for help with Panama's problems, she identified racism, not sexual sin, as the deciding factor hampering Maryknoll's work: "Have the children pray for their brothers and sisters in Panama. . . . Prejudice is very strong so that makes it hard for the Sisters since the Americans

FIGURE 5.4. Sister Loretta Kruegler and children in Panama, undated. Credit: Maryknoll Mission Archives

and Panamanians look down on the Negroes."[55] Although she was not ready to dismiss sexual sin as irrelevant, she pointed to the social sin of racism as the more pressing matter.

The vow of obedience ensured that concern about such ambiguities would occur in personal, rather than communal, contexts. The institutional church did not leave room for sisters to question their charge as they carried out the tasks of postwar reconstruction and religious revitalization. In the end, the pluralistic ideals articulated in the principles of the Mystical Body of Christ were countermanded by higher priority concerns among the ecclesiastical hierarchy. Religious orthodoxy was of utmost importance, but Cold War geopolitics consumed a comparable amount of attention. Maryknoll participated in the anticommunist crusade with vigor.

COLD WAR MISSION

In 1946, the sisters' promotional material goaded potential donors and recruits: "communism is a challenge—isn't it?—to those who possess the infinite wealth of Faith, which of its essence demands expansion." Warning that this anti-Christian doctrine of "hate and destruction" threatened "our potential converts," Maryknoll assured its donors that by taking the offensive and funding clinics and classrooms, Americans could triumph.[56] Postwar anticommunist preoccupations invested mission social services and religious outreach with a newly explicit political significance.

The tone of Maryknoll's internationalism was informed by US geopolitics, but it was also linked to the Vatican's social teachings. The Vatican had consistently expressed its antipathy to socialism, notably in a 1937 screed against "bolshevistic and atheistic Communism," the encyclical *Divini Redemptoris*.[57] Such work spoke to men. The popes addressed the laity as workers, employers, and heads of families, and they described the responsibilities of the church in terms of the priest's labors. This meant that the tasks of women religious went unspecified, except for their role in religious instruction. The Maryknoll Sisters added their own gloss to the cause by connecting their efforts to the triumphal and even bellicose liberalism shared in US Catholic circles. Maryknoll also emphasized the importance of women's domain as a safeguard against infiltration. In this, the congregation found an ally in consummate cold warrior Francis Spellman, the New York cardinal called the "most influential American Catholic prelate of his age." At the funeral of Mary Josephine Rogers in 1955, Spellman confided to Rogers's successor, Mother Mary Columba Tarpey, "there is no Community for whom I have a higher esteem than yours."[58]

In mission literature as well as individual accounts, Maryknollers expressed strong faith in the intellectual underpinnings of the liberal anticommunism that guided US policy making. Drawing on the premises of containment theory, sisters viewed communism as a contagion spread through devious means that could culminate in the destruction of Western, Christian civilization. Despite their on-the-ground presence in the Pacific and Latin America, Maryknoll women described Marxist political movements as the simple product of Soviet machinations. They failed to detect the local roots of discontent.

In contrast to the pacifism of Dorothy Day and the Catholic Workers, many Maryknollers believed that war might be necessary to secure peace. Sisters in Hawaii were dismayed at the limited scale of the Korean conflict and at the perceived weakness in the response of President Harry Truman. A diarist reported: "Naturally we are all shocked and grieved over the news report of the removal of General Douglas MacArthur from his command in the Far East." Truman's unwillingness to challenge China was, "of course, just what the Russians were looking for." The sister had recourse to a more amenable inter-cessor in the conflict: "May Our Lady respond to the urgent prayers of her children for peace!"[59] Peace could prevail only when communism was force-fully eliminated.

Like the International Rescue Committee (IRC), the organization that backed the "jungle doctor" Tom Dooley's celebrated anticommunist interven-tions in Southeast Asia, Maryknoll interpreted mission outreach as a quest for the hearts and minds of the developing world. It sought to deliver these hearts and minds to the Catholic Church, but it also identified social progress with the introduction of American values and capitalist development. Like the IRC, it partnered with the US government in aid projects; unlike the IRC, Maryknoll did not establish formal ties to the Central Intelligence Agency (CIA) or State Department. Instead, sisters and priests participated in programs like the Alli-ance for Progress and the Peace Corps, lending their labor to literacy campaigns, housing projects, and health care initiatives.[60]

A new line of work at what Maryknoll called the "bamboo gate"—lands adja-cent to the communist "bamboo curtain"—directly addressed the consequences of Communist revolution in China. In South Korea, Hong Kong, Macau, and Formosa (Taiwan), the congregation established emergency services for refu-gees. In Hong Kong, where the population increased fourfold between 1945 and 1951, sisters administered extensive social services in refugee colonies with the encouragement and financial assistance of the overwhelmed colonial govern-ment. Mission works included a housing project spearheaded and largely funded by the sisters and a community center that provided recreation, education, employment services, and relief to over 7,200 families. From this point on, refu-gee services were a regular part of the sisters' ministry.[61]

Maryknoll sisters not only demonstrated their expertise in these projects, but they also created public relations opportunities that dramatized their contributions to the Cold War effort. The medical ministry of the congregation's first doctor, Mercy Hirschboeck, in Pusan (Busan), Korea, was no mere publicity stunt, as the city quadrupled in size with the surge of refugees and orphans affected by the Korean conflict. At the same time, scholar Suzanne Thurman explains, "the image of American nuns bringing state-of-the-art medical care to the victims of Marxism struck a chord with the American public."[62] Inspired by an ostensibly selfless desire to serve and reaching a population in desperate need, the Maryknoll clinic evoked the idea of a battle waged not through violence but by altruism.

The sisters' more typical areas of labor also carried considerable value in the context of postwar recovery and anticommunist prophylaxis. The classroom was a particularly important site for exerting the type of soft power that might subdue communism without conflict. *Maryknoll* cautioned its readers that communists were poised to teach children "that American democracy is the real evil in the world, a thing to be purged in blood." The Maryknoll Sisters, a 1951 financial appeal highlighted, had the power to shape ideology. As the ideas encountered in the classroom could either "plunge the world into utter helplessness and despair or hold it steady on the way to heaven," sisters were positioned to supply the "RIGHT IDEAS" to their students—"South American boys, and Chinese and Filipino and African and Hawaiian youngsters."[63] The sisters' globe-spanning presence conferred advantages in confronting the shape-shifting enemy that knew no borders.

Maryknoll sisters and priests administered two ventures in community development designed to put a vision of cooperative capitalism into motion: labor collectives and credit unions. These projects resonated with the development goals espoused by liberal internationalists who sought to address the deprivations experienced in the so-called Third World with the capitalist development schemes of modernization theory. They also borrowed from the premises of Vatican social teachings, which held that economic harmony could be achieved among consumers, laborers, and managers when behavior was guided by the precepts of natural law. Labor collectives were not new to Maryknoll: in the 1920s the sisters' Hong Kong mission had commissioned local women to produce religious vestments for sale. After World War II, sisters conducted such activities with a more explicit intent of fostering solvency in a cash economy. Collectives like Hong Kong's Pope Pius XII Handicraft School were, according to a Maryknoll priest, "the embodiment of an idea that is calculated to transform the dependent and penniless squatter into an independent and self-reliant citizen and member of the community."[64] This approach to poverty rejected the supervisory function of the socialist state. Charitable organizations aimed to produce a capitalism built not on untrammeled competition but on mutual support between labor and management.

Maryknoll established credit unions with similar expectations of capitalist uplift. Taking their cues from a Catholic cooperative movement launched from Antigonish, Nova Scotia, in the 1930s, several Maryknoll priests introduced credit unions into missions to militate against usurious practices that locked workers into cycles of debt and peonage. Concerned with women's narrow horizons in patriarchal Korean families and inspired to spread democracy at the "bamboo gate," Maryknoll Sister Gabriella Mulherin trained with the founder of the Antigonish movement in 1958 and then introduced credit unions to South Korea.

There, she found that a "lack of mutual trust" hampered the establishment of groups where members would put up modest, regular deposits to be able to borrow at low rates when necessary. Mulherin drew upon her pastoral skills to overcome this obstacle, cultivating trust among the members in what might today be described as a microfinance project. The idea caught on and quickly spread from her single venture with 28 members in 1960 to fifty-two credit unions with 6,900 members collectively in 1963. The World Council of Credit Unions posthumously honored Mulherin's role in sparking credit union development throughout East Asia. Maryknoll historian Penny Lernoux concluded that Korean credit unions had indeed fostered political uplift as their early members "had risen in the ranks of democratic political movements, academia, and labor unions."[65]

At midcentury, *Maryknoll* was inclined to describe the popularity of credit unions in Cold War terms. The magazine explained: "Each new credit union . . . deals another blow to the distressing poverty of the villagers and weakens the forces of oppression. The quiet revolution of a young Maryknoller, which is elevating the dignity of man, might well replace the revolution of blood and slavery so vigorously sought by [the] Reds."[66] Here, reference to the dignity of man not only hearkened to the Mystical Body's emphasis on the sacredness of the individual but also evoked capitalist ideologies of economic individualism.

MADRE GO HOME

Sisters claimed to interrupt communist infiltration in crucial venues: refugee camps, schools, homes, and workplaces. Yet magazine profiles and diary boasts aside, the Catholic Church's schemes for social progress had a limited impact on the growing unrest and poverty in mission territories. Any doubts that these ambiguities and difficulties may have posed to Maryknoll's triumphalist projections remained hidden behind the unified front of its pietistic, anticommunist public identity.

However, the daily work of mission revealed tensions raised by the sisters' political and national allegiances. Nowhere was this more evident than in Latin

America. The influx of mission personnel to Bolivia, Chile, Guatemala, Nicaragua, Mexico, Panama, and Peru in the 1940s and 1950s occurred alongside heavy-handed US political and economic intrigue directed at suppressing leftist movements. Drawing on their authority as religious and expert humanitarians, sisters unwittingly helped foster climates of fear and despotism inimical to the spirit of love that was proclaimed to be the essence of evangelization. They expected mission populations to be grateful for American help. They were surprised when they met hostility or indifference to their efforts.

Disconcerting encounters peppered mission interactions even as the sisters' services were widely solicited and appreciated. In Cobija, Bolivia, an elderly woman, impatient to receive a clothing donation, shocked the sisters with her anti-American and anticlerical sentiments. She was overheard saying that "these foreigners will get what is coming to them when the persecution comes. They will be imprisoned and beaten just like those two nuns I was reading about." The convent diarist took it in stride: "What fiendish thoughts from a little old lady, who now cannot be sweet enough to us." Another group in Bolivia worried over the discovery that post office workers had contemptuously destroyed mail directed to the convent: "Some letters were partly burned and others were found being used for bathroom purposes. . . . A bit disheartening to say the least."[67]

Such everyday disruptions betrayed the fraught circumstances of the mission interactions. Though these small incidents bore little direct connection to political events, they revealed brewing resentments that pitted Latin American peoples' movements against US foreign policy and development aid. US women's religious outreach was centered on the premise that interpersonal encounters could shape broader political and economic developments. The reverse was evident in Maryknoll missions, where structural inequalities exerted their influence on person-to-person mission relationships.

As anti-Americanism spread through Latin America, sisters blamed discontent on aberrant individuals, figures like "a Russian trained communist" student leader who apparently saw fit to infiltrate the remote jungle town of Guayaramerín, Bolivia. Such agitators introduced misguided sentiments to Maryknoll students, who argued that "'Communism is wonderful; if you have rice and I don't have any, you must give me half of yours.'" A diarist acknowledged that "to many who never have enough to eat this is music to their ears."[68] The supposed communist influence undermined sisters' authority and challenged their theology. Students tested them: "'You can't be a Catholic and a Communist' say the padres but they don't know since they are only 'gringos. . . .' 'Why can't communists be Godparents since they are the best people in town, Madre.'" An anti-American demonstration in La Paz inspired one in Guayaramerín, but the demonstration did not trouble the diarist: "as there are only five Americans—all Maryknollers—it did not last long."[69] When sisters embraced their role as ambassadors of American liberalism, they rarely recognized why their allegiances stirred animosity.

The sisters found themselves embroiled in conflicts explicitly tied to US foreign policy in two prominent settings. First, during the sisters' inadvertent participation in the Guatemalan coup staged by the CIA in 1954, a Cold War myopia obscured the repressive circumstances underlying their presence. Second, skirmishes over nationalism in the Panama Canal Zone pitted sisters against the students they expected to influence.

In Guatemala, sisters stepped into a situation that outwardly confirmed the righteousness of US Catholic internationalism. They arrived in Guatemala City in 1953 to open the Colegio Monte María, an elite girls' school. They soon became aware that "Guatemala was a focal point for Communistic indoctrination of the Western hemisphere," which was evident in the labor and land reform schemes of the democratically elected reform government of Jacobo Árbenz Guzmán.[70] Sisters feared the threat of the persecution of the church and the domino effect by which Central America would be lost to the Soviets. Their faith gave them confidence that the forces of God would triumph.

When *Time* reported that the legislator Cesar Montenegro Paniagua had declared that "as soon as trouble starts they plan to decapitate all anti-communists without more ado," the Guatemala City diarist took satisfaction in the piety of a student, Maria Teresa Montenegro, "the precious little daughter of the man who is so anxious to make martyrs of all of us." Montenegro "says the prayers before and after class as though the salvation of the world rested on her little shoulders." Maryknoll maintained that the salvation of the world depended on inoculating children against communism. It now faced the task in a dramatically immediate form. The sisters felt the strategic importance of their connection with the Montenegros and were baffled at Cesar's apparent belligerence, for "Mrs. Montenegro is a sterling character and one of our most loyal mothers."[71] By that time, her husband's days in the government were limited. An exiled general, Carlos Castillo Armas, had entered Guatemala with a small army to unseat Árbenz.

Castillo Armas delivered the sisters from the martyrdom that they feared in a successful coup in mid-1954. When Castillo Armas took power on the feast of the Visitation of Mary, July 2, the sisters concluded that "Our Lady" had saved Guatemalans from communism "because of their devotion to Her." The "liberator" Castillo Armas made it possible for the sisters to continue their politically strategic religious mission.[72] A 1958 report of Colegio Monte María outlined that the girls' school, "based on Christian democratic principles, and organized according to U.S. standards suitably adapted to the needs of Guatemala . . . , would serve to build up a strong bulwark against prevailing Communism, and offer strong, continued counter-action against that modern evil." The rationale rested on the strategic significance of education, as "the past history of Central and South America showed clearly that revolutionary movements have originated in the schools in these countries." Their future in the country secured by the junta, sisters endeavored to instill social responsibility and Christian morality among Guatemala City's daughters of privilege. The sisters explained that this element of their curriculum might catalyze the spirit of uplift: "it is our persevering hope that Monte María's graduates, responding genuinely to the need of their own people for education, will give at least some years to the service of the forgotten children of the mountain pueblos."[73]

However, things in Guatemala were not as they appeared to the sisters. When they arrived, they were amid what can be recognized in retrospect as the CIA's covert campaign to topple Árbenz. When these activities accelerated in the spring of 1954, the sisters' diarist noted, not coincidentally, that "many rumors are beginning to reach us concerning the plans of the communists." To destabilize the popular regime, the CIA deployed extensive psychological operations designed to foment an internal revolt in advance of the junta's invasion. Or rather, as a sister understood such activities, "there began to operate from nowhere a phantom radio station, giving the real news to the people about the time of liberation that was upon Guatemala." Stories of the abuses of the Árbenz government were spread by word of mouth, newspapers, leaflets dropped from the sky, and graffiti. They told of communist control of the government, secret inquisitions, impending confiscation of property, and the repression of the church. They primed sisters and the families of their students for civil upheaval. "Everyone," the diarist wrote, "expects a revolution soon because things can't continue as they are."[74]

But the coup wasn't a revolution against Árbenz's apparent "Communistic indoctrination." His abortive prolabor policy and land reforms were intended to lessen the chokehold on the Guatemalan economy held by native oligarchs and the United Fruit Company. The coup was a reactionary strike carried out primarily by US secret forces to ensure the stability of this system. The contours of the sisters' daily life in Guatemala were determined by the close relationship between the Catholic Church and the ruling and business elite whose interests the coup protected. Sisters gained their perspective on Guatemala's economic needs and social problems in their encounters with wealthy Colegio families or in circumstances like visits with "Mr. Malamphy at United Fruit and Mr. Collins at Grace Line, both of whom are very good to us."[75] These two US companies, which extracted enormous profits out of Central America, did indeed treat the sisters well. The coffee they regularly received as a gift from Mr. Collins came as a result of an export economy that starved the population. The uplift model of social responsibility instituted by the preconciliar church did not inspire the sisters to examine the limits of charity or the abuses of the powerful.

Accordingly, the revolutionary activity that erupted into an undeclared civil war did not originate in the infiltration of Soviet agents. It developed along the existing fault lines in a society built on violent racial and class oppression. The sisters' absolutist understanding of communism and their insistence on a piety-driven, top-down model of social progress served as a theological accompaniment to US policy maneuvers that underwrote a horrific spiral of unrest. When Castillo Armas was assassinated in 1957, the diarist described him as "our martyr-president." But sisters had also struggled to make sense of his capriciously repressive presidency, which set the pace for subsequent ones. When he freed Communists he had imprisoned, the diarist marveled: "Castillo Armas himself officiated at the ceremony of release. Surely this is a hard country to understand!" Sisters expressed concern over the fate of Cesar Montenegro, the father of their model student, who—unlike his family—was not granted permission to leave the country: "we fear he is in for a hard time."[76]

Later events gave reasons for concern. The coup ushered in an era of presidential assassinations, increased disregard for democratic processes, and military control of the government. In 1970, Montenegro was assassinated, one of the many people killed in a convulsion of violence carried out by US-trained paramilitaries. The terrorism of the ruling class would reach genocidal proportions in its efforts to eliminate opposition from the left and indigenous Guatemalans. This regime was not the communist bulwark that the sisters envisioned, but it was the communist bulwark they defended. Inadvertently, they helped normalize antidemocratic militarism as the answer to socialist agitation.[77]

In the Panama Canal Zone, conflicts over US interventions in Central America reached the convent door. Cheering US occupation of the territory, sisters flew the American flag, celebrated the Fourth of July, and, on one occasion, also saluted the wife of the US vice president, who was passing through on a goodwill tour. When Richard and Patricia Nixon visited Panama in 1955, three years before their disastrous trip to Venezuela, Pat thrilled the sisters by stopping her motorcade next to Maryknoll schoolchildren, "dressed in their red plaid uniforms and waving American flags," to say hello. The diarist acknowledged that the move might have been made for publicity purposes, as "someone said later she was primed to be extra nice to religious since we are in a Catholic Country"—the Eisenhower administration was in the midst of treaty negotiations. Still, the sisters were delighted by the attention. In the face of anti-American agitation in the subsequent decade, the sisters complied with Nixon's parting words: "she told the children to keep waving their flags—and to wave them hard."[78]

As the promise of the Cuban revolution inspired protest movements throughout Central America, the sisters staffing Colegio San Vicente in Ancón became enmeshed in confrontations over US occupation. They maintained that faith in the US presence and Catholic ideals held the answer to Panama's struggles.

An increasingly vocal contingent of Panamanians disagreed. In 1958, the sisters observed a large student demonstration against the presidency of Ernesto de la Guardia Navarro, another oligarch supported by the United States. The national guard used tear gas to disperse the protestors, killing one student. The sisters kept their distance. As usual, they attributed organized nationalist and anti-imperialist movements to "the Communist influence . . . , operating underground in various disguises, but always boring into the vital fibers of the country." When a delegation visited the convent asking for a donation for a memorial mass for the slain student, the women responded "that we did not wish to be affiliated with this federation, and that we would have our own Mass for the same intention." They asserted their spiritual stewardship even as they rejected temporal association with the victim.[79]

The demonstrations turned into more explicit attacks on US imperialism. They targeted the sisters themselves, whose convent was located on the border between the Canal Zone and the Republic of Panama. Protestors "did their bit along the border street in front of the convent. We watched the youngsters and some older people parade up and down carrying their flags and shouting, 'Go home, Yankees!'" The diarist reflected that "it's sad to see the anti-U.S. feeling growing, but in a country with so many unemployed and destitute, Communist agitators build up 'Yankee imperialism' as the cause of everybody's trouble and they get a large, irresponsible group worked up to riots and vandalism." She concluded that this quest for self-determination thwarted Latin American development: "All this instability delays the progress and prosperity that everybody longs for." And much as the sisters insistently waved their flags in front of the convent, so demonstrators in this skirmish endeavored to plant a Panamanian flag in the Canal Zone. The sisters saw no equivalence between Panamanian calls for independence and their own nationalist enthusiasm.[80]

Faith in the Cold War gospel desensitized them to the organic development of anti-Americanism. They appraised the protestors much as they would schoolchildren, dismissing riots and vandalism as undisciplined, immature behavior. Just as they believed that educational methods that instilled restraint would improve life for their students, sisters expected the US carrot-and-stick pursuit of a Central American sphere of influence—the carrot of development aid, the stick of military interventions—would secure the progress that juvenile agitators obstructed through their lack of obedience.

In the 1940s and 1950s, Maryknoll ardently supported the Vatican's cautious pluralism and insistent anticommunism. The sisters' storied place in US Catholic life in the years after World War II reflected the convergence of ideals of the Catholic Church and US liberal internationalism, with new longings for racial harmony and a muscular commitment to the triumph of putatively democratic institutions over communism. Maryknoll's politicization under the influence of the Vatican's social teachings and US foreign policy confirmed the righteousness of church and nation.

This convergence soon came to a close. Pope John XXIII's 1959 call to update the Catholic Church ushered in the profound canonical and theological reforms of the Second Vatican Council (1962–65). At the same time, Maryknoll was roiled by social movements stirring outside of the church. With new opportunities for institutional reform and fractures in the Cold War consensus, the congregation pursued more expansive directions in theology and more oppositional angles in political commitments.

PART III "THE FERMENT OF FREEDOM"

   In the early 1960s, Maryknoll stood on the cusp of profound internal and external changes. The Second Vatican Council did not mandate radical reform in Catholic institutions. However, its directive to engage in self-scrutiny made radical reforms possible. As a participant in international and intercultural projects launched in a heated geopolitical context, and as a community that valued women's leadership, the Maryknoll Sisters were positioned to make such changes. With the fragmentation of the Cold War consensus as well as the growing momentum of civil rights, anticolonial, and antipoverty moments, Maryknoll was compelled to rethink the meanings of boundary-crossing evangelization.

   During the same period, the YWCA of the USA had emerged from the anticommunist attacks that had proven so vexing at the height of McCarthyism. As much as the New Right redefined the politics of Christianity after the midcentury, it could not suppress the Christian righteousness claimed by the civil rights movement. When the civil rights movement accrued national legitimacy and political traction, the YWCA's social consciousness regained its air of credibility. Seeds that had been sown in the early interracial work of constituency groups, which culminated in the 1946 Interracial Charter that pledged active involvement with desegregation, were coming to fruition.

   The YWCA's midcentury civil rights contributions constitute one of the more striking and well-documented chapters in its history.[1] With its members' extensive involvement in interracial advocacy and direct action, the association produced many of the foot soldiers of the movement and provided a wealth of organizing spaces. It nurtured the career of Dorothy Height, the lone woman among the so-called Big Six organizers of the 1963 March on Washington. Height created decades of innovative racial justice programming from her National Board staff position, but the YWCA also facilitated her innovative volunteer career. From the vantage point of 1986, Height explained the symbiosis: "One thing that is little known about my role in the civil rights movement is that the nature of my professional assignments and the conscious and deliberate involvement of the National Board in the quest for equality made it possible for me to carry, as a volunteer, my role in the United Civil Rights Leadership as president of the National Council of Negro Women. This was more than a cooperative relationship. There was always a wholeness for which I am deeply grateful."[2]

Madie Hall Xuma carried YWCA racial justice influences to the transnational context as she linked the uplift politics of African American clubwomen that she had honed first as a YWCA secretary in 1930s North Carolina and Virginia to the apartheid-era liberation struggle in South Africa. Xuma came to prominence in the 1940s and 1950s in the Women's League of the African National Congress (ANC) and as the wife of ANC president, A. B. Xuma. At the same time, she organized Zenzele (do-it-yourself) YWCAs dedicated to community-level women's empowerment and cross-racial fellowship. The historian Iris Berger concludes that Zenzele clubs "helped to nurture the locally based politics of the [South African] Black Consciousness Era during the 1970s."[3] Much as US YWCAs served as organizing spaces during the long civil rights movement, the Zenzele clubs provided the discursive insights and practical training for later grassroots mobilizations in South Africa.

Though the 1960s and 1970s were a period of turmoil in the United States, the YWCA's efforts to engage with progressive social movements evinced a certain institutional stability, given its historical moorings. The Maryknoll Sisters joined the YWCA in responding to the tumult by revisiting and reasserting their vision of socially relevant Christianity. The considerable political and institutional transformations undertaken by the Maryknoll Sisters set the congregation's religious ethics on a course of convergence with those of the YWCA. By the end of the period discussed in this part of the book, this convergence extended into the experience of red baiting.

The frames of feminism and human rights provide a way of interpreting how conceptions of women's community and political commitments brought the two groups into closer alignment. Both obliquely and directly, feminist insurgencies provided both groups with new energy. Popular feminist discourses that encompassed both the reformist spirit of liberal feminists and the provocations of radical women's liberation raised social issues and lent intellectual resources that invigorated long-standing commitments to women-centered community and politics. When the Second Vatican Council directed religious institutes to examine the charism of their founders, the Maryknoll Sisters discerned that Mary Josephine Rogers had laid foundations for the congregation to pursue modern directions in ministry and community identity. Through sometimes fractious soul-searching, sisters opted to jettison the habit that had given women religious such a distinctive outward identity. But innovations in approaches to pastoral and apostolic labors proved more consequential to their sense of purpose than elimination of mandates about clothing and cloister regimentation. While large numbers of women left the congregation after conciliar reforms, echoing wider vocational trends, Maryknoll found renewal in reexamining the meaning of religious vows. It established democratic governing structures and, because of changes in the Catholic Church more generally, it was no longer tethered to the responsibilities of maintaining large schools and medical facilities. Maryknoll recast its understanding of the role of the individual in community, expanding opportunities for women to forge their own path in a decentralized church and in a crisis-ridden geopolitical landscape.

It is ironic that, to an extent, the YWCA became a more separatist institution than the Maryknoll Sisters. Of course, as a congregation of women religious, sisters held themselves apart from men in fundamental ways. Yet they were not situated in exclusively female worlds. Their projects served a mixed clientele. In the early part of the congregation's existence, sisters usually worked under the supervision of the male church hierarchy. In later years, they used partnership models to conduct their work. This often meant working in concert with nonprofit organizations and social service agencies. Sisters frequently coordinated their efforts with their companion group of fathers and brothers, who wholeheartedly joined the quest to infuse mission with the insights of the Vatican Council and the liberation theology movement. Many Maryknoll sisters became interested in feminist issues as a result of the realization that "women are the most marginalized, anywhere and everywhere."[4] But their newly articulated dedication to the "spiritually dehumanized, socially oppressed, culturally marginated, or economically deprived" meant that the sites of their labors in the 1960s and 1970s continued to be largely heterosocial.[5]

In contrast, the YWCA regularly affirmed its commitment to remain a space by and for women. Pressured at an early point by the Young Men's Christian Association to merge, the YWCA's leaders maintained that an all-female institutional structure was fundamental to the group's identity. Not all YWCA constituents shared this belief. Indeed, several local associations staked their survival on mergers with the better-funded YMCA.[6] But the national leadership directed its work toward cultivating common ground among diverse women, which linked older models of bourgeois club life with the spirit of youth revolt.

To this end, the National Board enlisted the feminist theologian Letty Russell to create religious programming. Her output combined group work approaches to social change with 1970s-style consciousness-raising. "Let us try to help unlock the resources of spiritual power so that the ferment of freedom can aid in the struggle of liberation," she encouraged YWCA readers. One of the first women ordained by the United Presbyterian Church, Russell applied YWCA rhetoric of Christian social consciousness to the radical movements that stirred the interest of younger members. She asserted that "the biblical God does appear as the 'fighting liberator' who wants people to be free from all sorts of (not only 'spiritual') oppression." Putting the organization's democratic ethos in the parlance of the times, she designed her study guides and exegesis to "*set women free to do their own thing*," exhorting her audience "to free ourselves . . . from racism, from sexism, from colonialism—in short, from oppression in all its demonic manifestations."[7]

National Board leaders also mentored the members of a younger generation whose provocations called to mind the Social Gospel insurgency in the early organization. While in the 1920s Social Gospel politicization culminated in support of the working-class membership and an expansive legislative agenda, in the 1970s younger women pushed the YWCA to ally itself with liberation movements. Renetia Martin, a student radical recruited into the organization by

FIGURE P3.1. Dorothy Height, director of the YWCA Center for Racial Justice, reports on the YWCA Teen Counseling Project, 1974. Credit: Sophia Smith Collection, Smith College

Dorothy Height and her activist clubwomen colleagues, set the tenor of this new era in a 1970 convention speech that ended with the benediction, "in the name of Malcolm, Martin, and Jesus—Power to the struggle." That year, Martin and her cohort challenged the national assembly to make a more forceful commitment to racial equality by declaring "one imperative" to be the YWCA's foremost priority: "To thrust our collective power toward the elimination of racism wherever it exists and by any means necessary." As had been the case at the 1920 national convention, some delegates were discomfited by the boldness of the resolution, which invoked the cadences of Malcolm X, but they elected to adopt it, honoring the organization's tradition of democratic leadership and self-empowerment among young women.[8]

As was the case with the YWCA, the most potent challenges to the liberalism of the Maryknoll Sisters came from the left in this period. And like the YWCA, the sisters endeavored to be responsive to calls for revolution at the same time that they upheld their institutional heritage. As the next chapter shows, the sisters were able to draw on an unprecedentedly capacious body of Catholic social teachings to navigate these difficulties.

While the feminist movement gave new life to the organizations' single-sex configurations, the human rights movement, broadly considered, provided an extensive social movement infrastructure that gave life to their advocacy interests. The human rights movement as such came into its own in the 1970s, as indicated by the efflorescence of leverage politics advanced by such nongovernmental organizations (NGOs) as Amnesty International and Human Rights Watch. Yet the efforts of Maryknoll and the YWCA illustrate human rights activism as extending beyond the discourses and methods associated with this cluster of NGOs. The YWCA's participation in intergovernmental forums, beginning with the League of Nations, reflects one manifestation of this. The YWCA lent its resources to decades of consultative work on women's initiatives of the United Nations, notably including the push for a Commission on the Status of Women after World War II.[9] The two groups' involvement in the African American civil rights movement, connected as it was to midcentury global struggles over minority rights and white supremacy, should also be included under the umbrella of human rights. The turn from civil rights into ethnic nationalism in the United States echoed the Third World solidarity movements and revolts against repressive governments that posed unprecedented challenges to the colonialist world order.[10] Since the YWCA of the USA's international work had been gutted during the Great Depression, it had fewer ways to participate in on-the-ground transnational mobilizations, but the sisters' work in the field compelled them to reorient mission projects. The Maryknoll Sisters launched an advocacy office in 1974 as it became "more clearly aware of the increasing interdependence and inter-complicity of events, which . . . nurture injustice throughout the world."

The sisters used their transnational connections to respond vigorously to these types of injustices, contributing to the global dissemination of information among the international networks of NGOs that made up the bedrock of the human rights movement.[11]

Such activity, in concert with the liberation theology influences that inspired Maryknoll to stake its claim in the body politic, generated discontent among conservative forces who resented the postconciliar influence of the Catholic left. The final chapter of this book describes how their criticism created obstacles for Maryknoll much like those faced by the YWCA in the early 1900s and at mid-century. Compelled to answer charges of disloyalty to their nation and their faith, Maryknoll women were put on the defensive.

Although the YWCA found purpose in the era's political developments, it would also find this to be a challenging time. It was not politics but instead practical matters of budgetary shortfalls and administrative strain that set it on an uncertain path. Its top-heavy bureaucracy had been highly innovative in its earliest years, using an economy of scale to facilitate expansion and programming development. However, in the second half of the twentieth century, there were no longer the same organic relationships holding community associations together in a national federation. The antiracist "one imperative" established at the 1970 convention became the banner initiative of the national organization—though the National Board also administered grant-funded programs, particularly related to youth and health care. Community YWCAs, while delivering programming related to the "one imperative," found their niche as social service providers, with facilities that continued to be used for transitional housing, after-school and adult education, and emergency services for victims of domestic violence and sexual assault. The national organization struggled to find its place.

The remaining two chapters in this book discuss the ways in which Maryknoll joined the YWCA in making a leftward turn in its approach to Christian social change. The closing chapter visits the most famous—and wrenching—episode of Maryknoll history as it investigates just how instrumental this globally oriented Christian women's activism could be.

6 · "WE CHOOSE TO IDENTIFY WITH THE CHURCH OF THE POOR"

Preferential Option in Action

At Maryknoll's St. Anthony's school in Maui, Hawaii, the sisters played Camelot in celebration of John F. Kennedy's inauguration. They held a costume dinner, "complete with the Kennedys (the President, Sister Imelda Marie, and Jackie, Sister Louis Mary), their families, and the new White House entourage." Sisters "dined amid the splendor of candle light and sparkling tiaras" and filled the evening with "toasts, speeches and congratulatory telegrams."[1] Maryknoll sisters cherished these lighthearted moments, bursts of school-girl levity that Mary Josephine Rogers had introduced to women's religious life. The activities affirmed the Maryknoll spirit, an institutional identity that balanced disciplined sanctification with a cheerful dedication to spreading the Gospel. The priorities of the Kennedy presidency similarly affirmed the mission course charted by Maryknoll in the previous fifteen years. Though the sisters infrequently indulged in the Camelot lifestyle, the congregation's preoccupation with the contagion of communism aligned with the premises driving the administration's cultural, economic, and military interventions overseas. Maryknoll belonged to a cluster of Catholic groups that worked on Kennedy-era soft-power projects designed to promote political stability and economic modernization in the Third World.[2] The administration's attention to the hemispheric politics of Latin America matched Maryknoll's concern over leftist agitation in the region where one-quarter of its overseas personnel were stationed.

At the mock inauguration as well as at the motherhouse, it would have been difficult to detect impending changes in the congregation and the liberal consensus shoring up Kennedy's foreign policy. Maryknoll labored like never before to expand the reach of its message, and it attracted an unmatched number of recruits as Catholics achieved new influence in US public life. Between 1955 and 1960, the Maryknoll Sisters increased the number of personnel stationed in foreign countries from 323 to 458 out of a population of sisters (professed and nonprofessed) that had grown from 1,127 to 1,430. In 1966, the year of peak membership, the organization numbered 1,675 women, with around 600 stationed in foreign missions.[3]

Such growth registered the success of Maryknoll's midcentury vision. However, the numbers were not the whole story, and the dramatic changes that unfolded during the 1960s and 1970s unsettled the institutional stability that the congregation had achieved. A combination of factors rooted in the internal dynamics of the Catholic Church, the geopolitical context of US mission presence, and generational shifts that affected women coming of age as sisters ushered in an era of uncertainty, experimentation, and internal dissent. Just as Camelot gave way to a deeply divided national polity, countercultural impulses and searching political critique became ascendant at Maryknoll, displacing the triumphalism and anticommunism that once suffused its missiology.

Amid these realignments, no single factor can account for the transformation of the Maryknoll Sisters from passionate cold warriors to a force on the Catholic left. Maryknoll's reconfiguration was not simply set into motion by the Second Vatican Council, an event often described as unique in generating progressive church activism. Nor can these developments be attributed solely to the influence of ostensibly secular social movements, such as anticolonial and feminist insurgencies. While these factors affected the sisters deeply, Maryknoll's heritage and on-the-ground experience propelled its journey. As had been the case for the YWCA, a combination of single-sex institutional structures and politicized religious consciousness proved adaptable in the face of social upheaval. And again paralleling the YWCA, a sense of crisis rooted in struggles over race, class, and nation pushed Maryknoll toward an increasingly activist end of the political and religious spectrum. It was not a quick or easy journey, but the congregation faced the global struggles of the 1970s with a core of committed personnel and a revitalized sense of purpose.

Observing a leftward migration in political interests and a concurrent drop in vocations that occurred widely among religious institutes, commentators like Garry Wills and William F. Buckley Jr. sounded an alarm over the crisis in the postconciliar Catholic Church. The vibrancy of Maryknoll throughout this period requires a more complex perspective. The struggles of the age effected an evolution, not dissolution, of the community bonds that held the organization together. Significant numerical losses in the congregation over the 1960s did not reflect decline. The women who reshaped the destiny of the community affirmed Mary Josephine Rogers's vision of socially engaged evangelization. From this foundation, they positioned their work within the social justice wing of the church and a global human rights community. In so doing, they refashioned their vocation into a vehicle of both individual autonomy and progressive reform.

"A DUCK TAKES TO WATER"

Maryknoll publicity in the early 1960s sounded the familiar warnings and promises of Cold War Catholicism. "The Communist menace thrives on faithless souls and empty stomachs," a magazine advertisement read. "Our many missioners are working fervently to reach all peoples who seek God and his gospel."[4] The warning highlighted the religious dimensions of the conflict; the promise assured donors that their financial support contributed to a peaceful Christian triumph over the elusive enemy. Distributing US food and technical aid, the sisters had a place on the front lines of Cold War charity. Conditions in the field, however, raised important questions about the aims and efficacy of both evangelical and political dimensions of mission.

In 1962, Pope John XXIII opened the Second Vatican Council. With an unexpectedly sweeping ambition to update the church, the council was charged with modernizing institutional structures and doctrine. Informally, the pope spoke of "flinging open the windows" to let in air, and indeed a new spirit seemed to animate the proceedings. With an emphasis on self-scrutiny, ecumenicalism, and engagement with contemporary social issues, Vatican documents struck a different tone than the papal proclamations of previous years, which maintained a rigid, neo-Thomistic logic that centered on fealty to the Catholic Church. Though it was business as usual in terms of women's exclusion, the council proved to be a relatively democratic forum for male clergy. The impact of the reforms adopted during the three-year council would quickly be felt in Catholic life. It transformed worship in the pews, the lifeways of religious, the apostolic chain of authority, and techniques of evangelization and education. The council sparked both rebirth and backlash, opening the way for the revolutionary impulses of liberation theology and a reactionary insurgency that would bear fruit in the papacy of John Paul II.

The council provides a convenient, if clichéd, metric to assess the changes that shook Maryknoll over the 1960s, and the congregation's experience yields two perspectives on the impact of the council on religious institutes. On the one hand, its journey confirms conclusions of commentators who have questioned the council's instrumentality. In the estimation of the sociologist Helen Rose Ebaugh, "the Council was simply one event in a much broader historical process."[5] The council itself did not produce dramatic upheaval, she argues. Instead, decades of questions percolating within and beyond the church had produced the council. For Maryknoll, many of the concerns shaping the proceedings had come to the forefront as challenges particularly relevant to a missionary congregation. Most important, the extent of poverty and social unrest in the field brought awareness of the depth of global inequality to Maryknoll women in advance of conciliar proclamations on such issues.

On the other hand, the pace of change in Maryknoll identity and practices indicates that the congregation fully embarked on restructuring only when conciliar directives enabled it to do so. Helene O'Sullivan, who entered Maryknoll just as the council convened, remembers it as clearly a transitional time. She felt "the winds of change were in the air" at the same time that she experienced "a very good taste of old religious life." Reflecting on the early years when she was embedded in the dramas and debates that accompanied conciliar mandates, she concluded, "it was wonderful because I saw the change, and I could see how people changed." Perhaps an assessment by Sister Barbara Hendricks best captures the dynamic of a group that was primed to renew its identity in the mid-1960s: "Our community took to these principles of Vatican II like a duck takes to water."[6] Identifying themselves as handmaids to the church, Maryknoll sisters had hardly been a force for revolution. Yet embarking on vocational renewal, sisters at the grassroots seized the initiative and thrust Maryknoll into a new model of religious life: one that prioritized democracy over hierarchy, community development over proselytizing, and structural social change over toleration of inequalities of the status quo.

The council affected Maryknoll in a direct fashion, as decrees on missionary activity and religious life mandated reform, and in diffuse ways, as new principles in social teachings filtered into mission rhetoric and practice. Conciliar-era documents such as *Gaudium et Spes* and *Pacem in Terris* advanced themes that resonated with Maryknoll personnel, particularly an emphasis on the dignity of each person, "which demands that a more humane and just condition of life be brought about," and the call for the church to pursue social justice through the "integration of faith and action."[7] These two documents also confronted the Cold War mentality underlying Maryknoll's outreach. In the words of historian Mary Margaret Reher, "no longer was atheistic communism the sole object of papal criticism." Lengthy meditations on the relationship between the commandment of love and international relations moved away from the intensive attention to the "satanic scourge of communism" that had characterized the Catholic political agenda in the previous decades. The documents singled out international militarism as a threat to human survival and denounced unjust schemes for economic development. Such provocations invited scrutiny of Maryknoll mission goals.[8]

The documents provided the sisters with a wider set of spiritual resources for interpreting their faith. O'Sullivan characterized the canonical training she underwent as a novice as rote "formulaic doctrine," and she saw things change quickly as she completed her training. "All of the sudden, along came Vatican II," she remembered, and she described the impact of the new language of social justice and the democratizing of sacred texts as a continual source of renewal: "An emphasis on scripture, the Holy Spirit, Revelation, how it worked through human beings. A Gospel for justice and the poor. It just transformed everything." Drawing on a new emphasis on open inquiry into sources of religious revelation, many members of the congregation found a less legalistic, more prophetic faith than the one that had motivated their predecessors. O'Sullivan explained the crucifixion of Jesus, the story on which Christian salvation hinges, as the embodiment of a Gospel mandate for temporal justice. "Really studying the life of Jesus and parables," she discovered "why he was really crucified: he was a threat to the empire." He was a threat "because his emphasis was being so for the poor. Even the church was laying these burdens on the poor, these purity burdens. Then Romans laid the taxes on the poor and crushed them. . . . That's what got him killed, rather than any formula of sins and seven virtues." She realized then that following the Gospel message meant living her vocation "more like Jesus's life. Being totally with the poor, understanding, and being on their side." In the congregation's search for a more authentic Gospel life, "everything changed. The world flipped."[9]

The conciliar mission decree *Ad Gentes* heightened such impulses. Reframing the decidedly insular, Eurocentric organization as a world church, this set of directives rejected mission as an incursion into the foreign and, appropriate to the council's larger move toward ecumenicalism, appraised nonorthodox practice and non-Catholic religions in a more favorable light. A conciliar watchword was inculturation, the adaptation of the Gospel message to the surrounding culture. The historian Angelyn Dries concludes that the document "presented a positive evaluation of other religions, acknowledging the 'seeds of the word'"—an existence of the divine—"beyond the Catholic Church and present before the missionary's arrival."[10] Thereafter, mission personnel (increasingly called missioners rather than missionaries) received training centered on immersion in local cultures and indigenous religious practices, in contrast to years of attempts to institute sacramental uniformity based on the traditions of Europe.

According to Sister Betty Ann Maheu, this radically affected the congregation's spirituality. The prescriptions of *Ad Gentes* countered missionaries' tendencies to hold themselves apart from the local communities, as sisters did when they lived in inaccessible convents, staffed by housekeepers who prepared American food. The document cast mission populations not as objects to be instructed in the rigors of the faith but as neighbors who supplied sisters with the opportunity to grow. Maheu reflected that "we saw all as persons whom God has always loved, persons open to love; we saw more clearly the goodness of people which often put us to shame and we began to realize that evangelization is a two-way process, that in the very process of evangelizing we ourselves are being evangelized." Throughout Latin America, this shift was especially evident as missioners encouraged local communities to revive the syncretic traditions that had been so vilified in previous generations.[11]

Sisters working in Tanzania described everyday ways in which the rhetoric of the council transformed practice. Patricia Cain, stationed there in the early 1960s, believed that the "experience of working on the grassroots" provided a special perspective on the council. The rural isolation of the mission meant the sisters "read many books about Vatican II and the theological renewals that were going on at that time." These documents resonated with Cain's sense of what it truly meant to carry the Gospel message. "The best of those times were the celebrations when we would dance with the people under a starry sky or have a meaningful liturgy or just visiting friends in their home," she recalled, or "when you would get together with other Sisters you would laugh long into the night." This simple, direct openness to personal connection sparked "appreciation and love for people and their struggles and a new concept of accompanying people—not really bringing them something but sharing in their journey as a person, walking with them."[12] Likewise, the cultural relativism promoted by *Ad Gentes* increased awareness of the richness of community healing practices and indigenous spiritualities.

In her first mission assignment—in the late 1960s in Tanzania's capital, Dar es Salaam—Darlene Jacobs was led to a new avenue of service by the antipoverty emphasis of the Vatican Council. At first, she taught music in "a private little conservatoire run by a British lady." Sisters frequently provided various private lessons to offset the costs of their work. Jacobs enjoyed her occupation, but she recalled, "I just didn't think I should be doing that in Tanzania." Whether Tanzanian or European, her students "were all mostly people with privilege of some kind. They were not the neediest. They were not the poorest." She decided that "I could probably use my skills in a better way, in a more helpful way," and she started an informal school for young men who had no other educational or work opportunities. Jacobs elected to shift her attention away from patrons who could support the Catholic infrastructure and toward those in need.[13]

Such sensibilities prompted Maryknoll sisters stationed in the United States to participate in the "racial apostolate" described by the historian Amy Koehlinger as the "complex network of programs and activities" devised by US women religious as their contribution to the struggle against racial injustice in the 1960s.[14] In the Bronx, Maryknoll women participated in "Summer in the City," which continued traditional work of home visiting and community services, but they framed that work in a postconciliar language that sounded the tones of a struggle against poverty and racial alienation appropriate to the atmosphere of urban crisis. Efforts to help teenagers secure jobs were designed to help "keep them off streets and [gain] self-respect." Young peoples' problems weren't their souls but instead "robbery, assault, carrying weapons, a lot of trouble with dope." Sisters showed their penchant for fun by holding a street dance and a "hootenanny" that they described as "a great success, the people just loved it."[15]

Such efforts fit the template for the new nuns of the 1960s, with their iconoclastic idealism and immersion in liberal social thought. A conference paper about Maryknoll's New York City addiction services efforts captures this spirit. Three sisters who devised the project in 1966 set out "to reverse [the] tide of 'turning on and dropping out' and to move its current in the direction of . . . a fully responsible human community."[16] Providing educational assistance and research, sisters collaborated with the academics and counselors of the city's Human Resources Administration in a work setting that would become a primary site of labor for postconciliar women religious: the nonsectarian, nonprofit social service agency. In workshops with business and church groups, sisters used their formal training in social work to spread a gospel of self-realization and personal healing.

Of the council documents, the mandate for renewal contained in the 1965 decree *Perfectae Caritatis* ("On the Appropriate Renewal of Religious Life") had the most visible and contentious impact on the congregation.[17] *Perfectae Caritatis* instructed religious communities to make a structured inquiry into their institutional configuration and the charism of their founders—the God-given calling that inspired the formation of the group—in light of social changes. It required communities to undertake thorough self-examination and reform, but it allowed them to carry out the reform on their own terms. This directive underscored the importance of the unique calling of each community, affirming the integrity of these institutions independently from their function in the ecclesiastical hierarchy. The self-directed process reflected the democratic spirit of the council, and it allowed religious groups to explore renewal without the scrutiny of often-censorious church authorities. It conferred on them new autonomy in crafting an approach to evangelization.

Maryknoll launched a period of reflection, often fractious deliberation, and experimentation. Demographic shifts and wider social movements led to dramatic changes. While the disintegration of urban ethnic enclaves reduced demand for parochial institutions that enlisted the labor of women religious, the upward mobility of white Catholics altered links to the neighborhood parish culture that had steered large numbers of young people into religious life in the 1940s and 1950s. O'Sullivan describes a generational factor at play that influenced her decision to join Maryknoll just as these changes began: "When you got to the twelfth grade, they made you look at what you wanted to do in life. . . . In those days, you really made a decision." The options were limited: "You kind of knew it would be the religious life or marriage or maybe a very special career, like a girl who wanted to be a doctor. You had to do that single-minded thing."[18]

Congregational statistics suggest that this single-minded mentality would soon be on the wane when O'Sullivan applied to join Maryknoll in 1961. The novitiate would shrink over the course of the 1960s from roughly 260 women in 1960 to 25 in 1970, while the number of professed sisters held relatively steady throughout the 1960s.[19] The much diminished number of women entering the congregation at the end of the 1960s was the consequence of factors that included but went beyond the changes introduced by the Vatican Council. At the same time that liberal feminism reshaped perspectives on women's professional employment, the leadership of women religious labored to cut attrition and raise credentials among incoming sisters.[20] O'Sullivan was affected by this: her application to join the congregation was deferred until she had spent time at an outside college. The imposition of a mandated period of self-reflection preceded conciliar reform—and the 1963 publication of Betty Friedan's *The Feminine Mystique*. Declining numbers of entrants stemmed from secular changes that provided Catholic women with more options, but these circumstances had also been deliberately engineered by religious superiors, a strategy designed not for recruitment but retention. Though forces of disarray would contribute monumentally to an exodus from religious life at the end of the decade, Maryknoll and other congregations sought a more committed and better qualified cadre of religious in the 1960s, not simply larger memberships.

The Maryknoll Sisters embarked on the renewal process in 1964, the year before *Perfectae Caritatis* was formally adopted by the Vatican. Sisters determined that the charism that inspired Rogers was essentially "innovative and flexible." "Ahead of its time," the Maryknoll spirit emphasized individuality and an ethos of care. Rogers, Cain reflected, had encouraged missionaries "to be present—to the person you are with—to God—to where you are and who you are."[21] Though Rogers had considered the vow of obedience to be the "supreme vow," the congregation believed her respect for individuality anticipated the Vatican Council's affirmation of "collegiality and democracy." To that end, Maryknoll established an elected, consensus-oriented governing body that replaced the traditional hierarchy of a mother general and her appointed superiors. Rank-and-file-sisters together with the elected leaders reassessed the congregation's present needs.[22]

Reexamination of the charism was not a superficial inquiry. It involved questioning what the community meant and how its collective identity would be expressed. Owing to the Cold War boom in religious vocations, the sisters were a young cohort who proved to be as involved in the upheavals of the time as their peers outside of the church. Many established sisters also felt it was time to chart a new course. The congregational documents produced in this period relied on a language of psychological development and spiritual growth not unlike the psychological theory that had transformed the YWCA's religious discourse in the 1920s. With theories of self-realization and critiques of authority that received wide hearing in US society in the 1960s, the place of the individual in community emerged as a central concern in renewal.[23]

Perfectae Caritatis devoted special attention to the elimination of unnecessary restrictions and outdated clothing. Given the tenacity of cloister-influenced practices, such changes had a considerable impact. Maryknoll sisters quickly abandoned many of the congregation's more ascetic policies. They adjusted rules of silence and ceased reciting the Daily Office, a cycle of chanted prayers that punctuated the day. They eliminated the Chapter of Faults, a weekly ritual in which sisters would ask forgiveness for everyday mistakes. Professed and non-professed sisters could freely converse, even in groups of two. They received permission to watch television (but not to smoke). Their mail and reading materials were no longer censored.[24]

To both women religious and everyday observers, the conciliar directive to adopt a "simple and modest" style of clothing proved monumental.[25] The habit had often been an encumbrance for peripatetic missionaries. Sister Mary Shannon remembered the difficulties of the elaborate outfit in tropical climates: "The pins in the veil would rust, and you would have to pull the pins out with pliers. . . . I lost a lot of hair. . . . We had slips with sleeves. We wore a tunic covered by a scapular that came to the ankles and a cape with a high collar that had to be changed every day. You were always sweating." Sisters initially modified their outfit, discarding its many layers in favor of a "simple habit and veil."[26] They then created a Motherhouse Habit Committee to determine whether further measures needed to be taken.

Debates about the habit highlighted challenges to the vocational emphasis on self-abnegation. Citing those who deemed religious communities to be irrelevant to contemporary life, the committee suggested that archaic clothing had become a liability that threatened the congregation's future. The committee asserted that sisters still wanted "to be a living proof that virginal love"—that is, the consecrated life of women religious—"is not an obstacle to personal development but contributes positively to making a woman more personally enriched."[27] For religious life to stay vital, it needed to attend to the psychological needs of the individual. The habit had once been the proof of personal enrichment, the sign of dedication to God. Reform proponents proposed that sisters who presented themselves as unique, outwardly expressive women now would be the proof of the value of religious life.

Ironically, as the women's liberation movement shone a spotlight on the dehumanizing effects of beauty culture on women's development, sisters seeking change in the congregation placed new emphasis on personal appearance

Our look is different; *our love, the same!*

Today in mission lands, many Maryknoll Sisters are wearing a different style of dress. In keeping with the updating of religious congregations urged by Vatican II, we are continually trying to improve our mission methods. But some things never change. Our love for Christ's poor, our faith in His words and our need for your help grow with each year. **Please continue your prayers for our work and your generous material support. You will be providing happiness for many people, and God will bless your charity!**

- -

Maryknoll Sisters · Maryknoll, New York 10545

Please use my gift of $ . . . . to help your work wherever   JN1
it is needed most.

NAME . . . .

ADDRESS . . . .

CITY . . . . STATE . . . . ZIP CODE . . . .

FIGURE 6.1. "Our look is different; our love, the same!" *Maryknoll* financial appeal, 1968. Credit: Maryknoll Mission Archives as a site for self-fulfillment. In making recommendations for changes in clothing regulations, the committee highlighted that "the way we act and appear and feel does have a definite effect on our psychological makeup." Departing from the androgynous style of radical feminists, committed members described the performance of gender as central to self-development, and they insisted that the woman religious "must be allowed to express her individual femininity by the way she dresses and appears." She needed "to do things that are peculiarly feminine so as to feel and be and grow as a woman of her time." Placing young women in uniform "out-of-date clothing . . . at a time of development when they are still trying to discover what it is to be a woman" hampered emotional growth. It was nevertheless an "unnecessary and unjustified psychological hardship" to force sisters who preferred the habit to change. The community ultimately elected to adopt contemporary clothing while allowing sisters to retain the habit if they wished.[28]

Cultural debates of the 1960s fueled confrontations to the established order in all manners of American life, and sisters who supported congregational change posed challenges within and beyond their community. The symbolic jettisoning of the habit proved to be, in Darlene Jacobs's words, "a mind-set change, a significant change." It signified the emergence of the autonomous individual from obedient self-effacement. In Jacobs's encounter with a bishop in Tanzania, such an assertion of independence ran up against the traditional chain of command. She recounted an incident in which a cleric ordered Maryknoll women to wear veils; the sisters refused. Jacobs reflected on the sisters' response: "Because there were enough of us and because we were young and foolish or whatever, we said no, we're not going to." She laughed, "end of story." Though the Second Vatican Council may not have addressed issues of women's inequality as such, the changes it introduced in religious formation opened new space for sisters to take control of their vocation.[29]

In one sociological study, a former nun explained that in response to *Perfectae Caritatis*, "all of a sudden we changed from neuter to woman."[30] After this transition, an atmosphere of experimentation extended beyond the areas of concern delineated by the Vatican, and just as popular psychology and feminist yearnings for autonomy could be detected in Maryknoll's habit debates, the sexual revolution worked its way into congregational life. In contrast to the open dialogue about clothing, challenges to sexual strictures occurred surreptitiously. There was no indication from the ecclesiastical hierarchy that the vow of celibacy was up for reinterpretation, but some sisters wondered whether a life of dedication to God could be compatible with romantically expressive love. Marjorie Bradford, who entered Maryknoll in 1949, recollected that she began to wonder whether the vocation's sexual prohibitions placed an unnatural barrier between body and soul. Was the church's "distorted emphasis upon sex" an impediment to the

God-given "motivation to live and do so joyfully?" Did the obsession with sin drive people to a different kind of sin, the fear of that which is "most sacred—the reaching out to human beings"?[31]

Other women's doubts became obvious, if unspoken, when they left the congregation to marry, as Bradford did. The Maryknoll Sisters added a new article to their constitution in 1965 stating that a "sister who has run away with a man [or] who attempts or contracts marriage, even if it be a civil marriage" would be dismissed from the congregation. The change suggests that violations of chastity appeared to be a threat by the mid-1960s, requiring Maryknoll to spell out the consequences: heterosexual romance could not be reconciled with community life. A superior, Mary Naab, reiterated this prohibition in 1968 when she conceded that "there is no virtue in a narrow, cold, critical, selfish celibacy"—an unexamined rejection of romantic love—but reinforced that "obviously, neither is our objective here at Maryknoll to see how much good fellowship between priests, Sisters, and seminarians we can develop." Sisters had "had an opportunity for dating and socializing with young men" before entering the congregation. Vocational commitment still entailed a binding quest to "live out a life of celibate love."[32]

Yet a disconcerting number of men and women in religious life were rejecting this foundational vow. Worse, in a 1968 incident, members of the congregation assented to this unauthorized experimentation. After the defection of a sister to marry a Maryknoll priest, Naab issued a sharply worded statement condemning casual reactions to the marriage, "lest silence seem to lend consent to behavior." The marriage itself galled the congregation's leadership, but the presence of sisters from the motherhouse at the wedding prompted outrage. Naab made it clear that the marriage was nothing to be "celebrated and applauded" but was obviously at "variance with what the religious life of Maryknoll Sisters stands for." This religious life still stood for a celibacy that allowed women to become "what God wants us to be—wholly women, wholly loving, wholly God's." The wholeness derived from the sanctified transcendence of the attachments of romantic love. Naab affirmed that "one of the great strengths of Vatican II was to . . . emphasize for us the unique value and potential of each human being." This endorsement of the sisters' turn toward self-realization delineated that the "valuing of the individual is in counterpoint to the community, not to the obliteration of it."[33]

According to Naab, the experimental ethos of the 1960s had not only struck at the nature of community life in the challenge to celibacy. It had also induced an "unnatural tolerance of Sisters leading two lives," and their secret lives disrupted community bonds. Other threats included "not praying, or joining the Community in trying to pray; not carrying their share of chores and works; keeping and spending money; [and] smoking."[34] Sisters who engaged in such activities rejected the obedience that had once been intrinsic to the communitarianism of religious life. Naab maintained that religious vows included allegiance to those rules.

The difficulties experienced by Naab were shared by other women in the governing structure, including those who welcomed the renewal initiated by *Perfectae Caritatis*. Sister Virginia Flagg, who served as a superior in Hong Kong during the late 1960s, embraced many of the changes of the Vatican Council. However, she still struggled with discontent among the sisters. "When we changed, I enjoyed the change," she recollected, joking, "I like to wear regular clothes." But many issues could not be solved as easily as the clothing question. Sisters who arrived at the mission from the motherhouse had been influenced by the restive environment in the United States and "were of a totally different mind" than sisters who had been in Hong Kong carrying out day-to-day mission labors. In hindsight, Flagg negatively appraised this time, "where there was an emphasis on self-fulfillment. It would have been nice not to have been in charge of anything then." To her, it was not reform itself but the attitude, "I'm first, I must be fulfilled at all cost," that enervated the community. Flagg had the responsibility of mediating competing visions. She "didn't know whether I was supposed to stick to the old" or accommodate sisters who were "for the modern, modern ways." She tried to be fair, but as women took sides, the cooperative ethos degenerated into factionalism. The sisters could not "have a decent meeting without fighting."[35] When the nature of the vow of obedience became open to new interpretations and the vow of celibacy was privately questioned, community relationships were fundamentally altered.

The ferment inspired many sisters to take more daring, experimental approaches to their ministry. It also led to a considerable decline in the number of women religious. Jacobs remembered the exodus: "Sometimes things didn't change fast enough, sometimes things changed too fast perhaps." Both conservatives and radicals found reason to reject the new direction charted by the congregation. The most dramatic numerical loss was not in the withdrawal of professed sisters—though this rate increased during the 1960s—but in the sharp decline of new entrants. In 1962, 132 women entered formation, the period of religious training that previously had been known as the postulancy and novitiate. In 1966, the number dropped to 79. The next year saw only 32 new recruits. In 1969, 8 women joined, and thereafter, the annual number of entering sisters would stabilize in the low single digits.[36]

But if such benchmarks showed the effect of centrifugal forces on the congregation, the sisters who remained found new inspiration in the ministries made possible by the postconciliar Vatican. The liberation theology movement that gained traction in the Catholic Church in these years gave new life to Maryknoll. Recognition of the considerable impact of the liberation theology movement underscores that it was not the Second Vatican Council alone that prompted institutional change. For Maryknoll sisters and priests, liberation thought had almost a multiplier effect on their interest in social engagement. With a sense of collective purpose evolving from their sense of global crisis, sisters redoubled their commitment to the antipoverty emphasis of conciliar social teachings. They dedicated themselves to a missiology aimed at the political and spiritual empowerment of the poor.

Liberation thought became a force in global Catholicism after the 1968 conference of the Latin American Episcopal Council (Consejo Episcopal Latino-Americano, or CELAM) at Medellín, Colombia. The conference was convened with the goal of applying conciliar developments to the unique pastoral, economic, and political conditions of Latin America. It introduced to the larger church the foundational tenets of liberation thought, which had been circulating for years in leftist religious circles in South and Central America. Most of all, the conference affirmed that the Catholic Church was at its essence a church of the poor. This understanding of Jesus cast him as the savior to the segment of society to which he belonged during his time on earth—oppressed groups such as the poor, the sick, widows and orphans, foreigners, and the exiled. As the embodiment of poverty and suffering, Jesus shared a special, corporeal relationship to marginalized people, and honoring God meant securing justice for Jesus's people. The assembly, which included the Maryknoll Sisters' mother general, Mary Columba Tarpey, accordingly decreed that the church as a whole needed to dedicate itself to the poor as "a sign of the inestimable value of the poor in the eyes of God." The law of Christian love demanded an "obligation of solidarity with those who suffer." This obligation yielded what was designated the "preferential option for the poor," a ministry deemed preferential because it reflected the priorities of Jesus himself.[37]

Though CELAM may have given official sanction to the preferential option for the poor, the idea was not new to the Maryknoll Sisters. The women weren't simply an audience to wider developments in liberation theology, they were its interlocutors: discussion groups and course work were integral to the mission lifestyle. In conversation with other religious, they interrogated the changing context of their labors and vocational identity. Moreover, the sisters had quietly participated in the pastoral foundations of a movement identified more commonly with the output of prominent priests and bishops. (Many of these clerics and theologians found a print audience through Orbis Books, the publishing house established by the Maryknoll Fathers in 1970, which remains a leading source of works on socially engaged theology.)

The degree to which the congregation anticipated the Vatican's and CELAM's interest in poverty and social action is well represented by service projects carried out in Maryknoll schools before the council. Lima, Peru, was an important site in the development of such activities. There, sisters established the St. Rose of Lima school in the late 1950s at the local bishop's behest, as he sought to revitalize support of the church among the city's wealthy. The school offered an English-language education that held a particular attraction for local elites. A 1958 history of the school glibly concluded that "the poor . . . are excluded for admission for several reasons," including tuition costs and because "the development of their intellectual capacity is hindered by the conditions under which they live." Over time, such a laissez-faire attitude toward the poor proved unsatisfactory. "As we heard . . . the cry of the masses," Maryknoll sisters in Lima later recalled, "we questioned our own commitment to the relatively few who . . . could be served by our social institutions."[38]

Their concerns were shared by a newly ordained priest, Gustavo Gutiérrez, and a fellow cleric, Jorge Alvarez-Calderon, who embarked on a search for an effective Christian response to social divisions in a city bearing the strain of economic modernization schemes. The dark side of restructuring manifested itself in Lima through permanent squatter settlements, which hosted an influx of rural migrants seeking jobs in a market that had uprooted them from subsistence agricultural communities. The Peruvian priests introduced the sisters to the techniques of the Young Christian Workers (Jocists), a lay Catholic Action-inspired organization that bears some parallels to the YWCA's group work efforts. Jocist "Social Action Teams" engaged members in small-group study led by priests, and Maryknoll women found this model of social engagement to be a worthy platform for service projects carried out by their wealthy students.[39]

A squatter settlement, Ciudad de Dios, served as the site for these encounters. Working alongside Maryknoll priests, sisters initiated ventures supported by a Peruvian government that saw advantages in the third-party provision of social services in an unplanned community.[40] While Maryknoll men took on the rugged work of building houses, sisters established projects that connected the convent school with the slum. The girls of St. Rose volunteered in the settlement's service center, where they led reading and catechumenal instruction, prepared food, and watched children. A sister reported to the motherhouse how such everyday application of social ideals might have a wider, transformative effect: "We realize that to successfully produce leaders and socially conscious men and women, the school has the responsibility of not only teaching in the theory, but also of providing the opportunities of carrying on the action, under guidance."[41]

The participation of a young Gustavo Gutiérrez, who would become the figurehead of liberation theology, rendered the Peruvian initiative particularly notable. However, sisters in Lima were not the only Maryknollers responding to a crisis of poverty that overwhelmed the resources of the church and called into question its emphasis on noblesse oblige. At Guatemala City's Colegio Monte María, which was nicknamed the "Maryknoll Hilton" for its luxurious facilities and privileged clientele, comparable service projects sent students of the all-female school into slums and an indigenous mountain town. As in Lima, the projects transformed the consciousness of sisters as well as students, for they interrogated what it truly meant to help the poor. "Probably more than actual help offered to the poor," noted a Guatemala City diarist in 1962, "was the benefit to the girls themselves through the soul-shaking experience of seeing the stark poverty lived by fellow human beings, and knowing that there is no recourse because of social injustice and heartless indifference on the part of those who have." She delineated the special significance of small-group efforts in reshaping political and spiritual consciousness: the "project wasn't a big charitable work, but a splendid, person-to-person encounter with Christ-in-His-'least-brethren.'"[42] Whether in Latin America or East Asia, the sisters' increased responsibilities among the urban dispossessed, as well as their ongoing involvement with indigenous and rural communities, provided stark portraits of economic expropriation and marginalization.

Attention to poverty may not have been new to the sisters, but liberation theology's leftist perspective on political and economic change was. Liberation thinkers appropriated the Social Gospel in their denunciation of structural sin, the dehumanizing regimes responsible for poverty and oppression. Whereas the Catholic Church had historically emphasized salvation as a transcendent phenomenon and the kingdom of God as a future destination, liberation theologians placed their emphasis on the kingdom of God as a mandate for temporal action. The term "liberation" signified both salvation in the afterlife through faith in Jesus and freedom from oppressive conditions on earth. It demanded that the faithful be agents of this liberation through agitation for social change.

Many Maryknoll sisters found the preferential option to be a natural outgrowth of their mission heritage. Governing documents that marked the conclusion of the renewal period defined such ministry to be integral to the congregation. Sisters announced their commitment: "we choose to identify with the Church of the poor, not afraid of the risk and consequent insecurity this involves."[43] Instead of pursuing the salvation of souls, they embarked on a quest to build a "Kingdom of God . . . , a world where men strive to bridge ideological gaps and break the great economic barriers that divide people so that the riches of the world benefit not a few persons or nations, but all; where the discriminatory social barriers—those between men and women, races, religions, etc.—are broken down." The description of foreign mission itself had undergone a fundamental shift. A missionary congregation, the sisters explained in a 1969 governing document, was "to be the Church at the frontiers of society in ways which are not available to the rest of the Church." Maryknoll had once sought "geographical frontiers," but now sisters pursued "the frontiers of international life in a particular way, of world poverty, and of justice and peace."[44]

Many layers of Christian thought came through in statements like these: an assertion of the loving bonds connecting God and humankind, a liberation-style analysis of class struggle, and an ecumenicalism born of the Vatican Council. Maryknoll expressed an expansive sense of its allies in the effort to bring the poor into the world that God intended for them to have. "We wish to manifest our concern for and affirm our solidarity with all those struggling for justice and peace," the congregation declared, implying that loyalties to religious institutions had little relevance to mission. "We shall work in cooperation with all groups . . . who share this same concern"—perhaps even those groups, it remained unstated, that might struggle for political revolution. Still, the congregation downplayed the radical associations of liberation in declaring its affiliation with the poor. In Maryknoll's rendering of the preferential option, conciliar descriptions of social justice and interpersonal relationships took precedence over the type of neo-Marxist, social-scientific analysis employed by liberation theologians to theorize processes of social change. Though sisters discussed the structural underpinnings of unequal power relations, they used a language of personal growth and transcendent spiritual fulfillment. In this way, they repurposed the interpersonal approach to social change that was a hallmark of women's mission. Newly casting these encounters as part of the "liberating process," sisters aimed to participate in psychological and social transformations. While hoping to help "persons and communities to realize their full human potential as purposed by God," their work could create conditions for a more just social order. "We may not be a great force in social-economic development," they wrote, "but we are commissioned to a presence which strives with all men to work for a genuine openness and concern for the other."[45]

Such pronouncements evoke the YWCA's politicized Protestant therapeutics, but Maryknoll women elaborated these themes in a distinctively Catholic context. Reflecting on the storied Kaying ministry of the 1930s (discussed in chapter 3), which sent sisters in small catechetical teams into the countryside of southern China, Sister Betty Ann Maheu found preconciliar roots for the congregation's interest in the poor: "the sisters in China . . . would not have thought of their work as a preferential option . . . , but it was." The Kaying method, after all, placed sisters among the rural poor to make inroads that city missions could not.[46] In a similar fashion, sisters described Rogers as anticipating postconciliar conceptions of mission. Maheu drew connections to this heritage: "Mother Mary Joseph was very advanced in her day in her concept of doing mission." "Because you loved your neighbor," she explained, "you wanted to share the Good News of God's salvation; you wanted them to experience the power of God's healing love; you wanted to bring them to saving grace."[47] Some of this reimaging of Maryknoll's historic identity glossed over how different the congregation's sense of the sacred had become. The ecumenical impulse informing the new emphasis on the kingdom of God and the more confrontational politics explored by the sisters was at odds with the sacramental legalism and liberal anticommunism that had once prevailed. The sisters found much of value in their heritage and handily adapted their founder's vision to current mission circumstances, but the postconciliar interpretation of the congregation's charism quietly shed pieces of the past that were liabilities in their new pursuit of social justice.

Innovations tied to liberation theology gave the congregation a more unified sense of purpose and a more manageable sense of scale, the latter of which was particularly meaningful in light of Maryknoll's declining ability to maintain large institutions. One important line of work to emerge in this vein was health promoter programs, in which missioners trained catechists and local leaders in preventive care and hygiene. Aiming for grassroots empowerment and culturally appropriate treatment, health promoter initiatives adapted the tradition of charitable medicine to a new context of Catholic social services. Sisters endeavored to establish cooperative health care systems that communities could sustain with their own resources. These were public health innovations as well as attempts to contribute to the personal growth of the powerless, people who did not have access to formal education and credentialization. The model had wide utility, and in a number of countries it garnered official support when health departments issued certification to trained promoters. Indicative of the program's threat as a form of empowerment, health promoters in Guatemala became targets of military reprisals.[48]

The liberation movement gave rise to new governing structures and new directions in apostolic work such as medicine and education, but the pastoral side of mission work also shifted considerably. Beginning in the early 1960s in Latin America, Maryknoll oriented its catechumenal work toward the formation of base communities, a unit of ministry that was a hallmark of liberation theology. Sisters' pastoral efforts in youth groups and classroom instruction had long centered on the small-group educational encounter, which Gutiérrez called "an *essential infrastructure*" for liberation theology.[49] But these encounters were no longer designed to increase piety. They aimed to raise consciousness of social problems and instill a sense of belonging in an egalitarian kingdom of God. Like other innovations of this era, base communities democratized participation in religious life as they positioned church personnel to be facilitators, rather than authorities, in the process of self-realization. Leadership of small groups was transferred from the clergy and women religious to the laity, as individuals met on an equal footing for prayer, worship, and collective discussion of spiritual and secular matters.[50]

This was the practical work of conscientization, liberation theology's application of the pedagogy of Paolo Freire, which promoted self-awareness, recognition of social injustice, and subsequently liberation from oppression through action.

Conscientization provided a theory of social change that linked grassroots spiritual awakenings to self-knowledge and then mobilization. Maryknoll Sister Peg Dillon offered an informal account of how conscientization functioned in the course of mission, attributing such awakenings to everyday discussions about the personal relevance of Gospel principles. In a Nicaraguan squatter settlement, "we would read the stories from Scripture and then ask the people to relate those stories to the stories of their lives. Inevitably, as people grew in faith, they grew in their desire to serve their neighbors and the wider community, just as they grew in their criticism of injustice in society." Conscientization cast sisters as students and participants rather than authorities and teachers. Cain, stationed in Tanzania, called this a "mission vision [built on] an appreciation and love for people and their struggles."[51] A religious vocation did not entail bringing God's blessings to the people; instead, it was a matter of sisters opening themselves to the divine that dwelt in all of humanity.

Women religious had historically trained to perfect themselves as individuals to cultivate the indwelling of God. The idea of evangelization as accompaniment, of seeking the presence of God in others, marked a reconceptualization of divine immanence. The House of Prayer established by two Maryknoll sisters on the Lower East Side of Manhattan in the early 1970s gives evidence of changes in the contemplative dimension of vocation. Responding to a "deep call from

FIGURE 6.2. Sister Alice Morrison in Chimaltenango, Guatemala, after the 1976 earthquake. Credit: Maryknoll Mission Archives

God to share the life of the poor," the women established a "cloister in the city" to make the church present "through love, prayer and poverty in those sections of our cities where there is the most misery, violence and oppression."[52] This call was distinctly different from previous assignments the women had carried out during their long tenure in the congregation. One of the founders of the house was Mercy Hirschboeck, the famed doctor who had combated communism in Korea and segregation in Kansas City. Another participant had spent part of her career at the motherhouse's cloister as one of a small group of sisters who lived in enclosure. With the city cloister project, the women created a contemplative ministry attuned to the preferential option. They hoped to "witness . . . the unity of love through an emphasis on one aspect of evangelical poverty: social poverty." Quietly residing at a local parish, bypassing the Sturm und Drang of the new nuns' proclivities for direct action protest, these sisters came to a struggling neighborhood "to listen, to pray, to serve in some small ways—to befriend."[53]

As much as the sentiments of liberation theology resonated with the congregation's collective sense of purpose, Maryknoll leaders decisively rebuked several sisters' involvement with liberation-influenced militancy. Marjorie Bradford initiated the Maryknoll Sisters' most notorious brush with radicalism in 1967.[54] She had begun the decade as a teacher in Guatemala City's "Maryknoll Hilton," and as director of its antipoverty service projects, she had had a political awakening. She set off what came to be known as the "Melville incident" when a youth group that she organized with two Maryknoll priests made contact with leaders of the military contingent of the Guatemalan Communist Party. The youth group aimed to launch a "Christian revolutionary movement," mobilizing peasants into unions and cooperatives. "We would arm ourselves when the time came," she later wrote, "but our immediate plans were for organizing a base among peasant leaders."[55] The scheme was discovered, and the Maryknoll Fathers' superior ordered the Maryknollers involved to leave Guatemala. In response, Bradford and the two priests, brothers Arthur and Thomas Melville, defected to Mexico with intentions of joining a guerrilla underground. They were intercepted, sent to the United States, and expelled from Maryknoll. Though the *New York Times* reported that a Maryknoll spokesman called Bradford the "ringleader," the incident became known by the surname of two priests involved. Susan Fitzpatrick-Behrens concludes: "Gender norms granted [the men an] authority to speak that surpassed their role" in the activities.[56]

The incident produced some ambivalence in the congregation, for a Maryknoll superior publicly acknowledged that there had been "general sympathy" with the group's "belief that something like a social revolution would have to occur . . . before anything could be done about [Guatemala's] backwardness."[57] But the Maryknoll Sisters responded unequivocally in censuring Bradford and publicly denouncing the "naïve, impetuous, individualistic, and romantic reasoning which has now set back the authentic work of human and social development in Guatemala." The Melville incident in fact prompted the Guatemalan military to keep close watch on Maryknoll missions and, according to Fitzpatrick-Behrens, served as a reason "to identify all Catholics seeking to promote social change as potential 'Communists.'"[58]

Bradford continued a headline-grabbing political and spiritual journey after she left the congregation and married Thomas Melville, taking his surname. The couple joined a leftist Catholic circle in Washington, D.C., and within five months of returning to the United States, they and other members of a group that included Philip and Daniel Berrigan made their way to the Catonsville, Maryland, draft board office. The activists entered the facility, announced their opposition to US "militarism and imperialism," and destroyed draft files using homemade napalm. The "Catonsville Nine" were arrested and featured prominently in the press. As much as the trial highlighted the Vietnam protest movement, the Melvilles used their time on the stand to denounce US policy in Guatemala. Jane Fonda was initially slated to play Marjorie to Donald Sutherland's Tom in a film version, but such countercultural star power was ultimately not in evidence in the 1972 release of *The Trial of the Catonsville Nine*.[59]

The Melville story was the highest-profile example of tensions that accompanied the congregation's postconciliar journey. Still, the experience of Sister Cecilia Goldman, a white woman committed to the black freedom struggle in the midwestern United States, similarly made clear that Maryknoll's social consciousness remained, at its core, centered on liberal approaches to change. The child of a Catholic mother and Jewish father, Goldman had been inspired to join Maryknoll, she told a newspaper reporter, because it was "serving people all over the world regardless of race. It is a religious order concerned with humanity." Coming into "close contact with deprived blacks" in her assignment to teach "in the slums" of St. Louis, Missouri, she elected to "devote all my time to poverty programs in the area" rather than embark on foreign mission.[60] There, she also became involved with ACTION, an idiosyncratic, "stridently interracial" St. Louis civil rights and black power organization that bridged integrationist impulses to calls for revolution. Though the group never had more than a hundred active members, its dramatic protests and incendiary demands gave it a highly visible place in the local movement. Goldman chaired ACTION's Religion Committee, and she publicly established her credentials as a radical in December 1968 when she chained herself to the revolving doors of a downtown department store in an ACTION "Black Christmas" protest designed "to get Christians involved with the ghetto."[61]

Neither an arrest and conviction for disturbing the peace nor murmurs of disapproval from Maryknoll leadership dissuaded Goldman from standing in the forefront of ACTION's signature confrontational protests. The group's next

FIGURE 6.3. "Where Is the Church? Peace, Brotherhood, Justice, Where?": Sister Cecilia Goldman chained to door of the Famous-Barr department store in a "Black Christmas" protest, St. Louis, Missouri, 1968. Credit: Photo courtesy of the *St. Louis American*

campaign further threw the spotlight on tensions emerging in the civil rights commitments of liberal churches. ACTION mobilized behind the 1969 "Black Manifesto" of James Forman and the National Black Economic Development Conference, a short-lived coalition pursuing black economic autonomy. The document's demand that churches and synagogues provide $500 million as reparation to African Americans stupefied religious leaders. For the previous fifteen years, many major church bodies had understood themselves to be at the moral center of the civil rights struggle. They now were confronted by a screed that excoriated mealy-mouthed white liberals who profited from and perpetuated the enslavement of African Americans. As one self-described St. Louis "militant-at-large" explained: "Everybody asks why the churches? Yes, they marched in Selma [and] Birmingham. But then they went home and did the same old things."[62]

During the summer of 1969, demonstrators interrupted church services to present the manifesto in a set of protests they called Black Sundays. ACTION sent Goldman to give advance warning to the city's powerful Catholic archdiocese that the cathedral would be targeted, but church officials were not receptive to the manifesto's uncompromising demands that the church turn over 75 percent of its income for reparations, denounce the systemic brutality carried out by its parishioners who were police officers, and divest from slum properties and discriminatory businesses. Accordingly, when a protester at the cathedral announced through a bullhorn that Black Sunday visits would "subsequently take on various forms of uniqueness, such as spitting in the communion cup during communion service, a symbolic gesture of changing wine back to water, and/or taking the holy bread from the reverend and distributing it to the black poor," the archdiocese responded with indignant rage.[63] The cardinal insisted that the "church would not tolerate 'blasphemous threats.'" Further actions at Catholic churches resulted in scuffles and arrests, and the archdiocese ultimately secured an injunction against Black Sunday demonstrations, ironically under the authority of a Reconstruction era measure designed to protect blacks from racial violence.[64]

Local media highlighted Goldman as a particularly intriguing participant in the campaign because of her leadership role in ACTION and symbolic value as a militant new nun facing off against the Catholic hierarchy. Though the communion threat seems to have been a one-off provocation that was not representative of the techniques of the mobilization, the archdiocese and mainstream press used it to characterize and discredit Black Sunday protests. Goldman did not endorse the threat, but neither did she apologize for it. "Our whole movement has been one of peace. Peaceful disruptions," she told an interviewer. These disruptions followed the example of Jesus, who "was completely surrounded by violence." He, like ACTION, "perhaps created . . . violence or conflict of conscience."[65] Deeming Goldman's response insufficient, the Maryknoll governing board demanded that she resign from ACTION. She adamantly refused. "My dedication to humanity and Christianity comes before any institution," she stated at a press conference, dismissing the Maryknoll Sisters' growing interest in social justice efforts as outweighed by its institutional investment in unjust power structures. "The church . . . has white values," she told a reporter, "and it is keeping black people down."[66]

By petitioning the Vatican, Goldman successfully deflected Maryknoll's initial attempt to discipline her. But not content to quietly cooperate, she continued her public attack on the injustices perpetrated by the Catholic Church. Her final provocation was a renunciation of the vow of poverty. "The church is a million dollar racist institution," she charged, "and it would be hypocritical for me to consider myself a sister under the vow of poverty." This statement was designed as a "symbolic act" to dramatize the disingenuousness of declarations of religious poverty. The critique may have hit home for missioners who usually lived in more comfortable circumstances than the impoverished populations they served. While Goldman continued to air her grievances in the press, Maryknoll's governing board issued no public response when it expelled her for breaking her vows. A story reported that Goldman was then invited into a local Episcopal Church as "Sister Cecilia—sister of the people."[67]

Assigned to mission work in Bolivia in the early 1970s, Sister Mary Harding also learned the limits of Maryknoll's social commitments. Like Goldman, Harding came to find her faith-driven political consciousness incompatible with the operating practices of Catholic institutions. Harding began in antipoverty ministry when she took a job in a La Paz factory to live in solidarity with the poor. In a period of wrangling between military and leftist governments, she became involved in union activity and then joined a national liberation army. Harding explained her shift in consciousness in terms that evoked liberation theologians' orientation toward praxis, a Marxist-inflected conception of mobilizing faith to produce social revolution: "The union could do a few things, [but] I wanted to work for the liberation of the Bolivian people. . . . You can talk about social justice for just so long before putting it in concrete terms." For her, as with others on the radical side of liberation theology, social justice engendered opposition to capitalism—and the regimes that supported it. She "came to the conclusion that the answer was an armed group." Sensitive to the ticklish relationship between the Catholic Church and militant liberation movements, Harding left the congregation after she took up arms. She "'did not want to see the Maryknoll order compromised,'" acknowledging that her choices could well endanger Maryknoll's mission presence. She also recognized that despite CELAM's endorsement of liberation themes, the revolutionary ambitions of many liberation practitioners were more uncompromising, ambitious, and, she believed, effective than the vision of the institutional church. She determined that she could no longer define herself through the Maryknoll community. In turn, the congregation declined to associate itself with her after she staked such allegiances. When the Bolivian government detained Harding in 1973, Maryknoll was not among the pressure groups that lobbied for her release.[68]

Even as Maryknoll pushed its charism in innovative directions, the commitment to the poor and disenfranchised that drove Marjorie Bradford Melville, Cecilia Goldman, and Mary Harding into radical activity was deemed to be at variance with the community identity. The congregation's leadership was a younger and more progressive cohort than ever before, but they rejected associations between Maryknoll and those perceived as extremists, whether armed Marxists in Latin America or black power advocates in the United States. However, by the middle of the 1970s, a shift in climate was evident. The congregation took formal measures to participate vigorously and unapologetically in activism related to issues that its expelled radicals had prophetically warned of: dispossession, disappearances, torture, and the direct culpability of US business interests and the US government in such repression. Framing the task at hand not as a people's revolution, but instead as the pursuit of human rights, Maryknoll assumed an active role in combating abuses instead of distancing itself from political controversy. The sisters who made the confrontation of such injustice central to their ministry increasingly served as the public face of Maryknoll.

"I AM FULFILLING MY VOWS BY SUPPORTING THE LIBERATION OF PEOPLES"

The year 1973 provides a convenient watershed for interpreting this shift. On the US front, the Vietnam War dragged on despite movements toward "Vietnamization," and for many, burn-out settled in as the New Left and black power movements split into factionalism and fanaticism. Overseas, US gestures toward détente with Soviet Union hardly balanced proxy wars and Third World revolutionary struggles. Richard Nixon's reelection in 1972 pushed progressives into disarray and dismay, and a steady trickle of revelations about the Watergate cover-up undermined what little credibility the administration still had.

Another secret operation of the US government had a decisive impact on the development of advocacy work in Maryknoll: the Chilean coup. The coup unfolded in a fashion comparable to the 1954 ouster of Jacobo Árbenz Guzmán in Guatemala. In both cases, US secret operations were pivotal to the violent overthrow of democratically elected, left-friendly regimes. However, the aftermath of the two events played out differently. While the media and Maryknoll cheered Carlos Castillo Armas's assumption of the Guatemalan presidency, the "systematic brutality" of the Chilean junta inspired little enthusiasm. Mass arrests swept up two Maryknoll priests, who were interned with thousands of other foreigners in the national stadium. Knowledge of clandestine operations of the CIA in Salvador Allende's Chile—confirmed and defended by President Gerald Ford days after he pardoned Nixon—compounded the outrage.[69]

The Maryknoll Sisters responded with a collective letter of protest to Ford. They called his recourse to the threat of communism as a justification of the junta "unconscionable" and asked a question that was an about-face from Maryknoll's Cold War Catholic triumphalism: "by what arrogance do we decide what is in the best interests of Chile or any other nation?" Furthermore, in contrast to its actions in the Melville, Goldman, and Harding incidents, Maryknoll did not wash its hands of a sister detained in Chile: Peggy Lipsio had sheltered Salvador Allende's nephew and accordingly was hunted by security forces. Experiencing raids and other civil rights restrictions, sisters stationed in Chilean squatter settlements experienced firsthand the terroristic tactics of the regime of Augusto Pinochet—which, like other Latin American dictatorships, labored to suppress liberation-infused Catholic activism.[70] More generally, the logic of anticommunism had become deeply strained. Basic mission activity, when conducted among those who had gotten on the wrong side of authoritarian governments, would be indiscriminately tagged as subversive.

While the Catholic Church had long used the term "communism" to discredit a wide range of disruptive political sentiments, this technique lost its credibility as Third World people's movements took on new legitimacy and urgency. Information on CIA intrigue in Latin America aired in 1974 revealed extensive government infiltration of missionary efforts in service of military goals, and such revelations cast further doubts about the liberal anticommunism that had once defined Catholic mission. Maryknoll was not named in these revelations, but reports described a range of unsavory alliances between similar religious groups and the CIA.[71] Sisters who were attacked for their association with guerrilla groups at first seemed to be exceptional cases of radicalism, but as increasing numbers of religious personnel were targeted as political enemies, the congregation took a more jaundiced view of governments in power.

As a consequence of this awareness of "increasing oppression occurring in areas where Maryknoll Sisters were missioned," in 1974 the congregation created an advocacy department, the Office of Social Concerns, to establish a collective way to respond to social struggle. It entered the realm of international nongovernmental organizations, gaining consultative status with the United Nations. The office was designed as a clearinghouse for public education and lobbying efforts. Missioners could use their insider/outsider status to gain a hearing for previously untold stories of conflict, poverty, and human rights abuses. They were insiders in mission communities, witnesses to daily violence and deprivations. But they were also outsiders, US citizens with privileged standing who could not be disposed of as easily as quotidian political enemies. The Office of

Social Concerns prepared official letters of protest and congressional testimony, and it compiled research materials about local circumstances that would not otherwise have reached US policy makers and the general media. A wide range of issues stirred the office to action in the 1970s, including economic investment in apartheid South Africa, indigenous rights, the political abuses of Ferdinand Marcos in the Philippines and Park Chung-Hee in South Korea, and the environmental toll of World Bank development projects.[72] The office served a particularly valuable function in its affiliation with the Washington Office on Latin America (WOLA). The Latin American studies scholar Svenja Blanke identifies WOLA as a "key lobbying organization for the faith-based community" that "acquired an exceptional role as a broker in foreign affairs with Congress and became the most respected Latin America-oriented human rights interest group."[73] Using the congregation's transnational connections and media access, Maryknoll sisters (and priests, who created a corresponding Office of Justice and Peace in the same period) joined a liberal Christian bloc of international human rights observers, which was treated by many as a trusted source of information. This bloc publicized abuses that would otherwise have gone unnoticed, and it highlighted the role of US foreign aid in sustaining repressive governments.

As much as Maryknoll's advocacy offices may have challenged Catholic complacency, their methods fit in the mainstream of social movement activity: information sharing and political lobbying as well as providing individual testimony and witness. Sisters resisted overt clashes with the ecclesiastical hierarchy and, in fact, counted many priests and bishops as allies. The source of the congregation's influence as an international NGO lay in its access to multiple transnational advocacy networks—access that it had gained by virtue of its presence in diverse mission contexts. Maryknoll gave expression to antipoverty, Latin American solidarity, and human rights commitments through participating in such coalitions. With secular and religious affiliates, a stable organizational presence, and grassroots energy, these networks gave Maryknoll's advocacy efforts a broader reach than would have otherwise been possible in face of the congregation's shrinking numbers. As explained by Margaret Keck and Kathryn Sikkink, transnational advocacy networks achieve such reach by linking global partners who have differential access to power and resources: "For the less powerful third world actors, networks provide access, leverage, and information (and often money) they could not expect to have on their own; for northern groups, they make credible the assertion that they are struggling with, and not only for, their southern partners."[74]

With such machinery for advocacy in place, sisters who embraced activist causes consistently found support from the congregation's leadership. Janice McLaughlin was the most prominent of the activist sisters of the late 1970s. She entered Maryknoll in 1961, just before the Second Vatican Council. Like other members of this generation, she started formation under a model that emphasized ritual, obedience, and the intricacies of the institutional church. She remained with the congregation as it weathered the changes of the 1960s and was assigned to mission in Kenya, where she was responsible for media relations.[75] This was ample training for a stint in Rhodesia that flared into an international incident. There, she harnessed the power of the press to turn US and European attention toward an independence struggle that laid bare the lingering impact of colonialism and bolstered a righteous call for black nationalism.

When McLaughlin arrived in Rhodesia in 1977, a national liberation movement had coalesced into a potent threat to the rogue state, which had been formed when prime minister Ian Smith declared independence from the United Kingdom to maintain white minority rule. McLaughlin had been sent to assist Rhodesia's Catholic Peace and Justice Commission in documenting the violent reprisals directed at the Zimbabwean independence movement and distributing this information to the international press. With attention from the press, such efforts might lead to sanctions against Smith's government and garner material support for resistance movements.[76] Three months after McLaughlin arrived, as the British press prepared to release the commission's report, she and the report's other authors were arrested. McLaughlin alone was refused bail, tagged as a "'dedicated supporter of the terrorist cause'" based on personal writings that had been confiscated from her apartment. Moreover, lest her whiteness be a misleading indicator of her allegiances, investigators noted that she was "Afro-hairstyled."[77]

The trial gave McLaughlin an international platform to discredit the Rhodesian government, and her advocacy for Zimbabwean insurrectionary forces drew support in ways that Melville's and Goldman's activities did not. Rhodesia had virtually no allies, and the media turned a skeptical eye toward the charges against McLaughlin. The international press aired the commission's reports of state repression while they covered the trial, and McLaughlin's diary and courtroom responses cast her in a favorable light as she defended those whom she called "freedom fighters." "I feel I am fulfilling my vows by supporting the liberation of peoples," she testified. "I think the church has often supported violence—the violence of a just war." Penny Lernoux reported McLaughlin's appealing affirmation of black nationalist solidarity (in addition to her Afro): "The most widely quoted item from her diary, appearing in headlines . . . throughout Africa, was her passionate declaration: 'If I had a black skin, I would join the boys'"—the familiar term for Zimbabwean nationalist guerrillas.[78]

With a flurry of press coverage, the lobbying of the Maryknoll Sisters, and indirect pressure from the US government, which did not have a diplomatic relationship with Rhodesia, McLaughlin was deported to the United States after three weeks in prison. She told reporters that she "felt guilty winning release by outside intervention when hundreds of others without possible external assistance are still imprisoned," but immediately afterward she lent her support to the liberation struggle from the outside.[79] She had a bully pulpit. Working from the church-based Washington Office on Africa, she set out to educate Europeans and Americans about African liberation struggles while she raised funds for the Zimbabwean cause. After testifying to Congress in support of sanctions against Rhodesia, she returned to southeast Africa in 1979 to aid refugees. When Robert Mugabe—a Catholic, like Tanzania's President Julius Nyerere—took power in Zimbabwe in 1980, she was hired as an educational consultant for his administration.[80]

"A CHRISTIAN CANNOT REMAIN NEUTRAL"

McLaughlin's experience of government persecution had become a familiar one for Catholic religious and clergy engaged in liberation work in conflict situations. Nowhere was this more true than Latin America, where church personnel became enemies of the state. As documented by Lernoux, "between 1968 and 1978, over 850 bishops, priests, and nuns were threatened, arrested, tortured, exiled, or murdered."[81] Maryknoll was enmeshed in this context. In the 1970s, its personnel were spared the worst of these reprisals, but this security would not last.

In 1978, Nicaragua came to prominence as the central locus of Latin American revolutionary movements when the insurgency against the dynasty of Anastasio Somoza Debayle gained momentum, led by the armed liberation group known as the Sandinistas (the Frente Sandinista de Liberación Nacional, or FSLN). The country then became the focus of an emerging debate about human rights in US foreign policy, which President Jimmy Carter had named an international relations priority. The Maryknoll Sisters' experience with the Nicaraguan struggle represented the high-water mark of liberation-influenced missiology in the congregation. From the days of the noblesse oblige of the Somoza patriarch, Anastasio Somoza García, who had hosted sisters in the 1940s when they operated schools for the elite in a gold-mining company town, to the unraveling of his dynasty under his son, Maryknoll personnel stood party to both the operations of the state and the dramatic poverty of the people. As events unfolded, Maryknoll women on the ground in mission and in the congregation's leadership supported the revolution.

Though Sandinista military actions most directly prompted the ouster of Somoza in the summer of 1979, the revolution as a whole owed much to Catholic mobilizations. The Nicaraguan church hierarchy had been at odds with the government since publicly objecting to election fraud and the theft of humanitarian aid funds after the 1972 earthquake. Missionary orders stationed in Nicaragua

used their access to media in other countries to publicize the increasing poverty and repression. Liberation theology had a strong impact at the grassroots
level, with religious and clergy ministering from the base community setting in
the conscientization tradition. A commentator noted that as more Catholics
came to priests asking whether "it was morally acceptable to join the FSLN,"
the answer increasingly became that "it was a legitimate option for Christians."[82]
The depravity of the Somozas left few other options, and the Sandinistas proved
accommodating to the support of Catholic activists. Miguel D'Escoto Brockmann, a Maryknoll priest, became one of two priest spokesmen for the coalition opposing Somoza. After Somoza's defeat, D'Escoto was appointed foreign
minister of the Sandinista government, and he served in this capacity until 1990.
Two other priests, Ernesto and Fernando Cardenal (brothers who were both
Jesuits), also held long-term positions in the Sandinista government.[83]

During the saga of the Nicaragua insurgency, Maryknoll sisters labored on
the front lines. They had conducted base community work in squatter settlements and mining towns since the early 1960s, and when the Sandinista rebellion turned into open warfare, they established emergency refugee services. In
the *Washington Post*, Sister Julianne Warnshuis reiterated a fundamental premise
of liberation thought as she explained the church's open opposition to Somoza:
"A Christian cannot remain neutral in the reality of a dictatorship like this."
Clergy and religious no longer blanched at accusations of subversion, for these
accusations accompanied any action to provide for basic human needs. Maryknoll was suspect "for trying to organize people in the slums, trying to help them
improve their conditions. It was even subversive of us to ask for water."[84]

Fear of a Marxist menace and discontent at the US abrogation of its duties
of hemispheric policing in Nicaragua aroused anxiety among US business interests and their congressional advocates. The Maryknoll Sisters, however, publicly
commended "our Nicaraguan brothers and sisters in their struggle for justice
and self-determination." The congregation urged the United States to cut ties
with Somoza, citing missionary expertise as justification for its recommendations. Sisters "live and work with people in the pueblos. They know what the
people have suffered as a result of poverty, inadequate education, and lack of
proper health care. Most of all, they have witnessed the terrible oppression of a
dictatorial government which has become obsessed with power."[85] Sisters testified to the desperate conditions that the US government would hardly acknowledge in its effort to stave off a socialist revolution.

When the Somoza regime fell, Maryknoll was caught up in the excitement
over the possibilities of the Sandinista state. Sisters who had ministered to the
refugees enthusiastically reported to the congregation their hopes for the new
government: "The ideals of these Sandinista people are high and the struggle
to fulfill them will be difficult." The women believed that the Maryknoll Sisters

could have a part in infusing Sandinista Nicaragua with Christian love: "we have a unique opportunity to continue to build the Kingdom of Justice, Peace, and Brotherhood side by side within the Revolution whose ideals so echo the Gospels."[86]

Maryknoll women's enthusiasm for the promise of Christian revolution was met by a backlash from Catholic conservatives who had been pushed to the margins of the church after the Second Vatican Council. Rumblings of dissent had been heard before the Nicaraguan revolution, as when Maryknoll's magazine abandoned anticommunist rhetoric in the early 1970s and adopted the pacifist tones of conciliar documents. One subscriber complained that "every time I read [the magazine] I become more provoked at the anti-American sentiment in most of the articles." Another referred to the split that had divided mainline Protestantism in the early twentieth century: "I am dismayed to find that your society has, apparently, jumped on the bandwagon of 'social gospel.'" "The Church has no competence to speak on matters of economics and politics," this reader complained, stating that "the primary aim of the missioner should be to transmit the heritage of our faith."[87] The Wanderer, a leading conservative Catholic publication, lumped Maryknoll into a disreputable cast of characters in its reporting on planning sessions for the 1976 Call to Action conference in Detroit, Michigan. This hallmark event brought the acrimonious schism between liberal and conservative Catholics into the open. Disgusted by proposed resolutions supporting reevaluation of Catholic doctrine on celibacy, homosexuality, reproductive rights, and male clergy, the magazine wrote contemptuously of the "Justice and Peace types from neighboring dioceses, Maryknollers on furlough from Peru, hard-faced nuns in pantsuits, and a scattering of bureaucrats from the [US Conference of Catholic Bishops]" who "joyfully applauded the worst excesses."[88]

If Maryknoll represented just one part of a queer group of heretics in this 1975 view, critics singled the congregation out as a leading force of Catholic subversion after the Nicaraguan revolution. In a 1979 editorial praising Pope John Paul II's denunciation of liberation theology, Michael Novak took the lead in identifying Maryknoll as a Catholic institution where "the Marxists are plainly riding high." He pointed to Orbis Books and D'Escoto's Sandinista affiliations as proof that Maryknoll "was the headquarters for liberation theology in the United States, and perhaps in the entire world."[89] For people like Novak, nothing spelled doom for the church more than relenting on the battle against communism. In such quarters, anticommunist reductionism continued to prevail, and any critique of capitalism necessarily meant the endorsement of revolutionary Marxism, becoming the means by which liberation thought would destroy, rather than renew, the Catholic Church.

These expressions of discontent did not affect Sister Patricia Edmiston's mission responsibilities in 1979. In that year, she traveled to Nicaragua on a break from an assignment in El Salvador. She needed a rest. The Salvadoran military had ambushed a demonstration of over 200,000 people, and she had helped to embalm the mutilated bodies of seventeen victims that had been trapped inside a cathedral for a week. Her trip to Nicaragua did not provide much of a respite: "we took a vacation and went to a war." During the visit, the Sandinistas launched their final push against the National Guard. Unable to return to El Salvador, Edmiston joined the sisters stationed in Nicaragua and sat out the National Guard's siege of the Sandinista-held city of León. They provided food, shelter, and medicine to some three hundred refugees.[90]

Even more bewildering events followed Edmiston's accidental journey to the middle of the Nicaraguan revolution. The congregation reassigned her to Nicaragua, where she coordinated a Sandinista public health program for a barrio of 80,000 people. Meanwhile, sisters Carla Piette, Ita Ford, and Maura Clarke went to El Salvador as replacements. Within a year and a half, the three sisters in El Salvador died in horrific circumstances: Piette in an auto accident; Clarke and Ford in a kidnapping-murder. Edmiston could only wonder "why? For a while you start thinking should I have stayed, should I have been, was I supposed to be the one killed?"[91] Maryknoll once wore its connection to the cult of martyrdom like a badge, exalting those who lost their lives in mission. The El Salvador killings could not be placed neatly into those traditional narratives, and the tragedy put Maryknoll in the public eye like never before. The story of why and how the women died was indelibly tied to the political journey traversed by Maryknoll over the 1970s. The congregation's pursuit of justice changed the meaning of Catholic martyrdom in profound ways.[92]

7 · "THE NUNS WERE NOT JUST NUNS"
Foreign Mission and Foreign Policy

In the popular memory of recent years, Ronald Reagan has been credited with engineering a peaceful conclusion to the Cold War after the collapse of the Soviet Union. Rarely discussed is the fervor with which his presidential administration heated up the decades-long conflict by unleashing an astounding array of clandestine and brazen military interventions. The enduring power of the well-publicized story of the deaths of Maryknoll sisters Ita Ford and Maura Clarke alongside their mission colleagues Dorothy Kazel and Jean Donovan in El Salvador defies this tendency toward rose-tinted recollections of the Reagan years. The story of the women's fate provided, and continues to provide, a rare visibility of the appalling casualties of counterinsurgency campaigns. It is not hyperbolic to say that the murder of these four women determined the course of US policy toward Central America in the 1980s. The international incident was a definitive event of the first years of the Reagan presidency, a human rights tragedy that proved to be a public relations disaster for the renewed war on communism. With high drama, it played out in Congress, the executive offices of the US government, and communities throughout the country. It captured the imagination of a broad coalition of organized activists, elected officials, and everyday people—especially Catholics.

The churchwomen provided a symbolic touchstone that joined secular liberal-leftist protest movements to the peace and justice wing of the Catholic Church that gained influence after the Second Vatican Council. The strength and persistence of this coalition has been overshadowed by the undeniable conservative ascendancy in US public life. Maryknoll's effort to marshal the power of the women's story was more than symbolic, though. Its dedication to achieving justice in El Salvador—not only for those the congregation named its martyrs, but for Salvadorans suffering from the gross human rights violations of the US-fueled civil war—gave it significant leverage in the realm of advocacy. Quietly but determinedly, the organization invested the mobilization around the deaths with a belief that "effective love can form us into one people and overcome the barriers which separate us." Its message was both Catholic and catholic: born of the conciliar reimagining of the corporeality of Jesus in the lives of the poor and appealing to a universal ethics of cooperative care. The sisters faced off against "political structures which . . . destroy the image of God in the human person."[1]

The four churchwomen's deaths have been recounted exhaustively in histories of social movements in the United States and Central America in the late twentieth century, and they have been chronicled in the popular and religious media.[2] The complex narrative nevertheless continues to deserve sustained attention. While the impact of the incident has been given its due, the role of the Maryknoll Sisters in parlaying this tragedy into a formidable human rights battle tends to be underplayed. The reach of this event, which stretched from the end of the 1970s to 2016, had an instrumental effect on US foreign policy. It compelled those in seats of executive power to take extraordinary measures to implement their Latin America agenda. For the churchwomen's advocates, the campaign to secure justice fueled a social movement both in the United States and abroad, setting a precedent in human rights law. Moreover, this activism shaped a crucial transition in US Catholicism. In the beginning of the 1980s, conciliar and liberation ideas reached an apex of influence among grassroots Catholics and secular activists alike. By the end of the decade, a conservative turn in the church muted this dedication to social and political transformation. The Maryknoll Sisters, like other US women religious, may have aroused the disapproval of conservative elements who narrowed the parameters of the church's commitment to social change in the 1980s. However, the die had been cast for the unapologetically socially engaged ministry that the congregation carried into the twenty-first century.

"AM I WILLING TO SUFFER WITH THE PEOPLE HERE?"

A shadow already hung over the US political scene when the sisters were killed in early December 1980. The malaise of the Carter years had undone his presidency, and few knew quite what to make of the incoming Reagan administration. Indictments had been issued in the Abscam cases, an almost farcical sequel to Watergate that confirmed a certain hopelessness among the electorate. Internationally, clusters of revolutionary movements stoked strong emotions in the post-Vietnam cultural landscape: the stirring solidarity movement in Poland raised hopes of a new break in the struggle against communism at the same time that it aroused fears of a Soviet crackdown; the Iranian hostage crisis hit its one-year anniversary with few signs of resolution; and unrest throughout Central America brought the specter of Soviet world domination and the reality of war by proxy in the backyard of the United States.

As recounted in the previous chapter, the Sandinista uprising in Nicaragua was an invigorating experience for a number of sisters, a high point of synergy between liberation theology and Latin American people's movements. While the mainstream press and US policy makers wrung their hands over a revolution attributed to malign Soviet and Cuban influences, Catholic missioners remained convinced of the organic nature of the events. Maryknoll women were optimistic about the Sandinista regime, viewing its success as proof of the power of the preferential option for the poor to transform social conditions on the ground. Several of the women found opportunities to align their ministry with Sandinista social development initiatives.

If the Nicaraguan revolution demonstrated the great potential of liberation-inspired reform, the El Salvador conflict revealed the profound dangers such commitments entailed. Unlike Nicaragua, the escalating crisis in El Salvador in the late 1970s made few impressions on the US public. However, Catholic activists and a secular Latin American solidarity movement sounded an alarm over the cascade of atrocities that intensified after Carlos Humberto Romero's seizure of executive power in 1977. The country's young people and campesinos, crippled by the economic expropriation of the oligarchic ruling class, launched a protest movement that turned into armed revolt. Security forces answered the agitation with terrorism, indiscriminately casting the rural poor and their advocates in the Catholic Church as subversives. The notorious death squads, with shadowy ties to military and paramilitary groups, operated with anonymity and impunity as they unleashed horrific violence. The consequences of dangerous allegiances were spelled out by the omnipresence of armed soldiers, dead bodies that increasingly appeared on roadsides, and village raids in which mass torture, kidnapping, and murder elicited no response from law enforcement.[3]

A handful of Maryknoll sisters were working in El Salvador in the late 1970s when the country's archbishop, Óscar Romero, invited missionary religious to replace the dozens of Salvadoran church workers who had been killed or disappeared in the undeclared civil war, which claimed the lives of nearly a thousand people by mid-1980. Romero defied expectations that his leadership would bolster the power of Salvador's ruling class. Earning the devotion of campesinos, 73 percent of whom tuned in to his Sunday radio sermons, he became the paragon of liberation theology in action. The homilies described a military state of violent repression that the press ignored. Romero's call for missionary assistance in continuing the grassroots work of the church was also a plea for the international community to condemn the atrocities and eliminate the military aid fueling this violence. With the vision of working alongside the revered archbishop, Maryknoll sisters Carla Piette, Ita Ford, and Maura Clarke answered the request for volunteers and made arrangements to take positions in El Salvador in 1980.[4]

They were not able to arrive in time. After broadcasting a sermon that called for soldiers to disobey orders and lay down their arms, Romero was assassinated by a sniper while saying Mass in a small chapel on March 24, 1980. The tenor of the sisters' experience was set on the day that Carla Piette arrived, March 30—the day of Romero's funeral. Unknown parties directed smoke bombs and sniper fire at the fifty thousand people who had gathered for the funeral, killing thirty to fifty people. Each of the three sisters had had considerable experience in Latin American conflict regions. However, Ford and Piette's time in Chile during the 1973 coup and Clarke's in the Somozas' Nicaragua had not prepared them for the unvarnished repression that marked daily life in El Salvador. Several dozen religious and catechists had already been murdered for making the basic efforts of Catholic ministry, the provision of social services and accompaniment of the poor on a spiritual journey of self-empowerment. For the first few months following their arrival in El Salvador, Ford and Piette pondered how to navigate such a chaotic environment as they stayed with Maryknoll colleagues in the city of La Libertad. There, they worked with a tightly knit group of missioners sponsored by the Diocese of Cleveland, Ohio. The team included Jean Donovan, a lay missioner, and Dorothy Kazel, a member of the Ursuline Sisters. In the summer, Ford and Piette made their way to Chalatenango, the capital of a province that was a stronghold of leftist revolutionaries and accordingly a magnet for death squad reprisals. The town was overwhelmed by refugees as campesinos fled the isolated, violence-riddled countryside. Working with a parish priest, the two sisters distributed food and medicine, as well as comfort and care, to a traumatized population. Father Paul Schindler later reflected on some of the presumptions that guided the decision to use these sisters, instead of local priests, in carrying out the fraught tasks of refugee work. He believed that their presence as "blonde, blue-eyed women" would mitigate the danger. Privileges of gender, race, and nationality would shield them from being treated as disposable subversives.[5]

The women undertook their assignment with sorrow and trepidation. Salvadoran women and children certainly were not spared from atrocities. The sisters were deeply aware that they stood in the face of death in Chalatenango simply by performing the works of charity and mercy that had been conducted by the earliest apostolic women's congregations. Conciliar teachings gave them a framework for understanding the relationship between faith and the experience of repression; the desperate need of the people spurred them on and gave them purpose as women religious. Sister Madeline Dorsey, one of the Maryknoll women in La Libertad, rendered her role in these plain terms: "accompanying the people, being with them. . . . Right now all we can do is to be with these people, to share with them, because they are hurting very badly." Ita Ford similarly described the challenge of her ministry: "Am I willing to suffer with the people here, the suffering of the powerlessness? Can I say to my neighbors, 'I have no solution to this situation . . . ; but I will walk with you, search with you, be with you?'"[6] Maryknoll sisters had once endeavored to experience God through perfecting and purifying themselves. They envisioned themselves as the conduits of God's graces in their devout charity. The preferential option prompted them to seek God in those whom he loved, those who shared his persecution. In living this witness, they journeyed with the poor in a struggle for survival.

Tragedy struck early among the new arrivals. An August car accident in which Carla Piette died left Ford deeply shaken, having narrowly survived the experience that took her closest friend's life. Maura Clarke then arrived to take Piette's place. Army commander Ricardo Peña Arbaiza, whose office faced the dormitory where Clarke and Ford lived, made no pretense about his contempt for the work of the Catholic Church. Salvador's elites and military ruling class shared the view that Catholic pastoral work inspired communist revolt. Peña Arbaiza made clear to the women that they were viewed as collaborators in the rebels' cause. A 1983 report recounted his menacing hostility. In private and public meetings, he attacked church representatives for their subversive activity—subversive, Ford reported him saying, "because it's on the side of the weak." By the fall, soldiers "had virtually taken control of the church building," their presence a constant warning to church officials and potential parishioners.[7] In the last week of November, a note was posted over the door to Ford's room. An English-language translation read: "Every person who enters this house dies. We know that you are communists. If you don't believe this just try it. We know that the military takes no action against you, but we will execute you. . . . Death to Communism."[8] It was signed by the Mauricio Borgonovo Anti-Communist Brigade, an attribution that gave the impression that a right-wing paramilitary group was keeping watch.

It was not a paramilitary group, but instead National Guard soldiers, who kept surveillance on the sisters as they flew into the San Salvador airport on December 2, the night of their deaths. Ford and Clarke and their La Libertad colleagues Dorsey and Teresa Alexander were due to arrive from Nicaragua, where they had attended an annual meeting of Maryknoll personnel in Central America. Because the four Maryknollers could not get seats on the same return flight,

Dorothy Kazel and Jean Donovan drove to the airport twice to meet the travelers. Dorsey and Alexander arrived in the early evening, and after taking them to La Libertad, Kazel and Donovan returned for Ford and Clarke.

No single explanation has satisfactorily accounted for the motivation behind the kidnapping and murder of the four women that night. Five guardsmen, who carried out the crime in plainclothes, were ultimately convicted as the direct perpetrators. As the case unfolded over the years, some of the men said nothing about why they had intercepted the women's van, driven them to a remote field, assaulted them, shot them point-blank with high-power rifles, and left the bodies at the side of the road. A few of those involved explained that the women had attracted attention because guards spotted them with packages assumed to be weapons and subversive literature—items later inventoried as a handbag and a box of books.[9] The guards were on high alert, it was claimed, because leftist sympathizers were pouring into El Salvador for the funeral of several leaders of the guerrilla movement, whose kidnapping-murder had made international news. Other perpetrators insisted that their sergeant, Luis Colindres Aleman, told them to carry out the act because he had orders to do so. The men later agreed that they had been ordered to kill the women after Colindres made a phone call at the airport. This phone call would be one of several indications that commanders above the patrol unit had engineered the executions.[10]

The Maryknoll Sisters and their allies insisted that the case went beyond the individuals to whom US State Department officials would come to assign complete culpability: this handful of "low level police agents" working at the behest of Colindres, who was dismissed by a State Department attaché as a "a remarkably savage human being."[11] The deaths gave Maryknoll impetus to expose to the world the depravity of El Salvador's governing forces, a military that subdued the population with violent oppression. Moreover, these forces depended on the financial, military, and moral support of the US government.

For Maryknoll, these circumstances made it incumbent on US citizens to challenge the foreign policy that propped this regime. A new type of liberation theology politics emerged from Maryknoll's quest to secure justice for the churchwomen. While the small-scale ministry of pastoral accompaniment had drawn the sisters to Latin America, efforts to bring meaning and closure to churchwomen's deaths were charged with the potential of creating urgently needed structural change. When the churchwomen's deaths became an international incident, the quest to follow the path of the poor—Jesus's path—took Maryknoll out of base communities and put it into the center of national policy debates. With this attention, sisters redoubled their use of the language of liberation theology, announcing that "solidarity with the poor is not an option but a sign of the Kingdom that must be made explicit in our day."[12] Compelled to agitate for social change by the deaths of its sisters, which it interpreted through discourses of Christian martyrdom, Maryknoll deployed the liberation-inspired work of conscientization within the United States.

"A MOST IMPORTANT ISSUE FOR THE UNITED STATES GOVERNMENT"

Unraveling the contradictory accounts of the case and securing some measure of justice for the churchwomen proved to be a decades-long quest. It unfolded in multiple criminal and civil court cases as well as ongoing foreign policy debates. The churchwomen's cases intensified the polarization between those who supported escalation of anticommunist efforts and those who hoped to end the decades-long cycle of brinksmanship and proxy wars. Investigations of the deaths followed two distinct tracks and led to conflicting conclusions. The foreign policy arm of the US government narrated a tale that justified an ongoing alliance with the anticommunist Salvadoran regime. This galvanized an opposition movement that connected Maryknoll to a diverse group of advocates. Drawing on the resources of ordinary citizens, nongovernmental organizations, the victims' families, and religious communities, the alternative investigation launched a religiously informed critique of the underpinnings of foreign policy.

The investigations diverged almost immediately after revelation of the deaths. Though several days elapsed between the women's disappearance and press reports of the discoveries of their bodies, there were several direct witnesses to the crimes as they occurred. Hours before the sisters were abducted, a group of Canadian religious were stopped and interrogated at a roadblock outside the airport—a roadblock later revealed to be a means of isolating the churchwomen from other traffic. The experience left the Canadians so shaken that they contacted the US ambassador, Robert White, for help with the return trip. Later that night, campesinos heard gunfire and saw the women's van being driven to and from the death site. The next morning, a man notified the justice of the peace in Santiago Nonualco, a village fifteen miles from the airport, that bodies had been found at the edge of an isolated field. With a handful of police and national guardsmen looking on, the town official came to the site to authorize the burial of individuals classified as unknown, and villagers were directed to dig a common grave. The justice of the peace later stated that such "procedures . . . had become standard at the direction of the security forces." He told White that he oversaw "two or three such informal burials of unidentified bodies" every week. For most disappeared Salvadorans, that would have been the end of the story. One man, however, spoke of his discovery of four dead North American women to a priest. The information reached White and the sisters' colleagues, who by then had located the women's torched van on the side of the highway to the airport.[13]

White and the La Libertad missioners traveled to the unmarked grave on December 4, where they were joined by an international contingent of journalists who were in the country to cover the guerrillas' funeral. Reporters documented a scene of guardsmen with their weapons drawn, standing around campesinos who lifted the broken bodies, stacked on top of each other, out of the ground. An Associated Press photograph that appeared on the front page of many newspapers the next day left a haunting impression: a scene of dirt-flecked corpses, their disfigurement obscured by branches that had been placed over them by their colleagues, who knelt in prayer nearby. Press accounts conveyed that those with knowledge of the Salvadoran military agreed that this was not a random act of violence. The *New York Times* quoted an unnamed "foreign diplomat" as saying that "there is every reason to believe that Government security forces were involved."[14]

Perhaps this diplomat was Robert White. Because of his position and expertise, he would become one of the most important advocates for the churchwomen's cause. In so doing, he became the most outstanding, and outlying, example of a détente-era human rights diplomat. At the scene, he attracted press attention for his vocal outrage and aggressive questions to witnesses of the burial. "This time they won't get away with it," he was heard saying, "they just won't."[15] On camera, he sputtered, "I think people should stand guard over this thing while I go call on García and everyone else and raise holy hell," making clear his intention to compel the military high commander, José Guillermo García, to answer for the crimes.[16]

Though White, a practicing Catholic, would later explain his ongoing involvement with the churchwomen's case in the pragmatic tones of a career foreign service official, he may have experienced something of what Catholic doctrine would term the Mystical Body of Christ in this encounter with martyrdom. Dorsey, one of the women pictured praying over the bodies, termed the women's fate "our death, entombment, and resurrection story."[17] Her statement references Catholic interpretations of martyrdom as an experience of the incarnation of Jesus in his redemptive suffering that is unmatched in its immediacy. White had encountered the churchwomen in life, hosting Kazel and Donovan for an overnight visit the evening before their airport duty; his encounter with their deaths was even more intimate. When he described the scene later, his impressions conveyed a raw emotion that turned him from an agent of the US government into a staunch critic and human rights crusader: "When you saw the flies, the ropes, when you saw them uncovered, it was horrible and pitiable. . . . You see people you love beaten and broken." Sister Helene O'Sullivan vividly recalled White's apoplectic reaction, as well as that of a fellow foreign service officer who became determined to launch a full investigation: "They went berserk to see those women raped and killed. It just made them crazy!"[18] White's human rights leanings had already drawn the disgust of Latin America hawks in Congress—notably Senator Jesse Helms, who had held up White's appointment to El Salvador for four months. The combination of political commitment, in-depth knowledge of Salvadoran social conditions, and a "searing" memory of a scene of brutality—a memory that his wife, Mary Anne White, averred "made him determined that this was not going to happen again"—compelled him to insist that the Department of State prioritize scrutiny of the Salvadoran military.[19] Soon, it would become evident that he was odd man out.

Certainly, many people shared Robert White's visceral response to the sadistic acts, and a significant number of those who observed the scene from afar expressed a sense of emotional connection to the churchwomen. The unfathomable violence that already had displaced and killed thousands of Salvadorans was made legible when it was written onto the bodies of pious white women. But there were also tremendous political reverberations of these essentially transnational causalities of war. The massive aid long poured into Central America with the justification of suppressing communist revolution came under unprecedented scrutiny. The day after the disinterment, the Carter administration suspended the military portion of El Salvador's aid package and sent a team of advisors to establish a plan for a criminal investigation.

This get-tough posture proved a temporary response. US recognition of Sandinista Nicaragua and deoccupation of the Panama Canal Zone marked a certain détente in hemispheric relations. Still, the domino theory continued to trump such concerns in the Cabinet and Congress, and the rapidly changing situation on the ground in El Salvador created a complicated set of circumstances to navigate. The deaths occurred during pivotal transitions in the governments of both the United States and El Salvador. In the United States, the incoming Reagan administration adamantly repudiated human rights interests and declared an all-out offensive against the perceived threat of global communism. In El Salvador, the ruling military junta had been in flux, and by 1980 the US State Department was hopeful that a centrist government could be installed over the extremists on both the left and the right. In the days surrounding the women's deaths, several junta members had been removed, and a civilian, José Napoleón Duarte (who reportedly was on the payroll of the CIA) had been added. To the State Department, this was a "good coup," one that shuffled some of the hardline anticommunists, who had ties to the death squads, out of the seat of executive power. But another unnamed diplomat pointed out to the US press that hardliners remained in charge of defense forces: this was the true source of authority on the ground.[20] Leftists had announced an offensive at the end of 1980, declaring that popular support would carry them to victory. This spurred an intensification of death squad activity, and awareness that Soviets and Cubans had supplied the rebels with weapons was an irresistible provocation for the

United States to flood security forces with war materiel and counterinsurgency training. Even Carter's human rights interests could not hold him back from restoring aid on the last day of his administration. White continued to warn the press that something was amiss: "As far as I am concerned, there is no reason to believe that the Government of El Salvador is conducting a serious investigation. I am not going to be involved in a cover-up."[21]

In public, other spokesmen for the US government declined to provide information about the investigation, claiming that doing so would delay the process of Salvadoran justice. Behind the scenes, a team of federal agencies including the FBI, CIA, Department of State, and National Security Council mobilized a tremendous amount of resources to close the case. Internal documents gave a frank assessment of why the investigation mattered so much. According to them, it was not so much the tragedy or a desire for the truth that drove the quest to solve the murders. It was deemed "a most important issue for the United States government," according to an FBI legal attaché, because it incited protests against US military assistance to El Salvador.[22] The interdepartmental investigators hoped to convince security forces to flush out the perpetrators and distance themselves from acts of extrajudicial violence. This was not an entirely disingenuous effort. Personnel like White believed that pressure for a proper investigation would be incentive for the Salvadoran regime to adopt new operating procedures while it subdued revolutionary forces.[23]

To critics of US Central America policy, a more sinister strategy behind these measures seemed clear. The agencies coordinated their efforts to isolate a problem, "allay public opinion," and protect US military support of the quasidemocratic, anticommunist junta, which the incoming Reagan administration enthusiastically endorsed. To step up the endless fight against Marxist insurrection, still figured in the Manichean narrative of Soviet and Cuban infiltration, supporters of military escalation endeavored to demonstrate that their Salvadoran allies had instituted some semblance of the rule of law. The supporters especially needed to stave off the charge that the national military, and not the revolutionary left, was the country's terrorist force. In retrospect, White stated bluntly that Reagan and his foreign policy makers had engaged in "systematic misrepresentation to the U.S. Congress and American public . . . concerning the atrocities of the Salvadoran military."[24] Accordingly, the US government's investigation devoted extensive resources to tying the handful of rank-and-file guardsmen to the crime. It neglected to probe those higher in the chain of command who may have engineered the women's execution. Indications of the involvement of others could be identified at many junctures: individuals who radioed the airport with information about the sisters' travel plans; soldiers who boarded a Miami-bound plane in San Salvador the morning before the churchwomen were killed, singling out Maryknoll sister Maria Rieckleman for interrogation;

the anonymous man who handed a Chalatenango parish assistant a list of names, including Clarke's and Ford's, on the day of the deaths and said, "here is the list of the people we are going to kill, and today, this very night, we will begin." These events were documented by the US State Department, but there was no substantive follow-up on signs of command-level involvement.[25]

When Salvadoran military officials assumed control of the investigation, a US concession to noninterference in foreign governments, the State Department put the fox in charge of the henhouse. This predicament would be soon acknowledged but hardly rectified. From the start, the US government was thwarted by the obstructionist response of Salvadoran officials in its efforts to assuage the public. The culprits could not be singled out when law enforcement refused to do rudimentary investigative work. Even in the first month after the killing, internal State Department memoranda detailed irregularities that suggested a cover-up of National Guard activities at the airport.[26] The Salvadoran military commanders who headed the investigation flatly stated that it was impossible that national security forces had been involved, even though basic evidence of the guardsmen's guilt "was readily available for gathering," in the words of a State Department advisor. When the bodies were disinterred before White, public health officers refused to conduct autopsies on the grounds that they had no surgical masks. With the excuse of it being the Christmas holiday, forensic work was not initiated for several weeks after the disinterment. Once the bodies had been autopsied under the direction of the FBI, ballistics information led directly to the National Guard's guns. During that time, it would later be documented, one of the guardsmen told his superiors of the events, and commanders—including those heading the investigation—took measures to protect the perpetrators, a patrol of five men directed by Colindres. The men were transferred to different posts, and their service weapons were swapped with others that could not be tied to the shootings.[27]

Those who engineered the cover-up did a poor job concealing the murderers' trail. Using the leverage of US aid, the FBI demanded that the Salvadoran team provide fingerprints, weapons, and witness statements. H. Carl Gettinger, a State Department attaché, did intensive work on the ground, searching out witnesses and avoiding officials who obstructed the investigation. Within days, he had the name of Colindres, and in early 1981, he secured a recorded confession from Colindres using a National Guard officer who was a secret CIA informant.[28] These facts went unrecorded in official documents until the State Department declassified a trove of materials for the 1993 United Nations Truth Commission for El Salvador, a documentation project that assigned overwhelming culpability for human rights abuses to national security forces. The declassified documents finally confirmed the suspicions of Maryknoll and the human rights community: from the start, the US government knew much more about the crime than was ever acknowledged. By suppressing such information, the State Department had participated in the cover-up and defied accountability legislation enacted after Watergate and the Vietnam War. Foreign service personnel reasoned that only hard evidence—evidence admissible in a court system that was designed to protect the powerful—and legal convictions would successfully settle matters. To the churchwomen's supporters, who initiated a Freedom of Information Act lawsuit to open the government's investigation to scrutiny, the behavior smacked of complicity.

However much frustration US officials expressed behind the scenes about Salvadoran corruption, and however much they knew about the military's participation in the crime, they used their public relations efforts to bolster the ruling junta's credibility. For the incoming Reagan government, the spectacle proved an inconvenient obstacle to escalation of the anticommunist offensive, a priority articulated even as the deaths remained front page news. Central America would be the proving ground of the Reagan Doctrine, the generous and often clandestine financial and military support of anticommunist governments and armed opposition movements. The first attempts to manage public opinion on the matter played out poorly. Jeane Kirkpatrick, designated ambassador to the United Nations, fired an early volley, electing to discredit the sisters in an effort to justify increased military aid. She parroted the Salvadoran government's response to the murders, attributing the executions to a far right fringe group rather than the national military. In an interview published on Christmas, she further asserted that the sisters were responsible for their own deaths, having lent their services to guerrillas. Their religious vocation, she suggested, was a cover for something more sinister: "I don't think the government (of El Salvador) was responsible. The nuns were not just nuns; the nuns were political activists . . . on behalf of the Frente [Frente Farabundo Martí para la Liberación Nacional, a revolutionary coalition] and somebody who is using violence to oppose the Frente killed them."[29] Kirkpatrick was already an interested party. She had attracted the attention of Reagan's transition team as a neoconservative intellectual who made the case for prioritizing support of the anticommunist ventures of "moderately oppressive regimes" over human rights goals. When a Salvadoran lobbying delegation visited Washington during Carter's lame duck period, Kirkpatrick was among the advisors sent to "assure visitors . . . that the new administration will increase military aid," the New York Times reported.[30] Her tasteless, misleading comments about the churchwomen's deaths won few supporters for such a cause.

Secretary of State Alexander Haig also joined the fray, with the Salvadoran crisis dominating policy debates during his first months on the job. There had been no question that the former general and NATO commander sought to initiate an all-out war on communism, announcing in his first State Department press conference that "international terrorism will take the place of human rights."[31] He struggled to neutralize the challenge posed by the churchwomen's case. From the start, congressional foreign affairs committees pressed Haig to justify Reagan's Central American designs. Haig soon made what would come to be a characteristic public relations misstep when he insinuated that the churchwomen had died because of their involvement in armed resistance. He speculated that the women "might have run a road-block [and] there may have been an exchange of fire." When questioned about his suggestion that the women fired weapons, he laughed, saying "I haven't met any pistol-packing nuns in my day." Anthony Lewis of the *New York Times* expressed the revulsion felt by those moved by the sisters' tragedy: Haig, "talking about the vicious killing, suggested they were responsible in some measure for their fate." When challenged, "he tried to slither away, joking and expressing amazement and blaming the press."[32]

"CATHOLIC CHURCH ACTIVISM IS GETTING EXTRAORDINARY"

Haig's poor relations with the press would not be the only problem contributing to his short tenure as secretary of state. During his time in office, his call to invigorate Vietnam-style counterinsurgency met with widespread hostility as the US public persistently expressed opposition to military escalation in Central America. The Reagan administration's response to the churchwomen's death and its pursuit of massive military expenditures energized an activist coalition that had some success in checking the administration's foreign policy ambitions. Even as Reagan's inaugural parade coasted on the good feelings wrought by the homecoming of the Iran hostages, it passed by counterdemonstrators' placards that demanded "U.S. Out of El Salvador."[33]

A *Washington Post* story assessing the first months of the Reagan presidency reported that El Salvador, "which two months ago looked like a good place to 'draw the line' against communist expansion," had produced "the first notable backlash," with mail "running 10 to 1 against the administration's new emphasis on military aid and advisers" to the country. Critics were not only concerned about abstract military aid; Haig and others in the Cabinet had hinted that the United States would benefit from a stronger on-the-ground presence. Haig may have not made a compelling case for this to the electorate. He did succeed, however, in quickly removing White as ambassador. Though diplomatic turnover is standard, White attributes his sudden dismissal to his unwillingness to cooperate in a deceitful campaign to justify Salvadoran aid.[34]

Those who remained close to the US investigation knew that support for military escalation could not be achieved by casting the sisters as aggressors or by ignoring the institutionalization of human rights abuses. The difficulties of this case subsequently made Central America the most important foreign policy issue of the early Reagan administration and a potent threat to the Reagan Doctrine. Although the intensity of that struggle has been largely forgotten by the US public, it was Reagan's Vietnam. The Cold War was not over; neither was the antiwar movement. Reagan's run of unpopular foreign policy and controversial use of executive power may have played out in a less ignominious fashion than it did for Lyndon B. Johnson and Richard Nixon, but Central America posed a stumbling block at every point of Regan's tenure. Only when the fall of the Soviet Union cast a pleasant glow on his legacy would discontent about the military campaigns in Central America retreat into the background.

Advisors in the executive branch harangued, wheedled, and—when other methods failed—stole and lied to deliver military might to the right in Central America.[35] But their machinations unified diverse protest movements—antiwar, anti-imperialist, feminist, and religious. Maryknoll took a place of leadership in this coalition. Its vision of the purpose and scope of the churchwomen's investigation called for morally engaged policy change. Maryknoll and its advocates rallied against the government's vision of closure, which stopped with the prosecution of the guardsmen directly responsible. Instead they shone a spotlight on the structural violence fueled by the US government's military support and moral legitimization of the Salvadoran regime. The sisters' success at rallying a protest movement behind these issues can be attributed to two central factors. First, the deaths of its sisters provided a loose collection of activists with a moving narrative of the human cost of structural injustice. Second, because of its strong institutional commitment to public advocacy, the congregation's experience with on-the-ground transnational projects and human rights networks enabled it to influence the government and the press. Spiritual resources undergirded these institutional relations, and the sisters found meaning in the deaths by pursuing a Gospel mandate for the pursuit of justice. With grassroots efforts such as direct action and civic protest and a front-door lobby that directly engaged members of Congress, administration officials, and the US and Salvadoran judiciaries, Maryknoll brought liberation theology to the centers of power.

The symbolic importance of the sisters should not be underestimated. Their story immediately resonated with Catholic parishioners and religious throughout the United States. The murders of four highly visible American women, associated with the pure intentions of chastity and religious service, stirred indignation that had not been aroused by the abstract awareness of mass deaths in a foreign country. The modern narrative of martyrdom had an electrifying effect on those who might not have otherwise been interested in the policy questions at hand. The women became sanctified in their sacrifice to their faith, and this added a mystical valence to the antiwar, pro-poor cause. Describing the religious coalition that gave life to the US-Central America solidarity movement, Sharon

Nepstad emphasizes that social movement stories "engage people . . . when they dramatically portray a situation with moral clarity."[36] Even though the politicization of women religious drew criticism in the years after the Second Vatican Council, the perceived altruistic integrity of Catholic nuns still evoked a moral clarity that held Maryknoll in good stead. US foreign policy architects did not share such an upright reputation.

But Maryknoll women were not simply passive symbols of piety and vulnerability. Although the story of the sisters' deaths has figured prominently in histories of US-Central America relations, there has been little recognition of the degree to which the congregation became an instrumental actor in a powerful social movement. Maryknoll's initial response made clear that it would not be content to mourn quietly. Ford and Clarke's martyrdom was a consequence of their pledge "to announce the Good News of the Kingdom and to denounce that which diminishes the freedom, equality and dignity of people."[37] Paraphrasing Matthew 25:36, the presidents of the Fathers and Sisters described their congregations' purpose in a public statement: "Wherever we are called to work . . . , we will make our love active by feeding the hungry . . . , sheltering the homeless, visiting the sick . . . , and burying the dead." The women had died, they underscored, because of allegiance to a "Gospel imperative," which demanded not only charitable solicitude for the least of God's people but also that "justice be done for those who suffer hunger, who are naked and homeless . . . , and those who are persecuted." The statement connected scriptural mandates to the contemporary political context. Outrage over the women's deaths, it continued, "should not overshadow the murders of nearly 9,000 less known people in that country." The Gospel principles of justice and nonviolence included rejection of violence "in the hands of an assassin"—the actions of individuals who killed the churchwomen—as well as rejection of violence "in structures." US citizens accordingly had a moral responsibility to demand that "President Reagan not permit our government to send to the Salvadoran government any military aid to be used by security forces which would only serve to further the violence against their own people."[38]

Prompted by the social consciousness stoked by the Vatican Council and by the intensification of unrest in mission territories, the Maryknoll Sisters had inaugurated its Office of Social Concerns in 1974 as a means of sharing information and coordinating advocacy efforts. Its deep practical experience enabled the organization to put forward a forceful message after the Salvador deaths, even amid the trauma of the mourning process. The office, along with the Maryknoll Fathers' counterpart Office of Justice and Peace, encouraged Maryknollers to undertake reverse mission, raising awareness in the United States of the "interdependence and inter-complicity of events which . . . nurture injustice throughout the world." This task was one of conscientization, designed to make Americans aware of their own role in fostering violence in the developing world. Reasoning that "only a sister who has lived among the people for a number of years can present the reality of a people, a country, and a culture with the knowledge and empathy that is warranted," the sisters' office asserted that they were uniquely positioned "to speak of the needs of the peoples of the Third World and of minority groups in the US" in the face of the flurry of interest in Maryknoll. In this way, many ordinary Americans heard firsthand accounts of the impact of structural violence from sisters and human rights activists speaking at local churches and public talks and in press interviews.[39]

These small-scale educational encounters bore fruit. Catholics in the United States turned out for a "variety of protest activities," which a *Washington Post* reporter called "unmatched by few—if any—reactions to past issues, including the controversy over abortion." From the banner hung outside of the San Francisco cathedral that read "U.S. Dollars Kill U.S. Nuns" to countless memorial masses and statements of protest, a mobilization that stretched from the pews to the bishops endorsed Maryknoll's denunciation of the government's support of the Salvadoran right.[40] With telegrams and sermons, newspaper ads and mail campaigns, Maryknoll's Catholic supporters flexed their muscles and hounded elected officials to respond to the outcry. In Reagan's first term, many of these officials ran interference against his Central America maneuvers.

The first congressional challenge came in March 1981, when Ohio Representative Mary Rose Oakar, a Catholic Democrat enlisted by the victims' families, introduced a resolution calling for oversight of US aid to El Salvador. The idea gained momentum, and similar resolutions drew dozens of congressional signatories. Politicians running for election in 1982 marveled that "Catholic church activism is getting extraordinary." At town meetings and through the mail, voters called on elected officials to abandon US military expansion in Central America.[41]

It is important to note the extent to which the institutional Catholic Church contributed to the Maryknoll Sisters' continuing effort to seek political change. "The bishops were awesome," Helene O'Sullivan emphasized, and "American religious women were one hundred percent behind us." The National Conference of Catholic Bishops, highlighting its commitment to conciliar social reform, lent its voice to the sisters' cause. Organizations of laity and religious, including Pax Christi and Network, also gave El Salvador a central place in their 1980s agendas.[42]

Secular social movements likewise contributed critical support to Maryknoll. The fight over Central America brought to the surface much of the unfinished business of the American left: the betrayals of Vietnam; the nonsustainability of military-industrial culture; the endurance of empire; and the victimization of people of color, women, and the poor. Maryknoll was well connected in the wider human rights network. Affiliations with organizations like the Washington Office on Latin America (discussed in chapter 6) conferred credibility on the sisters' accounts of conflict regions. This had been helpful in the 1970s, when Sister Janice McLaughlin broke through a press blackout to document repressive white minority rule in Rhodesia, and it became even more important after the El Salvador deaths.

The religious human rights network coordinated its efforts with a range of secular organizations dedicated to opposing US military interventions and supporting people's movements in Latin America. This coalition of liberal, leftist, and religious groups, termed the solidarity movement, had a wealth of conflicts to address, but El Salvador and Nicaragua figured most prominently among them. The Committee in Solidarity with the People of El Salvador (CISPES) would become the largest of the solidarity groups focused specifically on that country, and at the movement's peak in the mid-1980s, there were two thousand local groups working on solidarity issues under a score of national organizations.[43] The bumper sticker "El Salvador Is Spanish for Vietnam" made its appearance after the churchwomen's deaths. Feminists, antinuclear activists, and antiwar protesters participated in major protest actions. A news story about a May 1981 demonstration that brought 25,000 people to the Pentagon focused on the motley crew of protesters, with a "flea market atmosphere, something for everyone," but the accompanying photo highlighted the central issue for the demonstration's organizers. The banner leading the march read "Make Jobs not War, U.S. out of El Salvador!"[44]

This is not to say that Maryknoll was universally respected for its human rights advocacy. Other activists contributed to the Reagan administration's attempts to, in the words of historian Roger Peace, "deflect the outpouring of criticism from the liberal religious community by insinuating that U.S. religious leaders were aiding American's Cold War enemy."[45] The Center for Inter-American Security, a conservative think tank, joined Kirkpatrick and Haig in claiming that the churchwomen "may have been working with left-wing guerrillas to overthrow the government." Still, as had been the case in campaigns to discredit the YWCA, most detractors described the sisters less as subversives and more as dupes. These gendered attacks avoided maligning a group that had high credibility among the American public. They cast the sisters' commitments as a result of ignorance and weakness, rather than as deliberate actions and ethical principles.[46] Indeed, Maryknoll's supporters may have found it strategically advantageous to have the sisters portrayed as passive innocents, unaware of the fraught political circumstances that surrounded them.

Conservative Catholic pundits weighed in with invective. An editorial in the March 1981 *National Review* painted a simplistic portrait of Maryknoll's Marxist folly. It juxtaposed the socialism of liberation theologians with the congregation's gentle language of social justice. The brief statement by the congregation's president, Melinda Roper, that "we have a mission based on the Gospel . . . which has political implications" was cited as "quite in keeping" with the socialism of Maryknoll priest Miguel d'Escoto Brockmann, vilified by anticommunists when he assumed a post in the Sandinista government. The editorial spelled out a vitriolic conclusion: "The Maryknoll leadership . . . espouses Christian Marxism in its grossest forms, inoculates its rank and file with these delusions, then sets them up like ducks in Central American shooting galleries. It does not lessen our abhorrence of murderous thugs"—the sisters' assassins—"to describe the order's conduct as despicable." Andrew Greeley appropriated the language of anticolonialism to invigorate the well-worn rhetoric of red baiting. He castigated "Maryknoll imperialists." These supporters of "Marxist-Leninist regimes" were, "without realizing it . . . , agents for Russian imperialism." Foolishly, "these fanatics [did] not deign to consider . . . a simple truth . . . that Marxism always means tyranny wherever it comes to power."[47] The supposedly delusional sisters had become handmaids to Marxism and had suffered the consequences. Notably, at this time, such conservative reactions came from the margins, rather than the centers, of US Catholic life.

Several participants in the Latin America solidarity movement were likewise targeted as subversives. After the actor Ed Asner spoke out against Salvadoran aid in a press conference prompted, he said, by an "emotional meeting with two Catholic nuns," CBS cancelled his well-regarded television show, *Lou Grant*. The FBI not only investigated Salvadoran security forces, but it also engaged in extensive clandestine surveillance of CISPES, the Maryknoll Sisters, participants in the Sanctuary effort to shelter undocumented refugees, and other Central America human rights activists.[48]

Even in the face of these critics, the sisters received sustained support from a Catholic voting bloc, which gave Maryknoll direct access to Congress. The *New York Times* presented the politicized religious commitments of Massachusetts Democrat Thomas "Tip" O'Neill, Speaker of the House and a "caustic" critic of Central America policy, as indicative of the influence of conciliar Catholicism on Washington. O'Neill named Maryknoll women—including Eunice Tolan, his aunt—as his "main sources of information about Central America." Bob Woodward deemed the Catholic influence on O'Neill to be "profound and almost mystical," writing that O'Neill became "a missionary in his opposition" to counterinsurgency campaigns and believed that the "nuns and priests spoke the truth" in a political environment full of obfuscation and self-interest. The influence prompted CIA director William Casey to grouse that "'if Tip O'Neill didn't have Maryknoll nuns who wrote letters,' the Nicaragua Contra campaign would have succeeded."[49] Senator Arlen Specter, a Pennsylvania Republican, also took special interest in the sisters' agitation for greater scrutiny over Salvadoran aid. In the early 1980s, sisters were called to testify before foreign relations committees on aid questions. To one such body, Melinda Roper explained the interconnections between Maryknoll's religious commitments and the impact of American foreign affairs: "the deaths of the four women cannot be separated from the general pattern of the persecution of the Church . . . and from the deaths of thousands of innocent Salvadorans," nor could they be "separated from U.S. policy toward that government."[50]

Under pressure from voters and using information shared by the religious lobbies, congresspeople pursued questions of human rights as Reagan and his advisors made their case for steep increases in aid to El Salvador. The churchwomen's supporters scored an important legislative victory in September 1981, when Congress made aid contingent on a biannual certification that the Salvadoran regime had made advances in human rights. Progress in the churchwomen's case was at the forefront of the issues that needed to be addressed.[51]

Though the certification measure fell far short of the goals of protestors, who sought nothing less than a fundamental dismantling of US military support for El Salvador, it threw a significant hurdle before the Reagan Cold War agenda. The requirement meant publicity for the case every six months from 1981 to 1984, when guardsmen were convicted of the deaths. In the estimation of Helene O'Sullivan, who directed the Office of Social Concerns during this period, the press became crucial allies, with "all these reporters from NBC and all these big channels . . . interviewing us right on TV, *all* the time. . . . When do you get interest like that?" The struggle, she contended, produced a true grassroots movement. "We had a lot of frustration," she stated, citing the obstructive tactics of the State Department, which withheld information and downplayed the documentation provided by Maryknoll throughout the investigative process. "Yet we had a staggering amount of support," she continued. "Just staggering. We couldn't have done it without the support of the American people." Civic protests, she argued, effected tangible change. Every six months, Reagan insisted on military aid increases to El Salvador, and for the most part during his first term, O'Sullivan pointed out, his demands were rebuffed.[52]

Nevertheless, Reagan's escalation of the Salvadoran conflict could not be thwarted. Though he did not receive the increases that he sought at every chance, he was able to divert an enormous amount of resources to accelerate the military offensive against the guerrillas and shore up political reform. David Duell Passage, US ambassador to El Salvador in the mid-1980s, called the country "*the* most important foreign issue to the United States." During his tenure, the number of staff members in the US embassy in El Salvador was exceeded only by the numbers of those in Cairo and New Delhi, and El Salvador received "the third largest disbursement of U.S. foreign aid." The amount of aid supplied over the 1980s is remarkable. Military aid to Salvador in 1981 totaled $5.9 million, it reached $206.6 million in 1984, and between 1984 and 1986 (after the guardsmen were prosecuted), combined economic and military disbursements totaled nearly $2 billion. "It was generally agreed," Latin America scholar Diana Villiers Negroponte concludes, "that without the funding, the Salvadoran government could not have survived one day."[53]

"THE TRUTH THIS TIME WILL COME BLASTING OUT"

The divergence between the US government's path to closure and that pursued by the sisters sharpened as the criminal investigation came to an end. Tenacious efforts to prosecute the guardsmen were ultimately successful. At the time the certification requirement was first implemented in 1981, the FBI had established a strong case against the low-rank patrolmen involved in the kidnapping and murders. Still, the intricacies of the Salvadoran criminal justice system and the outright deception of investigators slowed attempts to clear the aid pipeline. There was no question who had committed the direct crime; the most damning evidence was the suppressed secret recording of Colindres's confession. There were several false starts, with the very real fear of retaliation prompting jurists and jurors to steer clear of the case. Using autopsies, fingerprint and ballistics analysis, and polygraph tests, which elicited further confessions from participants, the FBI ultimately amassed proof that could be used for convictions in Salvadoran courts. With increasingly stringent threats to withhold aid, the State Department hectored officials to convene a criminal trial. In May 1984, a jury convicted five guardsmen of aggravated homicide, and each was sentenced to thirty years in prison. It was the first case in which members of the Salvadoran armed forces were convicted of murder in a civilian court.[54]

The trial elicited mixed emotions at Maryknoll. O'Sullivan felt confident that the criminal trial had produced tangible results: "when those five soldiers went to trial, the death squads stopped on a dime. . . . I think the soldiers realized, boy, nobody's backing us up." Accounts given to the Truth Commission corroborate a direct relationship between various incidents in which aid was threatened and a decline in indiscriminate death squad activity.[55] But the convictions by no means stopped the cycles of systematic violence. Nor did they solve conflicts in the United States about executive power and foreign policy in Central America. A shift in mood on Capitol Hill, which eased pressure on subsequent Salvadoran aid packages, was evident after the convictions, but as the controversy about El Salvador quieted, aid to the Contras in Nicaragua came to the fore in congressional opposition to Reagan's foreign policy.[56]

If this shift marked a turning point in the visibility of the churchwomen's case, it did not mark the conclusion of Maryknoll's conscientization of the public sphere. The limited scope of the US government's investigation had always been the sticking point for the churchwomen's supporters, who launched independent investigative efforts that yielded witnesses and documentation that kept the case alive against odds. "They kept repeating this mantra," a lawyer who assisted the sisters reported, "there is no evidence of any higher involvement."[57] Yet all of the documentation that had been released through the Freedom of Information Act showed that no sustained inquiry had been made beyond the level of the convicted guardsmen. The Tyler Report, an outside review of the investigation commissioned by the State Department, decisively concluded that Colindres alone was responsible for the killings and explained away evidence to the contrary. The State Department promised the churchwomen's advocates that secret evidence provided definite proof that the guardsmen acted alone, but when this evidence—the Colindres confession—was declassified, the documentation still showed the possibility of higher involvement.[58]

After the US government washed its hands of the problem, a team of human rights organizations, including the Office for Social Concerns, pressed for the inquiry to be extended into the high ranks of security forces. Maryknoll explained the tenacity of the legal campaign in terms of a faith-driven mission to achieve "true justice" through the prosecution of the "intellectual authors" of the crime. From that point onward, efforts hinged more on jurisprudence than on direct action. William "Bill" Ford, Ita Ford's brother, dedicated his legal career to bringing commanders in El Salvador to justice. For him, as for the Maryknoll Sisters, much more was at stake than solving the deaths of the churchwomen: those deaths were the consequence of a systemic culture of terror that needed to be rooted out at the source. O'Sullivan recalled the stakes of what would become a thirty-year mobilization: "When we started that case . . . ten thousand people had been killed by death squads. Not one iota of attention to ten thousand deaths." "By the time we finally brought it to trial five years ago," she continued, referring to subsequent civil cases, "seventy-six thousand people were dead . . . , just taken away. Men taken away, women taken away in the dead of night. . . . We pursued the case of our sisters to stop the death squads."[59]

With the help of the Lawyers Committee for International Human Rights, which endeavored to prosecute high-ranking personnel, a new stage of the fight began as the Salvadoran civil war wound down. The 1993 report of the United Nations Truth Commission provided new energy to the churchwomen's case. This was one of the first widely publicized official reports to maintain that the deaths had been ordered from someone with a higher rank than that of Colindres. But even this, along with a subsequent assertion from guardsmen that they had been ordered to carry out the deaths, did not provide explicit evidence of such official commands, which was a source of frustration to those seeking clarity.

However, the Truth Commission did make plain the scope of the cover-up, and the trail led to two top-ranked generals: José Guillermo García, minister of defense, and Carlos Eugenio Vides Casanova, head of the National Guard. To the surprise of the churchwomen's advocates, the generals had gained US residency and retired to Florida. "To think these people would have the nerve to seek out a comfortable retirement in the United States sent me into a rage," Bill Ford explained, and armed with this knowledge, he and the Lawyers Committee sued the generals under the provisions of the Torture Victim Protection Act of 1991. This act opened US courts to the civil prosecution of foreign nationals who engaged in gross human rights violations, a mark of "a growing U.S. assertiveness and recognition of its international obligations in the criminal jurisdictional sphere," according to a 1997 assessment.[60] Madeline Dorsey, who had worked alongside the slain women, reflected on a yearning to use tort law as a means of securing justice for all those who had suffered during the civil war: "We see so many connections with the victims and the causes of violence, and you hope the truth this time will come blasting out. I guess the hope is that the truth will be revealed and there will be an end to impunity."[61]

Ford lost his case in 2000, and subsequent appeals were unsuccessful. The case hinged on the principle of command responsibility, and jurors concluded that the chaos of the civil war meant that commanders could not control the actions of their troops. Ford was not disheartened, concluding that "we probably tried to prove too much. We were trying to prove everything that happened in Salvador for forty years." He hoped this case would encourage "more and more Salvadorans in the U.S. who were abused by this machine [to] come forward because now we have . . . a way of pursuing these things." This soon came to pass. His suit, *Ford et al v. Garcia and Vides Casanova*, began a conversation and made it possible for a human rights legal group, the Center for Justice and Accountability, to sue the two generals on behalf of three Salvadoran refugees whose experience of torture demonstrated command responsibility more successfully.[62] The success of that case, *Romagoza Arce et al v. Garcia and Vides Casanova*, established a precedent that assigned considerable responsibility for abuses to commanders who allowed them to flourish. With the 2006 *Romagoza* case, which levied $54 million in damages for the plaintiffs, the extension of liability established a new point of leverage in US human rights law.[63]

Ultimately, the *Romagoza* case, along with post-September 11, 2001 antiterrorism legislation, set into motion deportation proceedings against both García and Vides Casanova. Each case advanced in February 2014, with the deportation orders upheld after appeal. The decisions were a "an unusually expansive and scalding" acknowledgment from the US court that the country's allies had committed atrocities.[64] They supported an observation first made by Harold Tyler in his 1983 State Department-commissioned legal review of the churchwomen's case, which admitted that "officers of the Salvadoran military forces, whether by direction, inactivity or tolerance, encouraged the notion that their troops were above the law."[65] While the Tyler Report disregarded evidence that indicated the direct involvement of higher commanders in Colindres's crime, the Vides Casanova and García deportation judgments deemed commanders' assent to military lawlessness a constituent factor in systemic human rights abuse.

Robert White's testimony prevailed in these accounts of the ruling junta, and his reflections emphasized that the US government's public spin on the Salvadoran regime contrasted with the behind-the-scenes knowledge of the security forces' impunity. He recalled an exchange with García, then Vides Casanova's commander, in the days after the churchwomen's murders. García had asked White, "were these nuns wearing habits?" White explained the implication to the court: the military distinguished between "'good nuns,' who wore habits, and 'bad nuns,' who wore regular clothes." Vides Casanova, he concluded, had notified García of the fate of the women and "was building up a case against them."[66] The court concluded that the general's "lack of initiative" in investigating the case "sent a message to troops under his command that extrajudicial killings—even high profile murders of American church personnel—could be committed with impunity." When this information was added to several other documented cases in which he had failed to address extrajudicial killings, the court deemed Vides Casanova's actions to be a "pattern of behavior ranging from complicity . . . to outright support (by promoting individuals known to be involved in extrajudicial killings)."[67]

However, the decision did not address the culpability of the US government. In his defense Vides Casanova expressed surprise that he had been targeted in such fashion. He had worked closely with State Department personnel, at times meeting with the US ambassador on a weekly basis. Entrusted with instituting human rights reforms, he had twice been awarded the Legion of Merit by the US president for his service, crediting him with "'moving things forward'" in the Salvadoran struggle. The judge in the deportation case waved away the defense that the actions had been supported, even rewarded, by the United States. The "jurisdiction of the court," James Grim wrote, "does not extend to a review of foreign policy decisions." Vides Casanova's argument that "his actions were consistent with U.S. policy" was not relevant to the case. Vides Casanova and García were deported to El Salvador in 2015 and 2016, respectively.[68]

An uncollectible multimillion-dollar judgment against three individuals and the deportation of elderly generals is scant reparation for the damages of the Salvadoran civil war, and the conclusions of Truth Commission documents and immigration court cases did not elicit from the US government any sort of repudiation of Central America policy. Nevertheless, the Maryknoll Sisters and its allies had prevailed over powerful opponents to secure these measures of justice. On their journey to the left end of the liberal political spectrum, the Maryknoll Sisters had been subjected to techniques designed to suppress church-based activism, techniques pioneered in the days of the Dies Committee's assault on the YWCA's Rose Terlin (discussed in chapter 4): accusations of subversion lobbed from the highest levels of government, FBI harassment, and character assassination. Smear tactics raised questions about the Maryknoll Sisters' identity as women of faith, wholly dedicated to fulfilling the commands of Christianity. But in investing the missionary tradition of martyrdom with the weight of conciliar social teachings and liberation thought, the congregation's dedication to Gospel mandates for justice could not be suppressed.

EPILOGUE

In the first decade of the twenty-first century, a gulf widened between the ecclesiastical hierarchy of the Catholic Church and congregations of women religious working in liberal traditions. When research for this book began, Joseph Ratzinger became Pope Benedict XVI. His papacy continued the purge of liberation theology influences that had marked his tenure under Pope John Paul II as prefect of the Congregation for the Doctrine of the Faith, the Vatican office responsible for policing expressions of doctrine. The purge extended into a 2012 official inquiry into the Leadership Conference of Women Religious (LCWR), a federation of US women's congregations to which the Maryknoll Sisters of St. Dominic belongs. Expressing concerns about "radical feminist themes" in LCWR programming, among other divergences from ecclesiastical orthodoxy, Vatican investigators confirmed the impression that apostolic women religious in the United States had moved in opposite directions from clerical authorities over the thirty-two years since the US churchwomen's deaths in El Salvador.[1] During this time, some Maryknoll women expressed a sense of disconnection from the priorities of the institutional church. When asked about the problems facing the Catholic Church, Sister Darlene Jacobs reflected: "To tell you the honest truth, I don't have a lot of contact with 'the church' as such. I would like to see the church open to everybody. I would like to see the church be an example of justice and work toward this one world that I long for. But I don't see it, [and] as much as the church claims to follow the Gospel, it's a limited or a pick-and-choose kind of Gospel." Sister Anastasia Lott, who entered Maryknoll in 1986, similarly noted: "The whole thing is supposed to be good news . . . I don't know anybody who looks at the Catholic Church and says, wow, look at what a great job they're doing at proclaiming good news."[2]

As this book project came to a close, Jorge Bergoglio ascended to the papacy as Pope Francis. Though as a bishop he was by no means a supporter of liberation theology, his attention to the poor and his interest in reviving themes of social teachings from the Second Vatican Council brought about an obvious change in the church's mood. The Vatican investigation of the LCWR came to a sudden "friendly resolution" in 2015, with the LCWR and investigating bishops touting the "spirit of prayer, love for the church, mutual respect and cooperation" that had brought them to a place of reconciliation. Even as they acknowledged tensions within the Catholic Church, Maryknoll women did not express estrangement from their faith tradition. Lott pointed out that in religious life, "there's a freedom that we could exercise if we want." Mulling over debates about women's ordination, she gave a whimsical explanation of how little her vocation was defined by doctrinal mandates: "So I say half an hour of my day is 'abide by the rules of the Church,' but there's twenty-three and a half other hours . . . that I can call . . . anything I want. . . . We could sit here with bread and wine if we wanted and pray as much as we wanted in our own way and nobody's going to say anything about it."[3] Communion—both the rite and the collective expression of spiritual connection—was the inheritance of all God's people, not the reserved province of a particular religious vocation.

By holding to their heritage in the face of obstacles inside and outside of the church, Maryknoll sisters continue to approach religious service as an outpouring of care and as a quest for social justice. Susan Nchubiri, who made her profession of first vows at Maryknoll in 2006, reiterated what sisters seventy years before had said: "the Maryknoll spirit is a really, really free spirit." She entered the congregation because of what she had observed in a Maryknoll AIDS ministry in Kenya: "a love that has no boundaries that will make the Sisters wake up in the morning and go out to whichever place they have to go and just deal with those people as their own brothers and sisters. Without discriminating whether you were a Christian or Catholic or Muslim or Hindu or no religion at all. Having the same love for everybody." She was inspired to devote herself completely to a community still defined by a spiritual calling to cross boundaries and give "witness to God's love," in the words of the contemporary mission statement.[4]

Much has changed for the sisters, even if the Maryknoll spirit remains a touchstone. Nchubiri was one of 3 women taking vows that year, and none of them was from the United States. The situation couldn't be more different from that of the 1950s, when the congregation trained 100–200 novices a year, "a cross section of American womanhood."[5] The difference between the YWCA of the USA in its heyday and the present is similarly striking. While a focus on progressive social change remained consistent, the language of Christianity grew more and more scarce in the YWCA's programming over the 1970s. As foretold by Phyllis Schlafly's defection from the Alton YWCA, liberal mainline Protestantism no longer had the decisive influence in public life it once had. On the one hand, liberal Christianity lost ground to conservative and charismatic sects; on the other hand, activists on the left mobilized using social movement platforms that had primarily secular identities. The YWCA of the USA's formal identification with Christianity became attenuated until in 2009 it eliminated any reference to religion from its mission statement. It was renamed YWCA USA, no longer an acronym with a Christian association, under the explanation that this "more accurate name provides us with the opportunity to engage many more individuals in the important and inspiring work of our organization."[6]

Grace Hoadley Dodge once announced that with the creation of the National Board, "our great movement is going to live for centuries." A century later, the National Board no longer exists. It was replaced by a coordinating board headquartered in Washington, D.C. Its professional staff of fewer than 30 people marks a contrast from the 1920s, when 500 women worked directly for the National Board and community associations employed an additional 3,300. Like the Maryknoll Sisters, the YWCA USA soldiers on. It does not have nearly the reach it once had, but more than two hundred community associations provide vital social services in areas in which women are underserved. This once meant workers' housing and recreation; now it means child care and crisis shelters.[7]

From one vantage point, the groups' histories might reveal their institutional and ethical structures as part of an activist configuration that is disappearing. The time may have passed in which single-sex communities could serve as a popular outlet for women's activist and religious energies. The conservative ascendency in both Catholicism and Protestantism has overshadowed liberal Christian influences on the political sphere. The present state of the Maryknoll Sisters and YWCA could be seen as anemic in comparison to their former vitality.

A different vantage point, however, would underscore YWCA secretary Anna Rice's assessment that it is "not the numbers that we win, but the ideal that we lift up before the world will determine the worth of our work."[8] The organizations' endurance and contemporary relevance in the face of countervailing impulses are remarkable, but it is the historical scope and impact of these ideals that most clearly reveal their value. Foremost, the two groups' long histories provide sterling examples of the ways in which women were central actors in religious politics and social activism throughout the twentieth century. From its 1906 inception, the YWCA of the USA was a leading voice in uplift efforts to raise women's status. Influenced by the Social Gospel, the YWCA earned distinction—or notoriety, in some quarters—for enabling women workers to give voice to a labor agenda largely overlooked by unions. A cascade of other mobilizations sprung from these foundations. A Gospel-centered ethics of mutual care inspired multifaceted attempts to erase boundaries of nation and race. The National Board seized opportunities opened by women's newly won access to civic life to advance a nonpartisan political agenda designed to shape society according to Christian principles. The group later articulated a religious program that briefly incorporated the radical influences of the Popular Front. It dedicated itself more consistently to efforts to promote interracial and international fellowship.

The Maryknoll Sisters also began in the spirit of uplift. The early Cold War period was pivotal for the congregation, orienting it toward social reform as well as religious transformation. The gulf between the Cold War internationalism of the Maryknoll Sisters, acclaimed cold warriors, and that of the YWCA of the USA, regularly accused of subversion, particularly highlights the complexities of women's participation in religiously inspired political mobilizations. On the conservative side, women such as Schlafly, a disaffected YWCA volunteer, had an important place in organizing a right-wing revolt against the diplomatic and humanitarian maneuvers of liberal internationalism. Maryknoll and the YWCA shared an allegiance to liberal perspectives on the Cold War global order, expressing deep commitment to humanitarian interventions. Their divergent experiences in the McCarthy era shows a division in this liberalism between the enthusiastic anticommunism of the popularly celebrated Maryknoll Sisters and the YWCA's quiet resistance to the unilateralism that had displaced hopes for postwar cooperative world governance. When the Maryknoll Sisters drifted away from their support of militaristic US foreign policy in the 1970s and 1980s, the congregation would experience the type of repression already visited on the YWCA for its insistence on structural social change.

Across this spectrum of liberalism, from the irreproachable politics of uplift to brushes with radicalism, the groups persistently rejected restrictive expectations of women's roles while they maintained faith in their single-sex moorings. The YWCA branched off from denominational church life, endorsing women's diverse responsibilities as workers, activists, citizens, and neighbors. Following the modernist turn in mainline Protestantism, it repudiated fundamentalist restrictions on women's domain. At the same time that the preconciliar Maryknoll Sisters affirmed women's submissive position as handmaids to the church, they established an autonomous community life and pushed beyond the limited horizons of the cloister tradition.

The evolution and resiliency of the groups' ideals are apparent not only in the groups' dedication to single-sex organizing, but also in the ways they invigorated liberal Christian faith traditions. As the YWCA and Maryknoll expanded their interests in advocacy, they confronted conservative elements in their creeds. The YWCA particularly faced off against conservative Christian women: the women patriots of the 1920s, the radical right of the 1930s, and the insurgent New Right of the 1950s. The Maryknoll Sisters had their time of confrontation when reactionary Catholic cultural critics condemned the congregation's dedication to liberation theology. Sharing the ethical touchstone of Gospel accounts of Jesus's ministry, Maryknoll and the YWCA provide a corrective to a tendency—perhaps a mythology—to view Protestantism and Catholicism as mutually exclusive religions. The groups' histories suggest that the two branches of Christianity are hardly alien to each other, either in spirituality or politics. When liberal Christianity converged with women's movements, the commandment of Christian love was integral. The groups' concerns were not only eschatological; they were also pragmatic, dedicated to action on earth. Both groups moved steadily toward a religious practice that was ultimately experimental and politicized. These commonalities conflicted with shared beliefs that linked conservative Protestants and Catholics. In contrast to conservative Christian traditions, the two groups did not hearken back to a stable gender order premised on women's subordination. Ultimately, they conceived of God not as a judgmental and vengeful deity who demanded pious allegiance. Instead, they imagined a beneficent Jesus, full of mercy and solicitous care for the marginalized.

The power of the organizations' ideals should also be measured in their century-long pursuit of global community. This provides a history of international women's movements in which Christianity was both a vehicle of and a barrier to coalition. Foreign mission provided turn-of-the-century US women with an expansive realm for outreach, but the Christian mandate for evangelization produced contradictory impulses. Even as women of the YWCA and Maryknoll sought to unite humanity in fellowship, they went into the mission field with the expectation that they—as Westerners, Americans (most often white), and Christians—uniquely had the capacity for leadership in creating fellowship. Assured by triumphal narratives of the supremacy of US civilization, they hoped to transform non-Western cultures as well as religions. Their attempts to render national boundaries inconsequential paradoxically shored up exceptionalism.

The authoritarian model of mission was ultimately not tenable. In incremental and dramatic ways, the YWCA and Maryknoll adapted to the field. They were bound to be confronted by the disjuncture between the yearnings for cooperative Christian fellowship and the unequal power relations on which foreign mission was built. Their journeys illustrate that US Christian women's internationalism did not end after the heyday of missionary work had passed and the liabilities of the civilizing mission had become evident. The tension between an understanding of the message of Christianity as human unity and the power imbalances that continued to shape US women's international interventions did not disappear. Nevertheless, the groups came to envision Christianization as the extension of universal values to which they had particular allegiance as followers of Jesus: ideals of peace, justice, and fellowship. Ultimately, the universalizing gestures of liberal Christianity fed into a universalizing discourse of human rights.

From the nineteenth-century roots of Protestant evangelicalism and a foreign mission movement built on imperialist underpinnings, an ethos of cooperative care and religious service took the YWCA and Maryknoll Sisters outside of the churches and propelled their efforts to build institutions, provide social services, and participate in social movements. The perceived responsibilities of the commandment of Christian love began as a demand for allegiance to a religious creed and a way of life. They became something much more flexible and open, inspiring generations of women to turn the Gospel message into a force for progressive social change.

ACKNOWLEDGMENTS

The spirits that animate Smith College's Sophia Smith Collection inspired this project. The research began with my first encounter with the YWCA as a Sophia Smith Collection archives assistant, helping pack boxes for the transfer of the organization's records from its New York headquarters to the women's history archives at the college. The passing encounter with those documents awakened me to the richness and diversity of women's religious history. The support of my SSC colleagues and friends continues to sustain me. For everything from pot roast to photo permissions, I have depended on the dear friendship and historical expertise of Amy Hague. Maida Goodwin, "Y-brarian-in-chief," passed along scintillating documents and shared her sound perspective with me. I was fortunate to work alongside Joyce Follet, Margaret Jessup, Kathleen Banks Nutter, Sherrill Redmon, and Nanci Young, who have carried forward the mission of women's history archives in often daunting circumstances. The generous spirit and good counsel of Nancy Marie Robertson has been invaluable. The ongoing mentorship and kindness of Daniel and Helen Lefkowitz Horowitz is a source of inspiration.

The Women's Studies in Religion Program of the Harvard Divinity School generated similarly powerful energy. Ann Braude shared insights at every stage of the project, and the coven of research fellows Lihi Ben Shitrit, Sarah Bracke, Hsiao-wen Cheng, and Jacquelyn Williamson helped carry me through. The level of collegiality and collaboration that I have found in the larger community of women's religious history scholars stands out. There are too many such individuals to list here, but their names pepper the notes of this book.

Yale University supplied a productive environment for research and writing. The incomparable acumen and endless encouragement of Jon Butler and Joanne Meyerowitz made this book possible. I thank the MacMillan Center's Women, Religion, and Globalization Initiative for its international research support, and Jean-Christophe Agnew for his feedback. JoAnne Ghorai, Eric Hanthorne, Doug Havens, Marc LeBlanc, Amanda Ciafone, Daniel Gilbert, Jesse Gant, and Emily Lutenski provided valued input, friendship, and support.

I relied on the help of the stewards of the World YWCA and Maryknoll Mission Archives. At the World YWCA, Fiona Wilkie provided great hospitality. Many thanks as well to Ellen Pierce, Jennifer Halloran, and Stephanie Conning at Maryknoll. Deep gratitude is owed to the gracious Maryknoll sisters who shared their stories and time with me: Aurora de la Cruz, Patricia Edmiston,

Virginia Flagg, Darlene Jacobs, Loretta Kruegler, Anastasia Lott, Bernadette Lynch, Mary Mullady, Susan Nchubiri, and Helene O'Sullivan. I have donated transcripts of these interviews to the Maryknoll Mission Archives, and I hope other researchers will explore these resources, as this book captures only a small portion of the unique insights the sisters provided.

An earlier version of chapter 2 was previously published as "'By Love, Serve One Another': Foreign Mission and the Challenge of World Fellowship in the YWCAs of Japan and Turkey," *Journal of American-East Asian Relations* 24, no. 4 (2017); the materials are included here by permission of Koninklijke Brill.

I cannot thank my family enough. Much love to my grandparents, JoAnn and Patrick Izzo and Donna and Peter Grades; my mother, Donna Izzo; my father and wicked stepmother, Patrick and Patricia Izzo; and my brother, Patrick Izzo, and his family, Mandy Foote, Lea Izzo, Olivia Smith, J. J. Foote, and Patrick Izzo IV. Finally, Benjamin Looker, for everything.

NOTES

Works frequently cited have been identified by the following abbreviations:

FBI-Churchwomen "Undefined FBI File on the American Churchwomen Killed in El Salvador, December 1980," Federal Bureau of Investigation Library. Gale World Scholar: Latin America and the Caribbean.
MSA Maryknoll Sisters Archives, Maryknoll Mission Archives, Maryknoll, NY.
    Discourses: Mary Josephine Rogers. "Discourses of Mother Mary Joseph Rogers, M.M." Compiled by Mother Mary Coleman, 3 vols.
WYWCA World YWCA Archives, Geneva, Switzerland.
YWCA-SSC YWCA of the USA Records, Sophia Smith Collection, Smith College, Northampton, MA.
    Microfilm: Microfilmed Records of the YWCA of the USA.
    RG 2: Record Group 2. Predecessor Organizations and National Board.
    RG 3: Record Group 3. National Administrative Office.
    RG 4: Record Group 4. National Conventions and Conferences.
    RG 5: Record Group 5. International Work.
    RG 6: Record Group 6. Program.
    RG 7: Record Group 7. Student Work.
    RG 8: Record Group 8. Community Associations.

INTRODUCTION

1. The parochial educational system was then launching women's colleges designed to parallel schools like Smith College. See Kathleen Sprows Cummings, *New Women of the Old Faith: Gender and American Catholicism in the Progressive Era* (Chapel Hill: University of North Carolina Press, 2009), 66–67.
2. Sister Jeanne Marie, *Maryknoll's First Lady* (n.p.: Maryknoll Sisters of St. Dominic, 1964), 17. In the canonical taxonomy of the Catholic Church, as an apostolic, rather than contemplative group, the Maryknoll Sisters are a religious congregation, not an order, and members who have taken vows are called sisters rather than nuns. The term "women religious" is used throughout the book to refer to female members of vowed, canonically sanctioned religious communities. Jane Hunter notes the electric effect of missionary ceremonies on college students in *The Gospel of Gentility: American Women Missionaries in Turn-of-the-Century China*, (New Haven, CT: Yale University Press, 1984), 47–48.
3. Sidney Ahlstrom, *A Religious History of the American People*, 2nd ed. (New Haven, CT: Yale University Press, 2004), 804.
4. Mary van Kleeck, "Relation of the Young Women's Christian Association to the Problems of Labor," Printed Convention Proceedings, 1920, 249–50, RG 4, YWCA of the USA Records, Sophia Smith Collection, Smith College, Northampton, MA (hereafter YWCA-SSC). For van Kleeck's religious commitments, see Guy Alchon, "van Kleeck, Mary," in American National Biography Online, 2000, www.anb.org; Smith College Yearbook, 1904, and Smith

College Association of Christian Work files in the Smith College Archives, Northampton, MA; Mary van Kleeck Papers, Sophia Smith Collection.

5. This intervention is advocated by Ann Braude ("Women's History *Is* American Religious History" in *Retelling U.S. Religious History*, ed. Thomas Tweed [Berkeley: University of California Press, 1997], 87–107).

6. Estelle Freedman, "Separatism as Strategy: Female Institution Building and American Feminism, 1870–1930," *Feminist Studies* 5, no. 3 (1979): 521.

7. This history affirms Valentine Moghadam's assertion that global feminism "is predicated upon the notion that notwithstanding cultural, class and ideological differences among the women of the world, there is a commonality in the forms of women's disadvantage and the forms of women's organizations world-wide" but departs from her conclusion that this is a recent development ("Transnational Feminist Networks: Collective Action in an Era of Globalization," *International Sociology* 15, no. 1 [2000]: 62).

8. That trend has been countered recently, notably by David Hollinger in *After Cloven Tongues of Fire: Protestant Liberalism in Modern American History* (Princeton, NJ: Princeton University Press, 2013).

9. Mary Josephine Rogers, "The Student Volunteers," n.d., in "Discourses of Mother Mary Joseph Rogers, M.M.," comp. Mother Mary Coleman, 1982 (hereafter "Discourses") 2:464, Maryknoll Sisters Archives, Maryknoll Mission Archives, Maryknoll, NY (hereafter MSA); Agnes Gale Hill, "Our Foreign Call," Printed Convention Proceedings, 1909, 83, RG 4, YWCA-SSC.

10. Leila Rupp documents a secular side of this internationalism in *Worlds of Women: The Making of an International Women's Movement* (Princeton, NJ: Princeton University Press, 1997).

11. Barbara Reeves-Ellington, Kathryn Kish Sklar, and Connie Shemo, introduction to *Competing Kingdoms: Women, Mission, Nation, and the American Protestant Empire, 1812–1960*, ed. Barbara Reeves-Ellington, Kathryn Kish Sklar, and Connie Shemo (Durham, NC: Duke University Press, 2010), 6.

12. See, for example, Daniel Whelan, *Indivisible Human Rights: A History* (Philadelphia: University of Pennsylvania Press, 2010). Others touch on religious ethics, including Robert Drinan, *Cry of the Oppressed: The History and Hope of the Human Rights Revolution* (San Francisco: Harper and Row, 1987); Micheline Ishay, *The History of Human Rights: From Ancient Times to the Globalization Era* (Berkeley: University of California Press, 2008).

13. Verta Taylor and Leila Rupp examine the emotional ties of women's internationalism in "Loving Internationalism: The Emotion Culture of Transnational Women's Organizations, 1888–1945," *Mobilization* 7, no. 2 (2002): 141–58. For emotional attachment as a means of evangelization, see Hunter, *The Gospel of Gentility*, 174.

14. Ann Braude, "A Religious Feminist—Who Can Find Her? Historiographical Challenges from the National Organization for Women," *Journal of Religion* 84, no. 4 (2004): 555–72.

15. Hollinger attributes congregational attrition to these factors in *After Cloven Tongues of Fire*, xii.

16. Diane Winston, "Back to the Future: Religion, Politics, and the Media," *American Quarterly* 59, no. 3: especially 979–80.

17. This insight was first developed by Evelyn Brooks Higginbotham in *Righteous Discontent: The Women's Movement in the Black Baptist Church, 1880–1920* (Cambridge, MA: Harvard University Press, 1993).

18. Susan Lindley provides an overview of these trends in *"You Have Stept Out of Your Place": A History of Women and Religion in America* (Louisville, KY: Westminster John Knox Press,

1996), 385–406. See also Alice Knotts, *Fellowship of Love: Methodist Women Changing American Racial Attitudes, 1920–1968* (Nashville, TN: Kingswood, 1996); Amy Koehlinger, *The New Nuns: Racial Justice and Religious Reform in the 1960s* (Cambridge, MA: Harvard University Press, 2007); Gail Murray, ed., *Throwing Off the Cloak of Privilege: White Southern Women Activists in the Civil Rights Era* (Gainesville: University Press of Florida, 2004); Eleanor Stebner, *The Women of Hull House: A Study in Spirituality, Vocation, and Friendship* (Albany: State University Press of New York, 1997); Mary Irene Zotti, *A Time of Awakening: The Young Christian Worker Story in the United States, 1938–1970* (Chicago: Loyola University Press, 1991).

19. Joyce Antler, "Zion in Our Hearts: Henrietta Szold and the American Jewish Women's Movement," in *American Jewish Women's History: A Reader*, ed. Pamela Nadell (New York: New York University Press, 2003), 134. See also Faith Rogow, *Gone to Another Meeting: The National Council of Jewish Women, 1893–1993* (Tuscaloosa: University of Alabama Press, 1993).

20. Anne Firor Scott, *Natural Allies: Women's Associations in American History* (Urbana: University of Illinois Press, 1991), 215n58.

21. Book-length works include Karen Garner, *Precious Fire: Maud Russell and the Chinese Revolution* (Amherst: University of Massachusetts, 2003); Susan Lynn, *Progressive Women in Conservative Times: Racial Justice, Peace, and Feminism, 1945 to the 1960s* (New Brunswick, NJ: Rutgers University Press, 1992); Nina Mjagkij and Margaret Spratt, eds., *Men and Women Adrift: The YMCA and the YWCA in the City* (New York: New York University Press, 1997); Nancy Marie Robertson, *Christian Sisterhood, Race Relations, and the YWCA, 1906–46* (Urbana: University of Illinois Press, 2007); Daphne Spain, *How Women Saved the City* (Minneapolis: University of Minnesota Press, 2001); Judith Weisenfeld, *African American Women and Christian Activism: New York's Black YWCA, 1905–1945* (Cambridge, MA: Harvard University Press, 1997). In addition, there are scores of dissertations and articles.

22. Robertson calculated the comparative memberships (*Christian Sisterhood*, 74–75). For the other statistics, see Mary Sims, *The First Twenty-Five Years: Being a Summary of the Young Women's Christian Association of the United States of America, 1906–1931* (New York: Womans Press, 1932), 81. For unknown reasons, the Womans Press—the name given to the YWCA's publication wing and magazine—was spelled without an apostrophe until the 1940s.

23. Congregational statistics are from Office statistics files, MSA; Maryknoll Sisters, "Our Work," accessed September 13, 2016, https://Maryknollsisters.org/about-us/our-work. Comparative statistics were determined from *The Official Catholic Directory* (New York: P. J. Kenedy and Sons) in 1955, 1960, 1965, and 1970. Penny Lernoux provides a comprehensive congregational history (*Hearts on Fire: The Story of the Maryknoll Sisters* [Maryknoll, NY: Orbis, 1993]). Region-oriented accounts include Cindy Yik-Yi Chu, *Maryknoll Sisters in Hong Kong, 1921–1969: In Love with the Chinese* (New York: Palgrave Macmillan, 2004); Susan Fitzpatrick-Behrens, *The Maryknoll Catholic Mission in Peru, 1943–1989: Transnational Faith and Transformation* (Notre Dame, IN: University of Notre Dame Press, 2012); Jean-Paul Wiest, *Maryknoll in China: A History, 1918–1955* (Armonk, NY: M. E. Sharpe, 1998).

24. "Afield with the Maryknoll Sisters," *Maryknoll*, September 1949, 42.

25. Accordingly, this book will use YWCA or US YWCA to refer to the YWCA of the USA. Local association names, such as the Boston YWCA, YWCA of Japan, or World's YWCA will be used to specify other entities.

26. Grace Dodge, "President's Message," 60, and Mabel Cratty, "The National Movement," 35, both in Printed Convention Proceedings, 1909.

27. Constitution, Printed Convention Proceedings, 1909, 107–8; Anna Rice, "A Forward Look at Our Religious Work," *Association Monthly*, August 1916, 282.

28. Charlotte Adams, "The Spiritual Significance of the Summer Conference," *Association Monthly*, April 1916, 170.

29. Elizabeth Littell-Lamb, "Engendering a Class Revolution: The Chinese YWCA Industrial Reform Work in Shanghai, 1927–1939," *Women's History Review* 21, no. 2 (2012): 189–209.

30. Joseph Kamp, *Behind the Lace Curtains of the YWCA*, (New York: Constitutional Education League, 1948), 20, Controversy: Communism, RG 3, YWCA-SSC.

31. Sara Evans, ed., *Journeys that Opened Up the World: Women, Student Christian Movements, and Social Justice, 1955–1975* (New Brunswick, NJ: Rutgers University Press, 2003); Dorothy Height, *Open Wide the Freedom Gates* (New York: Public Affairs, 2003) and "'We Wanted the Voice of a Woman to Be Heard': Black Women and the 1963 March on Washington," in *Sisters in the Struggle: African American Women in the Civil Rights-Black Power Movement*, ed. V.P. Franklin and Bettye Collier-Thomas (New York: New York University Press, 2001), 83–91.

32. YWCA USA, "Annual Report, 2006–2007," "Mission," and "Advocacy," accessed June 26, 2010, http://www.ywca.org/site/pp.asp?c=djISI6PIKpG&b=281387.

33. "Constitution of the Foreign Mission Sisters of St. Dominic," 1931, chap. 1, no. 2, and chap. 22, no. 329, MSA.

34. Mrs. F. T. Thurston, "Christian Cooperation among Women in Social and Business Life," Printed Convention Proceedings, 1906, 56, RG 4, YWCA-SSC.

PART I   WOMEN AND CHRISTIAN FELLOWSHIP IN THE EARLY TWENTIETH CENTURY

1. Nancy Cott identifies a transformation in women's activism in the 1910s in the transition from the nineteenth-century language of the "woman movement" to feminism. See *The Grounding of Modern Feminism* (New Haven, CT: Yale University Press, 1987), 3–38.

2. For more on nineteenth-century transatlantic women's movements, see Bonnie Anderson, *Joyous Greetings: The First International Women's Movement* (New York: Oxford University Press, 2000). Anna Rice describes the YWCA's international work up to World War II in *A History of the World's Young Women's Christian Association* (New York: Woman's Press, 1947). Carole Seymour-Jones documents the postwar years in *Journey of Faith: The History of the World YWCA, 1945–1994* (London: Allison and Busby, 1994).

3. Anne Firor Scott, *Natural Allies: Women's Associations in American History* (Urbana: University of Illinois Press, 1991), 93.

4. "The Organization of a City Young Women's Christian Association," 1907, 13, Publications, RG 8, YWCA-SSC.

5. Mary Sims, *The Natural History of a Social Institution: The Young Women's Christian Association* (New York: Womans Press, 1936), 56.

6. "The Organization of a City Young Women's Christian Association," 1907, 13.

7. Nancy Marie Robertson, *Christian Sisterhood, Race Relations, and the YWCA, 1906–46* (Urbana: University of Illinois Press, 2007), 24. Glenda Gilmore explores this organizational landscape more generally in *Gender and Jim Crow: Women and the Politics of White Supremacy in North Carolina, 1896–1920* (Chapel Hill: University of North Carolina Press, 1996), 177–202.

8. The first meeting of the national YWCA occurred in December 1906. It was the result of negotiations between two predecessor umbrella groups, the International Board of Women's and Young Women's Christian Associations, which was primarily composed of northeastern city groups, and the American Committee of Young Women's Christian Association, formed mostly of midwestern campus groups. Though the works are dated, publications by YWCA of the USA writers continue to provide the association's most comprehensive organizational histories, particularly Mary Sims, *The YWCA: An Unfolding Purpose* (New York: Woman's Press, 1950). See also Robertson, *Christian Sisterhood*, 12–24.

9. Joyce Antler, "Zion in Our Hearts: Henrietta Szold and the American Jewish Women's Movement," in *American Jewish Women's History: A Reader*, ed. Pamela Nadell (New York: New York University Press, 2003), 129–52; Bettye Collier-Thomas, *Jesus, Jobs, and Justice: African American Women and Religion* (New York: Knopf, 2011), 279–283; Faith Rogow, *Gone to Another Meeting: The National Council of Jewish Women, 1893–1993* (Tuscaloosa: University of Alabama Press, 1993); Ian Tyrell, *Woman's World/Woman's Empire: The Woman's Christian Temperance Union in International Perspective, 1880–1930* (Chapel Hill: University of North Carolina Press, 2014).

10. This so-called Americanist controversy is discussed in Angelyn Dries, "The Foreign Mission Impulse of the American Catholic Church, 1893–1925," *International Bulletin of Missionary Research* 15, no. 2 (1991): 61–66; Margaret Mary Reher, "Americanism and Modernism: Continuity or Discontinuity?," *U.S. Catholic Historian* 1, no. 3 (1981): 87–100.

11. Angelyn Dries, *The Missionary Movement in American Catholic History* (Maryknoll, NY: Orbis Books, 1998), 38–39 and 63–64; David O'Brien, "Catholic Evangelization and American Culture," *U.S. Catholic Historian* 11, no. 2 (1993): 49–59.

12. Elizabeth Wilson, *Fifty Years of Association Work among Young Women, 1866–1916* (New York: National Board of the Young Women's Christian Associations of the United States of America, 1916), 225; National Board Report, 1924, RG 4, YWCA-SSC.

CHAPTER 1   "LIFE MORE ABUNDANT": THE YWCA AND THE SOCIAL GOSPEL

1. Remarks, Printed Convention Proceedings, 1906, 60 and 72–73, RG 4, YWCA-SSC.

2. Mrs. C. R. Springer, remarks, ibid., 21; Mrs. F. T. Thurston, remarks, ibid., 54.

3. Charles Howard Hopkins describes this central tenet of the Social Gospel in *The Rise of the Social Gospel in American Protestantism, 1865–1916* (New Haven, CT: Yale University Press, 1940), 107–8. See also Ronald White and Charles Howard Hopkins, *The Social Gospel: Religion and Reform in Changing America* (Philadelphia, PA: Temple University Press, 1976).

4. Constitution, Printed Convention Proceedings, 1909, 107–12, RG 4, YWCA-SSC.

5. Grace Hoadley Dodge, "A Voice from Yesterday" [reprint of a 1907 speech], *YWCA Magazine*, April 1954, 11.

6. For the International Migration Service, see National Board Report, 1924, 238–46, RG 4, YWCA-SSC. For Travelers Aid and the Federation of Business and Professional Women, see Mary Sims, *The Natural History of a Social Institution: The Young Women's Christian Association* (New York: Womans Press, 1936), 153–54. For the International Institute, see Celeste deRoche, "'How Wide the Circle of We': Cultural Pluralism and American Identity, 1910–1954" (PhD diss., University of Maine, 2000), 75–109.

7. National Board Report, 1909, 12, RG 4, YWCA-SSC.

8. "The Organization of a City Young Women's Christian Association," 1907, 10, Publications, RG 8, YWCA-SSC.

9. Nitza Berkovitch, *From Motherhood to Citizenship: Women's Rights and International Organizations* (Baltimore: Johns Hopkins University Press, 1999); Regina Kunzel, *Fallen Women, Problem Girls: Unmarried Mothers and the Professionalization of Social Work, 1890–1945* (New Haven, CT: Yale University Press, 1993); Peggy Pascoe, *Relations of Rescue: The Search for Female Moral Authority in the American West, 1874–1939* (New York: Oxford University Press, 1990).

10. National Board Report, 1909, 5; National Board Report, 1911, 5; National Board Report, 1913, 5; National Board Report, 1915, 7, all RG 4, YWCA-SSC.

11. "First Joint Convention Leaflet 1," 1906, RG 2, YWCA-SSC.

12. "The Organization of a City Young Women's Christian Association," 1907, 14.

13. Nancy Marie Robertson, *Christian Sisterhood, Race Relations, and the YWCA, 1906–46* (Urbana: University of Illinois Press, 2007), 24.

14. Judith Weisenfeld, *African American Women and Christian Activism: New York's Black YWCA, 1905–1945* (Cambridge, MA: Harvard University Press, 1997), 6.

15. Mrs. A. W. [Addie Waites] Hunton, "Beginnings among Colored Women," 1913, Publications: Interracial, RG 6, YWCA-SSC.

16. Edwin Wildman, "What Grace Dodge Has Done for the Working Woman," *World Today*, December 1910, 1363.

17. Esther Katz, "Grace Hoadley Dodge: Women and the Emerging Metropolis, 1856–1914" (PhD diss., New York University, 1980). On uplift and women's evangelicalism, see Lori Ginzberg, *Women and the Work of Benevolence: Morality, Politics, and Class in the Nineteenth-Century United States* (New Haven, CT: Yale University Press, 1990), 24.

18. Quoted in "Grace Dodge, 'Champion of Girls,'" 1961, General Biographical, Grace Hoadley Dodge Papers, Sophia Smith Collection, Smith College, Northampton, MA; Dodge, "A Voice from Yesterday," 11.

19. Katz, "Grace Hoadley Dodge."

20. Grace Hoadley Dodge, "President's Message," Printed Convention Proceedings, 1909, 60–61.

21. George Marsden, *Understanding Fundamentalism and Evangelicalism* (Grand Rapids, MI: William B. Eerdmans, 1991), 2. As modernist controversies created schisms within the Protestant churches, many fundamentalists claimed the term "evangelical" as their own.

22. "The Organization of a City Young Women's Christian Association," 1907, 13.

23. Mrs. C. R. Springer, remarks, Printed Convention Proceedings, 1906, 21.

24. Grace Hoadley Dodge, "A Private Letter to Girls," 1889, 10–11, General Writings, Grace Hoadley Dodge Papers.

25. Quoted in Karen Mittleman, "'A Spirit That Touches the Problems of Today': Women and Social Reform in the Philadelphia Young Women's Christian Association, 1920–1945," (PhD diss., University of Pennsylvania, 1987), 96. This underscores the significance of religious groups—including the National Council of Jewish Women and the National Council of Catholic Women—in the coalition of women's organizations behind the Women's Bureau. See Cynthia Harrison, *On Account of Sex: The Politics of Women's Issues, 1945–1968* (Berkeley: University of California Press, 1989), 8–9.

26. Guy Alchon, "van Kleeck, Mary"; Steven Niven, "Fauset, Crystal Bird"; and Maija Lutz, "Deloria, Ella Cara," all in American National Biography Online, 2000, www.anb.org.

27. Helen Barnes, "The Volunteer Worker," *Association Monthly*, November 1907, 450; Emma Bailey Speer, remarks, Subject Files: Convention Proceedings, 1926, 55, microfilm reel 29, YWCA-SSC.

28. Robertson, *Christian Sisterhood*, 78.

29. Quoted in Sidney Ahlstrom, *A Religious History of the American People*, 2nd ed. (New Haven, CT: Yale University Press, 2004), 786.

30. Ellen Fitzpatrick, *Endless Crusade: Women Social Scientists and Progressive Reform* (New York: Oxford University Press, 1990); J. Stanley Lemons, *Woman Citizen: Social Feminism in the 1920s* (Urbana: University of Illinois Press, 1973); Robyn Muncy, *Creating a Female Dominion in American Reform, 1890–1935* (New York: Oxford University Press, 1991); Kathryn Kish

Sklar, "Hull House Maps and Papers: Social Science as Women's Work in the 1890s," in *The Social Survey in Historical Perspective*, ed. Martin Bulmer, Kevin Bales, and Kathryn Kish Sklar (Cambridge: Cambridge University Press, 1991), 111–47.

31. Anna Rice, "A Forward Look at Our Religious Work," *Association Monthly*, August 1916, 282. For connections between the Social Gospel and evangelicalism, see Susan Curtis, "The Son of Man and God the Father: The Social Gospel and Victorian Masculinity," in *Meanings for Manhood: Constructions of Masculinity in Victorian America*, ed. Mark Carnes and Clyde Griffen (Chicago: University of Chicago Press, 1990), 71.

32. Ahlstrom, *A Religious History*, 804. *The Social Principles of Jesus* (New York: Association Press, 1916) was also the title of a student study guide written by Walter Rauschenbusch and distributed by the YWCA.

33. Ahlstrom, *A Religious History*, 85.

34. National Board Report, 1911, 28.

35. Remarks, Printed Convention Proceedings, 1911, 120, RG 4, YWCA-SSC. The resolution was drafted well in advance of the fire. See Robertson, *Christian Sisterhood*, 20.

36. National Board Report, 1911, 28–29.

37. Elizabeth Payne, *Reform, Labor, and Feminism: Margaret Dreier Robins and the Women's Trade Union League* (Urbana: University of Illinois Press, 1988), 132–36; Kathryn Kish Sklar, *Florence Kelley and the Nation's Work: The Rise of Women's Political Culture* (New Haven, CT: Yale University Press, 1995), 258–62.

38. Elizabeth Sweets, Mrs. William Slocum, and Blanche Geary, remarks, Printed Convention Proceedings, 1911, 121, 117, and 119.

39. Florence Simms, "The Association in Industry," *Association Monthly*, June 1911, 178.

40. Fitzpatrick, *Endless Crusade*; Kunzel, *Fallen Women, Problem Girls*; Daniel Walkowitz, *Working with Class: Social Workers and the Politics of Middle-Class Identity* (Chapel Hill: University of North Carolina Press, 1999).

41. Walter Rauschenbusch, address, Printed Convention Proceedings, 1915, 128, RG 4, YWCA-SSC; "Home Department Recommendations," Printed Convention Proceedings, 1909, 111.

42. Katz, "Grace Hoadley Dodge," 228; NTS Training School Catalogues, 1908, Training and Personnel, RG 6, YWCA-SSC. The NTS was not open to black women until 1911 (Robertson, *Christian Sisterhood*, 33).

43. Fitzpatrick, *Endless Crusade*, 73.

44. William Hutchison, *The Modernist Impulse in American Protestantism* (Cambridge, MA: Harvard University Press, 1976), 257–88. These individuals were among those who lectured or taught at the NTS between 1908 and 1920. Many of them spoke at other YWCA conferences and special events, and some served as consultants on projects or published works with the YWCA's press.

45. Annie MacLean, "Investigation into Social Conditions Finds Unselfish Life in Hop Fields," *Washington Post*, November 29, 1908. The *New York Times* concurred that it was a pioneering study ("Dancing—Preaching," November 29, 1908).

46. Grace Hoadley Dodge, "President's Message," Printed Convention Proceedings, 1909, 58–59; "Executive Committee Report," ibid., 7; MacLean, "Investigation into Social Conditions."

47. "Some Urgent Phases of Immigrant Life," 1910, 13, Constituent Groups: Immigration and Foreign Communities, RG 6, YWCA-SSC. See also deRoche, "'How Wide the Circle of We,'" 50–56.

48. Mary Sims, *The YWCA: An Unfolding Purpose* (New York: Woman's Press, 1950), 40.

49. Dorothea Browder, "A 'Christian Solution to the Labor Problem': How Workingwomen Reshaped the YWCA's Religious Mission and Politics," *Journal of Women's History* 19, no. 2 (2007): 87.

50. National Board Report, 1924, 156. Numbers from Browder, "A 'Christian Solution,'" 97.

51. "Year Book of Young Women's Christian Associations of the USA, 1916–17," 2, Publications: Data and Statistics, RG 3, YWCA-SSC.

52. Robertson, *Christian Sisterhood*, 58. For wartime mobilization, see "Report of the National War Work Council," National Board Report, 1920, RG 4, YWCA-SSC.

53. Lillian Chambers, letter to friends, March 31, 1919, Japan: Miscellaneous, World YWCA Archives, Geneva, Switzerland (hereafter WYWCA); Harriot Stanton Blatch, *A Woman's Point of View: Some Roads to Peace* (New York: Womans Press, 1920), 162–63.

54. Katherine Gerwick, "Women's Citizenship," reprinted in *Women and Leadership*, comp. Mary Sims and Rhoda McCulloch (New York: Womans Press, 1938), 68–69. Robertson examines Christian citizenship and racial politics in *Christian Sisterhood*, 74–100.

55. Gerwick, "Women's Citizenship," 68–69. See Leila Rupp, *Worlds of Women: The Making of an International Women's Movement* (Princeton, NJ: Princeton University Press, 1997), 101.

56. Resolution, Printed Convention Proceedings, 1920, 109–10, RG 4, YWCA-SSC. See also Browder, "A 'Christian Solution,'" 99–101; Robertson, *Christian Sisterhood*, 74–80. For more on the "Social Ideals of the Churches," see Charles MacFarland, *Christian Unity in the Making: The First Twenty-Five Years of the Federal Council of Churches of Christ in America, 1905–1930* (New York: Federal Council of Churches of Christ in America, 1948), 44–46.

57. Browder, "'A Christian Solution,'" 88.

58. Remarks, Printed Convention Proceedings, 1920, 71, 44, 45, 118, and 112.

59. The alternative pledge for student YWCAs replaced the requirement of church membership with a declaration from the prospective member: "It is my purpose to live as a true follower of the Lord Jesus Christ" ("Student Recommendations," Printed Convention Proceedings, 1920, 40). In 1930, full membership (with voting and office privileges) became available to those who made a simple declaration of dedication to Christian fellowship.

60. Typed notes on the *Manufacturers Record Daily Bulletin*, June 30, 1920, and "Letter of Employers Association of Pittsburgh," *New York Evening Post*, March 16, 1921, Public Advocacy: General Controversies, RG 6, YWCA-SSC. Other groups and publications are listed in a set of typed notes titled "Attacks Made on the YWCA," February 21, 1921, ibid.

61. Quoted in Edward Krehbiel, "The Attack on the Los Angeles YWCA," *Survey*, August 16, 1920, 612; typed notes on the *Manufacturers Record Daily Bulletin*, June 30, 1920.

62. Typed notes on the *Manufacturers Record Daily Bulletin*, June 30, 1920.

63. Quoted in "Don't Drive Labor Gompers Warns," *New York Times*, May 10, 1921.

64. "Disciplining YWCA," *Churchman*, February 26, 1921, 8; "The World of Today," *Christian Work*, February 12, 1921, 188; "Boycott: A New Phase," *Christian Advocate* (New York), February 10, 1921, 172.

65. The YWCA then trailed only the General Federation of Women's Clubs and the Woman's Christian Temperance Union in membership. See Robertson, *Christian Sisterhood*, 74–75.

66. "Citizen Education, 1922," Public Advocacy: Subject Files, RG 6, YWCA-SSC. For the comparison to the YMCA, see Robertson, *Christian Sisterhood*, 104–5.

67. National Board Report, 1922, 162, RG 4, YWCA-SSC.

68. "Citizenship Education in the YWCA," 1927, Public Advocacy: Subject Files, RG 6, YWCA-SSC; "Citizen Education, 1922."

69. Mrs. Harry Nims to Chairs, Legislative Committee Circulars, March 28, 1925, Public Advocacy: Committees and Subcommittees, RG 6, YWCA-SSC.

70. See Jan Doolittle Wilson, *The Women's Joint Congressional Committee and the Politics of Maternalism* (Urbana: University of Illinois Press, 2007). Subject files in the YWCA's Public

Advocacy files (RG 3) as well as Margaret Hiller's "Citizenship and Legislation" column in the *Womans Press* document the political endorsements made by the YWCA.

71. National Board Report, 1924, 124.

72. US Secretaries in Japan to Mrs. Paist, telegram, April 24, 1924, Public Advocacy: Ethnic Group Subject Files, RG 6, YWCA-SSC. Karen Seat documents this antixenophobic turn in US women's mission circles in *"Providence Has Freed Our Hands": Women's Missions and the American Encounter with Japan* (Syracuse, NY: Syracuse University Press, 2008).

73. National Board Report, 1922, 164.

74. Harriet Hyman Alonso, *Peace as a Women's Issue: A History of the U.S. Movement for World Peace and Women's Rights* (Syracuse, NY: Syracuse University Press, 1993), 109–13; Kim Nielsen, *Un-American Womanhood: Antiradicalism, Antifeminism, and the First Red Scare* (Columbus: Ohio State University Press, 2001), 73–83.

75. "Are Women's Clubs 'Used' by Socialists?" *Dearborn Independent*, March 22, 1924. For accounts of the controversy, see, for example, Lemons, *Woman Citizen*, 209–25; Wilson, *The Women's Joint Congressional Committee*, 148–70.

76. "Statement on Feminism and Bloc Dictatorship (Part I)," *Woman Patriot*, July 15, 1927. For this coalition of self-designated patriots, see Nielsen, *Un-American Womanhood*.

77. Henrietta Roelofs, "Memorandum on Attacks on the YWCA," June 25, 1927, General Controversy, RG3, YWCA-SSC; Rhoda McCulloch, "Criticism? Of Course," *Womans Press*, September 1927, 601.

CHAPTER 2   "BY LOVE, SERVE ONE ANOTHER": FOREIGN MISSION AND THE CHANGING MEANINGS OF EVANGELIZATION

1. Zech. 4:6 (KJV), quoted in Anna Rice, *A History of the World's Young Women's Christian Association* (New York: Woman's Press, 1947), 76. In 1955 the organization was renamed the World YWCA.

2. Gal. 5:13 (KJV). For examples of this motto, see Annual Report, Beyrouth, Lebanon, 1932–33, 3, Lebanon/Syria: National Programme Work, WYWCA; and Conference Report, 1945, 6, World Executive Committee: Eastern Mediterranean Federation, WYWCA.

3. Dana Robert, *American Women in Mission: A Social History of Their Thought and Practice* (Macon, GA: Mercer University Press, 1996), 133.

4. Barbara Reeves-Ellington, Kathryn Kish Sklar, and Connie Shemo, introduction to *Competing Kingdoms: Women, Mission, Nation, and the American Protestant Empire, 1812–1960*, ed. Barbara Reeves-Ellington, Kathryn Kish Sklar, and Connie Shemo (Durham, NC: Duke University Press, 2010), 4–6.

5. Sidney Ahlstrom, *A Religious History of the American People*, 2nd ed. (New Haven, CT: Yale University Press, 2004), 864–65.

6. Jane Hunter, "Women's Mission in Historical Perspective: American Identity and Christian Internationalism," in *Competing Kingdoms*, 36.

7. For the history of the world organization, see Nancy Boyd, *Emissaries: The Overseas Work of the American YWCA, 1895–1970* (New York: Woman's Press, 1986), 10–32; Rice, *A History of the World's Young Women's Christian Association*; Carole Seymour-Jones, *Journey of Faith: The History of the World YWCA, 1945–1994* (London: Allison and Busby, 1994).

8. G. Gollock, "World Wide," *World's Young Women's Christian Association Quarterly*, April 1896, 2.

9. Robert, *American Women in Mission*, 128–30.

10. World's Young Women's Christian Association, *A Study of the World's YWCA* (London: World's Young Women's Christian Association, 1924), 59.

11. N. Boyd, *Emissaries*, 34.

12. Quoted in Rice, *A History of the World's Young Women's Christian Association*, 116.

13. Leila Rupp, *Worlds of Women: The Making of an International Women's Movement* (Princeton, NJ: Princeton University Press, 1997), 3.

14. Mrs. J.H. [Lucy] Tritton, remarks, Printed Convention Proceedings, 1911, 27, RG 4, YWCA-SSC.

15. This complicates the history of internationalist Western feminism presented in Louise Newman, *White Women's Rights: The Racial Origins of Feminism in the United States* (New York: Oxford University Press, 1999). It affirms Jennifer Snow's description of Protestant missionaries' support of rights for Asians in the United States as a "racial project [that] competed with the racial project of scientific racism" (*Protestant Missionaries, Asian Immigrants, and Ideologies of Race in America, 1850–1924* [New York: Routledge, 2007], xiv). See also Karen Seat, *"Providence Has Freed Our Hands": Women's Missions and the American Encounter with Japan* (Syracuse, NY: Syracuse University Press, 2008).

16. Gal. 3:28 (KJV), quoted in Ethel Stevenson, "The World's Committee as a Pioneer and Unifying Force," 157; Mary Hill, remarks, 167; Tritton, remarks, 27, all in Printed Convention Proceedings, 1911.

17. Esther Pohl and Susan Orvis to Miss Gage, July 12, 1913, Turkey: Printed Material, WYWCA; Clarissa Spencer, remarks, Printed Convention Proceedings, 1913, 150, RG 4, YWCA-SSC.

18. Grace H. Dodge, "The Possibilities in the Young Women's Christian Association Movement," *Women's International Quarterly*, April 1913, 150; Agnes Gale Hill, "Our Foreign Call," Printed Convention Proceedings, 1909, 80, RG 4, YWCA-SSC.

19. "Foreign Division Statistics," January 15, 1922, USA: Reports, WYWCA.

20. "Does Japan Need the Social Message?" *Women's International Quarterly*, January 1914, 70; E. I. M. Boyd, "YWCA in Mission Lands," *Women's International Quarterly*, October 1914, 31. For foundational accounts of missionary discourses of women's empowerment, see Joan Jacobs Brumberg, "Zenanas and Girlless Villages: The Ethnology of American Evangelical Women, 1870–1910," *Journal of American History* 69, no. 2 (1982): 347–71; Jane Hunter, *The Gospel of Gentility: American Women Missionaries in Turn-of-the-Century China* (New Haven, CT: Yale University Press, 1984), 179–81; Robert, *American Women in Mission*, 133–37.

21. Mrs. Thomas Stantial [Effie Price] Gladding, "The Unique Responsibility of the American Associations to the World's Work," Printed Convention Proceedings, 1909, 63; Tritton, remarks, Printed Convention Proceedings, 1911, 27.

22. Elisa Cortéz, "Oriental Students in America," *Association Monthly*, July 1910, 243. Cortéz, a Mexican secretary employed by the US YWCA, identified herself as an "Occidental foreign student," but other YWCA sources sometimes listed the Latin American field as part of the orient. See, for example, "Foreign Division Statistics," 1922.

23. Mary Hill, remarks, Printed Convention Proceedings, 1911, 168; Inez Crawford, Quarterly Report, Fourth Quarter, 1917, Japan: Minutes and Reports, WYWCA; "World Fellowship Week of Prayer," 1920, 11, Projects and Programs, RG 5, YWCA-SSC.

24. Hunter, *The Gospel of Gentility*, 174.

25. "The World's Policy for the Next Four Years Adopted at the Berlin Conference," *Association Monthly*, September 1910, 320.

26. World Executive Committee Minutes, May 1919, 1–2, WYWCA.

27. World's Young Women's Christian Association, "Report of the Fifth Conference," 1914, 24, WYWCA.

28. Beth Baron, *Egypt as a Woman: Nationalism, Gender, and Politics* (Berkeley: University of California Press, 2005), 174–77; Insook Kwon, "Feminists Navigating the Shoals of Nationalism and Collaboration: The Post-Colonial Korean Debate over How to Remember Kim Hwallan," *Frontiers* 27, no. 1 (2006): 39–66.

29. National Board Report, 1915, 57, RG 4, YWCA-SSC; "The World's Young Women's Christian Association and Industry," 1920, History of Social and Industrial Work, WYWCA; "Biennial Report of Foreign Division and Excerpts from Education and Research Division," December 1929, 13, USA: Reports, WYWCA.

30. Karen Garner points out that racialized hierarchies underwriting YWCA expansion were difficult to displace because even after associations had been turned over to local control, "Western foreign secretaries played key policy-making roles" ("Global Feminism and Postwar Reconstruction: The World YWCA Visitation to Occupied Japan, 1947," *Journal of World History* 15, no. 2 [2004]: 198).

31. John McNab, "White Angel of Tokyo, Miss Caroline Macdonald, LL.D.," 1940s?, 15, WYWCA. Michi Kawai's autobiographies, *My Lantern* (privately printed, 1949) and *Sliding Doors* (Tokyo: Keisen-jo-gaju-en, 1950), are as yet the most comprehensive English-language sources of information on the educator and reformer.

32. Barbara Rose, *Tsuda Umeko and Women's Education in Japan* (New Haven, CT: Yale University Press, 1992), 124–41.

33. Sharon Nolte and Sally Ann Hastings, "The Meiji State's Policy toward Women, 1890–1910," in *Recreating Japanese Women, 1600–1945*, ed. Gail Lee Bernstein (Berkeley: University of California Press, 1991), 152. See also Rumi Yasutake, "Men, Women, and Temperance in Meiji Japan," *Japanese Journal of American Studies* 17 (2006): 91–111.

34. Secretary Katherine Hawes was one of many American women in the international field who characterized the Japanese as "imitators" ("Report of Visit to Japan," July 1919, 5, Japan: Minutes and Reports, WYWCA).

35. Michi Kawai to Misses Spencer, Stevenson, and Boyd, September 16, 1912, Japan: Miscellaneous, WYWCA.

36. Michi Kawai to Miss Taylor, September 1917?, Foreign, Japan: Staff Reports, microfilm reel 59, YWCA-SSC.

37. Jon Thares Davidann, *A World of Crisis and Progress: The American YMCA in Japan, 1890–1930* (Bethlehem, PA: Lehigh University Press, 1998), 81.

38. Hawes, "Report of Visit to Japan," 2.

39. Charlotte Adams to Miss Spencer, March 6, 1920, Japan: Miscellaneous, WYWCA; William Hutchison, *Errand to the World: American Protestant Thought and Foreign Missions* (Chicago: University of Chicago Press, 1987), 97.

40. Charlotte Adams, "Confidential Report on Japan," 1920, Foreign, Japan: Staff Reports, microfilm reel 59, YWCA-SSC.

41. Michi Kawai, "Japan's Present Need," Printed Convention Proceedings, 1915, 133–34, RG 4, YWCA-SSC.

42. Michi Kawai, "Japan," Printed Convention Proceedings, 1920, 314–16, RG 4, YWCA-SSC.

43. Jane Scott, report, June 1926, Japan: Minutes and Reports, WYWCA; Kawai, *My Lantern*, 167.

44. National Board Report, 1924, 226, RG 4, YWCA-SSC; "World's Young Women's Christian Association International Commission Findings," 1920, History of Social and Industrial Work, WYWCA.

45. Seat, *"Providence Has Freed Our Hands,"* xiii. For the shift to a discourse of "world friendship," see Robert, *American Women in Mission*, 272–73.

46. Tritton, remarks, Printed Convention Proceedings, 1911, 27; "Report of the General Secretary," 1924, Annual Reports, WYWCA.

47. "The World's Policy for the Next Four Years," 322; "Constantinople Conference," *World's Young Women's Christian Association Quarterly*, July 1911, 61.

48. *YWCA News*, February 1925, 1, WYWCA.

49. "Report from Miss Spencer," 1911, Foreign: Turkey Reports, microfilm reel 63, YWCA-SSC.

50. "Turkey, Our New Field," 1914, Country Files: Turkey Publications, RG 5, YWCA-SSC.

51. Margaret Stewart, report, 1921, Foreign: Turkey Girls Clubs, microfilm reel 63, YWCA-SSC.

52. Ruth Woodsmall, report, September 28, 1922, and "Report of the Smyrna Disaster," December 5, 1922, in World Executive Committee Regions: Near East, WYWCA; "Eyewitness Tells of Smyrna Horror," *New York Times*, October 10, 1922.

53. Elizabeth Wilson, "World Cooperation of the Young Women's Christian Associations of the United States of America, 1866–1929," circa 1929, 89, History, RG 5, YWCA-SSC.

54. Quoted in Margaret White, "Summary History," April 1934, Foreign: Turkey Reports, microfilm reel 63, YWCA-SSC.

55. Typed notes, May 28, 1923, World Executive Committee Regions: Near East, WYWCA. Clippings of hostile comments in the press can be found in Country Files: Turkey, RG 5, YWCA-SSC.

56. Ruth Woodsmall, "Report on the YWCA in the Near East," June 1, 1925, World's Executive Committee Regions: Near East, WYWCA. These transitions are recounted more generally in Deniz Kandiyoti, "End of Empire: Islam, Nationalism and Women in Turkey," in *Women, Islam, and the State*, ed. Deniz Kandiyoti (Houndmills, UK: Macmillan, 1991), 22–47; Roger Trask, "Unnamed Christianity in Turkey," *Muslim World* 55, no. 1 (1965): 66–76.

57. Woodsmall, "Report on the YWCA in the Near East"; Woodsmall, "How Would You Modify These Points?," n.d., Turkey: Industrial Work, WYWCA.

58. "Resumé of Discussion at a Meeting of the Foreign Division to Consider the Policy of the Association in Turkey," 1929, Foreign: Turkey History, microfilm reel 63, YWCA-SSC.

59. Ruth Woodsmall, "Memorandum on Present Position of the YWCA in Constantinople," October 27, 1925, World Executive Committee Regions: Near East, WYWCA; "Resumé of Discussion at a Meeting of the Foreign Division to Consider the Policy of the Association in Turkey," 1929.

60. Eurydice Akdjeoglou, speech, March 8, 1926, Foreign: Turkey Girls Clubs, microfilm reel 63, YWCA-SSC; Genevieve Lowry, "Inventory in Istanbul," *Womans Press*, February 1932, 88; Gal. 5:9 (KJV).

61. "YWCA in Turkey," 1925?, Foreign: Turkey History, microfilm reel 63, YWCA-SSC.

62. Quoted in untitled typescript, April 13, 1932, Turkey: Miscellaneous, WYWCA.

63. "Report by the General Secretary on the Work of the Executive Committee," June 1930–June 1934, 15, Annual Reports, WYWCA.

64. "Memorandum on the Interconfessional Position of the World's YWCA as Presented at the Budapest Conference," 1928, Ecumenical Work and Interconfessional Documents: History of Interconfessionalism, WYWCA; "Report by the General Secretary," June 1930–June 1934, 9. See also Rice, *A History of the World's Young Women's Christian Association*, 207.

65. American Liaison Committee files, Country Files: Turkey, RG 5, YWCA-SSC.

66. Tritton, remarks, Printed Convention Proceedings, 1911, 27.

CHAPTER 3   "HIDDEN AND EFFECTIVE SERVICE":
THE MARYKNOLL SISTERS ENTER THE MISSION FIELD

1. Sister Virginia Flagg, interview by the author, July 21, 2006, Maryknoll, NY; Office statistics files, MSA.

2. For "woman's work for woman," see Dana Robert, *American Women in Mission: A Social History of Their Thought and Practice* (Macon, GA: Mercer University Press, 1996), 130–37.

3. Amy Kaplan employs the term "domestic empire" to discuss the links between imperialism and nineteenth-century ideologies of domesticity ("Manifest Domesticity," in *The Futures of American Studies*, ed. Donald Pease and Robyn Wiegman [Durham, NC: Duke University Press, 2002], 120).

4. Mary Josephine Rogers, "The Student Volunteers," n.d., in Mary Josephine Rogers, "Discourses," 2:464. Here, Rogers quotes a New Testament verse often employed to explain the missionary vocation (Matt. 28:19).

5. Penny Lernoux, *Hearts on Fire: The Story of the Maryknoll Sisters* (Maryknoll, NY: Orbis, 1993), 43.

6. Angelyn Dries, *The Missionary Movement in American Catholic History* (Maryknoll, NY: Orbis Books, 1998), 22–57. Dries examines the Americanist controversy in light of the "missionary awakening" in "The Foreign Mission Impulse of the American Catholic Church, 1893–1925," *International Bulletin of Missionary Research* 15, no. 2 (1991): 61–66.

7. William Halsey describes Catholics' "quite vocal claim to America" in the years before the election of John F. Kennedy as president confirmed their sentiments (*The Survival of American Innocence: Catholicism in an Era of Disillusionment, 1920–1940* [Notre Dame, IN: University of Notre Dame Press, 1980], 169). For the effect of these developments on women religious, see Dorothy Brown and Elizabeth McKeown, *The Poor Belong to Us: Catholic Charities and American Welfare* (Cambridge, MA: Harvard University Press, 1997); Maureen Fitzgerald, *Habits of Compassion: Irish Catholic Nuns and the Origins of New York's Welfare System, 1830–1920* (Urbana: University of Illinois Press, 2006).

8. Alex Doyle, "Let Us Now Establish the Seminary for the Foreign Field," *The Field Afar,* October–November 1912, 3.

9. "Maryknoll," *The Field Afar,* December 1912, 6. The society also includes religious brothers, who, like Maryknoll sisters, take simple vows in contrast to the solemn vows taken by priests.

10. Lernoux, *Hearts on Fire,* 32, see also 38. The title "mother general" designates the superior heading the congregation.

11. "Constitution of the Foreign Mission Sisters of St. Dominic," 1931, chap. 1, no. 2, MSA.

12. Jean-Paul Wiest, *Maryknoll in China: A History, 1918–1955* (Armonk, NY: M. E. Sharpe, 1998), 60–61.

13. Wiest, *Maryknoll in China,* 130–65; Cindy Yik-Yi Chu, *Maryknoll Sisters in Hong Kong, 1921–1969: In Love with the Chinese* (New York: Palgrave Macmillan, 2004), 32–40.

14. Luke 1:38 (DV, Vulgate). See Sisters Mary Eunice Tolan and Mary Incarnata Farrelly, "Maryknoll Distaff: History of the Maryknoll Sisters, 1929–30," 1970, 4, MSA.

15. John 10:10 (KJV); Constitution, Printed Convention Proceedings, 1909, 107–12, RG 4, YWCA-SSC.

16. Jo Ann Kay McNamara, *Sisters in Arms: Catholic Nuns through Two Millennia* (Cambridge, MA: Harvard University Press, 1996), 385–88 and 461–65. Apostolic orders had an ambiguous legal standing until the 1918 revision of canon law that created the means for their official recognition, contingent on their adoption of many of the regulations that governed cloistered orders.

17. Brown and McKeown, *The Poor Belong to Us,* 86–89.

18. Fitzgerald, *Habits of Compassion*, 9.

19. Mary Josephine Rogers, "Our Vows," 1929, in "Discourses," 2:783; Helen Rose Fuchs Ebaugh, *Women in the Vanishing Cloister: Organizational Decline in Catholic Religious Orders in the United States* (New Brunswick, NJ: Rutgers University Press, 1993), 62.

20. Mary Josephine Rogers, "General Chapter, 1931: On Manners," in "Discourses," 2:500.

21. Mary Josephine Rogers, "Dominican Spirit—Maryknoll Spirit," 1932, in "Discourses," 2:627; Rogers, "General Chapter, 1931: On Manners," in ibid., 500.

22. Quoted in Lernoux, *Hearts on Fire*, 40.

23. Mary Josephine Rogers, "America's Contribution to the Personnel of Missions," 1927, in "Discourses," 2:437, and "The American Girl and Foreign Missions," 1932, in ibid., 470.

24. Rogers, "General Chapter, 1931: On Manners," 2:500, and "Dominican Spirit—Maryknoll Spirit," 1932, in ibid., 627.

25. Lernoux, *Hearts on Fire*, 39.

26. Diary, 426 So. Boyle Ave., Los Angeles, California, December 24, 1921, MSA. For the culture of women's colleges, see Helen Lefkowitz Horowitz, *Alma Mater: Design and Experience in the Women's Colleges from Their Nineteenth-Century Beginnings to the 1930s* (New York: Knopf, 1984), 147–78.

27. Flagg, interview. Patricia Byrne's account of cloister restrictions in US women's congregations indicates the relative freedom of Maryknoll ("In the Parish but Not of It: Sisters," in *Transforming Parish Ministry: The Changing Roles of Catholic Clergy, Laity, and Women Religious*, ed. Jay Dolan, et al. [New York: Crossroad, 1989], 128–32).

28. "PL Interview II at Monte Maria," July 1988, Penny Lernoux Book Collection, MSA.

29. Flagg, interview.

30. Erving Goffman describes religious orders as paradigmatic "total institutions," which he defined as existing when "a large number of like-situated individuals, cut off from the wider society for an appreciable period of time, together lead an enclosed, formally administered round of life" (*Asylums: Essays on the Social Situation of Mental Patients and Other Inmates* [Chicago: Aldine, 1962], xiii).

31. "Constitution of the Foreign Mission Sisters of St. Dominic," 1931, chap. 11, no. 144. Initially, novices trained at the motherhouse—the compound that housed the congregation near Ossining, New York. Houses were added in Clarks Summit, Pennsylvania; Valley Park, Missouri; and Topsfield, Massachusetts to accommodate the increasing number of entrants in the 1940s and 1950s. These additional houses were closed in the 1970s.

32. Mary Josephine Rogers, "Maryknoll Spirit," 1930, in "Discourses," 2:883; "Constitution of the Foreign Mission Sisters of St. Dominic," 1931, chap. 18, no. 277; "Motherhouse Rule Book/Handbook: Early Edition," circa 1962, Sisters Heritage Collection, MSA.

33. "Constitution of the Foreign Mission Sisters of St. Dominic," 1931, chap. 15, nos. 209–12.

34. Mary Josephine Rogers, "Fraternal Charity," 1932, in "Discourses," 2:610.

35. Mary Josephine Rogers, "Chastity," 1932, in "Discourses," 3:1051; and "Chastity," 1930, in ibid., 2:861. See also Horowitz, *Alma Mater*, 66–68.

36. "Motherhouse Rule Book/Handbook," circa 1962, 77.

37. Mary Josephine Rogers, "General Chapter, 1931: On Our Relationship with Men," in "Discourses," 2:535–36; "Constitution of the Foreign Mission Sisters of St. Dominic," 1931, chap. 22, no. 332.

38. Flagg, interview.

39. "Constitution of the Foreign Mission Sisters of St. Dominic," 1931, chap. 1, no. 3; "Overseas Notes," *The Field Afar*, September 1928, 257. Mission assignment statistics are calculated from *The Official Catholic Directory* (New York: P.J. Kenedy and Sons, 1933).

40. Diary, 426 So. Boyle Ave., Los Angeles, December 16, 1921.
41. "Jottings from the Diary of Maryknoll Sisters in China," *The Field Afar*, August 1922, 249; "From the Sisters in China," *The Field Afar*, December 1923, 352.
42. Wiest, *Maryknoll in China*, 100–109; Sister M. Marcelline, *Sisters Carry the Gospel* (Maryknoll, NY: Maryknoll Publications, 1956).
43. Ford quoted in Sister Jeanne Marie, *Maryknoll's First Lady* (n.p.: Maryknoll Sisters of St. Dominic, 1964), 166–67; M. Marcelline, *Sisters Carry the Gospel*, 16.
44. Pope Leo XIII, *Rerum Novarum*, 1891, accessed March 26, 2017, http://w2.vatican.va/content/leo-xiii/en/encyclicals/documents/hf_l-xiii_enc_15051891_rerum-novarum.html.
45. Pope Pius XI, *Rerum Ecclesiae*, 1926, accessed March 26, 2017, http://w2.vatican.va/content/pius-xi/en/encyclicals/documents/hf_p-xi_enc_28021926_rerum-ecclesiae.html.
46. "Constitution of the Foreign Mission Sisters of St. Dominic," 1931, chap. 22, no. 319.
47. "Life-Saving at Loting," *The Field Afar*, January 1938, 29; Sister Marya Thyne, "The Little Tin House," *The Field Afar*, June 1938, 188.
48. Diary, Kowloon Tong Convent, Hong Kong, April 1940, 4, MSA.
49. "Maryknoll's Russian School," *The Field Afar*, February 1938, 60. See also Paul Rivera, "'Field Found!' Establishing the Maryknoll Mission Enterprise in the United States and China, 1918–1928," *Catholic Historical Review* 84, no. 3 (1998): 477–517.
50. Sister Mary Paul McKenna, "Moving Along," *The Field Afar*, June 1922, 182; "The Maryknoll Sisters: To the Philippines via Typhoon," *The Field Afar*, July–August 1940, 18.
51. "Maryknoll Sisters' Apostolate of Kindness: Mission Work Is Social Work," circa 1930s, Direct Mail, MSA; Sister Victoria Francis Larmour, "Social Service and the Religious Life," circa 1930s, 9–10, Creative Works and Personal Papers, MSA.
52. Pope Pius XI, *Rerum Ecclesiae*.
53. Ibid.
54. "Constitution of the Foreign Mission Sisters of St. Dominic," 1931, chap. 22, no. 329; Sister Betty Ann Maheu, interview with Penny Lernoux, 1988, Vocation Problems, Penny Lernoux Book Collection, MSA.
55. "Constitution of the Foreign Mission Sisters of St. Dominic," 1931, chap. 22, no. 329; Flagg, interview.
56. Editorial, *The Field Afar*, May 1928, 133; S. M. I., "With the Japanese on the Pacific Coast," *The Field Afar*, March 1938, 93.
57. Diary, 426 So. Boyle Ave., Los Angeles, February 26, 1922.
58. Mary Josephine Rogers, "Opening Day of General Chapter," 1946, in "Discourses," 2:564.
59. Diary, St. Anthony's Convent, Maui, Hawaii, October 17, 1928, MSA.

PART II   FROM THE POPULAR FRONT AND AMERICAN CENTURY TO THE NEW FRONTIER

1. Henry Luce, "The American Century," *Life*, February 7, 1941, 65 and 63.

CHAPTER 4   "DARE WE BE AS RADICAL AS OUR RELIGION DEMANDS?": CHRISTIAN ACTIVISM AND THE LONG RED SCARE

1. Helen Gould Shepard, remarks, Printed Convention Proceedings, 1920, 45, RG 4, YWCA-SSC; "Mrs. Shepard Quits the Board of the YWCA," *New York Times*, April 18, 1920.
2. Elizabeth Dilling, *Should Christians Support the Y's?* (Chicago: Patriotic Research Bureau, [1938?]), 1–3.

3. Rose Terlin, *Christian Faith and Social Action* (New York: Womans Press, 1940), 34.

4. Mary Ely Lyman, "Is Worship a Lost Art? Or Is Our Generation Groping Its Way to a New Technique of Finding God?" *Womans Press*, May 1927, 325–26; Anna Rice, "The Religious Situation in the Association," Printed Convention Proceedings, 1928, 78, RG 4, YWCA-SSC.

5. Mary Sims, *The YWCA: An Unfolding Purpose* (New York: Woman's Press, 1950), 47–48.

6. Mary Sims, *The Natural History of a Social Institution: The Young Women's Christian Association* (New York: Womans Press, 1936), 115–16.

7. Winnifred Wygal, *The Good Life: A Discipline* (1936; reprint, New York: Womans Press, 1941), 12.

8. Sims, *The Natural History of a Social Institution*, 59.

9. Nancy Marie Robertson, *Christian Sisterhood, Race Relations, and the YWCA, 1906–46* (Urbana: University of Illinois Press, 2007), 89–94. Valerie Matsumoto documents similar dynamics in YWCAs serving West Coast Japanese communities, where the association "sought to include racial-minority girls without challenging racial lines" (*City Girls: The Nisei Social World in Los Angeles, 1920–1950* [New York: Oxford University Press, 2014], 26).

10. De Orona McCrorey, remarks, Printed Convention Proceedings, 1924, 117, RG 4, YWCA-SSC; "Women Working Together," *Association Monthly*, March 1920, 192.

11. Ruud Abma, "Madness and Mental Health," in *A Social History of Psychology*, eds. Jeroen Jansz and Peter van Drunen (Malden, MA: Blackwell, 2004), 112. For therapeutics in religious life, see Susan Curtis, *A Consuming Faith: The Social Gospel and Modern American Culture* (Baltimore, MD: Johns Hopkins University Press, 1991); Donald Meyer, *The Protestant Search for Political Realism, 1919–1941*, 2nd ed. (Middletown, CT: Wesleyan University Press, 1988), 136–44.

12. National Board Report, 1926, 99, RG 4, YWCA-SSC.

13. Rhoda McCulloch, *War and the Woman Point of View* (New York: Association Press, 1920), 29. For the wider influence of this rhetoric, see Elizabeth Lunbeck, *Psychiatric Persuasion: Knowledge, Gender, and Power in Modern America* (Princeton, NJ: Princeton University Press, 1994), 69.

14. Margaret Burton, "Releasing Personality," *Womans Press*, March 1924, 175.

15. See, for example, Heather Warren's assessment of Protestant religious education, which contends that, because of their adoption of therapeutic discourses, mainline churches in the 1930s and 1940s became "vulnerable to the charge that they abetted moral and religious laxity" in their "compartmentalization of private and public morality" ("The Shift from Character to Personality in Mainline Protestant Thought, 1935–1945," *Church History* 67, no. 3 [1998]: 537–38 and 544).

16. Burton, "Releasing Personality," 175.

17. "We Were Talking about Religion," *Womans Press*, January 1930, 9.

18. Jane Bellows, "The Health Way and Play," *Womans Press*, November 1924, 808.

19. Abbie Graham, "Four Services for Associations," 1927, 20–21, Religion Publications, RG 6, YWCA-SSC.

20. "Oath by the Students of the National YWCA School of Social Work, Delhi, for Gandhiji on His Birthday," 1947, India (Unprocessed): Minutes and Reports, WYWCA; National YWCA School of Social Work, brochure, 1948, India (Unprocessed): Social and Industrial, WYWCA.

21. Dorothy Height, *Open Wide the Freedom Gates* (New York: PublicAffairs, 2003), 223. See also Dorothy Height to friends, November 13, 1952, India (Unprocessed): Social and Industrial, WYWCA, and "A Woman's Word," *New York Amsterdam News*, January 29, 1966.

22. Grace Coyle, "Group Work and Social Change," in *Group Experience and Democratic Values* (New York: Womans Press, 1947), 142, and "Personal Significance and Social Action," Program and Convention Materials, 1934, 13, RG 4, YWCA-SSC.

23. Janice Andrews and Michael Reisch, "The Legacy of McCarthyism on Social Group Work: An Historical Analysis," *Journal of Sociology and Social Welfare* 24, no. 3 (1997): 215.

24. For example, see *An Adventure Book for Younger Girls*, 1927, 42, Teenage and Younger Girls: Publications, RG 6, YWCA-SSC; Rhoda McCulloch, "God Inspects the World," *Womans Press*, March 1931, 45.

25. Grace Coyle, "Social Groups and Program Development," *Womans Press*, January 1933, 17, and "Group Work and Social Change," 150–51.

26. Margaret Hiller, "Uncle Sam at Geneva: The United States and the League of Nations," 1938, 58, Public Advocacy Subject Files: League of Nations, RG 6, YWCA-SSC. Matsumoto documents the considerable popularity of YWCA clubs for adolescents, called the Girl Reserves, among second-generation Japanese Americans of Los Angeles in *City Girls*. For YWCA work in internment camps, see Abigail Lewis, "'The Barrier-Breaking Love of God': The Multiracial Activism of the Young Women's Christian Association, 1940s to 1970s." (PhD diss., Rutgers University, 2008), 17–70.

27. Elizabeth Wilson, *World Cooperation of the Young Women's Christian Associations of the United States of America*, circa 1929, 123, History, RG 5, YWCA-SSC.

28. "A Forum of Student Opinion," *Association Monthly*, November 1920, 543; Veleda Hoebel, "A Project in World Fellowship," *Womans Press*, September 1923, 559.

29. Annetta Dieckmann, "Toward Unity in Industry: How Various Organizations Are Studying the Problem of the Colored Worker in Industry," *Womans Press*, April 1927, 258–59; advertisement, *Association Monthly*, December 1921, 479. Dorothea Browder details staff members' efforts to address civil rights in such venues in "Working Out Their Economic Problems Together: World War I, Working Women, and Civil Rights in the YWCA," *Journal of the Gilded Age and Progressive Era* 14, no. 2 (2015): 243–65.

30. National Board Report, 1926, 101, RG 4, YWCA-SSC; "Student-in-Industry Projects," *Womans Press*, February 1930, 103. For an example of workers' writings, see Zora Cullati, "Spring Comes to a Factory Worker," *Womans Press*, May 1934, 247.

31. Dorothea Browder, "From Uplift to Agitation: Working Women, Race, and Coalition in the Young Women's Christian Association, 1908–1950" (PhD diss., University of Wisconsin-Madison, 2008), 149–50; National Board Report, 1924, 93, RG 4, YWCA-SSC.

32. National Board Report, 1924, 93.

33. Browder, "From Uplift to Agitation," 189.

34. National Board Report, 1924, 156. Robertson recounts African American secretaries' responses to the National Board (*Christian Sisterhood*, 81–91).

35. "How Would You Answer?" *Womans Press*, April 1923, 197; advertisement in ibid., 236.

36. Lucy Carner to Margaret Mead, October 1, 1935, Interracial/Racial Justice: Properties, Grace Dodge Hotel Policy, RG 6, YWCA-SSC. The National Board privately worried about the policy but resorted to dishonesty when put into a positon to publicly acknowledge it. When Walter White of the National Association for the Advancement of Colored People sought accommodations at the hotel for an African American group in 1934, the hotel's director deceitfully claimed that there were no vacancies to prevent "any further thought of using the Dodge Hotel for this group" (Elizabeth Eastman to Henrietta Roelofs, November 22, 1934, Interracial/Racial Justice: Properties, Grace Dodge Hotel Policy, RG 6, YWCA-SSC).

37. "Against Mob Rule," *Womans Press*, January 1934, 29; Resolutions, Printed Convention Proceedings 1946, 92–93, RG 4, YWCA-SSC. Community YWCAs were administered by a

central association, which had subsidiary branches. Many YWCAs serving African American communities were branches operating under the oversight of the "usually white-dominated" central association (Robertson, *Christian Sisterhood*, 39).

38. Resolution, Printed Convention Proceedings, 1920, 109–110; Public Affairs Committee, "Report of Resolutions," January 8, 1930, RG 6, Public Advocacy Subject Files: International Court of Justice, YWCA-SSC.

39. Karen Garner, *Precious Fire: Maud Russell and the Chinese Revolution* (Amherst: University of Massachusetts, 2003), 84–90.

40. Mrs. Robert E. [Emma Bailey] Speer to all members of the Senate Committee on Foreign Relations, April 8, 1924, Public Advocacy Subject Files: International Court of Justice, RG 6, YWCA-SSC.

41. Lucy Randolph Mason, remarks, Printed Convention Proceedings, 1924, 164.

42. "The International Labour Organisation and Asiatic Countries: Memorandum Prepared for the YWCA Regional Conference," October 1936, Program Guides, WYWCA; "Report of the Budapest Conference," June 1928, 12, WYWCA. Among other cooperative ventures, the World's YWCA assisted the ILO with reports on unscrupulous employment agencies, the traffic in women and children, Armenian refugees in Syria, and the legal status of women. See "Report by the General Secretary on the Work of the Executive Committee," June 1930–June 1934, and Annual Report of the Executive Committee, 1939–40, in Annual Reports, WYWCA. Carol Riegelman Lubin and Anne Winslow describe the ILO's relationship with women's organizations in *Social Justice for Women: The International Labor Organization and Women* (Durham, NC: Duke University Press, 1990).

43. "Public Affairs Chronology by Subject," 1938?, Public Advocacy: General/History, RG 6, YWCA-SSC.

44. Anne Firor Scott, *Natural Allies: Women's Associations in American History* (Urbana: University of Illinois Press, 1991), 85.

45. David Wyman, *The Abandonment of the Jews: America and the Holocaust, 1941–1945* (New York: Pantheon Books, 1984), 12.

46. Mary Schonberg to Henrietta Roelofs, June 16, 1933, and Henrietta Roelofs to Mary Schonberg, May 14, 1934, Public Advocacy Subject Files: Refugees, RG 6, YWCA-SSC.

47. Wyman, *The Abandonment of the Jews*, 12; Henrietta Roelofs to Mabel Ellis, March 28, 1938, and "Protest Committee of Non-Jewish Women against the Persecution of the Jews in Germany," circa 1933, Public Advocacy Subject Files: Refugees, RG 6, YWCA-SSC.

48. Susan Lynn underestimates the toll of the Red Scare on the YWCA, but she emphasizes how "religious ideals never lost their capacity to . . . inspire commitment to social change" at a time of an overall secularization of social reform (*Progressive Women in Conservative Times: Racial Justice, Peace, and Feminism, 1945 to the 1960s* [New Brunswick, NJ: Rutgers University Press, 1992], 10).

49. Meyer, *Protestant Search for Political Realism*. Richard Wightman Fox narrates the theological and political journey of Christian realism's most prominent representative in *Reinhold Niebuhr: A Biography* (Ithaca, NY: Cornell University Press, 1996).

50. Fox, *Reinhold Niebuhr*, 168. In 1940, the FSC was renamed the Frontier Fellowship, and *Radical Religion* became *Christianity and Society*. The organization disbanded in 1956.

51. Wygal, *The Good Life*, 23.

52. Winnifred Wygal, *The Superb Adventure: Acquiring a Theory of Living* (New York: Womans Press, 1934), foreword, 20.

53. Winnifred Wygal, "Religion in the Standards Study," *Womans Press*, October 1938, 435 and 450.

54. Winnifred Wygal, "What's the Use?," *Womans Press*, November 1939, 479.

55. Ibid.

56. Winnifred Wygal, "The Nature of Religion," 1936, 27, Religion Publications, RG 6, YWCA-SSC.

57. Winnifred Wygal, *Our Religious Vocabulary: A Glossary of Terms in Current Use* (New York: Womans Press, 1939), 7 and 19.

58. Rose Terlin, "Faith for Reconstruction," 1941, 6, Religion Publications, RG 6, YWCA-SSC, and *Christian Faith and Social Action*, 34–35.

59. Terlin, "Faith for Reconstruction," 11.

60. Rose Terlin, "Christian Basis of Our Public Affairs Work," *Public Affairs News Service*, March 11, 1940, Public Advocacy Publications, RG 6, YWCA-SSC.

61. Terlin, *Christian Faith and Social Action*, 19; Rose Terlin, "No Man unto Himself: Services of Worship on Interdependence," 1940, 11–13, Religion Publications, RG 6, YWCA-SSC.

62. Elizabeth Dilling, *Red Network: A "Who's Who" and Handbook of Radicalism for Patriots* (Kenilworth, IL: privately printed, 1935), 101; Glen Jeansonne, *Women of the Far Right: The Mothers' Movement and World War II* (Chicago: University of Chicago Press, 1996), 10.

63. Dilling, *Red Network*, dedication, 250–52.

64. Mrs. Frederic [Theresa] Paist, "Letter to Presidents of Local Associations," December 27, 1934, Public Advocacy: Controversy, Public Affairs Issues, RG 6, YWCA-SSC.

65. Robert Cohen, *When the Old Left Was Young: Student Radicals and America's First Mass Student Movement, 1929–1941* (New York: Oxford University Press, 1993), 226.

66. Printed Convention Actions Report, 1936, 22, RG 4, YWCA-SSC; "Public Affairs Chronology by Subject," 1938?

67. "Cabinet Meeting, 1967," radio play, 1937, and "American Youth Congress" brochure, 1937, in Outside Organizations: American Youth Congress, microfilm reel 123, YWCA-SSC.

68. George Rawick, "The New Deal and Youth: The Civilian Conservation Corps, the National Youth Administration, and the American Youth Congress" (PhD diss., University of Wisconsin, 1957), 319 and 323.

69. "Roosevelt Names Used by Red Chiefs, Says Dies Witness," *New York Times*, October 10, 1939.

70. "Two YWCA Groups Back Youth Congress," *New York Times*, April 15, 1940; "Summary of Principles Suggested in Discussion of Place of Communists in Our Organization," 1940, Outside Organizations: American Youth Congress, microfilm reel 123, YWCA-SSC. See also Cohen, *When the Old Left Was Young*, 298–304.

71. Ann Herlihy to Mrs. Bishop, July 1941, Outside Organizations: American Youth Congress, microfilm reel 123, YWCA-SSC.

72. Elsie Harper to Grace L. Elliot, February 9, 1948, Controversy: Communism, RG 3, YWCA-SSC.

73. George Dondero, "Americans, Take Notice—School of Political Action Techniques," June 11, 1946, Controversy: Communism, RG 3, YWCA-SSC. This file also contains clippings regarding the conservative press, including *Counterattack*, and Community Chest problems. See also "Correspondence Regarding Relations with Community Chests and Councils," 1947–48, Public Advocacy Controversy, RG 6, YWCA-SSC.

74. US House Committee on Un-American Activities, *100 Things You Should Know about Communism and Religion*, (Washington: Government Printing Office, 1949), 13.

75. Joseph Kamp, *Behind the Lace Curtains of the YWCA* (New York: Constitutional Educational League, 1948), 23, 37, and 64, Controversy: Communism, RG 3, YWCA-SSC. Kamp was the uncle of the actor Jon Voigt, now a pundit for the far right, and great-uncle of the

actress Angelina Jolie, who has pursued liberal channels of internationalist humanitarianism ("Behind the Lace Curtains of the YWCA," Conelrad Read Alert, accessed October 11, 2016, http://conelrad.com/books/spine.php?id=368_0_1_0_C). Several of the YWCA's accusers represented the far reaches of reactionary politics. Kamp and HUAC supplied each other with information, though Kamp was under investigation for more than a decade for possible connections to the German-American Bund. He was acquitted of contempt of Congress charges levied when he refused to turn over the financial records of the Constitutional Educational League. See Kenneth O'Reilly, *Hoover and the Un-Americans: The FBI, HUAC, and the Red Menace* (Philadelphia, PA: Temple University Press, 1983), 40; Joseph Paull, "Kamp Freed in Contempt Case," *Washington Post*, February 7, 1952. Elizabeth Dilling was indicted for fascist sedition during World War II, but the prosecution failed to secure a conviction. See Jeansonne, *Women of the Far Right*, 155–64. Kenneth Goff, the Dies Committee witness who named Rose Terlin as a party member, shifted from professional anticommunism to the anti-Semitic, survivalist Christian underground. See Jeffrey Kaplan, *Encyclopedia of White Power: A Sourcebook on the Radical Racist Right* (Walnut Creek, CA: AltaMira, 2000), 120–22.

76. Kamp, *Behind the Lace Curtains*, 12–13, 20–21, 28, and 44. In the 1932 poem, Hughes directs Jesus to step aside for men with no religion—Marx, Lenin, and Stalin—declaring that capitalistic Christianity stood in the way of justice. The poem generated considerable controversy on its publication, and Hughes later repudiated these Popular Front sentiments before HUAC. See Wallace Best, "Concerning 'Goodbye Christ': Langston Hughes, Political Poetry, and African American Religion," *Religion and Politics*, November 26, 2013, http://religionandpolitics.org/2013/11/26/concerning-goodbye-christ-langston-hughes-political-poetry-and-african-american-religion. Dilling first called attention to the YWCA's use of the poem (*Should Christians Support the Y's?*).

77. Kamp, *Behind the Lace Curtains*, 35; Edward Krehbiel, "The Attack on the Los Angeles YWCA," *Survey*, August 16, 1920, 612.

78. Kamp, *Behind the Lace Curtains*, 10 and afterword.

79. Jean Logan Buxton, "The Test of an Association," *Association Monthly*, April 1907, 101.

80. Dorothy Nossett to Mrs. [Constance] Forrest Anderson, February 19, 1951, Controversy: Schlafly, RG 3, YWCA-SSC. *Sweetheart of the Silent Majority* is the title of Carol Felsenthal's 1981 biography of Schlafly.

81. Nossett to Mrs. [Constance] Forrest Anderson, February 19, 1951.

82. Phyllis Schlafly, remarks, Printed Convention Proceedings, 1952, 112 and 159–60, RG 4, YWCA-SSC.

83. Phyllis Schlafly, "What's Happened to the C in YWCA?," 1953, Controversy: Schlafly, RG 3, YWCA-SSC.

84. Phyllis Schlafly, telephone interview by the author, April 1, 2014; Donald Critchlow, *Phyllis Schlafly and Grassroots Conservatism: A Woman's Crusade* (Princeton, NJ: Princeton University Press, 2005), 71–72.

85. SAC, New York, to Director, FBI, memorandum, December 3, 1954, Federal Bureau of Investigation Freedom of Information and Privacy Act request file number 1090772–000, Rose Terlin.

86. SAC, New York, to SAC, Albany, telegram, January 9, 1964, in ibid.

87. Landon R. Y. Storrs, "Red Scare Politics and the Suppression of Popular Front Feminism," *Journal of American History* 90, no. 2 (2003): 494.

88. Public Affairs Committee, minutes, October 20, 1948, Public Advocacy, RG 6, YWCA-SSC.

89. Kenyon and resolution quoted in Helen Laville, *Cold War Women: The International Activities of American Women's Organisations* (Manchester, UK: Manchester University Press, 2002), 111.

90. Critchlow, *Phyllis Schlafly and Grassroots Conservatism*, 217.

91. David Hollinger, *After Cloven Tongues of Fire: Protestant Liberalism in Modern American History* (Princeton, NJ: Princeton University Press, 2013), xii.

CHAPTER 5   A "FIFTH COLUMN FOR GOD": THE MARYKNOLL SISTERS AT MIDCENTURY

1. Maryknoll's numbers include professed and nonprofessed sisters. Office statistics files and "Statistics of the Maryknoll Sisters of St. Dominic," 1942–56, Mission Works: Statistics and Lists, MSA. For general growth in religious vocations, see Patricia Byrne, "In the Parish but Not of It: Sisters," in *Transforming Parish Ministry: The Changing Roles of Catholic Clergy, Laity, and Women Religious*, ed. Jay Dolan, R. Scott Appleby, Patricia Byrne, and Debra Campbell (New York: Crossroad, 1989), 135.

2. Henry Luce, "The American Century," *Life*, February 7, 1941, 65.

3. "Maryknoll Sisters," Lent 1952, Direct Mail, MSA.

4. Jean-Paul Wiest, *Maryknoll in China: A History, 1918–1955* (Armonk, NY: M. E. Sharpe, 1998), 318–408.

5. Richard Cushing, preface to Sister Mary de Paul Cogan, *Sisters of Maryknoll through Troubled Waters* (New York: Charles Scribner's Sons, 1947), v–vi. See also Penny Lernoux, *Hearts on Fire: The Story of the Maryknoll Sisters* (Maryknoll, NY: Orbis, 1993), 78–120.

6. Quoted in Albert Nevins, *The Meaning of Maryknoll* (New York: McMullen Books, 1954), 24–25.

7. Quoted in "Work of Missions Praised as War Aid," *New York Times*, October 19, 1942. The story of the repatriation is recounted in Lernoux, *Hearts on Fire*, 94–95.

8. Quoted in Josephine Loftus, "The Rosary Wins in Manila," *Maryknoll*, July–August 1945, 9. *The Field Afar* changed its name to *Maryknoll* in 1942.

9. "Afield with the Maryknoll Sisters," *Maryknoll*, January 1949, 41–42.

10. Diary, Convent and Home, Los Angeles, California, December 6 [*sic*], 1941, and March 30 and June 6, 1942, MSA.

11. Ibid., May 17, 1942; "Maryknoll Sisters," September 1944, Direct Mail, MSA.

12. Quoted in Angelyn Dries, *The Missionary Movement in American Catholic History* (Maryknoll, NY: Orbis Books, 1998), 180.

13. Josephine Loftus, "Departure Eve," *Maryknoll*, September 1945, 32; "Constitution of the Foreign Mission Sisters of St. Dominic," 1931, chap. 1, no. 2, MSA.

14. "Maryknoll Sisters," Spring 1947, Direct Mail, MSA.

15. Kathleen Sprows Cummings, *New Women of the Old Faith: Gender and American Catholicism in the Progressive Era* (Chapel Hill: University of North Carolina Press, 2009), 195. Susan Fitzpatrick-Behrens surveys demographic characteristics and examines Maryknoll's negotiation of the cult of domesticity in "From Symbols of the Sacred to Symbols of Subversion to Simply Obscure: Maryknoll Women Religious in Guatemala, 1953–1967," *Americas* 61, no. 2 (2004): 193–96. The Maryknoll Sisters operated the accredited three-year Maryknoll Teachers College at the New York motherhouse from 1934 to 1963. Superiors selected which novices received advanced training. Renamed Mary Rogers College in 1963, the school awarded bachelor's degrees to sisters and a general student population until its closure in 1973 (Rogers College finding aid, MSA).

16. Rebecca Sullivan, *Visual Habits: Nuns and American Postwar Popular Culture* (Toronto: University of Toronto Press, 2005), 24.

17. Byrne, "In the Parish but Not of It," 133.

18. Quoted in Helen Haig, "Through Mud to Stars," *Maryknoll*, January 1945, 38. For more on the People-to-People program, see Kenneth Osgood, *Total Cold War: Eisenhower's Secret Propaganda Battle at Home and Abroad* (Lawrence: University Press of Kansas, 2006), 232–44.

19. "Afield with the Maryknoll Sisters," *Maryknoll*, September 1949, 42.

20. "Who Are Maryknoll Sisters?," 1955, Direct Mail, MSA.

21. Cindy Yik-Yi Chu, *Maryknoll Sisters in Hong Kong, 1921–1969: In Love with the Chinese* (New York: Palgrave Macmillan, 2004), 9–10. Danforth used the pseudonym Sister Mary Victoria for *Nun in Red China* (New York: McGraw-Hill, 1953).

22. Scott Allen Nollen, *Three Bad Men: John Ford, John Wayne, Ward Bond* (Jefferson, NC: McFarland, 2013), 268. See also Ron Burton, "Jane Wyman Gets Help of Nun in Portraying Role," *Wilmington Morning-Star*, December 5, 1955.

23. "*Labore Est Orare*," *Time*, April 11, 1955, 76–81.

24. "Bernie Becomes a Nun," *Cosmopolitan*, December 1954, 119–27; "Last Word," *Cosmopolitan*, February 1955, 138.

25. Bernadette Lynch, interview by the author, July 20, 2006, Maryknoll, NY.

26. Ibid. See Sister Maria del Rey, *Bernie Becomes a Nun* (New York: Farrar, Straus, and Cudahy, 1956).

27. Diary, Nyegina, Tanganyika, November 19, 1957, MSA; "The Bush People," *Maryknoll*, January 1956, 16.

28. "Who Supports the Maryknoll Sisters?," *Maryknoll*, May 1956, 44.

29. John Considine, "The Last of the Founders," 1956?, Direct Mail, MSA.

30. Pope Pius XII, *Mystici Corporis Christi*, 1943, accessed March 28, 2017, http://w2.vatican.va/content/pius-xii/en/encyclicals/documents/hf_p-xii_enc_29061943_mystici-corporis-christi.html.

31. Monika Hellwig, "Mystical Body of Christ," in *The Modern Catholic Encyclopedia*, rev. ed., ed. Michael Glazier and Monika Hellwig (Collegeville, MN: Liturgical Press, 2004), 573.

32. Pope Pius XII, *Mystici Corporis Christi*. For more radical interpretations, see James Terence Fisher, *The Catholic Counterculture in America, 1933–1962* (Chapel Hill: University of North Carolina Press, 1989), 59–60.

33. Albert Nevins, "The Radical Popes," *Maryknoll*, July 1956, 31.

34. "Constitutions of the Foreign Mission Sisters of St. Dominic," 1952, pt. 1, chap. 1, MSA.

35. Bernadette and Robert Hoyt, "Hospital for the Sick," reprint from *Interracial Review*, September 1957, Direct Mail, MSA; Howard Rusk, "Racial Barrier Goes Down," *New York Times*, April 1, 1956.

36. "Maryknoll Sisters," Lent 1952; "Letters to the Editor," *Maryknoll*, January 1959, 62.

37. Amy Koehlinger, *The New Nuns: Racial Justice and Religious Reform in the 1960s* (Cambridge, MA: Harvard University Press, 2007), 3.

38. Peter D. Kramer, "Maryknoll Sister Recalls 'Bloody Sunday' in Selma," *Journal News*, March 9, 2015, http://www.lohud.com/story/news/local/2015/01/16/selma-Maryknoll-nun/21871169. Lernoux describes Maryknoll's presence in Selma and Kansas City in *Hearts on Fire*, 171 and 189–91.

39. Diary, St. Anthony of Padua, Bronx, New York, August 1944, MSA; "Maryknoll Sisters," Lent 1952.

40. "Constitution of the Foreign Mission Sisters of St. Dominic," 1931, chap. 22, no. 329.

41. Barbara Mann Wall describes the medical dimensions of Maryknoll's work in Tanzania in *Into Africa: A Transnational History of Catholic Medical Missions and Social Change* (New Brunswick, NJ: Rutgers University Press, 2015), especially 63–91.

42. Diary, Kowak, Tanganyika, January 13, 1949, MSA; "The Bush People," 15.

43. "Africa's Nonconformists," *Maryknoll*, April 1962, 47 and 50.

44. "Forever Africa," *Maryknoll*, March 1949.

45. "Two Thirds of Mankind," *Maryknoll*, January 1959, 56; Diary summaries, Kowak, Tanganyika, October 1960–June 1962; John Considine, "More Change to Come," *Maryknoll*, May 1971, 31.

46. Diary, Kowak, Tanganyika, February 8, 1949.

47. Ibid., September 29 and October 11, 1949.

48. "Afield with the Maryknoll Sisters," *Maryknoll*, April 1949; "A Decade in Kowak History," 1958, 9, Africa History, MSA.

49. Bishop Danehy, speech, 1942, Bolivia History, MSA.

50. Diary, San Jose Mission, Riberalta, Bolivia, July 3, 1944, and December 8, 1943, MSA.

51. Advertisements, *Maryknoll*, January 1959, 43 and 55.

52. Peter Sanchez, *Panama Lost? U.S. Hegemony, Democracy, and the Canal* (Gainesville: University Press of Florida, 2007), 67–68.

53. Diary, Ancón, Panama Canal Zone, November 11 and 19, 1943, MSA.

54. Loretta Kruegler to Mom and Dad, October 11, 1953, Sister Loretta Kruegler Letters, Creative Works and Personal Papers, MSA.

55. Ibid.; Loretta Kruegler, interview by the author, July 20, 2006, Maryknoll, NY.

56. "Maryknoll Sisters," May–June 1946, Direct Mail, MSA.

57. Pope Pius XI, *Divini Redemptoris*, accessed March 28, 2017, https://w2.vatican.va/content/pius-xi/en/encyclicals/documents/hf_p-xi_enc_19370319_divini-redemptoris.html. For postwar Vatican anticommunism, see Frank Coppa, "Pope Pius XII and the Cold War: The Post-War Confrontation between Catholicism and Communism," in *Religion and the Cold War*, ed. Dianne Kirby (New York: Palgrave Macmillan, 2003), 50–66; Peter Kent, "The Lonely Cold War of Pope Pius XII," in ibid., 67–76.

58. Patrick McNamara, *A Catholic Cold War: Edmund A. Walsh, S.J., and the Politics of American Anticommunism* (New York: Fordham University Press, 2015), 146; Spellman quoted in Mother Mary Columba to Sisters, October 20, 1955, Correspondence, Mother Mary Columba Tarpey, MSA.

59. Diary, St. Anthony's Convent, Maui, Hawaii, April 11, 1951, MSA.

60. James Terence Fisher, *Dr. America: The Lives of Thomas A. Dooley, 1927–1961* (Amherst: University of Massachusetts Press, 1997), 93–114.

61. Chu, *Maryknoll Sisters in Hong Kong*, 67–81.

62. Suzanne Thurman, "The Medical Mission Strategy of the Maryknoll Sisters," *Missiology* 30, no. 3 (2002): 361. For more on Hirschboeck, see Lernoux, *Hearts on Fire*, 177–94, and Sister Maria del Rey's hagiographic *Her Name Is Mercy* (New York: Scribner, 1957).

63. Advertisement, *Maryknoll*, September 1956, 11; "Maryknoll Sisters," September 1951, Direct Mail, MSA.

64. Quoted in "Spinning Their Way to Success," *Maryknoll*, March 1956, 26.

65. Lernoux, *Hearts on Fire*, 199–200.

66. Joseph Hahn, "The Quiet Revolution," *Maryknoll*, November 1963, 7.

67. Diary, Cobija, Bolivia, August 1952, MSA; Diary, Guayaramerín, Bolivia, February 1953, MSA.

68. Diary, Guayaramerín, Bolivia, April 1960.

69. Ibid., Report for October 1958–April 30, 1959 and April 1960.

70. "Colegio Monte María, Guatemala City, Central America," 1958, 1, Guatemala History, MSA. Fitzpatrick-Behrens recounts the sisters' Guatemala experience at length in "From Symbols of the Sacred."

71. Diary, Monte María, Guatemala City, Guatemala, December 3, 1953, and June 4, 1954, MSA; Sister Mary Martina to Mother Mary Columba, June 18, 1954, in Guatemala History, MSA.

72. Sister Mary Martina to Mother Mary Columba, June 18, 1954.

73. "Colegio Monte María, Guatemala City, Central America," 1958, 1; Diary, Monte María, Guatemala City, November 1960–November 1961.

74. Diary, Monte María, Guatemala City, May 12, 1954; Sister Mary Martina to Mother Mary Columba, June 18, 1954. For a detailed timeline of CIA activities, see Stephen Schlesinger and Stephen Kinzer, *Bitter Fruit: The Untold Story of the American Coup in Guatemala* (Garden City, NY: Doubleday, 1982), 165–204.

75. Diary, Monte María, Guatemala City, December 3, 1953. On the many indictments of US policy and business practices in Central America, see Greg Grandin, *The Last Colonial Massacre: Latin America in the Cold War* (Chicago: University of Chicago Press, 2004); Walter LaFeber, *Inevitable Revolutions: The United States in Central America*, 2nd ed. (New York: W.W. Norton, 1993).

76. Diary, Monte María, Guatemala City, July 18 and August 13, 1954, and July 29, 1957.

77. Harris Lentz, *Assassinations and Executions: An Encyclopedia of Political Violence, 1900 through 2000* (Jefferson, NC: McFarland, 2002), 161–62.

78. Diary, Ancón, Panama Canal Zone, February 24, 1955.

79. Ibid., January 1–December 31, 1961, and June 18, 1958.

80. Ibid., Annual Report for the Year Ending December 31, 1959. The symbolic importance of competing flags proved enduring, inspiring three days of riots in 1964 that eventually led to a short-term break in diplomatic relations between the two nations. Sanchez, *Panama Lost?*, 132–33.

PART III   "THE FERMENT OF FREEDOM"

1. See, in particular, Sara Evans, ed., *Journeys that Opened Up the World: Women, Student Christian Movements, and Social Justice, 1955–1975* (New Brunswick, NJ: Rutgers University Press, 2003); Abigail Lewis, "'The Barrier-Breaking Love of God': The Multiracial Activism of the Young Women's Christian Association, 1940s to 1970s" (PhD diss., Rutgers University, 2008); Susan Lynn, *Progressive Women in Conservative Times: Racial Justice, Peace, and Feminism, 1945 to the 1960s* (New Brunswick, NJ: Rutgers University Press, 1992).

2. Dorothy Height, remarks, Tribute Dinner, November 5, 1986, Dorothy Height Papers, Sophia Smith Collection, Smith College, Northampton, MA.

3. Iris Berger, "An African-American 'Mother of the Nation': Madie Hall Xuma in South Africa, 1940–1963," *Journal of South African Studies* 27, no. 3 (2001): 564. See also Carole Seymour-Jones, *Journey of Faith: The History of the World YWCA, 1945–1994* (London: Allison and Busby, 1994), 158–75.

4. Helene O'Sullivan, telephone interview by the author, February 12, 2014.

5. "Searching and Sharing: Mission Perspectives," 1970, 6, MSA.

6. Nancy Marie Robertson, *Christian Sisterhood, Race Relations, and the YWCA, 1906–46* (Urbana: University of Illinois Press, 2007), 101–3; Jodi Vandenberg-Daves, "The Manly Pursuit of a Partnership between the Sexes: The Debate over YMCA Programs for Women and Girls," *Journal of American History* 78, no. 4 (1992): 1324–46.

7. Letty Russell, *Ferment of Freedom*, 1972, 13, 16–17, and 12, Religion Publications, RG 6, YWCA-SSC.

8. Quoted in Sara Evans, introduction to *Journeys that Opened Up the World*, 8.

9. Helen Laville, "A New Era in International Women's Rights? American Women's Associations and the Establishment of the UN Commission on the Status of Women," *Journal of Women's History* 20, no. 4 (2008): 53n3, and *Cold War Women: The International Activities of American Women's Organisations* (Manchester, UK: Manchester University Press, 2002), 59.

10. Vijay Prashad, *The Darker Nations: A People's History of the Third World* (New York: New Press, 2007), 112–13.

11. Office of Social Concerns to Sisters, October 1981, Office of Social Concerns: Correspondence and Reports, MSA; Kenneth Cmiel, "The Emergence of Human Rights Politics in the United States," *Journal of American History* 86, no. 3 (1999): 1235–36.

CHAPTER 6   "WE CHOOSE TO IDENTIFY WITH THE CHURCH OF THE POOR": PREFERENTIAL OPTION IN ACTION

1. Diary, St. Anthony's, Maui, Hawaii, August 1960–July 1961, MSA.

2. James Terence Fisher, *Dr. America: The Lives of Thomas A. Dooley, 1927–1961* (Amherst: University of Massachusetts Press, 1997), 93–114. Such partnerships had deeper roots in Catholic relief after World War II. See Susan Fitzpatrick-Behrens, *The Maryknoll Catholic Mission in Peru, 1943–1989: Transnational Faith and Transformation* (Notre Dame, IN: University of Notre Dame Press, 2012), 108–11.

3. Advertisement, *Maryknoll*, November 1961, 65; Office statistics files, MSA.

4. Advertisement, *Maryknoll*, November 1961, 65.

5. Helen Rose Ebaugh, "Vatican II and the Revitalization Movement," in *Religion and the Social Order: Vatican II and U.S. Catholicism*, ed. Helen Rose Ebaugh (Greenwich, CT: JAI Press, 1991), 3.

6. Helene O'Sullivan, telephone interview by the author, February 12, 2014; quoted in Penny Lernoux, *Hearts on Fire: The Story of the Maryknoll Sisters* (Maryknoll, NY: Orbis, 1993), 176.

7. Pope Paul VI, *Gaudium et Spes*, 1965, accessed March 30, 2017, http://www.vatican.va/archive/hist_councils/ii_vatican_council/documents/vat-ii_const_19651207_gaudium-et-spes_en.html; Pope John XXIII, *Pacem in Terris*, 1963, accessed March 30, 2017, http://w2.vatican.va/content/john-xxiii/en/encyclicals/documents/hf_j-xxiii_enc_11041963_pacem.html.

8. Margaret Mary Reher, *Catholic Intellectual Life in America: A Historical Study of Persons and Movements* (New York: Macmillan, 1989), 135. For an evaluation of the general themes of the conciliar documents, see Gregory Baum and Jean-Guy Vaillancourt, "The Church and Modernization," in Ebaugh, *Religion and the Social Order*, 26–33.

9. O'Sullivan, interview.

10. Angelyn Dries, *The Missionary Movement in American Catholic History* (Maryknoll, NY: Orbis Books, 1998), 268.

11. "Interview with Sister Betty Ann Maheu," February 1988, 2, Vocation Problems, Penny Lernoux Book Collection, MSA. For inculturation in Latin America, see Fitzpatrick-Behrens, *Maryknoll Catholic Mission in Peru*, 149–50.

12. Patricia Cain, "Biography and Marsabit, Kenya," 1983–86, Mission Stories, Creative Works and Personal Papers, MSA.

13. Darlene Jacobs, interview by the author, July 19, 2006, Maryknoll, NY.

14. Amy Koehlinger, *The New Nuns: Racial Justice and Religious Reform in the 1960s* (Cambridge, MA: Harvard University Press, 2007), 3.

15. "Sister Margaret Francis on Summer Work Done in the Bronx," 1965, Administrative Papers: St. Anthony of Padua Parish, New York City, Eastern USA History, MSA.

16. Christiana Croake, "Revolution in Character and Community Development," 1968, Administrative Papers: New York City Addiction Services, Eastern USA History, MSA.

17. Pope Paul XI, *Perfectae Caritatis*, 1965, accessed March 30, 2017, http://www.vatican.va/archive/hist_councils/ii_vatican_council/documents/vat-ii_decree_19651028_perfectae-caritatis_en.html.

18. O'Sullivan, interview.

19. There are variations in the statistics owing to differing sources and data labeling. These numbers are taken from "Statistics of the Maryknoll Sisters of St. Dominic," 1942–56, and "Personnel, 1932–1994," both in Statistics and Lists, Mission Works History, MSA.

20. Amy Koehlinger, "Academia and 'Aggiornamento': The Social Sciences and Postconciliar Reform among American Sisters," *U.S. Catholic Historian* 25, no. 4 (2007): 63–64; Mary Schneider, "American Sisters and the Roots of Change: The 1950s," *U.S. Catholic Historian* 7, no. 1 (1988): 58–64.

21. Lernoux, *Hearts on Fire*, 144; Patricia Cain, biographical information, 1986, Creative Works and Personal Papers, MSA.

22. Mary Josephine Rogers, "Our Vows," 1929, in "Discourses," 2:783; Lernoux, *Hearts on Fire*, 176.

23. Koehlinger, "Academia and 'Aggiornamento,'" 81–82.

24. "Constitutions of the Maryknoll Sisters of Saint Dominic," 1965, MSA.

25. Pope Paul XI, *Perfectae Caritatis*.

26. Quoted in Lernoux, *Hearts on Fire*, 171; "Constitutions of the Maryknoll Sisters of Saint Dominic," 1965, chap. 1, no. 2.

27. Motherhouse Habit Committee, "Ultimate Goals of Motherhouse Clothing Experimentation and Background Psychology," October 20, 1967, Clothes (Habit) Experimentation, Motherhouse Center Governance and Lifestyle, MSA.

28. Ibid.

29. Jacobs, interview. See also Koehlinger, "Academia and 'Aggiornamento,'" 64–67.

30. Quoted in Helen Rose Fuchs Ebaugh, *Becoming an Ex: The Process of Role Exit* (Chicago: University of Chicago Press, 1988), 116.

31. Thomas Melville and Marjorie Melville, *Whose Heaven, Whose Earth?* (New York: Knopf, 1971), 178–79.

32. "Constitutions of the Maryknoll Sisters of Saint Dominic," 1965, chap. 13, no. 12; Sister Mary Naab, policy sheet, January 13, 1968, Motherhouse Center Governance and Lifestyle, MSA. The traditional prohibition on "particular friendships" in women's religious institutions, which Maryknoll eliminated in these years, had tacitly raised the question of homosexual attachments. In the 1980s, the best-selling *Lesbian Nuns: Breaking Silence* (Tallahassee, FL: Naiad Press, 1985), edited by Rosemary Curb and Nancy Manahan, a former Maryknoll sister, brought greater attention to same-sex intimacy among women religious.

33. "Talk to the Motherhouse Community by Sister Mary Naab," January 4, 1968, Motherhouse Center Governance and Lifestyle, MSA.

34. Ibid.

35. Virginia Flagg, interview by the author, July 21, 2006, Maryknoll, NY.

36. Jacobs, interview; Office statistics files, MSA.

37. Second General Conference of Latin American Bishops, "The Church in the Present-Day Transformation of Latin America in Light of the Council," in *Liberation Theology: A Documentary History*, ed. Alfred Hennelly (Maryknoll, NY: Orbis Books, 1990), 116.

38. Saint Rose of Lima mission history, 1958, 5–6, Peru History, MSA; quoted in Dana Robert, *American Women in Mission: A Social History of Their Thought and Practice* (Macon, GA: Mercer University Press, 1996), 386–87.

39. "Santa Rosa de Lima Convent," 1963, 11, Peru History, MSA. Maryknoll's Lima projects are discussed in Fitzpatrick-Behrens, *Maryknoll Catholic Mission in Peru*, 195–201; Robert, *American Women in Mission*, 382–98. For Jocists more generally, see Mary Irene Zotti, *A Time of Awakening: The Young Christian Worker Story in the United States, 1938–1970* (Chicago: Loyola University Press, 1991).

40. Fitzpatrick-Behrens, *Maryknoll Catholic Mission in Peru*, 134–37.

41. "Santa Rosa de Lima Convent," 1963, 11.

42. Diary, Monte María, Guatemala City, Guatemala, November 1961–November 1962, MSA. Fitzpatrick-Behrens examines the long-term impact of these efforts, asserting that Monte María graduates "have been at the forefront of struggles to transform Guatemalan society," in "Knowledge Is Not Enough: Creating a Culture of Social Justice, Dignity, and Human Rights in Guatemala: Maryknoll Sisters and the Monte María 'Girls,'" *U.S. Catholic Historian* 24, no. 3 (2006): 112.

43. "Searching and Sharing: Mission Perspectives," 1970, 6–7, MSA.

44. Special Chapter of Affairs, "Nature, Role, and Function of the Maryknoll Sisters," in *Missions Challenge Maryknoll Sisters: Background Papers and Enactments*, 1968–69, 3 and 8, MSA.

45. Ibid., 6.

46. Quoted in Lernoux, *Hearts on Fire*, 149.

47. "Interview with Sister Betty Ann Maheu," February 1988, 2, Vocation Problems, Penny Lernoux Book Collection, MSA.

48. Lernoux, *Hearts on Fire*, 164. Fitzpatrick-Behrens documents the interplay between the Maryknoll Sisters' postconciliar health delivery efforts and indigenous healing practices among Maya Guatemalans in "Maryknoll Sisters, Faith, Healing, and the Maya Construction of Catholic Communities in Guatemala," *Latin American Research Review* 44, no. 3 (2009): 27–49.

49. Quoted in Alfred Hennelly, introduction to *Liberation Theology*, xviii.

50. Sharon Erickson Nepstad, *Convictions of the Soul: Religion, Culture, and Agency in the Central America Solidarity Movement* (New York: Oxford University Press, 2004), 60–63.

51. Quoted in Lernoux, *Hearts on Fire*, 251; Patricia Cain, biographical information, 1986. For the impact of liberation theology on sisters in Tanzania, see Barbara Mann Wall, *Into Africa: A Transnational History of Catholic Medical Missions and Social Change* (New Brunswick, NJ: Rutgers University Press, 2015), 84–91.

52. "Missionary Prayer Presence in the Lower East Side of Manhattan," 1974, and Mercy Hirschboeck, "Cloister in the City," 1974, 10, in Mission Presence: St. Bridget's, New York City, Eastern USA History, MSA.

53. Quoted in Lernoux, *Hearts on Fire*, 193.

54. Susan Fitzpatrick-Behrens, "From Symbols of the Sacred to Symbols of Subversion to Simply Obscure: Maryknoll Women Religious in Guatemala, 1953–1967," *Americas* 61, no. 2 (2004): 205–16. Marjorie Melville, née Bradford, was known by her religious name, Marian Peter, in Guatemala. More recently, she has used the name Margarita Melville.

55. Melville and Melville, *Whose Heaven, Whose Earth?*, 257 and 261.

56. John Leo, "Nun Said to Lead Guatemala Plot," *New York Times*, January 22, 1968; Fitzpatrick-Behrens, "From Symbols of the Sacred," 212. Marian Mollin addresses such marginalization in "Communities of Resistance: Women and the Catholic Left of the Late 1960s," *Oral History Review* 31, no. 2 (2004): 29–51.

57. Quoted in Henry Giniger, "Maryknoll Fears Guatemala Mood," *New York Times*, January 21, 1968.

58. Quoted in Melville and Melville, *Whose Heaven, Whose Earth?*, 284; Fitzpatrick-Behrens, "From Symbols of the Sacred," 214.

59. Fitzpatrick-Behrens, "From Symbols of the Sacred," 213; "Filming Set on Two Draft Protesters," *Washington Post*, December 4, 1971; Shawn Francis Peter, *The Catonsville Nine: A Story of Faith and Resistance in the Vietnam Era* (New York: Oxford University Press, 2012), 320–321.

60. Quoted in Elizabeth Mulligan, "Sister Cecilia—Rebel Nun," *St. Louis Post-Dispatch*, August 17, 1969.

61. Clarence Lang, "Between Civil Rights and Black Power in the Gateway City: The Action Committee to Improve Opportunities for Negroes (ACTION), 1964–75," *Journal of Social History* 37, no. 3 (2004): 740; quoted in "Nun Arrested in Disturbance Here," *St. Louis Post-Dispatch*, December 5, 1968.

62. Quoted in Robert Adams, "Churches Here Caught up in Reparations Drive," *St. Louis Post-Dispatch*, June 9, 1969. See also "Sister Cecilia Says She Has Not Quit ACTION," *St. Louis American*, January 9, 1969; Robert Lecky and H. Elliott Wright, eds., *Black Manifesto: Religion, Racism, and Reparations* (New York: Sheed and Ward, 1969).

63. Quoted in "Blacks Disrupt Church Services," *St. Louis Post-Dispatch*, June 9, 1969. For more details about the St. Louis version of the Black Manifesto, which was revised to reflect local conditions, see Percy Green, "Statement, Black Sundays—Phase I," [1969], Eda Houwink Papers, Series II: Personal Correspondence (1964–70), Missouri Historical Society Archives, St. Louis, MO. For the Catholic Church's particular hostility toward the manifesto, see Robert Lecky and H. Elliott Wright, introduction to *Black Manifesto*, 18–21.

64. Louis Garinger, "Target: Roman Catholic Church," *Christian Science Monitor*, June 25, 1969; "'Black Law' Enjoins Black Invasion of St. Louis Cathedral," *Chicago Daily Defender*, September 8, 1969. Other parishes and Protestant churches continued to receive Black Sunday visits, which were conducted more peaceably. See "Hostility Ceases at Area Churches as Black Militants Are Welcomed," *St. Louis American*, July 17, 1969.

65. Quoted in Harry Cargas, "'There Will Be a New Form of Christianity,'" *FOCUS/Midwest* 8, no. 52 (1970): 12. Goldman and Walter Matheus, cochairs of ACTION's Religion Committee, filed a complaint with the Federal Communications Commission over biased television coverage. See "Pastard Says Whites, not Blacks, Initiated Pattern of Violence," *St. Louis American*, June 26, 1969.

66. "Maryknoll Nun, Civil Rights Activist, Ousted by Governing Board," *Washington Post*, June 17, 1969; quoted in Cargas, "'There Will Be a New Form of Christianity,'" 14.

67. Quoted in "Nun Renounces Poverty Vows as Hypocritical," *Hartford Courant*, January 24, 1970; "Names and Faces," *Arizona Republic*, March 20, 1970. Fitzpatrick-Behrens recounts how many Maryknollers embarking on mission to Peru found a similar incongruity in the church's pledge to poverty and the comfortable circumstances in which religious lived (*Maryknoll Catholic Mission in Peru*, 185–86).

68. Quoted in Terri Shaw, "Nun Turned Guerilla Tells of Torture as Bolivian Prisoner," *Washington Post*, May 6, 1973; quoted in Deirdre Carmody, "American Ex-Nun Held by Bolivia as a Guerrilla," *New York Times*, January 11, 1973.

69. Marvine Howe, "Two Britons Freed in Chile Report Brutal Conditions," *New York Times*, September 20, 1973; Philip Shabecoff, "President Publicly Backs Clandestine CIA Activity," *New York Times*, September 17, 1974.

70. Central Governing Board of Maryknoll Sisters to President Gerald Ford, October 2, 1974, Correspondence, Office of Social Concerns, MSA; "Chile Searches for Priest and Two U.S. Nuns Said to Help Rebels," *New York Times*, November 6, 1975; Judy Noone, *The Same Fate as the Poor*, rev. ed. (Maryknoll, NY: Orbis Books, 1995), 30–44.

71.　Marjorie Hyer, "Clergy Wary of CIA Approaches," *Washington Post*, August 5, 1975; Dries, *The Missionary Movement in American Catholic History*, 231–32.

72.　Office of Social Concerns finding aid, MSA; History fact sheet, 1983, Office of Social Concerns, MSA.

73.　Svenja Blanke, "Civic Foreign Policy: Human Rights, Faith-Based Groups, and U.S.-Salvadoran Relations in the 1970s," *Americas* 61, no. 2 (2004): 235–36.

74.　Margaret Keck and Kathryn Sikkink, *Activists Beyond Borders: Advocacy Networks in International Politics*, (Ithaca, NY: Cornell University Press, 1998), 13.

75.　Lernoux, *Hearts on Fire*, 218.

76.　Keck and Sikkink label this the "boomerang pattern of influence" (*Activists Beyond Borders*, 12).

77.　"Sister Refused Bail," *Los Angeles Times*, September 16, 1977; quoted in Gerald Horne, *From the Barrel of a Gun: The United States and the War against Zimbabwe, 1965–1980* (Chapel Hill: University of North Carolina Press, 2001), 101.

78.　Quoted in "Guerrillas' Role Defended by Nun in Rhodesia Trial," *Boston Globe*, September 14, 1977; Lernoux, *Hearts on Fire*, 221 and 223.

79.　Quoted in Robin Wright, "American Nun Freed, Expelled by Rhodesia," *Washington Post*, September 23, 1977.

80.　"Deported Nun Hits Catholics, U.S. for the Fate of Rhodesians," *New York Amsterdam News*, October 1, 1977; Ulish Carter, "Sister Janice: Guerillas Have Rhodesia Peoples' Support," *Pittsburgh Courier*, October 15, 1977; Janice McLaughlin, "Economic Sanctions against Rhodesia," *Hearings Before the Subcommittees on Africa and on International Organizations of the Committee on Foreign Affairs, House of Representatives*, 96th Congress, (April–May 1979).

81.　Penny Lernoux, "The Latin American Church," *Latin American Research Review* 15, no. 2 (1980): 201.

82.　Phillip Berryman, *The Religious Roots of Rebellion: Christians in Central American Revolutions* (Maryknoll, NY: Orbis Books, 1984), 72.

83.　Ray Holton, "Church Leaders Playing Important Role in New Nicaragua," *Washington Post*, August 17, 1979.

84.　Quoted in ibid.

85.　"Statement of the Maryknoll Sisters Regarding Nicaragua," July 12, 1979, Nicaragua Insurrection, Office of Social Concerns, MSA.

86.　Report, 1979, Nicaragua Insurrection, Office of Social Concerns, MSA.

87.　Barbara Worth and Paul Trouve, letters to the editor, *Maryknoll*, July 1973, 35.

88.　Editorial, *The Wanderer*, February 2, 1975.

89.　Michael Novak, "Liberation Theology and the Pope," *Commentary*, June 1979, 61.

90.　Patricia Edmiston, interview by the author, July 25, 2006, Maryknoll, NY; Alan Riding, "Nicaraguan Planes Hit Rebel-Held City," *New York Times*, June 15, 1979. Berryman recounts the cathedral killings in *The Religious Roots of Rebellion*, 138.

91.　Edmiston, interview. See also "Eileen Campion's Yonkers," July 13, 1979, Nicaragua Insurrection, Office of Social Concerns, MSA.

92.　Nepstad, *Convictions of the Soul*, 100–105.

CHAPTER 7　"THE NUNS WERE NOT JUST NUNS": FOREIGN MISSION AND FOREIGN POLICY

1.　"Joint Statement by Sr. Melinda Roper and Fr. James Noonan," February 1981, Maryknoll and Church: Immediate Responses, El Salvador Martyrs, MSA.

2. The most comprehensive history of the Maryknoll sisters' backgrounds and the circumstances of their deaths is Judy Noone, *The Same Fate as the Poor*, rev. ed. (Maryknoll, NY: Orbis Books, 1995). Other substantial works include Donna Whitson Brett and Edward Brett, *Murdered in Central America: The Stories of Eleven U.S. Missionaries* (Maryknoll, NY: Orbis Books, 1988); Timothy Byrnes, *Reverse Mission: Transnational Religious Communities and the Making of U.S. Foreign Policy* (Washington: Georgetown University Press, 2011); Jeanne Evans, *Here I Am Lord: The Letters and Writings of Ita Ford* (Maryknoll, NY: Orbis Books, 2005); Sharon Erickson Nepstad, *Convictions of the Soul: Religion, Culture, and Agency in the Central America Solidarity Movement* (New York: Oxford University Press, 2004). Popular media coverage included a fictionalized portrayal of the killings in Oliver Stone's 1986 film *Salvador*.

3. The military forces of the Salvadoran state during the civil war consisted of the armed forces (Army, Navy, and Air Force) and security forces (National Police, Treasury Police, and National Guard). What became known as the death squads had obscure relationships to the military. The United Nations Truth Commission differentiated the violence carried out by the death squads from that of the military. The National Guard was the force deemed most culpable in the churchwomen's deaths. See Robert White, testimony, Carlos Eugenio Vides Casanova Removal Proceedings, United States Department of Justice, Executive Office for Immigration Review, December 17, 2012, 11, Center for Justice and Accountability, http://cja.org/downloads/Vides%20Casanova%20Removal%20Proceedings.pdf; United Nations Commission on the Truth for El Salvador, *From Madness to Hope: The 12 Year War in El Salvador* (New York: United Nations, 1993), 62–66.

4. The timeline of events presented here uses Noone's *The Same Fate as the Poor* for general background.

5. Gail Pellett, *Justice and the Generals* (Brooklyn, NY: First Run/Icarus Films, 2002), videocassette (VHS).

6. Quoted in Loren Jenkins, "Maryknollers Reconsider Role in El Salvador after Action by Priest," *Washington Post*, May 14, 1981; quoted in Noone, *The Same Fate as the Poor*, 82.

7. Quoted in *Justice in El Salvador: A Case Study* (New York: The Lawyers Committee for International Human Rights, 1982), 21–23, in Section 10, Bureau File 163–49105, "Undefined FBI File on the American Churchwomen Killed in El Salvador, December 1980," Federal Bureau of Investigation Library, Gale World Scholar: Latin America and the Caribbean (hereafter, FBI-Churchwomen).

8. Quoted in Amembassy San Salvador, "Threats against U.S. Citizen Nuns Working in Chalatenango," December 11, 1980, U.S. Department of State El Salvador Declassification Project, accessed April 11, 2017, http://foia.state.gov/Search/Collections.aspx.

9. Margarito Perez Nieto, statement, December 22, 1981, Section 7, FBI-Churchwomen.

10. Larry Rohter, "4 Salvadorans Say They Killed U.S. Nuns on Orders of Military," *New York Times*, April 3, 1998; Pellett, *Justice and the Generals*.

11. H. Carl Gettinger, "The Secret Colindres Confession," July 19, 1983, US. Department of State El Salvador Declassification Project, accessed April 11, 2017, http://foia.state.gov/Search/Collections.aspx.

12. "Official Community Statement," December 4, 1980, El Salvador Martyrs, MSA.

13. Account from transcription of William Rogers and William Bowdler, "Report to the President of Special Mission to El Salvador," December 12, 1980, in *Justice in El Salvador*, 3–5.

14. Quoted in "Bodies of 4 American Women Are Found in El Salvador," *New York Times*, December 5, 1980.

15. Quoted in Christopher Dickey, "Four U.S. Catholics Killed in El Salvador," *Washington Post*, December 5, 1980; Betty Glad, *An Outsider in the White House: Jimmy Carter, His Advisors, and the Making of American Foreign Policy* (Ithaca, NY: Cornell University Press, 2009), 250–260; William LeoGrande, *Our Own Backyard: The United States in Central America, 1977–1992* (Chapel Hill: University of North Carolina Press, 1998), 43–46.

16. Pellett, *Justice and the Generals.*

17. Madeline Dorsey, "Remembering the Martyrs 30 Years Later," *Maryknoll*, accessed February 7, 2014, http://www.Maryknollmagazine.org/index.php/magazines/201-remembering -the-martyrs-30-years-later.

18. White quoted in LeoGrande, *Our Own Backyard*, 62; Helene O'Sullivan, telephone interview by the author, February 11, 2014.

19. Quoted in Margaret O'Brien Steinfels, "Death and Lies in El Salvador: The Ambassador's Tale," *Commonweal*, June 14, 2004, https://www.commonwealmagazine.org/death-lies -el-salvador-0.

20. Quoted in ibid.; White, testimony, Vides Casanova Removal Proceedings, 12.

21. "Salvador Junta Member Is Named First Civilian President in 49 Years," *New York Times*, December 14, 1980; quoted in Juan de Onis, "Envoy Disputes U.S. on Salvador Deaths," *New York Times*, January 22, 1981.

22. Legal Attaché Panama to Director, memorandum, April 1981, Section 2, FBI-Churchwomen.

23. Steinfels, "Death and Lies in El Salvador." Clearly, not all agencies and foreign service officials shared these goals. For example, the Atlacatl Battalion, trained by the US military at the School of the Americas, was deemed responsible for many atrocities, including the 1981 El Mozote massacre and the 1989 Universidad Centroamericana executions. See United Nations Commission on the Truth for El Salvador, *From Madness to Hope*, 45–54 and 114–21.

24. Quoted in *Justice in El Salvador*, 12; Steinfels, "Death and Lies in El Salvador."

25. *Justice in El Salvador*, 22–24.

26. Legal Attaché Panama to director, memorandum, January 1981, Section 1, FBI-Churchwomen; DCM to LEGATT, memorandum, December 3, 1981, Section 10, FBI-Churchwomen.

27. Harold Tyler Jr., "The Churchwomen Murders: A Report to the Secretary of State," December 2, 1983, 23, Section 10, FBI-Churchwomen.

28. Gettinger, "The Secret Colindres Confession."

29. "Reagan-Appointed Democrat Speaks Her Mind on World, Domestic Politics," *Tampa Tribune*, December 25, 1980.

30. Quoted in Mary McGrory, "Should Reagan Prop up This Junta?," *Chicago Tribune*, December 15, 1980; Juan de Onis, "Reagan Aides Promise Salvadorans More Military Help to Fight Rebels," *New York Times*, November 29, 1980.

31. Quoted in Don Oberdorfer, "Haig Calls Terrorism Top Priority," *Washington Post*, January 29, 1981.

32. Anthony Lewis, "Abroad at Home; Showing His Colors," *New York Times*, March 29, 1981.

33. LeoGrande, *Our Own Backyard*, 9.

34. Edward Walsh, "Reagan Gets First Public Opinion Backlash—on Salvador Policy," *Washington Post*, March 27, 1981; Steinfels, "Death and Lies in El Salvador"; White, testimony, Vides Casanova Removal Proceedings, 22.

35. LeoGrande, *Our Own Backyard*, 281–82.

36. Nepstad, *Convictions of the Soul*, 105. Anna Peterson provides a further account of the modern meanings of martyrdom—and divergences from doctrinal traditions—in the context of the Salvadoran popular church in *Martyrdom and the Politics of Religion: Progressive Catholicism in El Salvador's Civil War* (Albany: State University of New York Press, 1997), especially 103–10.

37. *Maryknoll Sisters in Mission*, rev. ed., 1978, 17, MSA.

38. "Joint Statement by Sr. Melinda Roper and Fr. James Noonan," February 1981.

39. Office of Social Concerns to Sisters, October 1981, Correspondence and Reports, Office of Social Concerns, MSA. For accounts of conscientization in the United States, see Svenja Blanke, "Civic Foreign Policy: Human Rights, Faith-Based Groups, and U.S.-Salvadoran Relations in the 1970s," *Americas* 61, no. 2 (2004): 227–29; Byrnes, *Reverse Mission*; Nepstad, *Convictions of the Soul*, 100–103.

40. Colman McCarthy, "The Maryknoll Order," *Washington Post*, April 19, 1981; Marjorie Hyer, "Four Murders Trigger US Catholic Protests," *Washington Post*, December 10, 1980.

41. Margot Hornblower, "Rumbles of War Give Hill the Jitters," *Washington Post*, March 8, 1982.

42. O'Sullivan, interview; "End Military Aid to El Salvador, Chief of Catholic Bishop Urges," *Washington Post*, February 10, 1982; Edward Brett, "The Attempts of Grassroots Religious Groups to Change U.S. Policy Towards Central America: Their Methods, Successes, and Failures," *Journal of Church and State* 36 (Autumn 1994): 787–88.

43. Roger Peace, *A Call to Conscience: The Anti-Contra War Campaign* (Amherst: University of Massachusetts Press, 2012), 53–80; Van Gosse, "'El Salvador Is Spanish for Vietnam': The Politics of Solidarity and the New Immigrant Left, 1955–1993," in *The Immigrant Left*, ed. Paul Buhle and Dan Georgakas (Albany: State University of New York Press, 1996), 318 and 327.

44. Mike Sager, "25,000 Demonstrators March on the Pentagon," *Washington Post*, May 4, 1981. Other demonstrations commemorating the churchwomen are discussed in Marjorie Hyer, "Demonstrations Mark Anniversary of Nuns' Slaying," *Washington Post*, December 3, 1981; Caryle Murphy, "Protest," *Washington Post*, March 28, 1982; Edward Walsh Washington, "El Salvador Protests Called 'Orchestrated' Communist Effort," *Washington Post*, March 24, 1981.

45. Peace, *A Call to Conscience*, 83.

46. Center for Inter-American Security, "Murdered Nuns in El Salvador Suspected of Aiding Guerrillas," March 1980, Section 10, FBI-Churchwomen. Such critiques would also characterize responses to the Maryknoll Sisters' opposition to Nicaragua Contra aid. See Theresa Keeley, "Reagan's Real Catholics vs. Tip O'Neill's Maryknoll Nuns: Gender, Intra-Catholic Conflict, and the Contras," *Diplomatic History* 40, no. 3 (2016): 532.

47. Editorial, "Murder Outside the Cathedral," *National Review*, March 20, 1981, 263; Andrew Greeley, "Missionary Imperialism," April 30, 1981, News Releases: Critical of Maryknoll, El Salvador Martyrs, MSA. Other prominent denunciations included a syndicated column by Pat Buchanan, "Maryknoll Dyes Its Roots Red" and a *New York Daily News* interview in which William F. Buckley called Maryknoll "pro-Marxist and anti-pope" (quoted in Lernoux, *Hearts on Fire*, 254).

48. Mark Dowi and David Talbot, "Asner: Too Hot for Medium Cool," *Mother Jones*, August 1982, 11; Lucy Thornton, "FBI Probed Foes of U.S.," *Washington Post*, January 28, 1988; Ross Gelbspan, *Break-Ins, Death Threats and the FBI: The Covert War against the Central America Movement* (Boston: South End Press, 1991), 98–99. A Freedom of Information Act request for files related to the Maryknoll Sisters yielded no documents, though the FBI and CIA have both released voluminous material about the churchwomen's case more generally.

49. Philip Taubman, "The Speaker and His Sources on Latin America," *New York Times*, September 12, 1984; Bob Woodward, *Veil: The Secret Wars of the CIA, 1981–1987* (New York:

Simon and Schuster, 1987), 225; quoted in Nepstad, *Convictions of the Soul*, 53. Representative David Bonior, Michigan Democrat and leader in the fight against Contra aid, similarly attributed his "interest in Central America" to his early education from "nuns interested in Haiti and Nicaragua." See Peace, *A Call to Conscience*, 93.

50. "Testimony of Melinda Roper before the Foreign Relations Committee of the US Senate," April 9, 1981, Responses to U.S.-El Salvador Policy, El Salvador Martyrs, MSA. See also Arlen Specter, "Visit to El Salvador," *Congressional Record*, May 19, 1983, Section 8, FBI-Churchwomen.

51. Bill Peterson, "Reagan Plea Rejected, Senate Votes Terms for Salvadoran Aid," *Washington Post*, September 25, 1981. Other cases affecting US citizens were bundled into certification reports, the most prominent of which was the assassination of two civilian labor advisors in the lobby of the San Salvador Sheraton Hotel.

52. O'Sullivan, interview. See also William Chapman, "Plea to Restore Aid to Salvador Does Not Persuade Congress," *Washington Post*, June 12, 1982; Margot Hornblower, "Panel Votes Most of El Salvador Aid," *Washington Post*, May 12, 1983; "House Votes to Extend Curbs on Military Aid to Salvador," *Washington Post*, October 1, 1983. At some points, Congress proved less of an obstruction, but notably, House Democrats successfully overturned a Reagan pocket veto of certification requirements. See Helen Dewar and Joanne Omang, "House Approves Aid to El Salvador, Not Nicaraguan Rebels," *Washington Post*, May 25, 1984; Ronald Kessler, "Pocket Veto by Reagan Overturned," *Washington Post*, August 30, 1984.

53. David Duell Passage, testimony, Vides Casanova Removal Proceedings, 71; Diana Villiers Negroponte, *Seeking Peace in El Salvador: The Struggle to Reconstruct a Nation at the End of the Cold War* (New York: Palgrave Macmillan, 2011), 26.

54. "6 Salvadoran Soldiers Are Arrested in Slaying of U.S. Church Workers," *New York Times*, May 10, 1981; Raymond Bonner, "Salvador's Inquiry into Nuns' Slaying Stalled," *New York Times*, November 13, 1981; "Salvadorans Again Face Trial in Killing of 4 Churchwomen," *New York Times*, October 29, 1983; Lydia Chavez, "5 Salvadorans Are Found Guilty in Slaying of U.S. Churchwomen," *New York Times*, May 25, 1984; United Nations Commission on the Truth for El Salvador, *From Madness to Hope*, 65. The men lost an appeal of their case under postwar political amnesty statutes because the killings were ruled to be nonpolitical and thus not protected by reconciliation measures. Three men, including Colindres, have since been paroled for good behavior.

55. O'Sullivan, interview; United Nations Commission on the Truth for El Salvador, *From Madness to Hope*, 31–33.

56. LeoGrande, *Our Own Backyard*, 231–257; United Nations Commission on the Truth for El Salvador, *From Madness to Hope*, 31; Vides Casanova Removal Proceedings, 61–63.

57. Scott Greathead in Pellett, *Justice and the Generals*.

58. Harold Tyler Jr., "The Churchwomen Murders: A Report to the Secretary of State," December 2, 1983, 54–82, Section 10, FBI-Churchwomen. The 1983 State Department memo about the Colindres confession acknowledged that there remained "important unanswered questions on how and why the crime was initiated" (Gettinger, "The Secret Colindres Confession," 3).

59. Quoted in Robert McCartney, "5 Salvadorans Get 30 Years for Killing Missionaries," *Washington Post*, June 20, 1984; O'Sullivan, interview.

60. William Ford in Pellett, *Justice and the Generals*; Hari Osofsky, "Domesticating International Criminal Law: Bringing Human Rights Violators to Justice," *Yale Law Journal* 107, no. 1 (1997): 193. See also Robert Drinan and Teresa Kuo, "Putting the World's Oppressors on Trial: The Torture Victim Protection Act," *Human Rights Quarterly* 15, no. 3 (1993): 605–24.

61. David Gonzalez, "Trial of Salvadoran Generals in Nuns' Deaths Hears Echoes of 1980," *New York Times*, October 21, 2000.

62. William Ford in Pellett, *Justice and the Generals*; David Gonzalez, "2 Salvador Generals Cleared by U.S. Jury in Nuns' Deaths," *New York Times*, November 4, 2000; Scott Greathead and Michael Posner, "Bill Ford, Remembered," *Nation*, June 18, 2008, https://www.thenation.com/article/bill-ford-remembered; Dennis Hevesi, "William P. Ford," obituary, *New York Times*, June 3, 2008.

63. According to the Center for Justice and Accountability, the plaintiffs donated most of what they received, which included $300,000 of Vides Casanova's personal assets—a fraction of the damages awarded—to charity ("*Romagoza Arce et al v. Garcia and Vides Casanova*: Alien Tort Statue/Torture Victims Protection Act," accessed April 11, 2017, http://cja.org/what-we-do/litigation/romagoza-arce-v-garcia-and-vides-casanova/uscourt-ats-tvpa/).

64. Lalita Clozel, "Salvadoran Cites U.S. Backing of Violence in Deportation Appeal," *Los Angeles Times*, February 6, 2014; Julia Preston, "Salvadoran General Accused in Killings Should Be Deported, Miami Judge Says," *New York Times*, April 11, 2014.

65. Tyler, "The Churchwomen Murders," 54.

66. White, testimony, Vides Casanova Removal Proceedings, 17. A reporting mistake in the testimony originally attributed the quote to Vides Casanova himself. The correction was entered on page 5 with the conclusion that it was not plausible that García would have known about the matter without Vides Casanova having known, too.

67. Vides Casanova Removal Proceedings, 113, 115, and 133.

68. Ibid., 81 and 149–50; Alphonso Chardy, "Deported Former Salvadoran Defense Minister Plans to Appeal His Removal," *Miami Herald*, January 15, 2016.

EPILOGUE

1. Congregatio pro Doctrina Fidei, "Doctrinal Assessment of the Leadership Conference of Women Religious," 2012, 3, United States Conference of Catholic Bishops, http://www.usccb.org/upload/Doctrinal_Assessment_Leadership_Conference_Women_Religious.pdf.

2. Darlene Jacobs, interview by the author, July 19, 2006, Maryknoll, NY; Anastasia Lott, interview by the author, July 25, 2006, Maryknoll, NY.

3. Quoted in Laurie Goodstein, "Vatican Ends Battle with U.S. Catholic Nuns' Group," *New York Times*, April 16, 2015; Anastasia Lott, interview by the author, April 16, 2014, Maryknoll, NY.

4. Susan Nchubiri, interview by the author, July 21, 2006, Maryknoll, NY; Maryknoll Sisters, "Our Work," accessed September 13, 2016, https://Maryknollsisters.org/about-us/our-work/.

5. "Who Are Maryknoll Sisters," 1955, Direct Mail, MSA. This change reflects wider post-conciliar trends toward a "steep decline in the number of nuns in the global North and a significant increase in the South," according to Anne O'Brien ("Catholic Nuns in Transnational Mission, 1528–2015," *Journal of Global History* 11, no. 3 [2016]: 402).

6. YWCA USA, "Mission," accessed June 26, 2010, www.ywca.org/mission; YWCA USA, "FAQ," accessed April 2, 2017, http://www.ywca.org/site/c.cuIRJ7NTKrLaG/b.7515903/k.ADCE/FAQ.htm.

7. Grace Hoadley Dodge, "President's Message," in Printed Convention Proceedings, 1909, 60, RG 4, YWCA-SSC; National Board Report, 1922, 117, RG 4, YWCA-SSC; YWCA USA, "FAQ."

8. Anna Rice, "A Forward Look at Our Religious Work," *Association Monthly*, August 1916, 282.

SELECTED BIBLIOGRAPHY

ARCHIVES

Maryknoll Mission Archives. Maryknoll, NY.
Missouri Historical Society Archives, St. Louis, MO.
Smith College Archives. Smith College, Northampton, MA.
Sophia Smith Collection. Smith College, Northampton, MA.
    Mary van Kleeck Papers.
    Dorothy Height Papers.
    Grace Hoadley Dodge Papers.
    YWCA of the USA Records.
World YWCA Archives. Geneva, Switzerland.

Abma, Ruud. "Madness and Mental Health." In *A Social History of Psychology*, edited by Jeroen Jansz and Peter van Drunen, 93–128. Malden, MA: Blackwell, 2004.

Ahlstrom, Sidney. *A Religious History of the American People*. 2nd ed. New Haven, CT: Yale University Press, 2004.

Alonso, Harriet Hyman. *Peace as a Women's Issue: A History of the U.S. Movement for World Peace and Women's Rights*. Syracuse, NY: Syracuse University Press, 1993.

Anderson, Bonnie. *Joyous Greetings: The First International Women's Movement*. New York: Oxford University Press, 2000.

Andrews, Janice, and Michael Reisch. "The Legacy of McCarthyism on Social Group Work: An Historical Analysis." *Journal of Sociology and Social Welfare* 24, no. 3 (1997): 211–35.

Antler, Joyce. "Zion in Our Hearts: Henrietta Szold and the American Jewish Women's Movement." In *American Jewish Women's History: A Reader*, edited by Pamela Nadell, 129–52. New York: New York University Press, 2003.

Baron, Beth. *Egypt as a Woman: Nationalism, Gender, and Politics*. Berkeley: University of California Press, 2005.

Baum, Gregory, and Jean-Guy Vaillancourt. "The Church and Modernization." In *Religion and the Social Order: Vatican II and U.S. Catholicism*, edited by Helen Rose Ebaugh, 21–33. Greenwich, CT: JAI Press, 1991.

Berger, Iris. "An African-American 'Mother of the Nation': Madie Hall Xuma in South Africa, 1940–1963." *Journal of South African Studies* 27, no. 3 (2001): 547–566.

Berkovitch, Nitza. *From Motherhood to Citizenship: Women's Rights and International Organizations*. Baltimore, MD: Johns Hopkins University Press, 1999.

Berryman, Phillip. *The Religious Roots of Rebellion: Christians in Central American Revolutions*. Maryknoll, NY: Orbis Books, 1984.

Best, Wallace. "Concerning 'Goodbye Christ': Langston Hughes, Political Poetry, and African American Religion." *Religion and Politics*, November 26, 2013. http://religionandpolitics .org/2013/11/26/concerning-goodbye-christ-langston-hughes-political-poetry-and -african-american-religion.

Blanke, Svenja. "Civic Foreign Policy: Human Rights, Faith-Based Groups, and U.S.-Salvadoran Relations in the 1970s." *Americas* 61, no. 2 (2004): 217–44.

Boyd, Nancy. *Emissaries: The Overseas Work of the American YWCA, 1895–1970.* New York: Woman's Press, 1986.

Braude, Ann. "A Religious Feminist: Who Can Find Her? Historiographical Challenges from the National Organization for Women." *Journal of Religion* 84, no. 4 (2004): 555–72.

———. "Women's History *Is* American Religious History." In *Retelling U.S. Religious History*, edited by Thomas Tweed, 87–107. Berkeley: University of California Press, 1997.

Brett, Donna Whitson, and Edward Brett. *Murdered in Central America: The Stories of Eleven U.S. Missionaries.* Maryknoll, NY: Orbis Books, 1988.

Brett, Edward. "The Attempts of Grassroots Religious Groups to Change U.S. Policy Towards Central America: Their Methods, Successes, and Failures." *Journal of Church and State* 36 (Autumn 1994): 773–94.

Browder, Dorothea. "A 'Christian Solution to the Labor Problem': How Workingwomen Reshaped the YWCA's Religious Mission and Politics." *Journal of Women's History* 19, no. 2 (2007): 85–110.

———. "From Uplift to Agitation: Working Women, Race, and Coalition in the Young Women's Christian Association, 1908–1950." PhD diss., University of Wisconsin-Madison, 2008.

———. "Working Out Their Economic Problems Together: World War I, Working Women, and Civil Rights in the YWCA." *Journal of the Gilded Age and Progressive Era* 14, no. 2 (2015): 243–65.

Brown, Dorothy, and Elizabeth McKeown. *The Poor Belong to Us: Catholic Charities and American Welfare.* Cambridge, MA: Harvard University Press, 1997.

Brumberg, Joan Jacobs. "Zenanas and Girlless Villages: The Ethnology of American Evangelical Women, 1870–1910." *Journal of American History* 69, no. 2 (1982): 347–71.

Byrne, Patricia. "In the Parish but Not of It: Sisters." In *Transforming Parish Ministry: The Changing Roles of Catholic Clergy, Laity, and Women Religious*, edited by Jay Dolan, R. Scott Appleby, Patricia Byrne, and Debra Campbell, 111–200. New York: Crossroad, 1989.

Byrnes, Timothy. *Reverse Mission: Transnational Religious Communities and the Making of U.S. Foreign Policy.* Washington: Georgetown University Press, 2011.

Chu, Cindy Yik-Yi. *Maryknoll Sisters in Hong Kong, 1921–1969: In Love with the Chinese.* New York: Palgrave Macmillan, 2004.

Cmiel, Kenneth. "The Emergence of Human Rights Politics in the United States." *Journal of American History* 86, no. 3 (1999): 1231–50.

Cohen, Robert. *When the Old Left Was Young: Student Radicals and America's First Mass Student Movement, 1929–1941.* New York: Oxford University Press, 1993.

Collier-Thomas, Bettye. *Jesus, Jobs, and Justice: African American Women and Religion.* New York: Knopf, 2011.

Coppa, Frank. "Pope Pius XII and the Cold War: The Post-War Confrontation between Catholicism and Communism." In *Religion and the Cold War*, edited by Dianne Kirby, 50–66. New York: Palgrave Macmillan, 2003.

Cott, Nancy. *The Grounding of Modern Feminism.* New Haven, CT: Yale University Press, 1987.

Critchlow, Donald. *Phyllis Schlafly and Grassroots Conservatism: A Woman's Crusade.* Princeton, NJ: Princeton University Press, 2005.

Cummings, Kathleen Sprows. *New Women of the Old Faith: Gender and American Catholicism in the Progressive Era.* Chapel Hill: University of North Carolina Press, 2009.

Curb, Rosemary, and Nancy Manahan, eds. *Lesbian Nuns: Breaking Silence.* Tallahassee, FL: Naiad Press, 1985.

Curtis, Susan. *A Consuming Faith: The Social Gospel and Modern American Culture*. Baltimore, MD: Johns Hopkins University Press, 1991.

———. "The Son of Man and God the Father: The Social Gospel and Victorian Masculinity." In *Meanings for Manhood: Constructions of Masculinity in Victorian America*, edited by Mark Carnes and Clyde Griffen, 67–78. Chicago: University of Chicago Press, 1990.

Davidann, Jon Thares. *A World of Crisis and Progress: The American YMCA in Japan, 1890–1930*. Bethlehem, PA: Lehigh University Press, 1998.

DeRoche, Celeste. "'How Wide the Circle of We': Cultural Pluralism and American Identity, 1910–1954." PhD diss., University of Maine, 2000.

Dries, Angelyn. "The Foreign Mission Impulse of the American Catholic Church, 1893–1925." *International Bulletin of Missionary Research* 15, no. 2 (1991): 61–66.

———. *The Missionary Movement in American Catholic History*. Maryknoll, NY: Orbis Books, 1998.

Drinan, Robert. *Cry of the Oppressed: The History and Hope of the Human Rights Revolution*. San Francisco: Harper and Row, 1987.

——— and Teresa Kuo. "Putting the World's Oppressors on Trial: The Torture Victim Protection Act." *Human Rights Quarterly* 15, no. 3 (1993): 605–24.

Ebaugh, Helen Rose Fuchs. *Becoming an Ex: The Process of Role Exit*. Chicago: University of Chicago Press, 1988.

———, ed. *Religion and the Social Order: Vatican II and U.S. Catholicism*. Greenwich, CT: JAI Press, 1991.

———. "Vatican II and the Revitalization Movement." In *Religion and the Social Order: Vatican II and U.S. Catholicism*, edited by Helen Rose Ebaugh, 3–19. Greenwich, CT: JAI Press, 1991.

———. *Women in the Vanishing Cloister: Organizational Decline in Catholic Religious Orders in the United States*. New Brunswick, NJ: Rutgers University Press, 1993.

Evans, Jeanne. *Here I Am Lord: The Letters and Writings of Ita Ford*. Maryknoll, NY: Orbis Books, 2005.

Evans, Sara. Introduction to *Journeys that Opened Up the World: Women, Student Christian Movements, and Social Justice, 1955–1975*, edited by Sara Evans, 1–14. New Brunswick, NJ: Rutgers University Press, 2003.

———, ed. *Journeys That Opened Up the World: Women, Student Christian Movements, and Social Justice 1955–1975*. New Brunswick, NJ: Rutgers University Press, 2003.

Fisher, James Terence. *The Catholic Counterculture in America, 1933–1962*. Chapel Hill: University of North Carolina Press, 1989.

———. *Dr. America: The Lives of Thomas A. Dooley, 1927–1961*. Amherst: University of Massachusetts Press, 1997.

Fitzgerald, Maureen. *Habits of Compassion: Irish Catholic Nuns and the Origins of New York's Welfare System, 1830–1920*. Urbana: University of Illinois Press, 2006.

Fitzpatrick, Ellen. *Endless Crusade: Women Social Scientists and Progressive Reform*. New York: Oxford University Press, 1990.

Fitzpatrick-Behrens, Susan. "From Symbols of the Sacred to Symbols of Subversion to Simply Obscure: Maryknoll Women Religious in Guatemala, 1953–1967." *Americas* 61, no. 2 (2004): 189–216.

———. "Knowledge Is Not Enough: Creating a Culture of Social Justice, Dignity, and Human Rights in Guatemala: Maryknoll Sisters and the Monte María 'Girls.'" *U.S. Catholic Historian* 24, no. 3 (2006): 111–28.

———. *The Maryknoll Catholic Mission in Peru, 1943–1989: Transnational Faith and Transformation*. Notre Dame, IN: University of Notre Dame Press, 2012.

———. "Maryknoll Sisters, Faith, Healing, and the Maya Construction of Catholic Communities in Guatemala." *Latin American Research Review* 44, no. 3 (2009): 27–49.

Fox, Richard Wightman. *Reinhold Niebuhr: A Biography*. Ithaca, NY: Cornell University Press, 1996.

Freedman, Estelle. "Separatism as Strategy: Female Institution Building and American Feminism, 1870–1930." *Feminist Studies* 5, no. 3 (1979): 512–29.

Garner, Karen. "Global Feminism and Postwar Reconstruction: The World YWCA Visitation to Occupied Japan, 1947." *Journal of World History* 15, no. 2 (2004): 191–227.

———. *Precious Fire: Maud Russell and the Chinese Revolution*. Amherst: University of Massachusetts Press, 2003.

Gelbspan, Ross. *Break-Ins, Death Threats and the FBI: The Covert War against the Central America Movement*. Boston, MA: South End Press, 1991.

Gilmore, Glenda. *Gender and Jim Crow: Women and the Politics of White Supremacy in North Carolina, 1896–1920*. Chapel Hill: University of North Carolina Press, 1996.

Ginzberg, Lori. *Women and the Work of Benevolence: Morality, Politics, and Class in the Nineteenth-Century United States*. New Haven, CT: Yale University Press, 1990.

Glad, Betty. *An Outsider in the White House: Jimmy Carter, His Advisors, and the Making of American Foreign Policy*. Ithaca, NY: Cornell University Press, 2009.

Goffman, Erving. *Asylums: Essays on the Social Situation of Mental Patients and Other Inmates*. Chicago: Aldine, 1962.

Gosse, Van. "'El Salvador Is Spanish for Vietnam': The Politics of Solidarity and the New Immigrant Left, 1955–1993." In *The Immigrant Left*, edited by Paul Buhle and Dan Georgakas, 301–329. Albany: State University of New York Press, 1996.

Grandin, Greg. *The Last Colonial Massacre: Latin America in the Cold War*. Chicago: University of Chicago Press, 2004.

Halsey, William. *The Survival of American Innocence: Catholicism in an Era of Disillusionment, 1920–1940*. Notre Dame, IN: University of Notre Dame Press, 1980.

Harrison, Cynthia. *On Account of Sex: The Politics of Women's Issues, 1945–1968*. Berkeley: University of California Press, 1989.

Height, Dorothy. *Open Wide the Freedom Gates*. New York: PublicAffairs, 2003.

———. "'We Wanted the Voice of a Woman to Be Heard': Black Women and the 1963 March on Washington." In *Sisters in the Struggle: African American Women in the Civil Rights–Black Power Movement*, edited by V. P. Franklin and Bettye Collier-Thomas, 83–91. New York: New York University Press, 2001.

Hellwig, Monika. "Mystical Body of Christ." In *The Modern Catholic Encyclopedia*, edited by Michael Glazier and Monika Hellwig, 573. Rev. ed. Collegeville, MN: Liturgical Press, 2004.

Hennelly, Alfred. Introduction to *Liberation Theology: A Documentary History*, edited by Alfred Hennelly, xv–xxi. Maryknoll, NY: Orbis Books, 1990.

———, ed. *Liberation Theology: A Documentary History*. Maryknoll, NY: Orbis Books, 1990.

Higginbotham, Evelyn Brooks. *Righteous Discontent: The Women's Movement in the Black Baptist Church, 1880–1920*. Cambridge, MA: Harvard University Press, 1993.

Hollinger, David. *After Cloven Tongues of Fire: Protestant Liberalism in Modern American History*. Princeton, NJ: Princeton University Press, 2013.

Hopkins, Charles Howard. *The Rise of the Social Gospel in American Protestantism, 1865–1916*. New Haven, CT: Yale University Press, 1940.

Horne, Gerald. *From the Barrel of a Gun: The United States and the War against Zimbabwe, 1965–1980*. Chapel Hill: University of North Carolina Press, 2001.

Horowitz, Helen Lefkowitz. *Alma Mater: Design and Experience in the Women's Colleges from Their Nineteenth-Century Beginnings to the 1930s*. New York: Knopf, 1984.

Hunter, Jane. *The Gospel of Gentility: American Women Missionaries in Turn-of-the-Century China*. New Haven, CT: Yale University Press, 1984.

———. "Women's Mission in Historical Perspective: American Identity and Christian Internationalism." In *Competing Kingdoms: Women, Mission, Nation, and the American Protestant Empire, 1812–1960*, edited by Barbara Reeves-Ellington, Kathryn Kish Sklar, and Connie Shemo, 19–42. Durham, NC: Duke University Press, 2010.

Hutchison, William. *Errand to the World: American Protestant Thought and Foreign Missions*. Chicago: University of Chicago Press, 1987.

———. *The Modernist Impulse in American Protestantism*. Cambridge, MA: Harvard University Press, 1976.

Ishay, Micheline. *The History of Human Rights: From Ancient Times to the Globalization Era*. Berkeley: University of California Press, 2008.

Jeanne Marie, Sister. *Maryknoll's First Lady*. N.p.: Maryknoll Sisters of St. Dominic, 1964.

Jeansonne, Glen. *Women of the Far Right: The Mothers' Movement and World War II*. Chicago: University of Chicago Press, 1996.

Kandiyoti, Deniz. "End of Empire: Islam, Nationalism and Women in Turkey." In *Women, Islam, and the State*, edited by Deniz Kandiyoti, 22–47. Houndmills, UK: Macmillan, 1991.

Kaplan, Amy. "Manifest Domesticity." In *The Futures of American Studies*, edited by Donald Pease and Robyn Wiegman, 111–34. Durham, NC: Duke University Press, 2002.

Kaplan, Jeffrey. *Encyclopedia of White Power: A Sourcebook on the Radical Racist Right*. Walnut Creek, CA: AltaMira, 2000.

Katz, Esther. "Grace Hoadley Dodge: Women and the Emerging Metropolis, 1856–1914." PhD diss., New York University, 1980.

Kawai, Michi. *My Lantern*. Privately printed, 1949.

———. *Sliding Doors*. Tokyo: Keisen-jo-gaju-en, 1950.

Keck, Margaret, and Kathryn Sikkink. *Activists Beyond Borders: Advocacy Networks in International Politics*. Ithaca, NY: Cornell University Press, 1998.

Keeley, Theresa. "Reagan's Real Catholics vs. Tip O'Neill's Maryknoll Nuns: Gender, Intra-Catholic Conflict, and the Contras." *Diplomatic History* 40, no. 3 (2016): 530–558.

Kent, Peter. "The Lonely Cold War of Pope Pius XII." In *Religion and the Cold War*, edited by Dianne Kirby, 67–76. New York: Palgrave Macmillan, 2003.

Kirby, Dianne, ed. *Religion and the Cold War*. New York: Palgrave Macmillan, 2003.

Knotts, Alice. *Fellowship of Love: Methodist Women Changing American Racial Attitudes, 1920–1968*. Nashville, TN: Kingswood, 1996.

Koehlinger, Amy. "Academia and 'Aggiornamento': The Social Sciences and Postconciliar Reform among American Sisters." *U.S. Catholic Historian* 25, no. 4 (2007): 63–83.

———. *The New Nuns: Racial Justice and Religious Reform in the 1960s*. Cambridge, MA: Harvard University Press, 2007.

Kunzel, Regina. *Fallen Women, Problem Girls: Unmarried Mothers and the Professionalization of Social Work, 1890–1945*. New Haven, CT: Yale University Press, 1993.

Kwon, Insook. "Feminists Navigating the Shoals of Nationalism and Collaboration: The Post-Colonial Korean Debate over How to Remember Kim Hwallan." *Frontiers* 27, no. 1 (2006): 39–66.

LaFeber, Walter. *Inevitable Revolutions: The United States in Central America*. 2nd ed. New York: W. W. Norton, 1993.

Lang, Clarence. "Between Civil Rights and Black Power in the Gateway City: The Action Committee to Improve Opportunities for Negroes (ACTION), 1964–75." *Journal of Social History* 37, no. 3 (2004): 725–754.

Laville, Helen. *Cold War Women: The International Activities of American Women's Organisations*. Manchester, UK: Manchester University Press, 2002.

———. "A New Era in International Women's Rights? American Women's Associations and the Establishment of the UN Commission on the Status of Women." *Journal of Women's History* 20, no. 4 (2008): 34–56.

Lecky, Robert, and H. Elliott Wright, eds. *Black Manifesto: Religion, Racism, and Reparations*. New York: Sheed and Ward, 1969.

———. Introduction to *Black Manifesto: Religion, Racism, and Reparations*, edited by Robert Lecky and H. Elliott Wright, 1–32. New York: Sheed and Ward, 1969.

Lemons, J. Stanley. *Woman Citizen: Social Feminism in the 1920s*. Urbana: University of Illinois Press, 1973.

Lentz, Harris. *Assassinations and Executions: An Encyclopedia of Political Violence, 1900 through 2000*. Jefferson, NC: McFarland, 2002.

LeoGrande, William. *Our Own Backyard: The United States in Central America, 1977–1992*. Chapel Hill: University of North Carolina Press, 1998.

Lernoux, Penny. *Hearts on Fire: The Story of the Maryknoll Sisters*. Maryknoll, NY: Orbis, 1993.

———. "The Latin American Church." *Latin American Research Review* 15, no. 2 (1980): 201–11.

Lewis, Abigail. "'The Barrier-Breaking Love of God': The Multiracial Activism of the Young Women's Christian Association, 1940s to 1970s." PhD diss., Rutgers University, 2008.

Lindley, Susan. *"You Have Stept Out of Your Place": A History of Women and Religion in America*. Louisville, KY: Westminster John Knox Press, 1996.

Littell-Lamb, Elizabeth. "Engendering a Class Revolution: The Chinese YWCA Industrial Reform Work in Shanghai, 1927–1939." *Women's History Review* 21, no. 2 (2012): 189–209.

Lubin, Carol Riegelman, and Anne Winslow. *Social Justice for Women: The International Labor Organization and Women*. Durham, NC: Duke University Press, 1990.

Lunbeck, Elizabeth. *Psychiatric Persuasion: Knowledge, Gender, and Power in Modern America*. Princeton, NJ: Princeton University Press, 1994.

Lynn, Susan. *Progressive Women in Conservative Times: Racial Justice, Peace, and Feminism, 1945 to the 1960s*. New Brunswick, NJ: Rutgers University Press, 1992.

MacFarland, Charles. *Christian Unity in the Making: The First Twenty-Five Years of the Federal Council of Churches of Christ in America, 1905–1930*. New York: Federal Council of Churches of Christ in America, 1948.

Marsden, George. *Understanding Fundamentalism and Evangelicalism*. Grand Rapids, MI: William B. Eerdmans, 1991.

Matsumoto, Valerie. *City Girls: The Nisei Social World in Los Angeles, 1920–1950*. New York: Oxford University Press, 2014.

McNamara, Jo Ann Kay. *Sisters in Arms: Catholic Nuns through Two Millennia*. Cambridge, MA: Harvard University Press, 1996.

McNamara, Patrick. *A Catholic Cold War: Edmund A. Walsh, S.J., and the Politics of American Anticommunism*. New York: Fordham University Press, 2015.

Melville, Thomas, and Marjorie Melville. *Whose Heaven, Whose Earth?* New York: Knopf, 1971.

Meyer, Donald. *The Protestant Search for Political Realism, 1919–1941.* 2nd ed. Middletown, CT: Wesleyan University Press, 1988.

Mittleman, Karen. "'A Spirit That Touches the Problems of Today': Women and Social Reform in the Philadelphia Young Women's Christian Association, 1920–1945." PhD diss., University of Pennsylvania, 1987.

Mjagkij, Nina, and Margaret Spratt, eds. *Men and Women Adrift: The YMCA and the YWCA in the City.* New York: New York University Press, 1997.

Moghadam, Valentine. "Transnational Feminist Networks: Collective Action in an Era of Globalization." *International Sociology* 15, no. 1 (2000): 57–85.

Mollin, Marian. "Communities of Resistance: Women and the Catholic Left of the Late 1960s." *Oral History Review* 31, no. 2 (2004): 29–51.

Muncy, Robyn. *Creating a Female Dominion in American Reform, 1890–1935.* New York: Oxford University Press, 1991.

Murray, Gail, ed. *Throwing Off the Cloak of Privilege: White Southern Women Activists in the Civil Rights Era.* Gainesville: University Press of Florida, 2004.

Negroponte, Diana Villiers. *Seeking Peace in El Salvador: The Struggle to Reconstruct a Nation at the End of the Cold War.* New York: Palgrave Macmillan, 2011.

Nepstad, Sharon Erickson. *Convictions of the Soul: Religion, Culture, and Agency in the Central America Solidarity Movement.* New York: Oxford University Press, 2004.

Newman, Louise. *White Women's Rights: The Racial Origins of Feminism in the United States.* New York: Oxford University Press, 1999.

Nielsen, Kim. *Un-American Womanhood: Antiradicalism, Antifeminism, and the First Red Scare.* Columbus: Ohio State University Press, 2001.

Nollen, Scott Allen. *Three Bad Men: John Ford, John Wayne, Ward Bond.* Jefferson, NC: McFarland, 2013.

Nolte, Sharon, and Sally Ann Hastings. "The Meiji State's Policy toward Women, 1890–1910," in *Recreating Japanese Women, 1600–1945,* edited by Gail Lee Bernstein, 151–74. Berkeley: University of California Press, 1991.

Noone, Judy. *The Same Fate as the Poor.* Rev. ed. Maryknoll, NY: Orbis Books, 1995.

O'Brien, Anne. "Catholic Nuns in Transnational Mission, 1528–2015." *Journal of Global History* 11, no. 3 (2016): 387–408.

O'Brien, David. "Catholic Evangelization and American Culture." *U.S. Catholic Historian* 11, no. 2 (1993): 49–59.

O'Reilly, Kenneth. *Hoover and the Un-Americans: The FBI, HUAC, and the Red Menace.* Philadelphia, PA: Temple University Press, 1983.

Osgood, Kenneth. *Total Cold War: Eisenhower's Secret Propaganda Battle at Home and Abroad.* Lawrence: University Press of Kansas, 2006.

Osofsky, Hari. "Domesticating International Criminal Law: Bringing Human Rights Violators to Justice." *Yale Law Journal* 107, no. 1 (1997): 191–226.

Pascoe, Peggy. *Relations of Rescue: The Search for Female Moral Authority in the American West, 1874–1939.* New York: Oxford University Press, 1990.

Payne, Elizabeth. *Reform, Labor, and Feminism: Margaret Dreier Robins and the Women's Trade Union League.* Urbana: University of Illinois Press, 1988.

Peace, Roger. *A Call to Conscience: The Anti-Contra War Campaign.* Amherst: University of Massachusetts Press, 2012.

Pellett, Gail. *Justice and the Generals*. Brooklyn, NY: First Run/Icarus Films, 2002. Video-cassette (VHS).

Peter, Shawn Francis. *The Catonsville Nine: A Story of Faith and Resistance in the Vietnam Era*. New York: Oxford University Press, 2012.

Peterson, Anna. *Martyrdom and the Politics of Religion: Progressive Catholicism in El Salvador's Civil War*. Albany: State University of New York Press, 1997.

Prashad, Vijay. *The Darker Nations: A People's History of the Third World*. New York: New Press, 2007.

Rawick, George. "The New Deal and Youth: The Civilian Conservation Corps, the National Youth Administration, and the American Youth Congress." PhD diss., University of Wisconsin, 1957.

Reeves-Ellington, Barbara, Kathryn Kish Sklar, and Connie Shemo, eds. *Competing Kingdoms: Women, Mission, Nation, and the American Protestant Empire, 1812–1960*. Durham, NC: Duke University Press, 2010.

———. Introduction to *Competing Kingdoms: Women, Mission, Nation, and the American Protestant Empire, 1812–1960*, edited by Barbara Reeves-Ellington, Kathryn Kish Sklar, and Connie Shemo, 1–16. Durham, NC: Duke University Press, 2010.

Reher, Margaret Mary. "Americanism and Modernism: Continuity or Discontinuity?" *U.S. Catholic Historian* 1, no. 3 (1981): 87–100.

———. *Catholic Intellectual Life in America: A Historical Study of Persons and Movements*. New York: Macmillan, 1989.

Rice, Anna. *A History of the World's Young Women's Christian Association*. New York: Woman's Press, 1947.

Rivera, Paul. "'Field Found!' Establishing the Maryknoll Mission Enterprise in the United States and China, 1918–1928." *Catholic Historical Review* 84, no. 3 (1998): 477–517.

Robert, Dana. *American Women in Mission: A Social History of Their Thought and Practice*. Macon, GA: Mercer University Press, 1996.

Robertson, Nancy Marie. *Christian Sisterhood, Race Relations, and the YWCA, 1906–46*. Urbana: University of Illinois Press, 2007.

Rogow, Faith. *Gone to Another Meeting: The National Council of Jewish Women, 1893–1993*. Tuscaloosa: University of Alabama Press, 1993.

Rose, Barbara. *Tsuda Umeko and Women's Education in Japan*. New Haven, CT: Yale University Press, 1992.

Rupp, Leila. *Worlds of Women: The Making of an International Women's Movement*. Princeton, NJ: Princeton University Press, 1997.

Sanchez, Peter. *Panama Lost? U.S. Hegemony, Democracy, and the Canal*. Gainesville: University Press of Florida, 2007.

Schlesinger, Stephen, and Stephen Kinzer. *Bitter Fruit: The Untold Story of the American Coup in Guatemala*. Garden City, NY: Doubleday, 1982.

Schneider, Mary. "American Sisters and the Roots of Change: The 1950s." *U.S. Catholic Historian* 7, no. 1 (1988): 55–72

Scott, Anne Firor. *Natural Allies: Women's Associations in American History*. Urbana: University of Illinois Press, 1991.

Seat, Karen. *"Providence Has Freed Our Hands": Women's Missions and the American Encounter with Japan*. Syracuse, NY: Syracuse University Press, 2008.

Seymour-Jones, Carole. *Journey of Faith: The History of the World YWCA, 1945–1994*. London: Allison and Busby, 1994.

Sims, Mary. *The First Twenty-Five Years: Being a Summary of the Young Women's Christian Association of the United States of America, 1906–1931*. New York: Womans Press, 1932.

———. *The Natural History of a Social Institution: The Young Women's Christian Association*. New York: Womans Press, 1936.

———. *The YWCA: An Unfolding Purpose*. New York: Woman's Press, 1950.

Sklar, Kathryn Kish. *Florence Kelley and the Nation's Work: The Rise of Women's Political Culture*. New Haven, CT: Yale University Press, 1995.

———. "Hull House Maps and Papers: Social Science as Women's Work in the 1890s." In *The Social Survey in Historical Perspective*, edited by Martin Bulmer, Kevin Bales, and Kathryn Kish Sklar, 111–47. Cambridge: Cambridge University Press, 1991.

Snow, Jennifer. *Protestant Missionaries, Asian Immigrants, and Ideologies of Race in America, 1850–1924*. New York: Routledge, 2007.

Spain, Daphne. *How Women Saved the City*. Minneapolis: University of Minnesota Press, 2001.

Stebner, Eleanor. *The Women of Hull House: A Study in Spirituality, Vocation, and Friendship*. Albany: State University Press of New York, 1997.

Storrs, Landon R. Y. "Red Scare Politics and the Suppression of Popular Front Feminism." *Journal of American History* 90, no. 2 (2003): 491–524.

Sullivan, Rebecca. *Visual Habits: Nuns and American Postwar Popular Culture*. Toronto: University of Toronto Press, 2005.

Taylor, Verta, and Leila Rupp. "Loving Internationalism: The Emotion Culture of Transnational Women's Organizations, 1888–1945." *Mobilization* 7, no. 2 (2002): 141–58.

Thurman, Suzanne. "The Medical Mission Strategy of the Maryknoll Sisters." *Missiology* 30, no. 3 (2002): 361–73.

Trask, Roger. "Unnamed Christianity in Turkey." *Muslim World* 55, no. 1 (1965): 66–76.

Tyrell, Ian. *Woman's World/Woman's Empire: The Woman's Christian Temperance Union in International Perspective, 1880–1930*. Chapel Hill: University of North Carolina Press, 2014.

United Nations Commission on the Truth for El Salvador. *From Madness to Hope: The 12 Year War in El Salvador*. New York: United Nations, 1993.

Vandenberg-Daves, Jodi. "The Manly Pursuit of a Partnership between the Sexes: The Debate over YMCA Programs for Women and Girls." *Journal of American History* 78, no. 4 (1992): 1324–46.

Walkowitz, Daniel. *Working with Class: Social Workers and the Politics of Middle-Class Identity*. Chapel Hill: University of North Carolina Press, 1999.

Wall, Barbara Mann. *Into Africa: A Transnational History of Catholic Medical Missions and Social Change*. New Brunswick, NJ: Rutgers University Press, 2015.

Warren, Heather. "The Shift from Character to Personality in Mainline Protestant Thought, 1935–1945." *Church History* 67, no. 3 (1998): 537–555.

Weisenfeld, Judith. *African American Women and Christian Activism: New York's Black YWCA, 1905–1945*. Cambridge, MA: Harvard University Press, 1997.

Whelan, Daniel. *Indivisible Human Rights: A History*. Philadelphia: University of Pennsylvania Press, 2010.

White, Ronald, and Charles Howard Hopkins. *The Social Gospel: Religion and Reform in Changing America*. Philadelphia, PA: Temple University Press, 1976.

Wiest, Jean-Paul. *Maryknoll in China: A History, 1918–1955*. Armonk, NY: M. E. Sharpe, 1998.

Wilson, Jan Doolittle. *The Women's Joint Congressional Committee and the Politics of Maternalism*. Urbana: University of Illinois Press, 2007.

Winston, Diane. "Back to the Future: Religion, Politics, and the Media." *American Quarterly* 59, no. 3 (2007): 969–89.

Woodward, Bob. *Veil: The Secret Wars of the CIA, 1981–1987.* New York: Simon and Schuster, 1987.

Wyman, David. *The Abandonment of the Jews: America and the Holocaust, 1941–1945.* New York: Pantheon Books, 1984.

Yasutake, Rumi. "Men, Women, and Temperance in Meiji Japan." *Japanese Journal of American Studies* 17 (2006): 91–111.

Zotti, Mary Irene. *A Time of Awakening: The Young Christian Worker Story in the United States, 1938–1970.* Chicago: Loyola University Press, 1991.

INDEX

ABOUT THE AUTHOR

AMANDA L. IZZO is an assistant professor of women's and gender studies at Saint Louis University.